Dear Reader:

The book you are about to read is the latest bestseller from the St. Martin's True Crime Library, the imprint the *New York Times* calls "the leader in true crime!" Each month, we offer you a fascinating account of the latest, most sensational crime that has captured the national attention. St. Martin's is the publisher of perennial bestselling true crime author Jack Olsen, whose SALT OF THE EARTH is the true story of one woman's triumph over life-shattering violence; Joseph Wambaugh called it "powerful and absorbing." Fannie Weinstein and Melinda Wilson tell the story of a beautiful honors student who was lured into the dark world of sex for hire in THE COED CALL GIRL MURDER. St. Martin's is also proud to publish two-time Edgar Award-winning author Carlton Stowers, whose TO THE LAST BREATH recounts a two-year-old girl's mysterious death, and the dogged investigation that led loved ones to the most unlikely murderer: her own father. In the book you now hold, THE SURGEON'S WIFE, veteran reporter and bestselling author Kieran Crowley documents the celebrated case of a "perfect" marriage that went horribly wrong. . . .

St. Martin's True Crime Library gives you the stories *behind* the headlines. Our authors take you right to the scene of the crime and into the minds of the most notorious murderers to show you what really makes them tick. St. Martin's True Crime Library paperbacks are better than the most terrifying thriller, because it's all true! The next time you want a crackling good read, make sure it's got the St. Martin's True Crime Library logo on the spine—you'll be up all night!

Charles E. Spicer, Jr.
Executive Editor, St. Martin's True Crime Library

MISSING PERSON

BOB DROVE TO WORK ON MONDAY MORNING, THE BEGIN-ning of another hot, steamy day. From there he called Beth Israel—but Gail had not shown up for her graduate work or to see her first patients. He also called her psychiatrist, and introduced himself.

"Is Gail there?" Bob asked.

"No, and she's always on time," Dr. Elsa Fairchild said, speaking to Bob for the first time.

Bob explained about their fight and that Gail had "gone off in a huff."

Bob also checked in with Gail's friends and family again, as well as his own family before he decided he had to report her missing.

"I'm concerned that Gail might do something to harm her-self," he told one of her friends.

After work that night, about 9 o'clock, Bob drove to the 19th Precinct on East 95th Street, where he was directed upstairs to the Detective Squad.

"I want to report my wife missing," Bob told an officer sit-ting at a desk . . . .

ST. MARTIN'S PAPERBACKS TRUE CRIME LIBRARY TITLES
BY KIERAN CROWLEY

SLEEP MY LITTLE DEAD
BURNED ALIVE
THE SURGEON'S WIFE

THE
SURGEON'S
WIFE

KIERAN CROWLEY

St. Martin's Paperbacks

THE SURGEON'S WIFE

Copyright © 2001 by Kieran Crowley.
Background cover photograph of Robert Bierenbaum courtesy AP/Wide World Photos. All photos used with permission.

All rights reserved. No part of this book may be used or reproduced in any manner whatsoever without written permission except in the case of brief quotations embodied in critical articles or reviews. For information address St. Martin's Press, 175 Fifth Avenue, New York, N.Y. 10010.

ISBN: 0-312-97641-0

Printed in the United States of America

St. Martin's Paperbacks edition / September 2001

10 9 8 7 6 5 4 3 2

For Kathy

ACKNOWLEDGMENTS

THIS book is based on scores of interviews—in several cities around the country—and thousands of pages of police reports, court papers, trial transcripts and other documents. There are no fictional or "composite" characters in this book, although some people are given pseudonyms, which are denoted by *asterisks the first time the name appears. Certain events, sequences and conversations were necessarily reconstructed from a synthesis of all the evidence, including interviews, police reports, court papers, trial transcripts and other documents and information.

While researching this book, I uncovered facts the police had not discovered—which led me to propose an alternate theory of the ultimate fate of the victim, Gail Katz Bierenbaum.

First, I would like to thank my editors at St. Martin's Press, Charlie Spicer and Joe Cleemann, for all of their help. My literary agent Jane Dystel has my eternal thanks for her genial expertise and sage advice.

I wish to thank my eminent editors at the *New York Post*—Managing Editor Stu Marques, former Metropolitan Editor John Mancini and former Associate Metropolitan Editor Maralyn Matlick—for arranging the affairs of a Great Metropolitan Newspaper to suit the schedule of a lowly reporter. I tip my thinking cap to *Post* Head Librarian Laura Harris and her adept staff, and I am very grateful to *Post* Photo Editor Gretchen Viehmann, assisted by Imaging Editor Dave Johnston, who located many of the photos for this book. Fred Bruder at Rainbow Photo turned them into 8-by-10's. Also, thanks to *Post* photographers Jim Alcorn, Bolivar Arellano, Tamara Beckwith, and Joey Newfield, for their fine photos. I thank prosecutors Dan Bibb, Stephen Saracco and Adam Kaufmann, and a special thank-you to two great reporters—my former *Post* colleagues Mike Pearl and Barbara Ross.

I tender my thanks to Geology professor Fred Bachhuber of the University of Nevada at Las Vegas for a brief history of the Las Vegas area. I am also grateful to Ralph Rohay, Patti McGill and Buffy Gustafson.

Annah Bierenbaum's former nanny Barb Scholler has my gratitude for all her help. I also thank Dr. Lee Trotter for his honesty and assistance.

Andy Rosenzweig is a gentleman and a master detective. I am grateful for his assistance and expect to be reading his books someday soon. Private detective Mike Race was also helpful.

I am very much obliged to psychiatrist Dr. Michael Stone, who gave me unique insights into a terrible—yet fascinating—human tragedy.

I also extend my thanks to forensic psychiatrist Dr. Michael Wellner, chairman of the Forensic Panel and associate professor of psychiatry at New York University, for another point of view on Bob Bierenbaum.

There are quite a few people I would like to thank but cannot—because they are unnamed sources or people who have been given pseudonyms in the book, for various reasons. Please consider this your thank-you. You know who you are.

My gratitude also goes out to two New Jersey officials— Phil White, spokesman for the Wanaque Reservoir, North Jersey District Water Supply Commission, and Mike Petonak, director of the Boonton Department of Public Works and overseer of the Boonton Reservoir. Sam DeBenedetto helped by locating a shot he took of Wanaque Reservoir years ago, and Richard L. Mariconda supplied background information.

I thank Alayne and Steven Katz for the help they were able to give me and I wish them the best of luck.

David Lewis, the prominent murder defender who represented Bob Bierenbaum at trial, also has my thanks for all his help.

I am especially indebted to Bob Bierenbaum's lawyer Scott Greenfield. The smart and successful lawyer shocked me by giving me access to the defense team—which gave me a unique window into a murder defense in progress. For more than a year, with his client's permission, he answered most of my thousands of questions and I thank him.

My heartfelt gratitude goes to my family, especially Al Nemser, Tess Nemser and Kathy Nemser for their various free services—including wisdom, love, support and proof-reading.

With her laughter, my 5-year-old daughter Ariel—who wants me to write a book in which no one dies—reminded me why I do all of this.

My final thanks and all my love go to my first and best editor—my wife Riki. She made it all possible by giving up rest, relaxation—and a life—for more than a year and doing everything else, while I wandered around the country, hung out of airplanes, attended the trial and sat at the computer.

"Physician, heal thyself."

—LUKE IV, 23

THE SURGEON'S WIFE

CHAPTER I

PARTY OF ONE

GAIL whizzed effortlessly down the linoleum aisle of the Manhattan supermarket on her roller skates, her wavy chestnut brown hair fluttering gently over her shoulders. A talented dancer, her fluid movements turned the heads of people pushing squeaky shopping carts. Petite and lithe in her shorts and a halter top that bared her back and slim midriff, Gail breezed past the brightly stocked shelves with feline grace. She rolled to a stop in the beverage aisle. Her hazel eyes scanned the prepared drink mixes until she found what she wanted—a bottle of pre-mixed, non-alcoholic piña colada drink. She took it off the shelf with a willowy hand, her thin fingers and thumb adorned with several rings, and took it to the express lane. It was a Friday afternoon in New York and it looked like the bright, sexy 23-year-old college dropout who worked as a bartender was on her way to a party. A piña colada party.

Gail Katz skated out into the warm afternoon and over the downtown pavement toward her fifth-floor walkup apartment on West 14th Street. She closed the door behind her but did not lock it. Alone in her apartment, she put the bottle of creamy coconut, pineapple juice and sugar syrup aside on the kitchen counter and picked up the phone. She called her parents on Long Island and chatted awhile. Manny and Sylvia Katz ran a stationery store on the Island where Gail grew up. Her younger sister Alayne was in college and their brother Steve was in the fourth grade. For a change, Gail did not squabble with her mother. Before hanging up, Gail made plans to get together with the family soon. She then called several friends, had similar conversations and made plans.

After she finished her calls, Gail put on some music, got a bottle of vodka out of the cabinet and blended it with ice and the piña colada mix, producing the familiar frothy, festive beverage. The sweet smell of coconut filled the small kitchen. Gail knew piña colada should be laced with rum but she didn't have any. Her favorite drinks were piña colada and a liqueur named Kir. She took the pitcher of the potent aperitif, a straw and a single glass, and headed for the bathroom.

Gail gazed briefly in the medicine cabinet mirror at the strong nose dividing the delicate features of her pretty, tanned oval face. From inside the medicine cabinet, she took a plastic bottle of thick, round white pills. She brought everything into the bedroom and put it on the night table. She got a pencil and a pad of paper and also put them on the night table before crawling into bed and pouring a frosty white glassful of piña colada. One by one, Gail popped snowy Quaaludes into her mouth and washed them down by sipping the milky white cocktail, which tasted like an ice cream soda, through the straw. When her glass was empty, she filled it and continued her task. She didn't cry or become emotional. She was cold, dispassionate, deliberate. Gail was distant from herself, determined to escape her unbearable feelings of loneliness and disappointment.

"People think I have everything to live for and be happy about but they don't understand," Gail thought, as she gulped the chalky tablets and washed them down with the icy cocktail.

She thought about people who tried to talk her out of her depression, who told her that she was young and smart and good-looking. She listened to her psychiatrist and her family and friends when they responded to her complaints but she couldn't help herself. Sometimes she could see their point—faintly, as if through a blizzard, but their logic froze in the cold blast of her pain and misery.

The avalanche of iced booze chilled Gail from the inside out but the alcohol warmed her a bit. She picked up the pencil and drunkenly began to scrawl on paper all the reasons why she wanted to die. Unemotionally, Gail had made her phone calls to her family and friends because she intended to mask her plans. She wanted them to have a pleasant final memory of her. She didn't want them to blame themselves.

"If our last conversation was pleasant," Gail thought, "they can't reprimand themselves for not responding to my depression or pain."

She was determined to make sure that there was absolutely no indication of any problem or difficulty that they could reproach themselves for not having acted upon. Gail did not see that her plan might make her death more of a shock—more powerful and mysterious—to those who loved her. If she had, the fact that her effort to end her pain might freeze their hearts forever was not enough to stop her at that point.

Partially under a white sheet, she passed from drunk to anaesthetized when the " 'ludes" kicked in. Their depressant effect further frosted her mind, like a frigid climber on Mount Everest attacked by both frostbite and numbing hypothermia.

"It feels like splitting," Gail decided. There were two opposing parts of her that were battling and she couldn't pacify either of them. "It doesn't make any sense," she thought "It eliminates and destroys."

The cold was separating Gail from herself but she was no longer in pain. Slumping into unconsciousness, she floated on a peaceful white cloud of sensual happiness.

Gail Katz whirled away in the wind like a snowflake.

Gail Beth Katz was born on March 8th, 1956, in Brooklyn. Almost two years later, her younger sister, brown-eyed Alayne, was born. They shared a red-and-white bedroom in their second-floor apartment. Little Gail had an imaginary friend in grammar school—an older girl who scolded her and, once, ordered her to crawl around the house on her knees until blisters formed on her skin.

When Gail was in the fourth grade, her parents moved the family to a large, brick-and-shingle split-level home in the suburbs. Gail was an adorable child, a good student, and close to her little sister. By the time Gail graduated from grammar school and moved up to junior high school, she had acquired adolescent insecurities. In private, when she was reading, watching television or sleeping, she still sucked on her finger like a small child.

Gail discovered the opposite sex in the seventh grade and went boy-crazy, even scratching one guy's name into the flesh of her left arm with a razor blade when she was fourteen. Her lack of self-confidence seemed to drive her to seek constant attention from boys. From that time on, Gail always had a boyfriend. She never broke up with one until she had the next one lined up.

To neighbors, the Katz family seemed like every other happy suburban family, but underneath—like most families—there were undercurrents of conflict and money worries. Manny was the president of a specialty advertising company called Columbia Pen & Pencil. When the business was sold to a large Florida firm, he planned to move his family to the Sunshine State and continue to run the concern as a division of the larger corporation. But his plans fell through and Manny was shut out of his ideal job among the beaches and palm trees. Instead, Manny took out a second mortgage on their nice split-level in order to buy a stationery store in West Hempstead. Running a little card shop in a quiet neighborhood was a big step down in the world for a guy who had run an entire company. Also, Sylvia was needed as an unpaid worker to help Manny in the shop, to make ends meet. In the summer, the kids sometimes helped with the family business. Disappointed, carrying more debt and looking at bills for three kids and college on the horizon, Manny became stressed out and unhappy.

Some observers thought Sylvia seemed very flighty and high-strung, like Gail. Sylvia always seemed to be quarreling with her daughters. Steve, who was still young, realized his dad was under pressure and noticed that there were fewer good times. Sometimes Gail had arguments with her father that would end with neither father nor daughter speaking to the other for weeks, even though they ate at the same table, sat in the same room to watch TV and rode in the same car. Manny favored Alayne, who was more like him. He couldn't deal with the emotionality of Gail, who took after her mother. It seemed to Alayne that Sylvia put all her energy into helping Gail—because she was so needy. Alayne would hear her parents arguing—and sometimes yelling—about Gail, with Sylvia trying to get Manny to be more sensitive to Gail's needs.

Gail was still an outstanding student and she graduated in 1973, a year early, from Mepham High School in Bellmore. She went to the State University of New York at Albany. The following year she roomed in an off-campus apartment with Alayne, who also came to the school. But Gail dropped out during her sophomore year, in 1975, when she lost interest in college and started using drugs. It did not please Manny and Sylvia, who had many arguments on the subject. Sylvia, of course, wanted her daughter to finish school and be able to make a living. But, being a Jewish mom from suburbia who had worked as a receptionist in a doctor's office, Sylvia had a rather typical ambition for her eldest daughter—she wanted her to marry a doctor.

Alayne also took a year off but dropped back in. She transferred to another state school on Long Island. She did well and decided to enter law school after she graduated.

After she dropped out, Gail moved to Manhattan and entered a dance program at New York University. She moved with an easy grace and was a natural dancer. But the college dance scene left her dissatisfied and she again dropped out. She took a course in social work that she also dropped out of, and went back upstate. She dated musicians and tried to become involved in music and choreography but it led nowhere. Alayne, who occasionally visited her sister upstate, thought that some of the musicians Gail dated were crazy. Alayne felt her sister was lost—she was going nowhere and didn't know how to get anywhere. Gail's family rejected her boyfriends as either too old, too young or not Jewish. They referred to her choices as "Gail's reformation projects." Alayne felt that her older sister did not feel good about who she was, so she found damaged goods and tried to fix them.

In 1976, Gail lived in Albany with *Phil Lester, a musician in a local band. She made some efforts to choreograph the musicians' movements. She wanted to somehow dance with the band during performances but that also never worked out.

Upstate, Gail became friends with another band member named *Amanda Klein, who played synthesizer and guitar and wrote songs. Amanda, who had been a model, was a striking 5-foot-11 beauty. The two discussed their lives and loves. Gail was torn between her love of creative people and her yearning to make a life for herself, to fulfill the goal she shared with her mother—to marry a doctor. In fact, Gail's therapist was also onboard with the doctor plan. They all felt that Gail needed security and stability. That way, she wouldn't have to work odd jobs to pay the rent and could go back to school and get a degree. Phil was a very handsome, talented musician and a nice guy but he wasn't a doctor and would probably never be rich.

So, while Gail was with Phil, she was secretly looking around for better prospects. That was her style—she would test-drive a new guy before she broke up with the old one.

Amanda liked Gail, who she thought was intelligent and a sweet person but very emotional. Sometimes it seemed all Gail did was complain about how miserable she was and how Phil did not measure up to her expectations. Gail had a lot of friendships with women and she seemed to get something emotionally from her girlfriends that she didn't get from her boyfriends. She was distrustful of men, perhaps with good reason, but saw them as potential rescuers who could save her from the life of a loser. Amanda wondered what fears Gail's mother had communicated to her daughter to make her such an insecure young woman, searching for a man to take care of her. Gail, thought Amanda, was definitely a glass-is-half-empty kind of person. She was having trouble finding a calling in life. She seemed to be always starting and stopping things. She loved dancing but it seemed her real passion was herself—her soul-searching, her pursuit of happiness. Maybe she wasn't so different from everybody else, after all, Amanda thought.

"I feel so sad," Gail repeatedly whined to Amanda. "I feel so depressed."

Often, Gail's solution was a night out. She pressed Amanda to go out dancing at a disco and meet guys. And sometimes Amanda said yes. One night they went to a dance club in Albany and the men noticed when they arrived. They were an arresting pair: Amanda, tall, slim and sexy with her Raquel Welch good looks and streaked long brown hair, and the smaller, exotic Gail who only came up to Amanda's shoulder. Amanda sat down with her drink and opened a book she'd brought to the club, *The Anatomy of Human Destructiveness* by Erich Fromm. The book examined man's misdeeds—especially murder and war—and suggested that human beings were not innately evil but did evil things when their needs were frustrated and they were unable to achieve wholeness, happiness. While Gail performed on the dance floor, Amanda sipped her drink and watched her friend, dancing to a song by Gail's favorite group, Supertramp.

Amanda returned to her book. She was fascinated by Fromm's idea that evil people were created by thwarted hopes. Turning a page, brushing her long, brown hair aside, Amanda looked up to see a darkly handsome guy with black hair and a mustache smiling at her.

"Hi," he said to her. "I'm Nick."

"Hi."

"Oh no," thought Amanda. "Here comes Disco Joe. At least he's good-looking." But Nick was no dummy. He began talking intelligently about the Fromm book and other subjects. He and Amanda hit it off right away. It turned out *Nick Edwards was a plastic surgery resident at the local hospital. A surprised Gail returned from the dance floor to find that Amanda—without even trying—had found a doctor. Nick was there with another resident and he and Gail began talking. Gail and the other physician never quite clicked and she later broke up with her boyfriend Phil. But Amanda and Nick fell in love and moved in together. A few years later, in 1979, Amanda lived Gail's dream—she married her doctor.

It was in that same year, 1979, that Gail whizzed uptown on her roller skates. She rolled over the dirty sidewalks and gutters and around pedestrians and cars on her way to her latest boyfriend *Ken Dahlberg's office. After seeing Ken, Gail planned to skate in Central Park. She loved the park, enjoyed skating or walking its shady paths, sunning herself in a bathing suit, meeting people. She felt Ken treated her badly. One week, Ken would act like they were getting married and then he would treat her like garbage. She and Ken had been fighting again and Gail stopped by to work things out.

When she arrived, Ken made it very clear that it was over. Gail stormed out of Ken's office and began skating toward the park. At first, she was angry and dejected. She did not have another boyfriend waiting in the wings.

"I'm not in love with Ken, so why am I so disturbed?" Gail asked herself.

His rebuff should not have had such a troubling effect on her. But it was the feeling of being rejected without any means to gain control that really got to Gail. She remembered all the other times it had happened and thought, "Here we go again." She felt that it was never going to be any different.

"I can't take this anymore," Gail decided.

She rolled to a halt. Standing still, she made a decision and her racing emotions faded away. Perfectly calm, Gail turned around and changed direction. She skated back toward her neighborhood. As her resolve strengthened, she skated faster. She remembered she had a bottle of vodka at home. "If forty Quaaludes don't do the trick, the combination of both will," she decided.

But that wouldn't taste good, Gail realized. She didn't like the taste of straight vodka. That was when she got the idea to go to the supermarket to get a piña colada mix to make the vodka more palatable. She didn't see it as a tantrum or a way of hurting Ken or her family—she saw it as a way to stop her misery.

But the pills and the booze didn't do the trick. Or, rather, they did it too well. Gail vomited up the piña colada and 'ludes. The alcohol caused the regurgitation, which removed most of the drug from her system before it could kill her. She woke up in her bed six hours later, her head spinning, groggy and disappointed at her failure to end her life. She was drunk, dopey and sick to her stomach. She felt empty, as if she was even a failure at failure. She should have been grateful that she was alive, thankful she had failed in her suicide attempt and horrified by what she had almost done—but she wasn't. She had been given a second chance at life but was only despondent that she was not dead. Gail panicked when she realized that *Susan, one of the friends she had made plans with, was due to arrive at her apartment soon. She had to escape.

Gail found some cleaning fluid under the sink and poured it down her throat. It burned on the way down but didn't have the effect she expected, because the coconut milk had coated her stomach. It tasted bad so she stopped drinking it. Desperate, Gail stumbled into the bathroom and grabbed a safety razor. She got into the bathtub and began slashing at her wrists. Gail went about her work calmly, without tears or hysteria. She slashed four veins vertically, opening up the walls of the vessels. The red liquid spurted out, dripped down her arms and splattered onto the white porcelain.

Susan rang the doorbell in Gail's metal apartment door and waited. When her friend did not answer, she rang it again, several times. She became impatient and knocked loudly. Worried, she tried the doorknob and found it was unlocked. Did Gail leave the door open because she was in the shower or was something wrong?

"Gail?" Susan called, stepping inside the dark living room.

She smelled rancid coconut and stale alcohol in the strangely silent apartment. Susan did not hear the shower but advanced cautiously toward the bedroom and bathroom—where she saw light coming from under the closed bathroom door.

"Gail?" she called.

Susan swung open the door and screamed.

CHAPTER 2

RAPTURE OF FLIGHT

BOB strummed his acoustic guitar quickly, with his graceful hands, and deftly picked individual strings, bending beautiful notes with intense precision. The rich sounds of the elaborate classical guitar piece filled Amanda and Nick Edwards' New Jersey living room. Bob's playing was so perfect and professional, it sounded like a record or a live concert. His curly black hair swayed to the rhythm of the piece as his left hand flashed over the guitar frets and his right thrummed the strings. When he was done, Amanda and Nick applauded. Bob's face burst into a friendly grin. He then played another instrumental song, one he had composed himself. The song was also quick and complicated, like the guitarist.

When Bob arrived for dinner that night in 1981, he focused his gaze on Amanda and wondered what had happened since he last saw her up in Albany.

"Amanda, how are you?" Bob asked, gazing into her eyes, ignoring all else. "What have you been doing?"

When Bob Bierenbaum talked, he spoke fast—as if his voice was in a rush to keep up with his lightning brain that seemed to fly ahead of everyone else in the room. Occasionally, when Bob made a joke, there was confused laughter because it seemed that Bob's mind had gone somewhere theirs had not. As Amanda told Bob about her songwriting efforts, he questioned her and seemed genuinely fascinated by her life, especially since he also wrote songs. Bob's large hazel eyes gazed intently at anyone he engaged in conversation. They were the sharp eyes of a doctor—calmly observing, appraising what they saw. Many were put off by Bob's strong, strange eyes and felt uneasy, as if they were being probed by dark searchlights. They read Bob's objectivity as coldness. But Amanda felt that Bob's

challenging look was part of his powerful intellect. Along
with Bob's genius came a certain endearing eccentricity,
she thought. After a performance worthy of Carnegie Hall,
Bob could break into a high-pitched giggle and betray himself as a Young Republican square from New Jersey—dent-
ing the image of the cool musician. He loved music—
classical, rock, folk, blues, almost all of it, especially the
virtuoso guitar music of Leo Kottke, the delta pickin' guitar
of John Fahey, such as featured in his "On Doing an Evil
Deed Blues," and the rock stylings and rich harmonies of
the pop group Supertramp in hits like "The Logical Song."
He always had the latest stereo and computer gadgets. He
had passions—such as food and photography and flying a
plane—that filled what little spare time he had and betrayed
a love of life.

But no matter what his accomplishments, Bob remained
part geek, a bit goofy and nerdy, Amanda thought. Combined with his rumpled flannel shirt, faded jeans and silly
smile, he seemed to her like a big, brilliant, lovable boy.
But Bob was a kid who had always sought mastery of difficult undertakings. He was a young doctor who worked
long hours at Mount Sinai Hospital in Manhattan, repairing
people, saving lives. To some people it seemed odd that
after a long day and night of stressful life-and-death responsibility, Bob chose for recreation the complicated, difficult task of piloting a single engine plane, in which every
passenger's life—including his own—was in his hands. To
those who feared flying, Bob might have seemed like a
control freak, but he loved being up in the sky. He took his
pilot responsibilities seriously and also enjoyed teaching
others to fly.

"Let's get high," Bob often joked to friends—but he
meant going for a ride in his flying machine.

Bob had taken Nick up and begun teaching him how to
fly. Amanda heard from Nick and Bob how great their
flights were, so she decided to go also. It sounded like fun.
The three drove to the nearby Caldwell Airport, a small
field in the Jersey hills that had been a plane engine testing

facility and a P-40 fighter squadron base during World War II. It had a tower manned by federal air traffic controllers, who directed the landings and takeoffs by radio. Nick and Amanda were struck by the fact that pilots could drive their cars right onto the area where the planes were sitting. Bob took them through a large open concrete hangar with a Quonset hut roof and into an outside corner office with glass on two sides, the home of *Sky King Aviation Services, Inc. He arranged for the rental of a Cessna 172 Skyhawk, got the keys, checked the weather report, and entered the date and departure point of the flight in his personal flight log before walking his friends out onto the tarmac to the plane.

The aircraft, which featured a red stripe along the fuselage and a picture of a skyhawk on the tail, was one of three dozen single-engine planes that had a single wing above the small passenger cabin and one small door on either side. It was equipped with a "Hobbs meter" device that acted like a taxi meter and registered the number of hours the engine was running. The passenger area was as small as an ultra-compact car, with two seats in the front and two in the back. A small cargo area behind the seats had a little side door for loading and unloading baggage.

Amanda watched, fascinated, as Bob busied himself with his pre-flight checks. He deposited his maps and flight bag on the front, left pilot seat. He worked various controls that moved control surfaces on the outside of the aircraft. He walked around and fiddled with the tail, the flaps on the wings and the tires, then climbed up on one of the side wheel struts. He unscrewed a gas tank cap on top of the wing and peered inside. Satisfied, he climbed down and continued his inspection. It was almost like the plane was one of Bob's patients and he was conducting a medical examination on the metal bird.

When he was done, Bob put Nick in the back seat and strapped Amanda into the right front passenger seat next to him. It was hot and stuffy in the little cabin and Bob opened the small bottom-opening windows in either door as he readied for takeoff. The whole thing made Amanda slightly uneasy. There was a black, U-shaped steering wheel directly in front of each forward seat, making it possible for either person to pilot the craft.

"Clear!" Bob said loudly out the window, even though there was no one anywhere near the dangerous propeller. Bob turned the key on the dashboard. The two-bladed prop outside the front windshield spun and disappeared, as a loud, vibrating noise filled the cabin, making talking difficult. Bob gave Amanda a set of black headphones with a suspended microphone on the side, allowing them to hear each other and speak over the thrumming engine. Bob spoke to the tower and received clearance to taxi into position on the runway. He was flying VFR, he explained—Visual Flight Rules. On the runway, Bob pushed the throttle forward to do a "run-up" with the brakes on, to test the engine before takeoff. The cabin vibrated strongly as he revved the engine. He then received radio clearance for takeoff from the controller. As they spoke, a tape recorder in the tower recorded their conversation—which would be saved for two weeks and then be erased. Bob released the brakes and throttled up for real. The plane gained speed on the runway and Bob pulled back on the wheel. It suddenly jumped into the air, giving Amanda a giddy floating sensation. Winds buffeted the craft, wobbling it. Bob responded with small adjustments on the control yoke, smoothing out the ride as they climbed west above the airport and over the green hills of New Jersey at eighty miles per hour. Bob obviously loved being in charge. He was still the same guy, but there was also a "this-is-your-captain-speaking" authority in his voice. As they climbed to several thousand feet, they picked up speed to one hundred and ten miles per hour as they headed west. Amanda saw a winding river and a large reservoir with a wide waterfall far below.

Flying in the Cessna was a very different feeling from sitting in a huge 747 jetliner and being served dinner and a drink by flight attendants. Amanda's stomach sank. Even though it was now cool in the cabin, her palms began to sweat. A wave of electric fear washed over her. Her breathing became short and shallow and her heart raced. The walls of the cabin felt like they were closing in on her. She closed her eyes but that only made it worse. The walls were closer. She had to get out.

"Ummm . . . Bob . . ." Amanda stammered, panic in her voice. "I'm not doing so well . . ." was all she could manage.

Bob instantly turned his head and saw that Amanda was in trouble. Her cheeks were ashen and her beautiful features were contorted with anxiety. Terror flashed in her eyes as they darted around the cabin. Bob took Amanda's left hand. It was cold and clammy. Her hand felt rigid with fear. She appeared to be having a panic attack. In a small plane, one terrified person could create havoc. The control yoke and all of the controls were within arm's length. All she had to do was reach out and grab them.

Bob's training had conditioned him to respond to danger with precision. In a very calm voice, still holding her hand, Bob asked Amanda what was wrong. She told him her symptoms. She felt silly but she couldn't help herself. She couldn't shake the panic. Amanda felt she was going to die. If she'd had a parachute, she would have jumped out the door. Bob turned the plane and told Amanda they were going back.

"Look at the clouds," Bob told her, nodding his head to the cottony puffs suspended in blue outside the cramped cabin. "Look straight ahead. Focus on the clouds. Aren't they beautiful?" Bob suggested in a measured voice filled with wonder. "Look at the way the sun plays off the edges of the clouds."

Amanda did as Bob suggested. She looked straight ahead. The fat, snowy sunlit clouds were indeed beautiful in the baby blue sea. She gazed at the luminous coronas of light surrounding a puffy cumulus cloud, the taffy-like wisps of white made iridescent with pink and blue light. Bob kept talking to her, telling her how amazing and magnificent things were outside. It wasn't just a ploy to calm her, Amanda felt. Bob really loved being there and was deeply concerned about her. Even the plane was incredible, Bob explained. It had a powerful engine.

"Listen to it," Bob directed. Amanda kept her eyes on the heavenly sky but listened to the rhythmic humming of the engine, like the vibrant voice of a strong creature.

"Isn't it powerful?" Bob asked. Yes, Amanda agreed. It was powerful.

"You can feel the currents of air underneath the wings," Bob continued. He explained the shape of the wings—just like a bird's wing—and how the rushing air gave lift, held the plane up and allowed it to soar through the sky. It was incredible, miraculous. In fact, said Bob, flying in a small plane was much safer than flying in a giant jet, in which hundreds of people could all pretend together that they were in a large room—not hurtling through the sky at 600 miles per hour. A jumbo jet, Bob said, would sink like a rock if the engines cut out. But in a small plane it was different. They were lighter, with more wing space in relation to their weight.

"We would be able to glide to safety if the engines died," Bob assured her.

By the time they had landed, Amanda was fine. Bob had transformed a terrifying environment into a friendly one, a realm of beauty. With his compelling bedside manner, Bob had talked Amanda down.

Robert Bierenbaum was born in Newark, New Jersey, on July 22, 1955, the first son of internist Dr. Marvin Bierenbaum and his wife Nettie. One of little Bobby's first words was "plane!" It was the beginning of a lifelong fascination with flight. He grew up in West Orange, New Jersey, just over a dozen square miles sprawled over the rolling ridges and valleys of the Watchung Mountains. Bob was raised a child of privilege in a large, white house with pillars in an upscale suburban development on Waddington Avenue. His father was a doctor and his mother had worked in her husband's medical office.

Bob's intelligence showed at an early age: he excelled in the sciences, and took piano and guitar lessons. He loved science and his favorite toy was his ham radio, with which he used to talk to people all over the world while he was in grammar school. In 1962, Bob took an evening course in astronomy at the Hayden Planetarium in Manhattan. Though he was not old enough to take the course, he got in when the teacher asked him why he wanted to take the class.

"I want to be the first to land on the moon," little Bobby told the teacher.

In junior high school, Bob taught a friend, Scott Baranoff, how to ski. By the time he was a teenager at West Orange High School, Bob was a computer whiz and an honor student who scored 800s on his college boards. He also loved sports and made the varsity cross-country team. And he loved to ski almost as much as he loved piloting planes. On the slopes or in the air, he reveled in the feeling of flying—alone, free from gravity.

Bob took Judo lessons. Through the use of choke holds, he learned how to render a person unconscious within seconds. Choking holds, including the open-handed "shimewaza" move that jabbed at the neck, caused asphyxia by compressing the carotid artery on the left side of the throat that supplied blood to the brain. Other choke holds, if prolonged, could even kill. The advantage of the moves was that they were much faster than the hands-around-the throat approach.

As a teenager, Bob was well on the road to follow in his father's footsteps and become a doctor. He began learning all about the human body—how it was constructed, what could go wrong with it and how to fix it. He had virtually a photographic memory, which sometimes gave people the impression they were talking to an encyclopedia. Bob felt he could accomplish almost anything if he went by the book. The only problem was that Bob had not read any books on personal relationships and social interaction. He would learn that there were many things in life that were not printed in black and white and bound between two covers.

Bob finally began college at Rensselaer Polytech in up-state Troy, New York, in September 1972, at the age of 17. He went on to study medicine at Albany Medical College and graduated at the age of 22. By then, he had also been granted a pilot's license.

At medical school graduations, the rows of new doctors in caps and gowns were encouraged to stand, raise their right hands and take an ancient medical vow—the oath of Hippocrates. The Hippocratic oath binds healers to teach their craft to the sons of other doctors, among other things. It also forbade the dispensation of any deadly medicine. It was somewhat quaint in the modern age, but the words still defined for society the time-honored moral difference between a physician and an ordinary person: "I will abstain from all intentional wrong-doing and harm," the physicians swear. "Now, if I carry out this oath and break it not, may I gain forever reputation among all men for my life and for my art; but if I transgress it and forswear myself, may the opposite befall me."

Bob's parents were very proud of their brilliant son but they noticed his accelerated education had taken a toll on his social development, depriving him of the opportunity for normal socializing with people his own age. They noticed how his lapses of social grace or seemingly inappropriate behavior were sometimes misinterpreted. Bob was blisteringly honest, which occasionally caused discomfort or hurt feelings. Marvin and Nettie blamed themselves for allowing Bob to rely too much on his brain and to grow up too fast.

Bob still loved his expensive hobby of flying but it was much more than a hobby to him—he wanted to be the first Jewish astronaut. He applied to NASA when he got out of medical school but got turned down. He did, however, briefly study space medicine at the Johnson Space Center in Clear Lake, Texas, where they advised him to serve a residency in internal medicine—because it would give him a better shot at getting on the shuttle. Bob fulfilled the residency but NASA again turned him down, without saying why—one of the few things in life at which he did not succeed.

Earlier that year, Amanda had renewed her friendship with Gail. Two years after Gail had overdosed and slashed her wrists, the friends had gotten together for lunch at a Midtown restaurant. When Gail showed Amanda her razor scars, she winced at the pale lines on her wrists and arms. Gail explained that she had cut that way, following the line of the blood vessel, in order to drain her body of blood more quickly and avoid clotting. Amanda was shocked. She couldn't imagine the pain and loneliness that had driven Gail to do such a thing to herself.

Gail told Amanda how her friend had found her bleeding in the bathtub and dialed 911. Paramedics had bandaged Gail's self-inflicted wounds and rushed her in their ambulance to the New York Hospital–Cornell Medical Center emergency room, where doctors pumped her stomach and patched up her body. But healing her emotional wounds was proving to be more difficult. She was transferred to the nearby Gothic Payne Whitney Clinic for two months of psychiatric treatment. As she recovered, Gail would learn that what she believed before her suicide attempt was in many ways true. Compared to slowly, painfully rebuilding your shattered psyche after a nervous breakdown, death by piña colada was easy. After she got out of the hospital, Gail told Amanda, she continued to see a psychiatrist. Gail talked about her shrink and about a guy who helped her get over her depression.

Fortunately, two years after the event, Gail seemed to be on the other side of whatever it was that caused it and was apparently back to normal. That is, she still complained about her life and how unhappy she was.

Amanda remembered how she told Gail that she and Nick had gone from being a struggling couple in a small apartment—when Nick was a resident—to their new life.

Nick was a practicing plastic surgeon and, suddenly, they had money, a new house, new cars and nice vacations. Amanda did not have to work and she was pursuing her dream—writing music at home. Gail had said that she, too, wanted that life. She told her she needed someone and—like Amanda—wanted to meet a doctor and live happily ever after.

The night Bob played guitar for his friends in New Jersey, he had just broken up with his fiancée *Marcy, who was also a young physician, a resident working 120 hours a week, like Bob. Bob told people that he and Marcy had parted but most people, including Amanda, had never heard the details of the breakup.

When Bob finished playing the guitar and stood up, Amanda silently sized up the handsome, 6-foot-2 surgeon. He was a resident in Manhattan studying cardio-thoracic surgery. He had an athletic build, a straight nose, a strong chin and full, red sensual lips. Bob was also a genius, with perfect musical pitch, and a pilot. He came from a good family who lived only a few miles away in West Orange. He was a catch, the pick of the litter, Amanda concluded. Over dinner, Bob said he was in between girlfriends and a bit lonely in the city. Amanda asked Bob what kind of a girl he was looking for.

"Simple," said Bob. "Somebody who's pretty, bright and interesting."

It didn't sound so simple to Amanda. A girl would have to be bright to keep up with Bob, Amanda thought. Bob wanted what his friend Nick had—a beautiful, charming wife who made him happy. Amanda thought of her friend Gail—she was pretty, bright and interesting. While Bob was brilliant, outgoing and accomplished, Gail was introspective and lost. They were both lonely and lived in Manhattan. Perhaps opposites would attract, Amanda thought. Maybe Bob and Gail would like to date and have some fun.

After her weekend chat with Bob, Amanda decided she would do a little matchmaking and picked up the phone.

"Gail, how would you like to meet a doctor?"

CHAPTER 3

THE SURGEON'S WIFE

BOB nosed the Cessna north, high over the dark waters of New York Harbor. Lit by floodlights, the pale green figure of the Statue of Liberty stood sentinel with her glowing torch. The sprawling, sparkling stone forest of Manhattan slowly passed the window, as Bob guided the craft over the Brooklyn Bridge. A full, white moon hung in the sky over Queens and its reflection rippled in the dark river below. Even for a New Yorker, the sight was magnificent, a view Gail had never seen before—the New York skyline at night from her own private plane.

Bob could fly at night because he had obtained his instrument rating, which enabled him to use the plane's compass, altimeter, directional radios and other gadgets to pilot and land the aircraft while flying blind in the dead of night or in fog. Next, they soared over the Manhattan Bridge and the Williamsburg Bridge, glittering arcs over the East River. Bob was showing Gail his sky, sharing his first great love with the woman he loved. The flight and the new relationship took Gail out of herself, lifting her to new heights. It was quite a date. Theirs was a match made—if not in heaven—at least in the sky.

But Gail did not just look at the awesome view. She also looked at Bob and gazed deeply into his eyes. Gail was not put off by Bob's penetrating eyes—she was mesmerized by them. She was infatuated with Bob, swept off her feet and into the sky.

She later wrote a poem, in which Gail told Bob that he was master of the heavens and that "Moonbeams danced in your hair and a glow radiated from your eyes, /Engulfing me, and drawing me into you . . ."

Gail declared that Bob banished all her problems and depression, and she vowed her undying love for him.

Bob and Gail began to engage in wholesome outdoor activities together, like flying and hiking and biking and skiing. That seemed to be good for Gail. On the weekends, they would fly to scenic airports, such as rural Greenwood Lake Airport in Northern New Jersey, which was close to mountain trails, ski slopes and lakes that featured boating and swimming.

When they stood together and Bob put his arm around Gail's shoulder, she only came up to his chin. They were a pretty couple, the surgeon and the receptionist. Gail had been working at an entry-level job at a Manhattan ad agency. Very quickly, they had become close, even though they were very different. Bob spoke to Gail about his work as a surgical resident. He lived in a luxury one-bedroom condo but made almost nothing.

Amanda had no idea that Bob and Gail would get so serious so quickly. They had little in common: Bob was the first conservative Republican Gail had ever dated and they disagreed on most political issues. He was a dog person, she was a cat person. When they first met, it seemed all they each needed to hear was that they were both Jewish. Even though neither one seemed to be very religious, it was apparently very important to both of them.

Bob couldn't resist Gail sexually, and she made sure he was satisfied. After Gail and Bob began dating exclusively, with Gail spending most of her time at Bob's place, their relationship seemed to come down to earth.

As for their differences . . . stress. Bob was an uptown kind of guy. He had trouble with the idea of marrying someone who was a dropout, working at a non-professional job. He wanted Gail to go back to school and get her degree. Gail had already resigned herself to going back to school, even though it seemed like a task.

Bob noticed Gail's suicide scars and, eventually, she told him how she got them. It gave Bob pause but he was already infatuated with her. It seemed to Gail that she was marked, that she could never get a fresh start, that people would always look down on her because of her past—her drug days, her suicide attempt, her hospitalizations.

As their differences became plain, they began to have fights. Bob worked 120 hours a week in a cardio-vascular surgery program and was under tremendous stress.

Bob's parents met Gail and liked her, but thought she was very high strung. They urged Bob not to rush into anything, but he did not listen.

Gail confided her problems to Amanda, who thought that, at times, their relationship seemed to be more of a negotiation than a courtship. When Bob and Gail came over for dinner, the difference between the two was obvious. Bob was intellectually-based and Gail was emotionally-based, Amanda decided. While Bob asked his hosts about their own lives, Gail still talked mostly about herself—her feelings, her problems, how long the car ride was because of the traffic, how tired she was, how hungry she was but that she didn't want to eat too much because of her diet. Whatever his criticisms of Gail, Bob was obviously in love with her. He looked at her with puppy dog eyes, a big grin on his face all the time. Underneath the surface, Amanda saw one person who was in love, Bob, and one person who wanted security, Gail.

"I'm not sure if I'm in love," Gail confided in Amanda one day.

Gail told her friend about her huge misunderstandings with Bob. She seemed really angry at him for not being perfect for her. She had serious doubts but was trying to make it work, anyway.

"Am I doing the right thing? Is he the right one?" she asked.

Amanda told her she shouldn't get married if she wasn't in love—not if she didn't have an incredible emotional connection with Bob—because it wouldn't be a good idea for either one of them. It just didn't feel right to Gail but she was still willing to get married, even though that special spark was missing.

"If only he would be different . . ." Gail said, listing changes she wanted to make in Bob.

Meanwhile, Bob was making changes in Gail. Gail secretly resented Bob's program to correct her. Perhaps the worst was the smoking. Bob did not smoke and detested being around those who did. To him, it was an irrational, unhealthy, filthy habit. He warned Gail about lung cancer and heart disease, and reduced skin elasticity. "Smoking gives you wrinkles," he scolded her.

Bob did not give Gail an engagement ring, as he had with Marcy. Bob took the stone from his previous fiancée's engagement ring, and the stone from an engagement ring Gail had received from a prior suitor, and made them into earrings for her. It was a statement that they both had loved and lost in the past—and now had each other. But even when she wore the beautiful earrings, it did not seem as if Gail was preparing for the most joyous event of her life. It was as if she was about to swallow a distasteful pill that she knew would be good for her. Gail's mother and shrink had the same prescription for what ailed Gail—marry a doctor, get a degree and live a life of luxury. Gail explained to Amanda that she could return to school and complete her degree without having to work. If she married Bob, Gail knew she would make him and her parents happy. It seemed like a safe harbor, a promise to end her pain.

"Well, if it doesn't work out, at least I'll be farther along," Gail sighed. Not exactly a marriage made in heaven, Amanda thought.

In her talks with Gail, Amanda also sensed sexual problems, and she asked about them. Bob was satisfied but Gail was not. She just wasn't turned on by Bob. It was as if Gail was the one piece missing from Bob and he was now complete. She was obviously angry at him for being so perfect, so happy. Although she felt in control sexually, it pissed her off that she really satisfied him but she felt unsatisfied. Just like all her previous paramours, Bob wasn't good enough. Gail also wanted him to be suave, dashing. Amanda thought it was silly, unrealistic and immature. The guy was a genius, a surgeon, a musician, a skier—but he wasn't Richard Gere, too. Amanda thought there was no such person in the world. Bob's voice actually sounded just like another handsome actor—Kevin Costner—but he did not have Costner's suave charm. Gail could close her eyes and hear what sounded like Kevin Costner playing the part of a young surgeon, but when she opened her eyes, she saw Bob.

If Bob had a major shortcoming, Amanda thought, it was that he was too childlike. He was a stupid genius who couldn't see that his lady wasn't complete, like he was. He didn't want to know that she wasn't in love like him. If he wasn't a Jewish doctor, he would already be history, Amanda decided. She told Nick what Gail had said but neither of them warned Bob about what they thought he was getting into, what they thought he didn't see. Amanda thought Bob was like the nerd who got the beautiful, sexy girl in the movies. The real problem was obvious to Amanda—Bob loved Gail and Gail did not love Bob.

Perhaps Gail was not capable of achieving happiness or of loving someone, Amanda thought. She certainly wouldn't get happy by marrying a person she wasn't in love with. For some reason, Gail had bad taste in men and was attracted to bad boys, controlling, abusive types who might mistreat her. But Amanda wondered whether the men were abusive, or if her friend just found all men to be that way. One thing was certain—Bob lacked excitement for her because he wasn't a bad boy. Gail wasn't really attracted to Bob because he wasn't dangerous.

Gail complained about her life to most of her friends and many of her classmates. She gossiped to her hairdresser, a Lebanese-born woman who went by the single professional name of Ouidad, pronounced Wee-dod. Ouidad, who cut Gail's hair at her penthouse salon atop a small brownstone building on Seventh Avenue, liked Gail and thought she was funny, a real riot. But she was surprised, as Gail spoke of landing a doctor, to hear that her client had a family—since she had never spoken about them before. Gail detailed fights with her mother, who nagged her, and her disagreements with her sister Alayne. As Ouidad listened sympathetically, she got the impression that Gail was marrying the doctor to please her mother and sister.

But Gail was finally back in the good graces of her mother and father, who were very happy at the approaching wedding of their wayward daughter to someone who seemed to be Prince Charming after a long line of toads. Gail's parents seemed a lot happier about Gail becoming Mrs. Dr. Robert Bierenbaum than she was. Sylvia was ecstatic that Gail seemed to be on the right track, at last. Bob was a doctor, they were close to the same age, he was nice-looking, they were the same religion, he came from a comfortable family and he wanted to get married. Manny agreed. This was the way for Gail to get hold of her life and give it direction. Alayne thought that her parents were relieved when Gail brought Bob home, because "somebody else was going to take care of her." Bob seemed to want many of the same things for Gail that her parents did—he wanted her to settle down, go back to school and get a degree and have kids. Bob also insisted Gail stop smoking. He was taking her in hand.

The young couple drove out to Long Island for dinners in Bob's snazzy Datsun 280Z sports car that featured a license plate bearing Bob's initials and the MD designation. In the summer of 1982, they splashed around in the Katzes' backyard pool with Manny, Sylvia, Alayne and Steve. Sometimes neighbors and friends would drop by for fun in the pool or for barbecues.

Alayne liked Bob immediately. He was smart, he was attractive, successful and good at everything he tried.

Sylvia was "kvelling"—the Yiddish word for being overcome with pride and joy. Her heart swelled with "naches"—parental pride. To the same neighbors and friends that she had for years confided her hopes that Gail would find a nice Jewish doctor, Sylvia now announced her mission accomplished, after seven years of "tsores"—aggravation—from Gail.

"My daughter's marrying a doctor," Sylvia told her

neighbor *Tess Feinstein. Tess knew Sylvia had been a doctor's receptionist and had hoped for years to marry Gail off to a doctor. She had seen Bob at the house and thought he was adorable. She was glad for Sylvia, who was obviously very happy.

Having her weekly haircut between mirrored walls that caused her reflection to be repeated endlessly—the images fading away into infinity, Sylvia couldn't resist bragging. "My daughter Gail is marrying a doctor," she proudly told her hairdresser, as if Gail had completed medical school herself.

"Oh, that's great," the stylist responded, as he trimmed Sylvia's coif. "Congratulations."

"Thank you. He's a surgeon, he's Jewish, he's a okler and so good-looking," Sylvia beamed into the endless mirror. "He even flies a plane."

CHAPTER 4

CATS

GAIL saw the homeless cat hanging around the Caldwell Airport after she and Bob returned from a Saturday in the air. She convinced Bob to adopt the cat, whom they named Amelia—after Amelia Earhart, the aviatrix.

Months before Gail and Bob's wedding, Gail phoned Amanda and said she was very upset and had a story to tell about Bob. He had told his future bride about his breakup with Marcy, who also was a doctor. Bob said he was transporting Marcy's belongings back to her apartment—including her cat. During the car trip, the animal became very agitated and began skittering around the inside of the vehicle, making it dangerous to drive, Bob told Gail, so Bob drove with one hand on the wheel and tried to grab the panicky creature with the other. After several tries, Bob got ahold of the cat—who struggled fiercely to get free. In the struggle, Bob's hand ended up around the cat's neck. Because the cat was endangering the vehicle, Bob held it tightly and inadvertently strangled it to death. Gail was horrified when Bob related the tale and was still in shock repeating it to her girlfriend.

"Yow! That's some yucky story," Amanda thought, also appalled.

Amanda felt the incident didn't mesh with the Bob she knew. He was gentle and sweet around animals. Bob expressed remorse over the death but Gail told Amanda she didn't believe Bob, that he was a liar. She believed Bob coldly, intentionally killed the animal. It didn't seem to make any sense. If the animal was running around the car, why interfere? The cat couldn't crash the car. For some reason, despite Bob's version, Gail was convinced Bob had killed the cat on purpose—to exact revenge on the girlfriend who kicked him out. Gail told Amanda she was afraid Bob might hurt her cat. Bob, she said, thought she loved her cat more than him. Amanda wondered whether Bob was right.

"I'm scared of him," she told Amanda.

Gail claimed her cat acted strange around Bob and would run away from him or avoid him. She thought Bob was sick, and Amanda told her that if she thought someone was trying to kill her cats, she shouldn't marry that person. But the reluctant bride had no intention of canceling the nuptials.

The next time Amanda and Nick went to their friends' apartment in Manhattan, they seemed like the ideal couple. Gail snuggled up to Bob on the couch after the meal, as if they were deeply in love, and they chatted and laughed happily with their guests.

"This is whacky," Amanda thought. "Will the real Gail Katz please stand up?"

Bob picked up Gail's brown, striped tabby, and put her on his lap, stroking her neck and back, his palm running slowly down her soft fur before starting again at the head. Bob's contented smile gave Amanda a chill. Did he know that Gail had told her about the choking incident? Was Bob trying to make a point? How could Gail marry someone she feared? Was Bob a cat killer or did Gail exaggerate everything? Or did this latest piece of information about her fiancé inspire Gail to take him more to her heart—because Bob was now dangerous?

One hot August night in 1982, three weeks before the wedding, Bob and Gail decided to stop in Chinatown for something to eat. Gail felt that Bob was driving like a lunatic and when they began to argue about where to park, the dispute turned nasty. Gail felt Bob was berating her, and not because he believed the things he was saying, but for some other purpose.

"If I put up with it, he'll drop the subject," Gail thought.

Bob never parked the car. He drove them home in tense silence. They went to bed angry, each facing away from the other. Amelia, purring, jumped up on the bed and affectionately curled up with Gail.

Alayne Katz's phone rang in her Manhattan apartment. It was Gail and she was hysterical.

"Bob tried to strangle the kitten in the toilet bowl," Gail said quickly. "He had the cat's head under water and he had his fingers around the throat. You've got to help me."

It was a bizarre story to wake up to in the middle of the night. Alayne asked her sister the obvious question.

"Why?"

"He's jealous of me loving the cat," Gail replied. "He wants my full and undivided attention."

It was all very strange. Gail asked Alayne to come over the next morning and help her bring the cat to an animal shelter and not to tell their parents. Alayne agreed to help— even though she was allergic to cats.

The next day, when Alayne arrived outside Gail's apartment, Amelia, held in Gail's arms, was unhurt, but still meowing. Again, Alayne asked Gail why Bob would attack a little cat.

"Bob thinks I love the cat more than him," Gail explained.

"So we're calling the wedding off?" Alayne asked, hopefully.

"No, I love him," Gail protested. "I love this man. The invitations are out. I can make this work. I can change him." Alayne was still trying to adjust to the fact that Bob—the stable, wonderful, calm surgeon—was supposedly some kind of sick, insecure child who tried to drown kittens.

While the sisters were taking Amelia to an animal shelter, Alayne told her sister she had trouble believing that a brilliant professional like Bob could be so twisted as to try to kill a beloved pet with his bare hands.

"Bob looks good on paper—until you meet him," was Gail's reply. "That's when you see he's a social moron."

Alayne decided then that she disagreed with Gail, her shrink and their parents. Gail didn't need a husband, she thought—she needed some self-respect, motivation, ambition and direction. That would come from herself and from the right therapist—not from a husband.

"Why don't we keep the cat and get rid of Bob?" Alayne suggested. "There's something really wrong here and this is really scary."

No, said Gail. The cat was safe from Bob. Gail had no life to go back to. She had no choice but to marry Bob, she felt. She did not want to be single. Gail had a plan: all she had to do was make Bob content and happy—no matter what it took—and then she would change him.

Later, Gail told an older confidante about the incident and the woman tried to shock Gail into re-evaluating her life.

"Why are you always putting yourself in situations where things will blow up in your face?" the woman asked "Why are you putting yourself in the position of the cat?"

Gail did not answer. She just sat there silently, thinking.

CHAPTER 5

PERFECT LIFE

GAIL and her mother planned a perfect wedding—with white, blue and purple as her colors—but the day itself did not begin perfectly. Gail had convinced Ouidad to come out to Bellmore to fix her hair but when the hairdresser and her husband arrived, they walked into a tense house. There was no lunch, or even coffee, available, and Gail and her sister Alayne got into a screaming fight with each other. It was very awkward to witness an ugly family squabble but Ouidad had no choice. She set to work and resigned to finish as quickly as possible. Her husband, however, did have a choice and he fled outside to his car rather than remain in the house. When Ouidad was done, Gail was ready for the limousine trip into Manhattan.

Bob and Gail were married on Sunday, August 29, 1982, a sunny, not-too-hot, perfect summer day. The couple stood together, hand-in-hand beneath the customary "chupeh" shelter in a large Manhattan synagogue. Gail, who had dieted until she seemed almost too thin, was a beautiful bride, resplendent in a traditional white, lacy wedding gown. She wore a strand of white pearls around her neck, a garland crown of delicate white blossoms, baby's breath and a gossamer veil on her head. Bob was also dressed from head-to-toe in white—an ivory silk suit, shirt, tie and shoes, a matching white yarmulke on his head and a white floral boutonniere on his lapel.

The happy couple honeymooned in sunny Crete, where they stayed in a beautiful villa that belonged to one of Bob's doctor friends. There they sunned on the baking sand, swam in the azure sea under a bright cobalt sky and feasted on delicious local dishes, washed down with good, inexpensive wine. At the palace at Knossos, they walked the legendary labyrinth that might have inspired the mythological tale of Theseus and the Minotaur. Together, they wandered through its ancient twists and turns that legend said once concealed a deadly monster.

Like many young couples, Bob and Gail had spats on their honeymoon, interspersed with lovemaking. Once, while sightseeing on a dusty cliff overlooking the sea, Gail backed away from the brink because she had a sudden giddy terror that Bob might shove her over. But despite their occasional quarrels, they enjoyed their honeymoon and were reluctant to return home—especially Gail. En route back to Manhattan, she became very apprehensive. "There's a lot of mail waiting at home," Gail thought, in quiet terror.

The closer she got to the home she shared with Bob, the closer she got back to her new life, the more panicky she became. She was obsessed about the mail; In addition to the usual run of correspondence, bills and circulars, Bob received mail regarding the interests that comprised his busy life. He received hospital and doctor mail, as well as medical magazines, skiing magazines, computer and stereo magazines and large aviation maps for flying. Was there a lot of it waiting for them? Gail did not know why, but the thought of a large pile of unopened mail really frightened her. She knew it wasn't fear of some impending bill or some expected bad news—it went far beyond any explainable fear.

After the honeymoon, Gail began school and Bob returned to his long, exhausting, hours at the hospital. A month before the wedding, Bob had begun as a fellow in cardio-thoracic surgery. In addition, he worked with his father Marvin at the World Trade Center and at 26 Federal Plaza, reviewing medical charts of Social Security claimants—looking for fraudulent filings.

Bob pampered Gail, opening doors and turning on lights for her. Though Gail seemed to thrive on the constant attention, she told others she felt stifled by it.

Bob was studying to be a flight instructor and his goal was to log as many hours in the air as he could. The couple continued to fly on the weekends. Sometimes to different cities and other times, just to have fun in the sky, looking down on suburban New Jersey, the dramatic city skyline and the blue rippled ocean. Every time they went away, Gail's bizarre fear of the mail would reappear.

Gail saw a psychiatrist, *Elsa Fairchild, twice a week. If Gail became extremely anxious, Elsa would arrange for a third session. The same subject dominated every session— Bob. Over and over, Gail discussed her fear of staying with Bob and her fear of leaving him. She experienced chronic fear that she would make him angry. Elsa helped Gail explore her feelings on the subject but did not encourage her to stay or to leave. Bob, of course, paid the bill.

To unwind after a day on the job, Bob got an Atari home computer. He loved to play the games, especially the Flight Simulator program, so that even when he was earthbound, he could fly a virtual airplane and put his head back up in the clouds.

Sometimes, the young bride chided her husband because he was busy playing with the beeping computer when she wanted attention. She also used the computer to compose her term papers at Hunter College. Gail applied herself and maintained a perfect 4.0 grade average. She seemed to have motivation and ambition for the first time in years. Bob liked Gail to be thin, to work hard and not to smoke, and she was doing it all. Sometimes she felt Bob wanted her to be perfect—like him. There are few things as annoying or stressful as someone who accomplishes, seemingly without effort, that which others cannot do without grinding toil. And being perfect, for Gail, took a lot of hard work.

Gail began dressing the part of a doctor's wife, wearing more conservative and less revealing clothing. She still worked as a bartender—because they needed the money. But she did not like it and neither did Bob.

In 1982, Bob and Gail flew down to visit Alayne in Virginia, where she was living while attending law school in Washington. They were not exactly the jet set, but certainly the prop set. Bob and Gail and Alayne and her new boyfriend also flew together on ski trips. Though Alayne felt she could never be close to Bob, after what Gail had told her, she noted that they seemed to be happy, or at least friendly, and Gail finally had a goal and a life of her own.

Outwardly, Gail seemed like someone to envy but her mysterious inner turmoil was growing. From time to time, she jotted down some of her apprehensions in a small daily diary and address book that she carried with her. She was always on a diet. And when she went off her diet plan, she thought, "Well, today I won't be dieting and I'll start fresh tomorrow." Once she had decided that, Gail would eat everything she could get her hands on until she was stuffed. Once she had achieved that bloated, sated distension in her abdomen, she felt a wave of regret. And she would do it again and again.

Riding the subway alone one afternoon, on her way to school, Gail sat on a plastic seat, lost in thought. She was thinking about her tendency to be overly sensitive and completely withdraw from anyone she felt had been unfair or nasty to her.

"I actually feel that I hate them and I can't even stand to be in the same room with them anymore," Gail decided. "That goes for anyone—my family, my friends, employers, teachers."

Of course, this impulse of Gail's made it difficult for her to function and she needed to learn to deal with such situations in a different way. That was why she saw a shrink. "I end up hurting myself, rather than the person who hurt me," Gail concluded. As she thought about the things that were troubling her, she suddenly realized that her face had been very animated, as if she were reacting to a conversation with another person. As she caught herself frowning, she became embarrassed.

"I hope no one thinks I'm crazy," she thought.

Another time, Gail was at her weekly dance class at Hunter College, a short subway ride from her East 85th Street home. Dance was Gail's first love and she signed up for the class because she needed joy in her life. In her leotards and dancing shoes, Gail limbered up with the rest of the class. The professor described and demonstrated the dance steps, which were pretty basic. Gail had done them all before. But when it was her turn to perform, she felt inhibited, self-conscious. As she began the routine, her movements no longer seemed to flow with natural, sensual delight and her gestures were an imitation of grace. The steps were easy, but Gail's concentration was gone. She was convinced she was clumsy, terrible, the worst in the class—counting her own mistakes as she made them.

"I've been dancing since I was young," Gail thought. "I know the steps and the movements the professor is asking for but, time and time again, I screw up." For her, it was more than a dance. It was the one thing she was supposed to do beautifully, effortlessly, perfectly.

It broke Gail's heart that she felt she could no longer dance.

At college, Gail made several new friends. Marianne DeCesare, another psych major, sat next to Gail in her Abnormal Psych class. They were both married and older than the other undergraduate students in the class. They went out for coffee and talked about how they both wanted to be psychotherapists, the difficulty of making ends meet, and about opening a catering business to make money for grad school. Gail told Marianne about Bob and how much she wanted financial independence from him. After Gail had a fight with Bob, she would ask Marianne for advice. "What would you do?" Gail would ask. Marianne would tell her and Gail would listen very carefully—but never seemed to act on her suggestions.

Gail told her that Bob was very possessive and had threatened to strangle her if she ever left him. After watching a TV movie about socialite Claus von Bülow, who was charged with trying to kill his wife, Gail said Bob told her he would not leave a body to connect him to a crime.

"The problem with the von Bülow case is that he left evidence," said Bob. "I would not leave evidence."

Gail decided to start her own business, which offered catering and other services for busy professionals. She took out an ad in the trendy *New York* magazine. Francesca Beale, a high-powered attorney for CBS network, was one of those who answered the ad. Gail cooked a couple of meals in advance every week and stored them in Francesca's refrigerator. She also ran errands for the busy executive, walked her dog and watched Francesca's children until she got home from the office. Francesca liked Gail's work and recommended her to several other Upper East Side yuppie women. So Gail got a close look at the life she wanted, but not the way she wanted—as a servant, as a rent-a-wife. Francesca was shocked to discover that Gail was married to a doctor and had to work. Gail told her about her problems as well.

But things were looking up for Gail. Four months after the wedding, in January 1983, the couple moved into a grander two-bedroom place on the fashionable, high-rent Upper East Side of Manhattan—Nirvana by comparison to Gail's former residence. Bob used the spare bedroom, which doubled as a guest room, as his office. The $900 rent for their twelfth-floor apartment at 185 East 85th Street, in the Yorkville section, was paid for by Bob's father Marvin. The home had just been vacated by Bob's sister Michelle, a psychiatrist, and her husband.

The apartment house had a great location, uniformed doormen, great security and a spectacular view of the Manhattan skyline and the East River Bridges. The high-rise was featured on network television every week—as an example of success—on the opening of the network sitcom "The Jeffersons." As a camera panned up the front of the building, the show began with a catchy theme song, called "Movin' On Up," written and performed by Ja'net DuBois. The mock-spiritual praised the virtues of the elegant address in terms of a rollicking gospel hymn of thanksgiving that viewers, including Gail Katz and her parents, could appreciate. The theme song rejoiced that the couple was moving on up to the East Side, "To a deluxe apartment in the sky" and had "finally got a piece of the pie."

CHAPTER 6

IMPERFECTION

GAIL noticed that, although she was doing well in school, her level of anxiety was rising. She had always been nervous about speaking before large groups but it seemed to have gotten worse. Knowing that she had to speak in class the next day made it difficult for Gail to sleep. And when she gave her talks on psychology, her voice trembled.

Often, her tension came out when she was alone in her car. If someone cut her off, Gail would erupt into a rage, yelling and screaming. She knew the other driver couldn't hear her, but she would go absolutely nuts.

In college, Gail studied different methods of psychotherapy, including a new, controversial confrontational approach called STAP—short for Short-Term Anxiety-Provoking psychotherapy. It was a radical departure from other soothing brands of treatment. The goal was not to avoid anxiety but to provoke it—in order to quickly get to the base of problems. STAP required the therapist to enrage and incite the patient with probing questions and in-your-face observations that would force her to face her own denials and repressed rage that had led to personal problems. One of the most debated features of the therapy was the focus on submerged murderous thoughts. Encouraging a patient to express homicidal fantasies could liberate repressed anger and clear up relationships, many therapists felt. But the treatment mode was not for everyone and the method was aimed at a very specific, limited group of mildly neurotic individuals of above average intelligence, who were motivated to change. Therapists had to screen potential STAP patients very carefully: one of the scenarios to be avoided at all costs was encouraging a dangerous psychopath to express and explore his murderous fantasies. The result might be very unpleasant.

Gail became involved with a project that had begun to evaluate STAP therapy—by watching videotapes of sessions. She observed the head-on collisions between therapist and patient and then scored each session as to whether it had been successful, ineffective or harmful. Gail's boss at the research program was *Jane Dunne, an attractive 39-year-old clinical psychologist with a Ph.D. Jane felt fortunate to have Gail working for her because she was a bright, dedicated, hard worker, who labored long hours. But after a few weeks, Jane noticed that Gail had a tendency to be a bit neurotic and tempestuous, with occasional histrionic episodes. She still thought Gail would make a good therapist.

As they became friends, Gail spoke more and more about her problems. She told Jane she was unhappy in her marriage but was afraid to leave her husband because she was afraid to be alone. Gail's weekly bitching sessions about Bob became a regular feature of their working relationship and Jane listened with the sympathetic ear of an older woman—one who had been there. As Gail described a domineering husband who belittled her and controlled her, it resonated painfully with Jane. As she heard how cold Bob could be, Jane remembered her own failed marriage to a man she believed was a dangerous psychopath. The man Gail was describing seemed very much like her own ex-husband, who had put her through hell. He had beaten her and once almost killed her. One night, she had to jump out a window to escape his wrath. When Gail described how Bob had tried to kill her cat, Jane became alarmed and felt she had to warn the younger woman. She was also concerned that Gail seemed inclined to provoke her husband the way STAP therapists goaded patients. She tried to tell Gail that she needed to change her situation but Gail believed she could control things.

"I have a friend who was abused by her husband," said Jane, attributing her own terrifying experiences to another woman. It all just bounced right off Gail. Jane asked if Bob had ever attacked her.

"No."

"It's just a matter of time," she warned.

One of the people Gail met in her clinical work at Beth Israel Hospital was a *Dr. Ali Abdul, a physician. Gail flirted with Ali and, she would later tell Jane, she began a casual affair with him. She said that Bob, a staunch supporter of Israel, would be especially jealous if he knew Ali was of Arabic descent. Gail seemed pleased when she described how hurt her husband would be if he found out.

One night, about 11 P.M., as Gail was jogging down Sixth Avenue, she noticed a shabby young man, with wild, glaring eyes, walking in the middle of the street, directly into the oncoming traffic. He was obviously homeless, deranged, possibly drug addicted. The man playing chicken with the deadly line of vehicles did not speak but he emanated rage, as the autos swerved wildly to avoid killing him. He ignored the humans inside and concentrated on the screeching vehicles, as if the cars were living things.

"How fascinating," Gail thought. "I've got to follow this person."

Gail did not call the police but saw it as an opportunity to observe and understand both the disturbed individual and the reactions of normal people to him. As she followed the dangerous scene, she noticed that there was a method to his madness. Although he was staggering headlong toward the onrushing cars, he didn't actually change his course and throw himself under any of them. Gail could think of more practical ways to kill oneself. She could not look away. It seemed he would be smashed by the next car, but that, too, screeched and turned aside at the last second.

"He's trying to kill himself," Gail decided finally. "But he wants the cars to hit him. What a strange form of suicide."

Gail was attracted by this abnormal self-destructive behavior. Such moments seemed charged with meaning, almost as if Gail were meant to see them and learn from them. The way to fathom yourself was to understand others, Gail believed.

Bob and Gail's neighbors in the apartments on either side of theirs often heard Gail's taunting voice screaming at Bob, goading him. *Mae Eisenhower, a woman living on the floor beneath them, could hear them stomping across the floor and shouting. Sunday mornings seemed to be their favorite time: Like clockwork, Mae would hear the shouting and the furniture being shoved every Sunday. She decided they fought on Sunday mornings because that was the time they were both home.

Like many couples, Gail and Bob fought over money. Gail was not yet able to live like a doctor's wife because Bob made no more than $35,000 a year as a surgical resident. They would not have been able to live in their deluxe apartment in the sky without generous help from Bob's dad. When Bob returned from a long day and night of dealing with life and death at work, he began to get impatient with what he considered Gail's petty, self-centered bitching and demands.

The neighbors couldn't hear it but Gail occasionally became so enraged at Bob that she hit him. Like many men, Bob did not physically strike back but kept his own rage bottled up. Sometimes one or the other stormed out of the apartment, slamming the door. They were always drawn back together. Neither one could break it off or make it work. Bob was locked in by love and could not imagine Gail leaving him. Gail imagined leaving Bob but, as yet, had nowhere else to go. Arguments had become chronic, with Gail demanding attention that Bob had no time to provide. She wanted him to do things differently. Bob felt she wanted him to be someone he was not. He felt that he worked very hard, yet she was never satisfied. They each felt unloved.

During one argument between the couple, emotions ran very high and—unusually—Bob lost his composure. Gail was angry that Bob refused to attend a party she wanted to go to. Fed up, Bob grabbed a large, shiny knife from the kitchen and turned it toward his stomach. Eventually, he put the knife down, but their arguments had crossed a line from shouting to histrionic acting-out. During yet another shouting match in their car, while Gail was at the wheel on the FDR Drive, Bob flung open the car door and threatened to jump out. It was odd that Bob would threaten suicide to prove his love for Gail, who had actually tried to kill herself. They again reconciled and went on with their daily routine but their dramatic spats had raised the issue of death. It was used as a theatrical device to trump an argument but it also implied the possibility of death as one way out—a violent solution to their dilemma.

Sometimes, after the battles, Gail shared her woes with her friend Amanda, who listened with growing sadness. Gail complained that Bob was very controlling, unreasonably jealous and usually uncommunicative. Gail did not tell Amanda that Bob actually had reason to be jealous, although he only had suspicions. Also, said Gail, Bob refused to seek therapy. His message was: Gail was the crazy one. But Bob was no longer the cheerful guy Amanda once knew, either. She didn't tell Gail, but Amanda concluded that Bob had not saved Gail, as everyone had hoped. She wondered if Gail was capable of being in love with anyone. Gail, she decided, was dragging Bob down, emotionally. She regretted that she had introduced them.

While Gail was getting her hair cut one Saturday, Ouidad noticed that, after her big marriage, Gail had simply stopped talking about her doctor husband—as if she had married him and just filed him away.

"So, how's your husband?" Ouidad asked.

"Great," said Gail, in an artificial way, dropping the subject.

But Gail did talk about her boyfriends, without being asked. She described, graphically, what she did with other men and how exciting it was.

"Oh, this guy I'm seeing, he's wonderful," Gail gushed. "I feel so bad but I need it."

On Tuesday night, November 8, 1983, Gail was up late studying for her Graduate Record Exam, which would determine whether she got into graduate school. About 11 P.M., she decided she needed a smoke to lessen the tension and took a pack of cigarettes and a lighter out to the terrace and placed them on the table between two chairs. Bob wouldn't be home for quite some time, so Gail looked out at the uptown skyline lights and the sparkling bridges. She did not hear the apartment door open behind her, did not see Bob standing in the doorway. When he saw the pack of hated butts sitting on the terrace table, his look instantly distorted into raw rage. Gail turned, too late, saw Bob, and realized that she had finally been caught. Bob thought smoking was terrible but the issue had taken on much greater meaning between them. It was all the things they didn't like about each other, all the things they fought about. It was also all the things they did not discuss. Gail felt that Bob saw it as her intention to leave him. What would Bob do?

Gail's sudden fear caused adrenaline to surge through her system. Her breathing became rapid and her heart rate doubled, fluttering in her chest. Bob strode over to the table, scooped up the hated cigarette pack and tossed it contemptuously over the railing. Suddenly, Bob jumped over the terrace rail and onto the other side, with nothing keeping him from the 12-story drop but his hands and feet on the railing.

"It's all over," Bob said, in a matter-of-fact tone—as if he were about to let go and follow the cigarettes down, as if that were what Gail wanted him to do.

"No!" Gail yelled.

Gail was stunned. She felt that Bob had tried to manipulate her with dramatic threats before but this seemed real. After his gesture had its effect on Gail, Bob climbed back and sat down at the table.

"Why did you do that?" Gail demanded.

Bob listened sedately as Gail began to berate him and list all the things he did that she didn't like. She began to pound him with insults. She criticized his driving and told him he was a pathological liar. She said nasty, confrontational things about his mind, about how he didn't stand up to people, about how he did not measure up as a man.

"You're making the cigarette issue have more meaning than it really has," Gail said. Bob fixed her with a cold stare and answered her in a very calm and sincere voice: "I'm going to kill you."

Gail froze. Bob leaped up. His flattened hands darted toward her throat, his gold wedding band flashing, before Gail could react. His hands slammed into the base of her neck, his thumbs apart—the old judo choke hold he had learned as a youth. The sides of Bob's hands jabbed painfully into both sides of Gail's neck at the same time, compressing the carotid artery on her left side and instantly interrupting the flow of blood to Gail's brain. Deprived of oxygen-rich blood, her brain began to faint. The pain around her throat faded away, as did Bob's tranquil face.

"I'm dying," thought Gail, crumpling onto the floor like a rag doll.

As she lost consciousness, the city lights winked out and her vision dimmed to darkness, as a rushing sound flooded into her ears—like the sound of many waters bearing her down to a sunless sea.

CHAPTER 7

PSYCHOPATHY

GAIL awoke, coughing and gasping for air, moments later. She had a headache and her throat was sore and throbbed with pain. Her neck bore two oval red marks, where Bob had jabbed her.

Above her, Gail saw Bob's face talking to her.

"I'm sorry! Please forgive me!" Bob pleaded, like a child. "I'll never do it again."

He was frantic. He tearfully told Gail he loved her and pleaded with her not to leave him.

Gail got up, with Bob's help, and sat down in the chair. Hanging in the air was the fact that Bob had hurt her and she now had power over him. All she had to do was pick up the phone and dial 911 and his career would be ruined. If it were not for her test the next morning, Gail would have left the house or called the cops. She was scared and angry but did not call the police. She did not even immediately tell her family. She went inside, away from the edge of the porch.

Amazingly, Gail did well on her test the next morning but she had to wear a turtleneck top and use makeup to hide developing bruises on her neck. When she got home from school, about five o'clock, Gail called her older cousin Hillard Wiese, who was a Legal Aid lawyer in Manhattan.

"Hello?"

"Hillard?" said a hushed woman's voice.

"Who is this?"

"Hi, this is Gail, your cousin Gail."

"Oh, hi, Gail."

"Do you have a moment? I want to discuss something with you."

"Sure."

Gail, who sounded extremely upset, told him about her fight with Bob and his assault on her.

"It wasn't the first time he choked me but it was the first time I became unconscious," said Gail. "I'm just afraid it will happen again. He might still be angry."

"Is he there with you?" Hillard asked.

"No, but I'm expecting him. What should I do? Should I leave? What would happen to me if I pick up and walk out? Wouldn't I lose rights to matrimonial property?"

"Don't worry about that," Hillard told her. "If you are physically concerned for your safety, I want you to leave the apartment—immediately, tonight. I don't want for him to come home. I don't want you to try to work things out. You must leave the apartment right now. You can come stay with me, if you like, or you can go stay with your grandfather—but you must get out of that apartment! I want you to call me back to let me know where you are. I don't want you in the apartment."

Gail took his advice, packed a few things, and drove out to her grandfather's three-bedroom attached home on East 24th Street in the Sheepshead Bay section of Brooklyn.

The next day, Gail called Hillard and told her she was at her grandfather's place.

"Are you okay?" he asked.

"Yeah," she said. "If it's necessary, can you put me in touch with a lawyer—to talk about a possible divorce?" Gail asked.

Possible divorce? Hillard wondered.

"Sure," he said.

Gail called Amanda, told her she was at her grandfather's house and explained what had happened.

"I was smoking a cigarette and Bob caught me," Gail said. "He snapped. He attacked me and choked me. That's why I'm at my grandfather's."

Amanda knew that Gail was not allowed to smoke. But Gail said she was still in touch with Bob and was trying to rescue the relationship and make it work, especially now that she had a little leverage—the upper hand. She felt therapy would help.

"Oh my God," Amanda replied. "Why are you thinking about staying? Go! Get out of it—end of discussion!"

"Well . . ." Gail protested, explaining that she was now in a better position because Bob had attacked her.

"If he did this to you, that's it," Amanda said.

Again, Gail came up with reasons she should not leave Bob. Loving him was not one of them. Amanda was disgusted. Gail was still jockeying for position instead of cutting it off. Amanda tried to convince Gail to leave but realized she was wasting her time and gave up. Gail seemed locked in. Listing Bob's faults, Gail again told her girlfriend that he was unreasonably jealous but did not mention that she was cheating on him. Amanda was not surprised that Gail did not contact her parents or go home to Bellmore. She knew Gail would rather have been homeless on the street than go back to her parents' home.

Gail also called her customer Francesca Beale at her summer estate in the Hamptons and asked if she could move into the guest room in Francesca's Manhattan apartment. When asked why, Gail said she needed to leave her husband.

"I'm afraid of him—he has a terrible temper," Gail explained. "I'm afraid Bob will do something terrible."

"It probably won't work out," Francesca responded, turning Gail down.

Gail felt humiliated and angry and slammed the phone down. Francesca thought Gail's request was odd and wondered why she didn't go to her own family in time of trouble.

"Why would she want to live with me?" Francesca wondered. "I mean, she's not an immigrant, is she?"

Gail called her admirer, Dr. Ali. She told him her situation and asked to spend the weekend at his place. He also refused her.

She told one friend that Bob had had a problem reviving her and had to call 911, which was not true.

At Beth Israel, she told Jane Dunne that Bob's parents had asked her not to leave him. Jane noticed amorphous red marks on the sides of Gail's neck that looked like hickeys.

It was only after speaking to her girlfriends that Gail decided to report the choking incident to police.

She told her sister Alayne that "smoking was synonymous with saying, 'I'm leaving you.' It was such a violation of the rules of the marriage for me to be smoking, that I think when he saw me smoking, it was like I told him I was leaving him."

Once again, Gail asked her sister to keep the information from their parents—for the moment.

Gail did not tell Bob she was reporting him to the cops. She called the police to find out what to do and was told to go to her local precinct to report the incident. On Saturday, November 12, 1983, she walked into the 19th Precinct. She told the uniformed sergeant sitting behind the large counter inside why she was there and was directed to the complaint room. A civilian police aide took the information for a criminal complaint of assault, third degree. The aide typed that Gail's husband, "did strangle her to the point of unconsciousness."

A police lieutenant signed the form and the matter was referred to Family Court—that is, it was filed away. There was no investigation and Bob was not arrested.

Gail wanted to use the event to force Bob to do something he had absolutely refused to do—seek psychiatric counseling. As a result, Bob called his psychiatrist sister Michelle and asked for her help.

"Gail and I have a problem," Bob said. "We need to see a psychiatrist. Who's a good person to go to?"

Michelle sent Bob to a psychologist named Shelly Juran, who spoke to Bob several times on the phone and had one session with him in her Brooklyn office. After the session with Bob, during which she discussed with him recent events and his strong feelings toward his wife, the therapist became alarmed. She told Bob to go home and put Gail on the phone with her.

"I want to speak to your wife, to make sure she's okay," said Juran.

She gave him several reasons she wanted to speak to Gail, but she did not mention the most important.

"Okay," said Bob.

The psychologist was concerned for Gail's safety and urgently needed to speak to her to make sure she was still alive. She had doubts that she would hear Gail's voice, given Bob's expression of visceral passion about her, which she decided had triggered her duty-to-warn responsibility, the obligation of a mental health professional to alert anyone who is in danger from a patient.

But Bob did call the therapist and put Gail on the line.

"Are you okay?" Juran asked Gail.

"Yes, I'm okay."

Juran was reassured that Gail was safe, and, while Bob listened openly on an extension, she warned Gail that Bob might be dangerous. Juran did not take the case but referred it to Dr. Stanley Bone in Manhattan, whom she called. She told Bone that she believed Bob was a dangerous psychopath and a possible danger to his wife.

Dr. Bone met with Bob twice, on November 12 and November 16, and also asked Bob's permission to talk to Gail. Bob gave it and the psychiatrist called Gail at home—also to warn her about Bob. Bone told Bob he could not enter into treatment with him because Bone's schedule was too crowded.

Bone called Dr. Michael Stone on Central Park West and explained what he and the previous therapist had been told, as well as their conclusions about the threat Bob represented to Gail. Stone, who was given information on other past violent incidents, agreed to see Bob.

Michael, a well-dressed and erudite man with a gentle voice and a professorial air, was an eminent therapist and the author of three books on psychiatry. He had extensive research experience with patients suffering from personality disorders. His first two books were on borderline disorders and the third was on treating schizophrenic patients. He had also developed interests in other areas of psychiatry—especially forensic psychiatry, the study of the criminal mind. It was arranged that Stone would see Bob and Gail separately for several ninety-minute sessions during the consultation period, which was a time for the patients and therapist to see if they were comfortable with each other and wished to enter therapy on a regular basis. The reluctant Bob would be the first to have a session.

On Saturday, November 19, a casually dressed Bob arrived at Dr. Michael Stone's tan sandstone building facing Central Park. Bob walked into the lobby and up to the security desk and was directed to Stone's first-floor office. The soft-spoken older man in a dark suit and tie greeted Bob in a foyer reception area. They stepped into a large living room with a twelve-foot ceiling. Bob ignored the small couches and sat in the leather chair, farthest away from Michael.

Michael had been told by Bone that both of the potential new patients, a husband and wife, might suffer from Borderline Personality Disorder. The traits of BPD are those of intensity, of an all-or-nothing approach to life, with an underlying aggression. They could be alternately worshipful or contemptuous of the same person, as well as childish, clingy, demanding, fickle, fragile, manipulative, moody, seductive and unreasonable. BPD sufferers were capable of "frantic efforts to avoid real or imagined abandonment," according to the *Diagnostic and Statistical Manual of Mental Disorders*, third edition—known as the *DSM-III*, the "Shrink's Bible" of mental illness.

Bob seemed to radiate evil and immediately impressed Michael as a scary presence. He fixed Michael with a menacing predator's glare. Michael first asked about general biographical information and about his relationship with his wife. Bob described their history of fighting and said they had not had sex in three months. As Bob spoke, Michael wrote down his words verbatim on a pad he balanced on his crossed knee. He asked Bob about the recent strangling episode and Bob, unruffled, described it. He did not apologize.

Michael became very alert. He asked Bob if he had ever gotten violent or contemplated violence with anyone else in his life. Yes, said Bob. He had attacked Gail's cat last year—before they were married. He said he'd tried to strangle it to death because it didn't listen to him. Also, Bob said he had choked his previous fiancée, Marcy, during an argument, which caused her to break off the engagement. After Marcy kicked him out, Bob said he still had a key and went back into her apartment and strangled her cat to death.

Michael knew from his study of murderers that serial killers often started out killing animals—particularly cats. As Bob described these things, Michael noticed that he did not become excited or angry but spoke with a kind of calm, unexcited hatred. Michael was impressed by the coldness and indifference of Bob's emotions as he confessed these terrible deeds. There was a glint, a kind of glee in his eyes, a triumphant "I showed them" pride. He seemed to be telling Michael that he was a macho man, with a "don't fuck with me" attitude. Michael suspected he was simply a violent wimp.

The patient then spoke frankly about his past drug use—marijuana, cocaine and LSD when he was young—and mentioned that he had fought with his dad over drugs.

"I kicked my father in the balls when he tried to stop me from using LSD," Bob said.

Also, Bob said he once felt like murdering a college roommate who had made an anti-Semitic remark.

"I wanted to buy a gun and kill him," said Bob.

After the session, Michael made arrangements to see Bob again later in the week and ushered him out the door. Alone, Michael reviewed his notes. There was a passive quality to Bob, Michael thought, and yet he seemed to radiate menace—as though he were desperately trying to compensate for his wimpiness by being domineering and vicious and subjugating women. Bob was narcissistic and insecure and apparently predisposed to use bad solutions. He also seemed without scruples; he had apparently not internalized the rules of society. There seemed to be nothing to prevent him from carrying out any nefarious plans. "This is not a person I would want to be angry at me," Michael decided, remembering a classmate at medical school who had a similar personality.

Bob was obviously highly intelligent and superficially charming but underneath the social mask, Michael felt, he was devious, impulsive, insincere and egocentric and showed no remorse or shame for bad things he had done. He actually seemed defiantly proud of them which meant he was capable of repeating or expanding on such acts. He seemed to lack a conscience. There was a psychiatric diagnosis for such a group of traits but it wasn't a treatable Borderline Personality Disorder, as Michael had been told. In Michael's opinion, the patient had a condition called psychopathy which was widely believed to be incurable.

That didn't by itself mean Bob was a criminal or a likely murderer. A certain percentage of society was comprised of psychopaths who were used car salesmen, doctors, politicians, stock swindlers, journalists, lawyers, corporate CEOs and everything else under the sun. Psychopaths were disconnected from the physical effects of their emotions, so that they felt shallowly, if at all. Interestingly, one study concluded that, as a result, psychopaths did not physically experience fear—which might make them very brave on the battlefield or perhaps even allow them to pass lie detector tests they should fail. In Michael's opinion, after just ninety minutes of conversation, what made Bob dangerous was that he was not in control of his impulses—nor likely to be.

"His wife is at risk," and must be warned, Michael concluded.

That was not a problem, since she was scheduled to come in the next day and could be warned, in order to prevent uxoricide—the murder of a wife.

He also decided that he himself might also be at risk if he ever got on the bad side of Bob Bierenbaum.

"There's no way I can treat this guy," Michael concluded. "He's scary and he has an untreatable condition."

But, if Bob was a psychopath, rejecting him would not be a good idea.

"How can I tell him no," Michael wondered, "without saying no?"

CHAPTER 8

BORDERLINE

GAIL had her first session with Michael the next day. She described the recent choking incident and, when asked, said that she and Bob had not had sex in a month. Michael made a note and remembered that the day before Bob had said there had been no intercourse for three months.

"I had thought about getting separated. Four years ago, I made a suicide attempt, taking forty pills of Quaaludes and I cut my wrists in four places," after an argument with a boyfriend, said Gail.

She told Michael about her feelings of hopelessness and emptiness after years of a life filled with aimless promiscuity, kinky sex, drugs and shallow relationships.

"I had gone too far off the right path ever to get on it again," Gail said, dramatically. "I left psychology school, got into an arty life with musicians. I felt I was living in somebody else's body."

She related her brief happiness at meeting Bob, a doctor, and their wedded bliss, which did not even last until the wedding.

"He's a pathological liar, even about simple things," said Gail. "He says whatever is most convenient, the least trouble. Sometimes, he actually thinks he's telling the truth or it doesn't matter. Once, I threatened to write down all the lies on a notepad and he got hysterical. He promised to go to his folks' house for dinner, knowing full well that he couldn't, only saying, 'Gail made other plans.' He would throw all the responsibility on me, as if I was the bad guy. I lost all respect for Bob. It seemed such an unmanly thing to do. He shrunk as a man."

Gail thought Bob's parents were in denial about Bob, but that the choking incident twelve days earlier would finally bring his problems to light. And she seemed triumphant at the opportunity to demonstrate that "perfect" Bob was mentally ill—especially to his parents, who disliked her.

Michael suspected that Bob did not want Gail to become a full person. If she became independent and had her own career, she wouldn't need him. It also seemed like Gail didn't really smoke anymore and had provoked Bob—"accidentally on purpose."

"I knew Bob would be angry," she remembered. "I studied until eleven at night, then I figured I'd smoke for a bit on the terrace. He came home around eleven and saw the cigarettes on the terrace table. I was just about to have a cigarette."

She described how Bob had threatened to jump off the terrace, and his attack on her. She also mentioned the other arguments during which he had pointed a knife at his stomach and opened the moving car door. Then Gail told Michael about the attack on her cat.

Gail said it was the middle of the night, when she felt Bob get out of bed and go to the bathroom. Moments later, she heard Amelia meowing. Something was wrong. She jumped out of bed and went to the bathroom. She saw a naked Bob doing something with the toilet. A wet fur ball jumped away from Bob with a yowl and Gail realized with horror that he had been pushing Amelia down into the bowl.

"I was trying to kill your cat!" Bob yelled.

Gail's eyes were wide in astonishment and she realized Bob was saying something about doing it several other times without her knowing.

"I hate it!" Bob had spat at the cat. "She's so ungrateful. I strangled her."

"Did you try to drown her?" Gail asked.

"No, but that's a good idea," Bob replied lightly, and grabbed the wet feline again and shoved her struggling head down into the toilet water. "I really want to kill her."

Michael made a note that Bob's comments were an obvious projection of his feelings about Gail. He wanted to choke the life out of the soft, ungrateful female with big eyes. It was Gail's cat—a word that even sounded like her maiden name, Katz. Gail, Michael concluded, saw her marriage as a meal ticket to a better life. Bob was pulling her up a social rung, so she denied the risk factors. Or was there more to it?

"The cat attack didn't inspire you to call off the wedding?" Michael asked, incredulously.

"A wife's place is by her husband's side," Gail replied mechanically.

"Holy Jesus," Michael thought. "I've got to talk stronger to this babe or else she's gonna end up in a funeral parlor."

Michael had lost two similar patients—who were warned but returned to abusive men—to murder.

Michael made a note that Gail had seven out of nine symptoms of Borderline Personality Disorder—two more than needed to qualify. They were: frenzied attempts to avoid imagined abandonment; a history of passionate but unstable relationships; confusion of identity; impulsivity in sex, drugs and eating; suicidal behavior and self-mutilation; feelings of constant emptiness; and inappropriate fits of temper and sadness.

Returning to the strangling event, Michael asked Gail to explain why she did not notify authorities of the assault or leave a husband who had brutalized her.

"I chose to cool it, so I could take the test the next morning," she responded. "If not for that, I would have left the house or called the police."

"Fat chance," Michael quipped.

"Why did you say that?"

"If not for that, as you put it, he wouldn't have strangled you in the first place. He chose the night when you would be least likely in your whole life to turn him in."

Gail did not seem to follow the logic of Michael's analysis and did not see any danger. He asked her about her career plans.

"I hope to become a clinical psychologist. I had straight A's," said Gail. "My sister said last year, 'Bob likes you to be beneath him—he wouldn't like you to be success-ful.' "

"But you can't see what she and I are onto?"

"No . . ." said Gail, the bright student—who had already changed the subject and was objectively pondering psycho-logical symbolism, rather than her own safety.

"The smoking means infidelity, I guess?" she asked.

"Yes, absolutely."

CHAPTER 9
CARMEN SYNDROME

MICHAEL met next with Bob that same Sunday afternoon. He told the young doctor he was suffering from a serious condition that involved "dangerousness and significant risk."

The psychiatrist said he also needed to talk to Bob's parents and would have a separate forty-five-minute session with them. Then he informed Bob of the two security conditions he had to comply with, in order for Michael to agree to treat Bob on a regular basis. They were extraordinary protocols that Michael had come up with for the first time in his career, probably for the first time in anyone's career.

"First, I will make two audio tapes of each session," Michael began. "At the end of each session, you will take one of the tapes and I will put the other into an envelope. I will address it to my lawyer and drop it in the mail box down the hall as you leave."

Bob sat and waited for the second condition, something Michael said Bob's parents would have to pay for.

"Lloyd's of London would have to insure my life with a policy that would pay four million dollars—two million dollars for each of my sons—if I am killed."

It took Bob a few moments before the demand sank in. His mother and father, in addition to paying for his and Gail's therapy, would have to pay a large sum to insure Bob's psychiatrist.

Michael had come up with the protocols as a way to reject Bob without seeming to reject him. The conditions were incredible and treated Bob—a nice, Jewish doctor who had never been arrested—as if he were Jack the Ripper. Michael figured that if Bob agreed, it might mean that he was sincere about changing his behavior. If Bob balked, it would indicate that he was not serious about getting better and was probably incurable, as Michael assumed. Bob would be in the position of rejecting Michael, rather than the other way around. It was a win–win situation for Michael.

Bob, however, was quite angry. He felt that Gail had somehow chosen Dr. Stone and now Bob was convinced he had been set up by Stone and Gail. Bob did not need to discuss the proposed plan with his parents—he quickly rejected the whole scheme and told Michael he was ending the consultation. Then he stormed out.

Michael met again with Gail the next day and made another attempt to shake her out of her denial of how much danger he thought she was in. He was so troubled by Gail's attitude, that he did something else he had never done before in all his years of practice—he wrote a warning letter to Gail.

It was called a Tarasoff letter, after a landmark 1976 California court case that found a psychiatrist was at fault because he kept his patient's murderous plans confidential and did not warn a woman the man had said he intended to kill. Michael, who felt the letter was a professional and moral responsibility, had it waiting for Gail's signature when she arrived.

Gail seemed relatively relaxed, considering the alarming things that had happened to her, and Michael's interpretation of them. Unlike Bob, Gail had a hipness about her despite her chronic blues. Her denial was not the result of naïveté. Michael believed Gail was in danger because of her risk-taking, thrill-seeking behavior. She was also moody, depressed, irritable, manipulative and quite self-destructive—she liked living on the edge of danger.

He had diagnosed Gail as a borderline patient, one who had an urge to "get even" with men, but, in this case, Michael thought of it as "the Carmen Syndrome," after the opera about the beautiful but maddening Gypsy thief who caused her own murder by taunting her lover. Gail did not feel really alive unless she was flirting with death. For her, sex and aggression were fused. Like Carmen, Gail seemed to prefer death to admitting fear of her lover. Gail even resembled the fictional gypsy. Perhaps she had a background of abuse, or perhaps Gail's brain was simply deficient in the production or processing of dopamine—the opium-like chemical that produces sensations of pleasure in the human body. Perhaps she had guilt about something in her past and picked brutal men who would abuse her as a way to expiate her guilt. Because sex is seen as bad, getting beaten up is the price these women pay for sexual pleasure.

One thing seemed clear to Michael—Gail's confrontations with her husband, her taunting, were like waving a red cape in front of a bull. The pairing of a violent psychopath and a self-destructive borderline personality was perfect—they were a matched set. Bob's tab fit Gail's slot. If she ended up dead, it might be called murder but it would really be a victim-precipitated homicide.

"Bob is—apart from his craziness—what I want," Gail explained to Michael. "I've been with playboys, billionaires, scary situations, promiscuous sex. . . . All I want to do is get back where I was and marry a nice, Jewish boy. Except that he's crazy."

"So, all-in-all, you could summarize your life by saying, 'Why fuck with suicide when you can marry a killer?' "

Gail seemed startled by the provocative comment.

"You're in great danger," Michael explained. "You talk of denial on the part of Bierenbaum Senior—your denial is far greater than theirs. It beggars description. You're supposed to be joining the psychology profession. Every predictor of murderous capacity is there. He tried to kill you, he's been violent to animals, which is the strongest predictor of violence to be had among people."

"I dispute that," Gail shot back.

"I don't care—I know a lot more about this than you do."

"I was afraid on my honeymoon to stand near him when we'd be on the cliff, lest he push me off, so it's no different."

"What's no different?"

"He was threatening then, and he didn't do anything—so what's the danger?"

"Allow me to remind you that he just tried to strangle you."

When Gail continued to pooh-pooh the idea that her life was in danger, Michael presented her with the letter.

"Please read it and I'd like you to sign it, please," Michael said.

Gail read the short letter, shaking her head negatively as she read:

I have been advised by Dr. Stone that, for reasons of my own safety, I should at this time live apart from my husband, Dr. Robert Bierenbaum, and until such time as it would appear that the risk of injury to my person has been significantly reduced.

I further understand that, owing to the unpredictable nature of my husband's physical assaults and to the chronic nature of the characterological abnormalities that underlie these assaults no firm date can as yet be fixed as to when it might be safe to resume living together.

If I do not heed this advice, I must accept the consequences, including the possibility of personal injury, or death, at the hands of my husband, and absolve Dr. Stone of responsibility for any such eventuality.

Dr. Stone, meantime, promises to warn me and my parents of when he deems any such risk to be particularly intense and imminent, to the best of his ability—should he undertake to treat my husband, and will also give such warning, if indicated, during this consultation period.

When she was finished reading the letter, Gail put it down and declined to sign it.

"I'd like to notify your parents," said Michael, refusing to give up. "Please give me their address and phone number."

Again, Gail adamantly refused. She took the unsigned copy of the letter with her and walked out the door. For the third time in a month, Gail had been warned by a shrink that Bob was dangerous and, for a third time, she'd ignored it.

The next day, Michael mailed another copy to Gail's home address by registered, return receipt requested mail, for his records. If Gail would not listen to him, then at least he would be protected from a medical malpractice lawsuit.

When Gail arrived back at the apartment, she showed Bob the letter and told him she had refused to sign it. Bob was pleased. He read the letter and told her he had walked out on Dr. Stone. "He's off the wall," Bob told her. Gail agreed. They would go to another psychiatrist, he said.

But she did not toss the letter in the garbage. She put it in a bank safe deposit box for safekeeping.

About a week later, Michael met with Nettie and Marvin Bierenbaum and Marvin explained why their son was dangerous and why he could not treat him.

After Bob's parents left, Michael was finished with the Bierenbaums, who had taken their problems elsewhere. Perhaps, Michael thought, they'd found some naïve schmuck downtown to treat Bob, someone who didn't know what he was doing, who didn't have the training he did to recognize the danger. He was glad to be rid of the problem but uneasy that nothing had been resolved.

Michael wondered if that was the last he would ever hear of Bob and Gail Bierenbaum.

CHAPTER 10

GLASS CASSEROLE

ANTHONY strode up the well-lit semi-circular driveway entrance to the 36-story apartment tower at 185 E. 85th Street. *Carlos, the young uniformed doorman behind the desk in the outer vestibule, watched as Anthony approached and pulled open one of the large glass doors. He did not get up from behind his desk to open the door for the handsome, dark-haired gentleman who strongly resembled actor Treat Williams.

"May I help you, sir?" Carlos asked, even though he had seen Anthony before.

"Anthony for Doctor Bierenbaum, please," Anthony Segalas replied, with a smile.

Carlos picked up his house phone and dialed a number.

"Hello, Mrs. Bierenbaum? Anthony is here to see Doctor Bierenbaum. He's not? Oh, okay." Carlos hung up and turned back to the visitor.

"Doctor Bierenbaum is not home yet but you can go up. Apartment 12C, sir. The elevator to your left," said Carlos, who knew that Bob was not home because he had seen him leave hours earlier.

"Thank you."

The doorman shook his head. He liked both Bob and Gail. They were nice people. It was none of his business but he also knew that Bob was working late at the hospital, like he did every Monday night. He never saw Anthony around when Bob was home.

Gail opened the apartment door and admitted Anthony with a smile. A constellation of city lights sparkled outside the living room window. Gail's eyes also sparkled at Anthony but her eyeballs had been made glassy by the cocaine she had snorted a bit earlier. After she closed the door, Anthony kissed her passionately and Gail responded. Bob and Gail's smiling faces looked on from a large color photograph taken at their wedding, as Gail and Anthony snorted some coke together and laughed. The stimulant, once inhaled, produced a rush of euphoria and energy and the couple soon repaired to the bedroom, to put their energy to good use. Anthony made love to Gail on the bed, as loud rock 'n' roll played on the stereo.

After sex, Gail got dressed, got her cigarettes and lighter out of their hiding place and walked out to the breezy terrace. She lit a cigarette and inhaled the sinfully sensual smoke. She had become adept at sneaking sex, drugs and cigarettes when her husband was at the hospital. Gail exhaled, looking absently at the skyline and the shimmering necklaces of light strung across the Triboro Bridge. When she finished her forbidden cigarette, Gail flicked the evidence off the porch before going back inside to take a shower.

Bob and Gail had decided to seek a second opinion after they left Michael Stone eight months earlier. In November 1983, they went to a psychiatrist on West 13th Street for consultation and then treatment. That psychiatrist did not label Bob a dangerous psychopath or Gail a self-destructive borderline case. He simply labeled them a dysfunctional couple. He diagnosed Bob as suffering from a lesser adjustment disorder "with mixed disturbance of emotions and conduct." The shrink concluded that Gail suffered from a "Partner Relational Problem" that was characterized by poor communication and a pattern of criticism, as well as "unrealistic expectations." Bob liked these diagnoses much more than Michael Stone's unusual and confrontational conclusions.

After a few weeks, Gail moved back into the apartment with Bob. They underwent therapy for four months, in individual and some joint sessions, and it seemed to improve their ability to talk to each other and live together. For Bob, the crisis seemed to be over and they celebrated the holidays as if nothing had happened. Gail later got two new cats.

But on April 3, 1984, Gail met with a Manhattan divorce

lawyer to discuss her situation. She told her that she was planning to leave her husband but she needed several months to arrange her affairs. The attorney could bill her husband. She made a second appointment to return in August. Gail presented Bob with a written list of six divorce demands and sixteen items she intended to take from their apartment.

She wanted Bob to pay her $1,200 a month to cover her rent, utilities, food, transportation, clothing and veterinary care for her cats—for two years. Gail also demanded relocation expenses, including moving, furnishings and brokers' fees. Bob was to pay her lawyer's bill. He was also to pay the interest on her entire school loan. She also asked to be carried on his health insurance policy. Her last demand was that he pay her rent for a third year, if necessary. It all came to $49,280.

Gail's second list itemized what she would remove from the apartment, which included the telephone, the computer, the television, her bicycle, a book case, chairs, lamps and other furnishings, valuable prints by Picasso and Erté, towels and bathroom fixtures. She also listed eleven items she was not taking and that she would have to purchase, costing $3000.

Once again, Bob told Gail he loved her and would do anything for her, anything to keep her. They agreed to postpone the divorce if Bob treated her better. Gail told herself that she was in charge. She never returned to the divorce lawyer.

In May, Gail got a BA from Hunter College and went on to grad school at Long Island University in Brooklyn, while continuing with her work at Beth Israel Hospital. Bob continued to work long hours as a surgical resident at Maimonides Hospital in Brooklyn. He still had little time to meet Gail's needs or to keep track of her.

Bob and Gail had received treatment but it did not guarantee happiness. Rather, it brought a kind of polite ceasefire that satisfied neither one. Gail stopped wearing her dowdy "doctor's wife" outfits and returned to her former

revealing, sexy style. She and Bob socialized, went on vacations and attended family events, as usual—and even had
fun—but, in Gail's mind, everything had changed.

Gail and Anthony had first met at a diner several blocks
from Gail's apartment in July of 1984. The up-and-coming
investment banker, a bachelor, had been sitting alone when
he noticed the pretty, sad girl also sitting alone. Their eyes
met and they gave each other flirtatious looks. Anthony
finished his meal first. He paid and waited outside in the
warm sunshine for Gail to emerge and they introduced
themselves.

"Would you like to have a drink sometime?" Anthony
asked.

"Okay," said Gail.

Anthony asked for her phone number but Gail said it
would be better if he gave her his. She called a few days
later and they went to the beach, where their relationship
became physical. That summer, they met at Gail's or Anthony's place for sex. One hot day, Anthony drove with
Gail out to her parents' home on Long Island because Gail
had to babysit her younger brother. Anthony and 14-year-
old Steve shot a few baskets in the driveway before they
went to Jones Beach. While Steve was in the water, Anthony and Gail made out on the blanket, like teenagers.

Anthony liked Gail and he liked the sex but he did not
volunteer to be her next husband. Borrowing a phrase from
fighter pilots, Anthony thought the sleek but needy Gail
was "low drag, high maintenance." When the summer
ended and Gail went back to school, the romance petered
out.

Bob and Gail continued to argue and the neighbors heard
the fights through the walls. In the apartment below theirs,
Mae Eisenhower often heard Gail shouting, sometimes Bob
shouting back, and always Gail's angry shoe heels clicking
on the wooden floor. It was awkward for some of the neighbors, who heard the shouting matches, to smile and say

hello in the elevator or in the lobby or hallways. Most found Gail very friendly but several people felt that Bob seemed cold.

*Dr. Ralph Sugarman, the best man at Bob's wedding, was walking on the Upper East Side, huddled against a cold crosstown wind early in 1985, when he saw his old friend Bob walking toward him.

"Bob! How are you doing?"

Bob greeted Ralph, who asked after Gail. Bob shook his head. Ralph noticed his once-jovial buddy seemed both withdrawn and furious at the same time.

"I'm so angry with Gail, I don't know what I'm doing," Bob said. "I hate her so much, I could kill her."

Bob added that he was on his way to an appointment with a psychiatrist to discuss his problem.

"You'd better get this sorted out," Ralph said. "You should talk to your psychiatrist about this."

Bob said he was going to the shrink "to work things out" and get "cured of my anger and hostility."

He said Gail was seeing someone else, was "running with a drug crowd" and was just "using me to get through school.

"I want to make the marriage work but I'll let her finish school and then divorce her," Bob said.

Just before Valentine's Day, 1985, Gail was riding the Lexington Avenue Subway and reading an illustrated magazine article on self-mutilation—which caught the eye of another psychology grad student named Ken Feiner. Gail noticed Ken looking at her and smiled. He had bushy black hair and looked like a younger, more handsome version of consumer advocate Ralph Nader. Ken struck up a conversation, then asked for her telephone number. Gail told him it would be better if he gave her his. She later called and they went to a lecture on psychoanalysis together. Gail told Ken about her situation, and that she wanted out.

As usual, Gail was infatuated at the beginning of their

relationship. She was deeply in love and Ken was the ideal man. They became very close and met at Ken's apartment or at Gail's place—when Bob was at work.

Gail had not told Bob about her boyfriends but even someone as busy and focused as Bob noticed that something basic had changed. Bob told Alayne that he and her sister had not had sex for more than a year. Shocked, Alayne asked Gail, who told her in confidence that she didn't want to have sex with Bob because she was getting what she needed from a boyfriend. Gail also told her sister about Michael Stone's letter and how she intended to use it to pressure Bob to give her what she wanted in a divorce. Alayne who was in law school, saw nothing horribly wrong with Gail's plan and did not try to talk her out of it. The sisters spoke about the future and joked that when Alayne was a trial lawyer, she could call on Gail the clinical psychologist as an expert witness on some big case.

In the meantime Gail began looking at ads for apartments in the newspaper, to get an idea of how much money she would need to go out on her own. She decided it would take a lot of planning and preparation before she could leave Bob.

One of the major reasons Gail went into psychology was her desire to solve the mystery of her own heart and her behavior. During the spring semester, Gail took an abnormal psychology course called "Psychopathy." For five months, on Thursday afternoons, from 2 to 4:45, she studied the symptoms of psychopaths and the human consequences of their actions. Then she went home to Bob. The more Gail learned, the more she began to think that perhaps Dr. Michael Stone wasn't so "off the wall," after all.

In May, Gail studied for her Psychopathy final exam. On paper, at least, she mastered the subject—she got an "A" on the final.

At the end of June, Gail told her mother about her continuing problems with Bob and finally revealed that Bob had choked her into unconsciousness a year and a half earlier. She also confessed that she was considering divorcing Bob and that she was seeing another man who was not a doctor. Sylvia was unhappy that Gail was thinking of leaving her doctor husband. It was the end of the wonderful life she thought she had helped Gail achieve, after years of terrible struggling.

But Sylvia realized that Gail was in a better position to get a good divorce settlement because she had something on Bob that he did not know about—a copy of the 1983 police report of the choking incident. The original was tucked away in NYPD files. Also, Gail told her mother about Dr. Stone's letter and said she intended to blackmail Bob with it when she announced she was leaving him. Gail told her mother—who also saw nothing wrong with her daughter's plan—that she would put the letter in a safe deposit box.

After the conversation, Sylvia decided to cook for Gail, to comfort her with food. She began preparing one of Gail's favorite dishes—tuna casserole.

The next Thursday, while she was working at Beth Israel, Gail told Jane Dunne a bizarre story: Sylvia, like a good Jewish mom, had baked a delicious tuna casserole for her daughter. But, Sylvia warned Gail, a glass salt shaker had fallen from her grasp and shattered on her kitchen counter next to the casserole dish before it was cooked.

"I don't think any got into the casserole," Sylvia assured her daughter.

"There was glass in it!" Gail said, suddenly bursting into tears. "There were big pieces of glass in it—what does that mean?

"I picked hunks of glass out of the casserole," Gail moaned. "Can you imagine that my mother did this? She wants to kill me! How could she do this to me? She wants me to swallow glass?"

Jane suggested that an older woman with bad eyes might miss small shards of glass.

"Jane, they weren't just tiny slivers that you could overlook—there were hunks of glass!" Gail wailed.

Gail said she threw out the casserole but never confronted her mother about the glass. She launched into a self-pitying diatribe against her parents, essentially saying they did not love her or care about her. Jane was worried that Gail lacked any self-protective instinct and, in fact, seemed self-destructive, helpless, resigned to her fate. Jane gave Gail a supportive talk about how she needed to protect herself, emotionally, and deal with her problems—especially Bob.

Gail said she wanted to leave Bob but she feared his reaction. She wanted to marry Ken, but feared he wouldn't have anything to do with her until she left Bob.

"Gail, you can't stay in an abusive relationship—you've got to get out."

"But I have no money to get my own apartment," Gail moaned.

Jane was tired of hearing Gail complain but never taking any advice, never doing anything about her problems. She reached for her purse. She didn't have much money in the bank but this was an emergency.

"Here," said Jane, opening her checkbook and writing a check to Gail for $500, ripping it out of the book and handing it to her. "Get out this weekend."

Gail thanked Jane and told her she had a plan to get away from Bob and make him do what she wanted in a divorce. Her anger flowed and hate flared in her eyes. "I'm going to destroy Bob's career with a letter." She said she'd nail Bob and his father for Medicaid fraud, ending both their careers.

"If there's a lot of money involved, you're in danger," Jane warned. "Don't do that! Why would you do that? You'll get killed if you do."

CHAPTER 11

PLANNING A SURPRISE

GAIL worked her way through the address book, calling her friends and Bob's friends, as well as Bob's parents and his sister Michelle—to invite them to a gathering.

"I'm giving a surprise birthday party for Bob's thirtieth birthday," Gail happily told *Ray Solano, a doctor colleague of Bob's from the hospital.

Gail kept a guest list and checked off names as she made her calls. She chatted with the invitees, laughing about how Bob had no idea about the surprise and discussing the gourmet menu for the event. Just below her "Party" list of 37 guests, Gail had written her menu, which included hors d'oeuvres, fruit, cheeses, two types of pâté, vegetables, dips, breads, meat dishes and drinks, including Gail's favorite—piña colada.

When she was done with her phone calls, Gail's forced gaiety vanished and she turned her attention to another secret—a much bigger surprise for Bob.

She took out a second sheet of paper that also contained several handwritten lists of tasks—56 in all. Some were to be accomplished "Soon," such as a haircut and pedicure and a vet appointment for the cat. Others, such as "Sell weight bench, piano," "cash bonds," "clear all credit," and "loan—next year," were long-range plans. Gail stared at the two lists, which mirrored her two minds on the subject—to be or not to be, to stay or to go.

She pulled out a newspaper and dialed a number she had circled in the classified real estate section. She set a time to view an apartment the next day, thanked the woman and hung up. Gail had told several friends, as well as her mother and sister that she intended to leave Bob. She'd told Alayne the month before that she had confronted Bob about using the psychiatrist's letter against him unless he gave her what she wanted. She was working methodically to outsmart Bob about the party and about the apartment she wanted—until she was ready to spring both surprises. Gail believed she had been successful at keeping her husband in the dark about Anthony and Ken. She was certain that Bob was without a clue—but she was wrong. It never occurred to her that Bob might be planning a surprise of his own for her.

Gail insisted they rent a place in the Hamptons for the summer.

On Friday, June 21, Bob and Gail drove out to Long Island for their first weekend at their summer rental "share" house. They loaded their suitcases and Bob's laptop into the car and drove into Queens, where they picked up the Long Island Expressway for the two-hour trip out to South-ampton. They were greeted by the owner of the house, Do-lores Erickson, a slim, striking blonde whose husband ran an ad agency.

Gail confided to Dolores, whom she hardly knew, that she was very unhappy and wanted a divorce because she couldn't stand the fact that they had no money.

"But he's going to be a surgeon—you'll have money soon," Dolores assured her.

"Oh, that's going to take too long," said Gail. "That'll take at least three years—I can't wait that long."

Gail had renewed her association with Anthony in the spring of 1985 and began having sex with him again at his apartment and at her place when Bob was not around. The following Saturday, while Bob was working a long shift at the hospital, Anthony arrived at the front desk of Bob and Gail's apartment building. Later, while Anthony was up-stairs in bed having sex with Gail, the telephone rang. The sweaty pair disengaged and Gail picked up the phone.

"Hello?"

"Hi, it's me."

Gail's eyes widened. It was Bob, calling from the hos-pital. Anthony froze in the bed.

She chatted with her husband for a few moments about

what was up, when Bob would get home, and their dinner plans and then she hung up.

The naked couple looked at each other and exhaled. Gail became very nervous. She had been sure that Bob knew nothing about her boyfriends but the call had unnerved her. Bob was very casual on the phone—but what if he knew? What if he was playing with her? If he could prove she had committed adultery, would she be screwed in the divorce? Would all of her careful plans fall apart? The cocaine coursing through her brain fueled her paranoia. She told Anthony she thought Bob might be getting suspicious because there had been several hang-ups on the answering machine lately.

"Was that you?" Gail asked, panic creeping into her voice.

"No."

Anthony left quickly. Suddenly, far too late, Gail became cautious.

Gail met her friend from school Marianne DeCesare and told her she was about to ask Bob for a divorce because she was finally financially prepared to do it. "I've met someone else and I'm very happy," she told Marianne. "I'm in love for the first time. I've got $10,000 in a safe deposit box that Bob doesn't know about. It's to pay for my first year of grad school, after I leave him."

Gail then brought up a different aspect of her problem. "Is it okay to bring Anthony and Ken up to the apartment when Bob's not home?" she asked.

"I don't think that's a good idea," Marianne said. "It's a doorman building and the doorman knows Bob's family."

"I think I'm being followed," Gail confided. "I was walking on Lexington Avenue when I saw a person following me. I turned around and the person disappeared into a doorway."

By the first week of July, Gail's psychiatrist felt that after three years of waffling, her patient seemed more inclined to leave her husband than to stay. Gail told her she was very optimistic because she had gotten a wealthy gentleman to guarantee the security on an apartment for her—

something that was going to rescue her from her bad situation. The psychiatrist had never heard her mention the name before and was under the impression that he was someone Gail had recently met. The shrink did not write the name down and promptly forgot it. It didn't seem important. She did notice, however, that Gail had gotten a very nice pedicure, with dark red polish.

On Wednesday, July 3, Bob drove out to New Jersey to say hello to his childhood friends Dave Ostrow and Scott Baranoff, who were home from school. The trio were reunited for the first time in four years and had a fun evening with Scott's family and other friends. Bob mentioned his problems to Baranoff, who advised Bob to get a divorce and be done with it.

Bob worked on the Fourth of July holiday. There were always people who blew off their fingers or burned themselves with fireworks—in addition to the usual gunshots, stabbings and car accidents. It meant a busy overnight shift at the hospital.

Gail had a date. She and Ken went out to dinner and watched the pyrotechnic display from an East Side rooftop. They hugged as the petals of light exploded over the East River.

After the show was over, Gail and Ken went back to his apartment. Their ears still ringing from the blasts, they began to kiss, tenderly at first and then more deeply. Later, they made plans to rendezvous in the Hamptons on Saturday, July 13, when Gail would be out there with Bob. She told Ken she might move out soon and live temporarily with a friend in Connecticut, although it was inconvenient. Ken did not offer her a place to stay while she was married to Bob.

"I hate Bob," Gail said.

Later, Ken kissed Gail goodnight and put her into a cab. Gail sat alone in the dark back seat, thinking. Out the open cab window, she heard the sounds of thousands of fireworks. Close by, someone detonated a cherry bomb and Gail flinched at the bang. As the cab headed uptown toward home, Gail stared out the window and listened to the sharp salvos and volleys filling the night, as if she were driving, unarmed, into a war.

The next morning, Gail told Bob that she wanted them to spend the whole weekend together—without the distraction of parties or friends or family—to decide their future. Bob was very reluctant to agree. He knew it meant facing what they had not faced, talking about what they did not talk about. Gail presented it as a very adult weekend—but they could also go on a "date" together to the movies and have a romantic dinner at home on Saturday night.

Bob did not want a divorce, and he wanted to talk Gail out of a separation. He thought that's what married life was: You had fun, you had fights, you made up ... you still loved each other. He said yes to Gail's weekend plans because the psychiatrist's letter that she had could destroy his career. The last thing he wanted was for her to show it to his boss, as she had threatened. Bob did not like it and he suspected he would like her terms even less but he had little choice—Gail was in charge at the moment.

Bob called an 800 flight service number, checking on weather for the weekend. The recorded message made it clear that Saturday would not be a safe flying day but Sunday looked good.

The next day, Bob worked at Maimonides Hospital until 5 o'clock. It was still sunny and muggy and in the 90s when Bob went to a garage in Bay Ridge, Brooklyn, to check on his car. It had not been repaired, so he borrowed a car from a friend overnight—a tan Datsun 610. Bob drove home to Manhattan and parked the car in his rented spot in a parking garage on Second Avenue, around the corner from his apartment building, and got home at 7 o'clock.

Bob's old friend Dave Ostrow called a few minutes later from New Jersey. He told Bob he was still at Scott Baranoff's house and he wanted to get the old gang together one last time that night—because everyone was leaving in the morning.

"C'mon, Bobby—come out here," Dave urged.

Dave could hear Gail's voice in the background, telling Bob he couldn't go out.

"I can't," Bob reluctantly told his pal. "I have to go out to dinner and a movie with Gail."

"Hey, we came all this way. It's been four years since we've seen each other. Bobby, you can see her every night," Dave laughed.

Bob said he couldn't do it.

"You can bring Gail, we like Gail," Dave persisted.

Again, he heard Gail's voice, screeching and yelling at Bob.

"She's henpecking him," Dave thought.

"You can't go out!" Gail yelled. "We have a date!"

"I can't go out, we have a date," Bob repeated.

He tried one more time, suggesting that they all come into town and all go out to dinner together but Bob just repeated his regrets. Dave was frustrated and decided to use the ultimate macho insult, hoping it would work.

"You are pussy-whipped," Dave said, with a chuckle— loud enough for everyone at his end to hear.

Bob could hear the laughter through the phone. He was angry that he had to say no to his old friends but he went on his date with Gail.

Bob and Gail ate dinner out and decided to catch a 10 o'clock late show. The film they saw was *The Shooting Party*, a masterful 1984 British movie about, among other things, deceit and adultery starring a cast of excellent actors headed by James Mason, Edward Fox and John Gielgud. It was a strange choice of movie for a woman cheating on her husband, especially for a wife trying to arrange an amicable divorce settlement.

The next morning, Saturday, Bob was up early and off to work at seven in his borrowed car, which he had to return to his friend. Gail told Bob she had two morning appointments that day—at the hairdresser's and at her gynecologist. Bob was going to work a short day at the hospital, stop at his other job and get home early. They had plans to go to Gail's friend Debra Nudel's house that evening but

Gail said they were not going because it would interfere with their encounter-style weekend. Gail looked out on the terrace. It was warm and cloudy. The weather report called for temperatures in the upper 80s and said showers and thunderstorms were likely that night.

Gail had breakfast, showered, dressed and left to take care of business. She met a real estate agent and checked out an apartment, which was already rented. On her way to another appointment, she ran into Anthony on the street. He was dressed in a tennis shirt and shorts and carrying his racquet; he was late for a game at a nearby sports club.

"How are you doing?" Anthony asked.

"Oh, Bob's treating me better. . . ."

"I'm running late—we'll talk later," Anthony said, dashing off.

Gail went to her gynecologist to check the placement of the IUD birth control device that had been inserted two weeks earlier. Gail's doctor noticed that her patient—who was usually morose and withdrawn—seemed very happy and even jovial, as she made an appointment to return in January of the next year for a checkup.

"See you in six months," Gail smiled before she left.

"Gail seemed very cheerful," the nurse said, after she left.

But by 11 A.M., when Gail had an appointment at Ouidad's, the hairdresser found her in an opposite mood. She seemed very quiet, subdued. Something had apparently happened between her two morning appointments to lower her spirits. Ouidad was concerned for Gail because she liked her. She had no idea that Gail had a history of problems with depression and suicidal thoughts.

Gail told Ouidad the story of the glass-laced casserole. Ouidad thought it sounded unlikely and a little bit exaggerated. It was bizarre. What mother, thought Ouidad, herself a mother of two children, would try to give glass to her child—and then tell her about it, so she could find it? Either this was a very strange mother or this was a very strange daughter.

Gail surprised her stylist by suddenly saying, "I'm having a hard time with my husband," after about a year without mentioning him. She told Ouidad that she may have made a mistake marrying Bob and was apartment hunting. In the next chair was a real estate broker. Gail introduced herself and began quizzing her about apartments. Was there any way she could get an apartment but put in someone else's name, so no one would know it was hers? Ouidad thought that was strange. She didn't know if Gail wanted to set up a love nest on the side for her and her boyfriend or if she was really leaving her husband and wanted to hide from him.

Ken Feiner, one of Gail's new boyfriends, had picked Gail up from Ouidad's several times in the previous months, but he was not around that day. In fact, Gail feared that his feelings for her might be cooling.

When Gail got home, her mother called. Gail told her about her new haircut and her mother told her she disapproved, even though she had not seen it. They argued pointlessly about it for several minutes.

Bob left the hospital by 11 A.M. His car was still being repaired, so he took a subway to Manhattan, where he borrowed his dad's large, blue Cadillac. Bob arrived at the apartment at noon. As he changed for lunch, the phone rang and Gail picked it up.

"Hello?"

"Hi, Gail. It's Anthony. There was a hang-up on my machine—did you call me?"

"No, I didn't," Gail said, in a strange voice.

"What's the matter? Is Bob there?"

"I'll talk to you later."

They both hung up.

"Who was that?" Bob asked.

"My mother," Gail lied.

After Gail got off the phone, they went out to a new bagel store four blocks away, on Third Avenue, at 88th Street. As they walked along the warm pavement, the city appeared partially deserted. It seemed everyone was away for the weekend or for the day or for the summer. A warm Manhattan without crowds was the way it was meant to be—no lines for lunch or dinner or at the movies, no shoving hordes on the subway, no jammed stores. But Gail did not seem to be enjoying herself.

"What's bothering you?" Bob asked, as they sat down to lunch.

Gail claimed she was upset because she had had an argument with her mother over her new haircut.

After lunch, Gail said she had to shop for underwear, so they walked uptown and over to East 91st Street. Bob waited awkwardly in the high-priced lingerie shop, while Gail tried on a series of lacy underthings in a dressing room, inspecting her toned body in a mirror. Bob's face betrayed an expression far beyond the usual awkward-husband face, as he sat there and watched Gail use his money to buy sexy underwear for another man.

On their walk home, the air had become oppressive and a storm wind had come up. The cloud cover darkened and descended over the city. Their next stop was a pet store where they bought food for their two cats. Bob carried the heavy boxes of cat food, while Gail swung the dainty boutique bag of lingerie on her arm. Walking down Madison Avenue, they got into an argument because Bob said he had had enough shopping and enough baggage and wanted to go home but Gail wanted to make several more stops.

They were both worried about their upcoming talk. Bob knew Gail wanted a divorce but he loved her and did not want to lose her. Gail felt she was in control but was terrified that Bob might know about her boyfriends.

The bad weather prevented Bob from taking a plane up but that did not mean he couldn't fly. When he got home, he turned on his Atari. The computer screen beeped as Bob loaded in the Flight Simulator program. Daredevil computer pilots like Bob, flying the virtual skies in their living rooms, could risk their lives flying in bad weather or try acrobatics or dangerous maneuvers that might get them killed in a real plane. How slow could you really go in a

Cessna before it stalled? It was much better to first try out a questionable aerial tactic on the computer before attempting it in reality. He pre-flighted his aircraft, checked his instruments and weather conditions and taxied onto the runway for takeoff.

Gail paid no attention whatsoever to what Bob was doing. While he flew through a virtual stratosphere, she went out to shop for dinner, since they were eating at home that night.

After his successful cyber-flight, Bob came back to earth and grilled a thick steak and potatoes on the hibachi grill on the porch, while Gail prepared a salad and vegetables in the kitchen, then set the table, turned down the lights and lit two candles for dinner. Bob didn't have a drink but Gail made herself a cool summer cocktail, a rum and tonic.

A stranger with a telescope looking into the picture window of Bob and Gail's living room would have seen a handsome young couple with their whole lives ahead of them, sitting down to a romantic candlelit dinner, in elegant surroundings.

Of course, it wasn't the beginning of a romance but the end of one. Gail and Bob were cordial to each other but it was, in a sense, a business dinner and it was time for Gail to dictate her terms.

She told Bob that she still loved him but needed her own space to work things out. Gail said it was better for both of them that she leave, that they would both be happier in the long run. Maybe, she said in an upbeat tone—in the way that women lie to men to avoid conflict—it would only be a temporary separation. Bob did not want to be let down easy. He loved her. They went around and around. Gail made it clear that she wanted a quick, uncontested and generous settlement—and expected to be supported in the style to which she had become accustomed. She needed to finish school—without the inconvenience of a job—and become a clinical psychologist, so she could help people with emotional problems. On Tuesday, Gail was actually scheduled to have her first session with her first patient, something that excited her. She wanted nothing to stand in the way of that.

When Bob balked at giving Gail half of his earnings for as long as she stayed single, Gail went to the whip hand. She reminded Bob about Michael Stone's letter. She repeated her threat to show it to the chief of surgery at Maimonides—as well as any other hospital in the country that Bob might go to. Bob believed her threat—she would do it.

She also told Bob she had gone to the police after he had choked her, almost two years earlier, and had a copy of the police report. Bob did not believe that claim and wanted to see copies of both documents. Gail showed him a copy of the shrink's letter because an extra one had been mailed to her. She told Bob that another copy and the police report were somewhere in a safe deposit box.

Bob read over the letter. It didn't use the word "psychopath" but any professional would read between the lines. If his boss saw the letter, his career was finished.

But, if Gail blew the whistle on Bob and he could no longer work as a surgeon, he pointed out, she could kiss her fat divorce settlement goodbye. She would kill the goose that laid the golden eggs.

Bob, his voice getting louder, told Gail he knew she was cheating on him and she wouldn't get a dime in a divorce—because she was the adulterer.

Gail's worst fear had been confirmed. Had she been followed by a private detective? She screamed that she had evidence that would ruin Bob and his father. Her hatred of Bob was so great that she almost seemed more interested in destroying him than working out a deal.

They each said terrible, hateful things to each other, some of which they had never said before. They each felt belittled and vengeful. It was a lopsided Mexican standoff. Nothing was settled but the cards were on the table. Gail could shoot Bob's life as a physician down in flames but he could not end her career—only delay or reduce her divorce settlement in court. In a showdown, Bob had a lot more to lose.

They argued until the early hours of the morning and went to bed, turning away from each other. Although they had failed to reach an agreement, two things had changed—they both knew that Gail was finally leaving Bob for good and that Gail had Bob over a barrel.

Eventually, Gail, fully clothed to avoid sex with her husband, fell asleep, as thunder rumbled in the wet sky outside their bedroom window.

But Bob lay awake for hours, his finely-tuned brain calmly turning the problem over and over. Like Tom Swift Jr. from the science fiction books of his youth, Bob needed to invent a way to solve his impossible problem, overcome the evil force and get to a happy ending.

He examined all possible moves and options, as he would in a chess game, but most scenarios left him without her and without a life—or without half of his money for the foreseeable future. In every case, she would win and be left with a life and a career.

The worst that could happen to Gail was that she would lose the comfort his money could provide.

The worst that could happen to him was that he would lose everything he had ever worked for in his life.

Bob lay there in the dark next to the sleeping Gail with his eyes open for a long time—thinking and thinking and thinking.

CHAPTER 12

THIN AIR

BOB woke up and saw that the sky was clearing and the heat had returned. The forecast was for a hot, mostly sunny day. He called the flight service weather line and listened to detailed information about barometric pressure, humidity, temperatures, winds and the altitudes of cloud cover over the land and ocean.

Bob decided he would rent a plane from Caldwell. He dialed Sky King at the airport and reserved a Cessna. As usual, after he hung up, he opened his personal flight log book and wrote "7/7" in the date box and jotted "CDW" in the departure space. He would fill in the times and details of the flight later.

Bob and Gail were expected at Michelle's house in New Jersey for a birthday party for Bob's nephew that evening, so Bob had arranged for a late afternoon flight.

"You want breakfast?" he asked Gail.

"No," she replied.

Gail got dressed in pink shorts, a white halter top with the word APARADOS—a Brazilian beach—across the front and brown sandals.

The next week was going to be a busy one for Gail. In addition to having appointments with her own therapist, Gail had sessions scheduled with two patients who were to undergo therapy with her. But it was another meeting that had Gail on edge. She had an engagement the next morning that was the most important interview of her life—a meeting to qualify for her PhD doctoral program in psychology. It was a big step in her plan to become independent from Bob—to be a clinical psychologist. She was nervous about the interview and she was concerned about something else, something that Michael Stone had said almost two years earlier. The psychiatrist had told her that Bob attacked her on the one night that he knew she would not turn him in—the night before her graduate record exam.

It was the day before another most-important date. Gail was wary of Bob, treading lightly. On that warm, pleasant summer Sunday morning, the atmosphere in the apartment was like a frigid mountaintop overburdened with snow. The slightest disturbance could trigger an avalanche.

Bob showered, dressed and made breakfast. While he was eating, the phone rang and Gail answered it. It was 10:11 A.M., Sunday, July 7, 1985.

"Hello?"

"Hello, Gail. It's Francesca."

Gail had not heard from Francesca Beale in more than a year—not since she had turned down Gail's request to move in with her. The call seemed like wonderful luck out of the blue. Gail was elated. Perhaps she might be able to stay with Francesca until she got settled.

"Hi, how are you?" Gail's happy voice asked.

But Gail's friendliness turned instantly frosty when Francesca told her the reason for her call. She had not called to renew their friendship but because she wanted Gail to ask Bob to recommend a surgeon. She wasn't even asking for a referral for herself, but for a friend who needed some kind of surgery. Francesca was confused when Gail suddenly became angry and depressed, her voice flat and empty.

Gail slammed down the phone; the avalanche had started. She began screaming at Bob, instantly picking up where they had left off the night before, with the blackmail and the threats.

But this argument was different—neither one of them held back.

Gail, her pretty face contorted red with rage, screeched a final ultimatum at Bob. She told him he was pathetic. She revealed her affairs, including her claimed liaison with an Arab. She declared that she loved another man and that she had never loved Bob.

Bob no longer held back his anger. His rage exploded out of him, like a living thing.

The next-door neighbors were away on vacation but, in the apartment below, Mae Eisenhower heard Gail yelling at Bob—as usual on a Sunday morning. She couldn't hear what Gail was saying but could tell that she was furious. Then she heard Bob yelling back. Gail's heels clacked on the wooden floor and furniture legs scraped across Mae's ceiling, as the shouting reached a crescendo—and then ended with a loud bang, which was followed by welcome silence. Mae was used to the pattern—yelling, heel clicks, furniture scraping and then a door slamming—as one of them stormed out of the apartment or banged into the bedroom. Mae just wished they would get carpeting, so she wouldn't have to listen to them all the time.

A bit more than an hour later, an annoyed Debra Nudel called to find out why Bob and Gail had not shown up for the party she'd thrown the night before.

"Hello?"

"Hi, Bob, it's Debra. Is Gail there?"

"No, she went out."

Bob told Debra he would have Gail give her a call as soon as she got back.

At 3 o'clock that afternoon, Joel Davis looked up from his bagel and lox when the sexy brunette walked into H & H Bagels on East 81st Street with another woman and stood on the counter line. The happy, laughing women were fifteen years younger than Joel and paid no attention to the man sitting at a table with a woman. Joel Davis noticed the first girl's tanned body and her unusual T-shirt, which bore some kind of foreign phrase or a map of some kind of tropical island. A retired textile company president, Joel was almost as interested in the four-color silk screen job as the body underneath it. She reminded him of his ex-wife. Her firm, young body was slathered and glistening with suntan oil, as was her friend's. They each carried a beach bag and one of them was toting a folded beach chair. They looked like they had just come back from the park or a "tar beach"—a rooftop.

"She must have picked that shirt up in the islands," Joel said.

Joel's girlfriend Sue, whose back was to the women, noticed him ogling them but had no intention of turning to look.

At 3:30, Bob—lugging his large, heavy duffel bag—left the apartment and walked to his garage where he'd parked his father's big blue Caddy. He drove east and got on the northbound FDR Drive, cruising along the East River and then the Harlem River. He took the exit for the George Washington Bridge and passed over the Hudson. Once in New Jersey, Bob took the turnoff for Route 80 West. The journey to the Caldwell Airport was a familiar one and traffic was light. He arrived at the field before 4:30, parked on nearby Passaic Avenue and walked into the office of Sky King Flight Service. The woman behind the desk scratched out another name in the flying log and, misspelling Bob's name, wrote "Bob Berbaum" into a 4:30 to 6:30 slot on the flying log for the 1223F aircraft, which Bob had used several times previously. Bob did not file a flight plan for his trip. He performed his usual exhaustive pre-flight checkup, taxied onto the runway, and did his prescribed "run-up" of the engine in preparation for flight, then radioed to the tower for clearance.

"Tower, 23Foxtrot ready for takeoff on runway 2 west."

"Roger, 23Foxtrot, clear for takeoff."

In the tower, a tape slowly turned, recording the exchange. The tapes of that day's activity would be stored for two weeks—in case they were needed in an investigation by the Federal Aviation Administration, or any other agency—and then erased.

Bob pushed the throttles down, pulled the wheel back and the Cessna accelerated down the concrete runway, picking up speed until the small aircraft lifted off the runway. Leaving the airport behind, Bob steadily gained altitude. He pushed his controls to the right and began a turn. He set a course north-by-northwest—a flight path that would take him in a straight line to the Greenwood Lake Airport, just eighteen miles away—while climbing over suburban New Jersey, cruising at ninety knots. As long as he avoided major airport control areas, Bob could fly wherever he wanted without anyone tracking, directing or questioning his path.

Within ten minutes, Bob passed directly over the long, shimmering blue waters of the Wanaque Reservoir. It was a pretty sight. The reservoir, which stretched out to Bob's right, was almost seven miles long, the longest in New Jersey. Its still waters ran deep, from thirty-five to ninety feet. Unlike the nearby Greenwood Lake, which would be packed with swimmers, boaters, water skiers and fishermen on such a nice day, the reservoir was deserted. Because it supplied drinking water, no fishing, swimming or boating was allowed. It was surrounded by thousands of acres of forest and enclosed by a fence. The silver afternoon sun glinted invitingly across the calm water as Bob soared overhead.

The Greenwood Lake Airport, a few miles past the reservoir, had no control tower. Pilots who intended to land or take off from the small field simply announced their intention, and part of their tail number by radio, before doing it.

"Greenwood Lake, this is twenty-three Foxtrot, coming in for a touch-and-go on runway two-four—any other traffic, over?"

He repeated the message several times but got no response, meaning he was free to proceed. Bob came around to the left and made a perfect landing at the airport, powered back up and lifted off again.

He then flew low over the length of the peaceful reservoir. Scenic Wanaque, a manmade body of water completed in 1930, was the final resting place of numerous people. Several construction workers were killed and buried under tons of earth that comprised part of the dam at the southern end. Four cemeteries had to be moved before the valley was flooded, but authorities were never able to locate all of the remains from one old, colonial graveyard. Some were entombed forever under thirty billion gallons of water.

The valley that became the reservoir was named Wanaque, which was an old Native American term for "place of sassafras," but it had another meaning—it came from an Algonquin root meaning "rest and repose."

When he was done, Bob turned his aircraft away from the restful reservoir and headed south. Alone, he continued his ascent, climbing higher and higher into the thin air.

He returned to the airport almost exactly two hours later, at 6:25. Flying at ninety knots cruising speed, Bob could have flown almost anywhere in a circle with a diameter of 180 miles—an area of over 25,000 square miles—and then returned. When he paid for his plane rental, back at the Sky King counter, no one asked him where he had been.

Bob then drove to his sister Michelle's house in nearby Upper Montclair, a trip of less than five miles, to attend the birthday party for his nephew. He announced that Gail was not with him because she had gone out and had not returned. He did not mention that he had just gone flying for two hours. Bob partied with the birthday boy and his family, and sang "Happy Birthday" to his nephew, who blew out all his birthday cake candles. For photographs taken by his sister, Bob gave a big, happy smile for the camera.

When Marvin and Nettie left, Bob was stretched out on the living room couch, sleeping like a baby.

Bob stayed until 9 o'clock and then made an unplanned stop at the nearby home of Scott Baranoff. Scott was out to dinner but Bob visited with Scott's mom until he returned home. When he did, Scott was pleasantly surprised to see Bob, who seemed to have gotten some time away from Gail. Bob said he was able to drop by because he and Gail had had a fight and she had walked out and had not returned. Twice, Bob excused himself and called to see if

Gail was home. The answering machine was on and Gail did not pick up.

Bob arrived home at 11:30 that night. Gail was not there and there were no messages from her on the machine. He picked up the phone and dialed the Katzes' number on Long Island. Sylvia answered the phone.

"Hello?"

"Hi, it's Bob. Is Gail there?"

"No," said Sylvia, immediately worried.

Bob explained that he and Gail had had a fight that morning and Gail had walked out to cool off. Bob and his mother-in-law each promised they would call if they heard from her. Bob then called two of Gail's girlfriends, Debra Nudel, who had called earlier in the day, and Ellen Schwartz—who told him they had not seen or heard from Gail. Both women were concerned about Gail going missing.

He also spoke to one of Gail's professors, neuropsychologist Yvette Feis, and told her that Gail was not home. "We had an argument this morning and she went out to the park to cool off. She's still missing," Bob said.

"Bob, you have to call the police and report her missing," Yvette urged.

"I guess that's a good idea . . ." Bob said, but then told her he didn't want to involve the police in his personal business yet. Even if Bob had reported her missing the police were very reluctant to take missing persons reports until the adult had been gone for 24 hours.

Sylvia Katz could not sleep. She called her daughter Alayne in Virginia, who had just graduated from law school and was still up, studying for her upcoming Bar Exam. Alayne had been in New York for the wedding of a friend that weekend and had only arrived home a few hours earlier. Sylvia told Alayne about Bob's call and how Gail had left in a huff and not returned. Alayne knew how troubled her sister's marriage was and told her mother that Gail might indeed have just left Bob and gone off on her own, assuring her mother that Gail would contact her soon and explain what had happened.

Bob opened his flight log and stared at the date and departure entry he had made at the beginning of that very long day. Bob did not write down "4N1," the designation for the Greenwood Lake Airport, where he had been. Instead, he put the log book aside, along with several other items he had located. He intended to take them all with him the next morning.

Late that night, May Eisenhower was again disturbed by noise coming from above. But she did not hear any yelling or Gail's heels on the wood—only the scraping sounds of furniture being moved, as if someone were cleaning up or searching the apartment for something—and then more silence. May looked at her bedside clock—it was 1 A.M.

Bob did not call the police to report his wife missing. He had to work in the morning. Instead, he brushed his teeth and went to sleep in a half-empty bed.

CHAPTER 13

MISSING PERSON

BOB drove to work on Monday morning, the beginning of another hot, steamy day. From there he called Beth Israel—but Gail had not shown up for her graduate work or to see her first patients. He also called her psychiatrist, and introduced himself.

"Is Gail there?" Bob asked.

"No and she's always on time," Dr. Elsa Fairchild said, speaking to Bob for the first time.

Bob explained about their fight and that Gail had "gone off in a huff."

Bob also checked in with Gail's friends and family again, as well as his own family before he decided he had to report her missing.

"I'm concerned that Gail might do something to harm herself," he told one of her friends.

After work that night, about 9 o'clock, Bob drove to the 19th Precinct on East 95th Street, where he was directed upstairs to the Detective Squad.

"I want to report my wife missing," Bob told an officer sitting at a desk.

Bob said he had had a fight with Gail the day before and she'd walked out about 11 in the morning but did not come back. The cop filled in the date and time, asked Bob questions and wrote his answers into the boxes on the "51" form, a triplicate "Missing/Unidentified Person Report." The officer wrote "had argument with spouse" as the cause of Gail's absence. Her probable destination was "unknown." She was described as 5-foot-3-inches tall, petite, weighing 107 pounds, and having brown hair and hazel eyes. Her clothing and rings were described. Under scars, the cop wrote "Wrist/forearms 10 years old." In the remarks box, he wrote that she had a "history of psychiatric problems, presently in therapy. May have went [sic] to Central Park."

A second missing persons report was filled out by a police aide ten minutes later, adding further details. The cause of absence box was "EDP," cop shorthand for Emotionally Disturbed Person. A "Black wallet" was listed as the only property she had on her person, other than her rings.

In response to questions, Bob told police that he and Gail had been fighting over the weekend and that they had seen a marriage counselor. He told them that Gail had been twice treated for depression and had attempted suicide. When the paperwork was done, Bob went home.

The desk officer ordered a search in Central Park. A few officers drove around looking for Gail for about two hours but found nothing. Since it was dark and they did not have her picture, it wasn't much of a search. Notifications were made to the Transit Police and the Housing Police and a teletype alarm was transmitted, alerting all commands to the missing person. Everything was routine. Detective Virgillio Dalsass of the 19th Detective Squad was assigned to the case, as was Detective Thomas O'Malley of the Missing Persons Squad at Police Headquarters. Gail Katz Bierenbaum had become one of the thousands who disappear in New York City every year: Missing Persons Squad Case Number 7816.

Bob continued to go to the hospital that week but regularly heard from friends and family, who called to see if Gail had come home. She hadn't. Bob spoke to the doormen and went door-to-door on his floor, talking to his neighbors.

Bob knocked on neighbor Mario Villaverde's apartment door. Mario opened his door and saw the young doctor from down the hall.

"Hi," said Bob. "Have you seen my wife lately? Has she come back while I was away?"

"No, I didn't see her," said Mario. "Why?"

"I'm very worried because she disappeared," said Bob.

"She went out and never came back. She's disappeared and we can't find her."

The last time Mario had seen Gail, she had been leaving her apartment with a blond, blue-eyed woman but he didn't mention it to Bob. Later, after cops came around asking Mario the same question, he didn't mention it to them either—not even after he heard a rumor that Gail had a girlfriend and had run off with her. Mario thought Bob loved his pretty wife and was genuinely upset by her mysterious departure. When the other tenants began hushed conversations that maybe something bad had happened to their missing neighbor, Mario put no faith in the gossip. Bob didn't look like a killer. Besides, Mario reasoned, how could he have gotten her out of the building without anyone seeing anything? Mario had been in show business, as a dancer and actor, and Bob seemed genuinely worried—he didn't look like he was putting on a show.

Bob called his best man Ralph Sugarman and gave him the news that Gail had run off.

"I believe that she had been seeing someone," Bob explained.

Ralph thought Bob seemed numb and very distraught.

Gail's parents drove into the city every day with Steve and joined Bob searching the city streets and the park for Gail. By Tuesday morning, when Gail had not called her—or anyone else—or kept her appointments, Alayne was convinced that something awful had happened. She rushed back to New York and joined in the search for Gail. Bob's in-laws virtually lived in his apartment while they searched.

During the week, a very pretty blond nurse named Karen Caruana saw Bob at the hospital and noticed that he was exhausted and disheveled. He looked like he hadn't slept in days.

"Bob, what's wrong?"

He explained about Gail's disappearance. Karen had heard Bob argue with Gail on the phone and wasn't tremendously surprised that she had left.

"I'm really sorry, Bob," Karen said, sincerely. "Is there anything I can do to help?"

"No, thanks, Karen."

"Okay," she said with a comforting smile. "But if there's anything I can ever do, please let me know, okay?"

"Okay. I will."

Sylvia called Amanda, hoping that Gail was with her but she was not. Then Bob called her, asking the same thing. Bob said that Gail had gone jogging, although he didn't explain why Gail would go running in leather sandals. She detected panic in Bob's voice. It appeared to Amanda that Bob and Sylvia were both going through Gail's address book. The third call was Sylvia again—asking Amanda if she had anything bad to tell her about Bob. She didn't.

Bob had a MISSING poster made up, with a smiling picture of Gail and a brief description of her. It said she was a "Graduate student at Long Island University. Last seen 11 AM, Sunday, July 7, 1985. May have been in the vicinity of Metropolitan Museum in Central Park." The poster offered a "REWARD for any information concerning her whereabouts and leading to her return" and asked anyone with information to call Detective O'Malley at a Missing Persons Squad phone number.

Bob, along with Manny, Sylvia, Alayne and Steve, began taping the posters around the Yorkville neighborhood and close to Central Park. They walked all over the park, leaving posters on poles and trees and showing Gail's picture to people. Everyone just shook their heads. No, they hadn't seen her.

The more she heard about what had happened, the more people she stopped who had not seen Gail, the less sense it made to Alayne. Why would Gail just vanish? Alayne did not think her sister had been depressed or suicidal and she discounted the possibility that she had wandered off and jumped in the river. In her last conversations with her mother and sister, Gail discussed possible future plans and did not seem at all like someone about to do away with herself. And if Gail intended to leave, why didn't she take anything but the clothes on her back? Besides, no matter how much she squabbled with her parents or sister, they were her family. Gail might leave a husband or a boyfriend but how could she ever leave her family? Alayne was sure she knew the answer—Gail had run off with a boyfriend.

Anthony found two messages on his answering machine when he got home. The first was from Gail's brother Steve, who said Gail was missing. The second message was from Bob, with a similar message. Anthony took a deep breath and called Bob.

"Hello?"

"Bob?"

"Yes?"

"This is Anthony. I know that Gail is missing. I'm sorry to hear that—I'll do anything to help."

Bob seemed to know exactly who Anthony was. He did not ask what his relationship was with his wife and, more strangely, he did not even ask if Gail was with him.

"You were here the other night, weren't you?" Bob asked.

"Yes," Anthony replied, at a loss for any other words.

Bob asked Anthony if he would help look for Gail and he quickly agreed to come over on the weekend and help with the search.

Alayne got Ken's phone number out of Gail's date book and called him.

"I haven't heard from her in days," Ken told her. "If she went off with somebody, Alayne, it would have been me, so something terrible has happened."

"No, she would have been with *me*," Alayne protested.

Next, after Alayne spoke to Anthony, her heart began to sink. The boyfriends were their last hope. Gail had already confronted Bob with the psychiatrist's letter. What if Bob had found out that Gail was cheating on him? The Katz family also thought it was suspicious that Gail had vanished off the face of the earth wearing all of the expensive rings Bob had given her. It wasn't odd that she had been wearing her wedding band and diamond engagement ring but why would she have been wearing her aquamarine ring to the park?

Alayne decided that she was released from her vow not to tell her parents bad things about Bob. Alayne didn't trust Bob, and she didn't like the answers he gave about the argument. She felt he was hiding something. If he'd choked Gail once, maybe he'd done it again. Sylvia only knew a few bad things Gail had told her about Bob but Gail had told Alayne more. She told her parents about Bob strangling the cat and strangling Gail, and she discussed her fears with them. As they shared information, the whole picture became more and more alarming. Who else could it be? They decided Bob was acting weird, as if he was just pretending to look for Gail—as if he knew they weren't going to find her. He seemed not to be worrying with them in the same way. They thought he wasn't acting like a man whose wife was missing. But if they were right, it meant that something terrible had happened to Gail.

In Bob's apartment, Sylvia found Gail's pocketbook, which held her cigarettes, her address book, her house keys and her wallet with her credit cards. Why, Sylvia asked her family, would Gail run away without money or credit cards or identification or her cigarettes—or even her keys? But would Bob the genius do away with Gail only to leave all her things in the apartment for her family to find—when it would have been just as easy to get rid of them also?

The Katz family did not accuse Bob of anything but the air in the apartment became charged with suspicion. That was when Alayne decided to test Bob's assertion that Carlos the doorman had seen Gail leave the building on Sunday morning. When Carlos told Alayne that he saw Gail leave the building, not on Sunday morning, but on Saturday— the day before—Alayne's worst fears seemed to be confirmed.

Alayne was now convinced that Bob was responsible for Gail's disappearance. It was time to go to the police with her fears. From that moment on, the Katz family pretended to help Bob look for Gail but they had begun to look for evidence that he had killed her. When they stopped people on the street, they no longer hoped to find someone who had seen Gail alive. Their grim hope was to find someone who had seen Bob do something. They wanted Bob to be punished. But first they had to prove there had been a crime.

Alayne, searching for information, called Jane Dunne at Beth Israel and told her what she had already told Gail's friends: "Gail has disappeared and we think Bob did it."

Jane was saddened but not surprised. Along with a male colleague and two graduate students, she made arrangements with Alayne to help search for Gail.

When they arrived at 185 E. 85th Street, Jane and Gail's schoolmates discussed what Bob might have done with Gail's body.

"Maybe he threw her down the garbage chute," one of them suggested.

Playing detective, the academics walked around the building and came across a Dumpster in the rear of the high-rise. They all looked at each other and decided that, because Bob was a surgeon, he must have cut Gail up and dumped her remains into the large, steel trash container. They agreed it was a logical way to get her out of the building without being observed.

In seconds, the psychologist and the graduate students had climbed into the smelly box and were eagerly rooting around in the pile of refuse—looking for pieces of Gail's corpse. They found nothing there or anywhere else in the neighborhood but that did not alter their conviction that Bob was a killer.

For Gail's family, it was a maddening and surreal experience to look for their loved one with the person they believed was her killer. Every endless day they were forced to spend time being cordial to Bob was agony. The intolerable sadness in their hearts was quickly turning to seething hatred.

On the other side of Central Park, Dr. Michael Stone had just finished with a patient when his wife came back from a walk in the park.

"Guess what? Gail's missing—can you imagine?"

She held up a MISSING poster bearing the name and face of Gail Katz Bierenbaum, and said they were plastered on lampposts and trees all over the park. She knew her husband would be upset but he still could not tell the police what Bob had told him in therapy. The doctor–patient confidentiality rendered Bob's words virtually as sacrosanct as sins confessed to a priest, although he had discussed the unusual case with his wife.

"It's not a surprise," Michael said, shaking his head sadly. "He killed her."

CHAPTER 14

ON THE GRILL

BOB called the Missing Persons Squad from the hospital on a cloudy Wednesday afternoon and asked for Detective Tom O'Malley. What was being done to find Gail? Was there anything he could do to help find his wife? Tom asked the young doctor for a recent photo of Gail for a glossy, 3-by-5 NYPD MISSING PERSON card. The card would be distributed to all commands of the police department. It could be handed out to the public and it would be small enough to fit in a cop's pocket. Bob said he would drop off a picture on his way home from work.

"Do you know of anyone who may have seen your wife leave the building?" Tom asked.

"Yes. The doorman downstairs told me that he saw her leave a little after eleven," said Bob.

"What's his name?"

"Carlos."

Tom asked what happened before Gail left.

"We had an argument and she left the apartment," said Bob. "She told me she was going to Central Park to cool off and that was the last time I saw her."

It was agreed that the police department would alert the media, in an effort to locate Gail, and Bob would cooperate.

At that point Tom thought almost anything could have happened. The woman might have run away from her husband, maybe with a boyfriend—or even a girlfriend—or she might have been the victim of an accident or crime. Perhaps she was unconscious in a hospital somewhere or lying on a slab in the morgue. She had little or no identification on her and was wearing almost $10,000 worth of jewelry in a town where people got killed for a couple of bucks. She was tiny and would have not presented much of a threat to a mugger, rapist or killer. But she could have killed herself or ended up in a mental ward somewhere as a "Jane Doe." Maybe the teletype to the precincts and commands would turn up something.

Tom wanted to reconstruct Gail's last week and he needed to speak to all the people Gail had seen. He also asked Bob to bring in Gail's address book, so it could be copied and all the people in it could be contacted.

The next day, Thursday, Bob got calls from the press. Reporters came to his apartment and he gave them copies of pictures and told the *New York Post*, the *Daily News*, and television and radio stations how Gail had walked out the previous Sunday morning.

"I am concerned about her safety," Bob told a reporter for the *News*. "This is totally out of character. I'm really worried. She had an appointment to see a patient Monday at Beth Israel Hospital and to do some data research there Tuesday. She missed both appointments."

Bob sat on the couch in his living room and taped an interview that aired that night on WNBC-TV.

"I think, no matter what, she wouldn't abandon her patients," the soft-spoken physician said.

"What do you think happened to your wife?" the reporter asked.

"I don't know. I don't know—but I'm worried," Bob replied, looking at the floor.

The next morning, Friday, the story broke in the papers. "SURGEON'S WIFE VANISHES," read the headline in the *Post*, above a picture of a stern-faced Gail. "Police are hunting for a surgeon's wife today after her husband said she vanished after a domestic fight," it read. The phrase "her husband said" represented journalistic caution—in case the husband was later arrested. The story described Bob and Gail's "three-year, childless marriage" as "rocky." The piece also mentioned that Gail's white T-shirt was emblazoned with the name APARADOS, a beach in Brazil.

The story ended with an appeal for anyone with information to call detectives at the Missing Persons Squad.

Tom O'Malley, a husky, red-faced twelve-year veteran,

thought it might be a routine runaway wife case—until he got a call from Gail's family.

Her parents told O'Malley that Bob had choked Gail into unconsciousness about a year and a half earlier: he'd climbed out on a porch and threatened to jump after he caught her smoking a cigarette—and then choked her until she passed out. Just before their wedding, they said, Bob had tried to kill Gail's cat by strangling it and shoving it in the toilet. The missing woman had at least two boyfriends, her family said. They feared that Bob had discovered Gail was committing adultery and had done away with her. They also said that the doorman had not seen Gail leave the building alive and well on the day she disappeared—as Bob had told police—but the day before.

The detective's Missing Persons case was now a possible homicide but Tom had no body and no proof. The husband and the last person to see the victim, were always suspects until they could be eliminated—and Bob was both. He was a solid citizen and had never before been arrested but the guy was a surgeon who cut people up for a living. Tom told Gail's parents he had no evidence to get a search warrant for Bob and Gail's apartment. If they could get a warrant, police investigators would examine the bathroom drains to look for signs of foul play, he explained. The grisly possibility was chilling to the Katzes but they agreed to help.

While the Katz family was out distributing posters with Bob, Steve Katz stayed at the apartment to answer the phone. The police wanted him to check the apartment—especially the bathtub—for signs of anything suspicious, so he looked in the tub and peered into the drain and around the bathroom but did not find any traces of blood or pieces of his sister. The failure of his mission did not make him think that he and his family were wrong about Bob.

"He's a smart guy," Steve thought. "He covered his tracks."

Tom called Gail's parents and asked them to come to see him on Saturday to discuss the case. When Bob heard that Sylvia and Manny were going to see the detective, he called Tom and asked if he also wanted him to come. Tom said yes and Bob arrived that afternoon with a bundle of MISSING flyers. After their meeting, Bob was going to leave with Manny and Sylvia and distribute the flyers uptown.

Questioning a murder suspect is a delicate thing. Experienced homicide detectives know that usually you could only subject a person to hard questioning once—before he "lawyered-up" and stopped talking to you. The secret to interrogation is to keep the suspect away from an attorney and talking to you, until you have enough evidence and are ready to go hard at him. To let someone under suspicion know that they are the prime suspect—before you have the ammunition to make him crack—is something done only as a last resort.

"Hi, Tom," Bob said, smiling and shaking hands with the older detective.

Tom gripped Bob's hand and looked him in the eye. Bob looked away, suddenly interested in the floor, as he took a seat.

"This genius thinks I'm a dumb flatfoot that he can bullshit," Tom thought, smiling back at Bob. "He won't look me in the eye because he thinks I'll just go away."

The first thing Tom asked was for Bob to tell him the same story he had told him on the phone three days earlier about Carlos the doorman. Tom wanted Bob to repeat his story, to lock him into it—because he knew it was not true. Another detective had already been told by Carlos that he had not seen Gail walk out under her own steam on the day in question. Carlos said he had told Bob the same thing—and that men had been coming up to his apartment to see Gail while he was at work.

"You know, let's get right to Carlos, the doorman, because he saw your wife leave," Tom said.

It was a simple trap—too simple—and Bob did not fall into it.

"I made a mistake there," Bob said, apologetically. "Carlos didn't see her leave on Sunday. He saw her leave on Saturday."

Bob did not mention that Carlos had also told him that men were going up to the apartment—a rather significant fact, now that Gail had disappeared.

"He's a real cool cracker," Tom thought. "He's lying because he did it—he killed her."

Tom forged ahead, and asked Bob to detail his whereabouts after Gail left on Sunday morning. As Bob spoke, Tom took notes, which he would later type up in a DD-5 detective report on the case.

"I waited in the apartment for a period of time . . . as to how long, I don't recall," Bob said, vaguely.

Bob said he then walked to his garage on East 86th Street to pick up his father's car.

"What time was this?" Tom demanded.

"I don't recall," Bob replied, looking at the floor again.

The young doctor was unable to recall the timing of events that had occurred less than a week earlier. Was he some kind of absent-minded professor, or was he lying? The problem was that Tom had no hard evidence on what time Bob left the apartment or on what he had done from 11 A.M. until he arrived at a family party in New Jersey that night—a hole of at least seven hours. A lot of things could happen in seven hours. Bob's story was that he was home with Gail, then home alone, then in his car alone—until that night. In other words, he had no alibi. Bob then told Tom about his drive to the Garden State and attending his nephew David's ninth birthday party at Michelle's home—but said he was unsure what time he'd arrived.

Bob did not mention his first destination in New Jersey—the Caldwell Airport—or that he went flying that day. Instead, he told Tom he went directly to his nephew's party, and then to a friend's house.

"What time was that?" Tom asked.

"I don't recall," said Bob. "I called home to see if Gail had come home yet."

"Which phone number did you call?"

"I don't recall."

Bob recalled staying at Scott's house until 11 or 11:30 that night, when he left to drive back home to Manhattan. Once he got home, Gail was not there and he checked the answering machine to see if there were any messages from her —but there were none.

"Were there any other messages on the answering machine?"

"I can't recall."

"Were there any messages of any kind?"

Tom would not have been surprised to hear Bob say that only his message to Gail from Scott's house was on the machine.

"I can't recall if there were."

But Bob had no trouble remembering his subsequent calls to Sylvia Katz and Gail's friends Debra and Ellen that night.

"Why did you wait until Monday to report your wife missing?" Tom asked.

"I thought for sure she would return," Bob answered. "Some friends told me I should leave her in Central Park all night by herself."

He said by Monday his friends told him not to wait any longer and he called police.

"Which friends?" Tom asked.

"I don't remember," Bob said.

"He did it," Tom thought again. "I'll try my damnedest to prove it."

Tom switched gears and asked Bob about the state of his marriage.

"Pretty bad. My marriage is in bad shape. My wife and I are always having fights."

"Did you ever hit your wife?"

"No," said Bob, sitting up straight in his chair at the harder tone in Tom's voice. "I love my wife. We're trying to make it work . . . even to the point of going for therapy."

"Did you ever attempt to strangle your wife?"

Bob shifted uneasily in his chair and replied to the detective abruptly: "I don't want to talk about it."

"Did you ever strangle her cat?"

"No," he replied, looking at the floor once more.

"Did you ever threaten to jump from your window during an argument with your wife?"

"Yes, but I don't want to go there, either."

"Why?"

"I don't want to talk about it."

"Do you know anybody by the name of Ken or Anthony?"

"Yes. Those names are in her book."

Tom let the first mention of Gail's boyfriends hang in the air for a while.

When Tom asked about the information he had given about Gail's hospitalization, he didn't mind going there.

"She was depressed and suicidal," he declared.

Tom knew it was possible, given her background, that Gail had taken her own life. But suicides didn't hide themselves—they usually wanted to be found. If she had jumped off a bridge somewhere, hopefully they would find her soon, in time to identify her by fingerprints or dental records. To Tom, the longer she stayed missing, the more likely it was that her successful doctor husband had murdered her.

Bob looked very uncomfortable. Was he ill-at-ease because he was an innocent man outraged by insulting personal questions about his runaway wife—or was he nervous that the police were on to him? It was apparent that Bob had just been questioned as a suspect but Tom stopped short of an accusation or of asking Bob if he had killed Gail and cut up her body in the bathtub. He didn't have the ammunition he needed to continue and he didn't want Bob to lawyer-up. He wanted to keep his complainant talking and cooperative.

That was the game.

It was just as apparent to Bob that Gail's family and friends were giving negative information about him to the cops. Tom asked Bob to come in the next day, Sunday, to talk again. As the interview ended, Bob stood to leave. Gail's parents were waiting outside to distribute posters with him. Bob was agitated and shook his head. He had entered a worried husband helping the police look for his troubled wife and was exiting as a murder suspect.

"This doesn't look right and people are going to wonder," Bob blurted, looking at his in-laws.

"What do you mean?" Tom asked.

"It's obvious, isn't it?"

CHAPTER 15

SUNDAY IN THE PARK

MARIANNE and her husband greeted Bob and his parents Marvin and Nettie when she arrived at the apartment on Sunday, one week after Gail had vanished. Gail's mom and dad, Sylvia and Manny, were also there, along with Gail's friend Yvette Feis and a few others. Marvin was in charge. He gave everyone assignments, different areas of street and Central Park to search, question people, and put up the MISSING posters with Gail's face on them.

It was a hot day. In the park, Marianne and the others stopped joggers, dog walkers, anyone who would listen, and asked them about Gail. No one remembered seeing her. They stapled posters to trees and taped them to lampposts and stuck them in store windows. At one point that day, as Marianne and Bob talked to joggers near the metal gate on the track around the reservoir in the park, Marianne turned to Bob.

"Where do you think Gail is?"

"I think she's on a shopping spree at Bloomingdale's— you know what a JAP she is," Bob replied, with a smirk.

Marianne was appalled at the bad "Jewish American Princess" joke. Bob explained what he said happened that morning, that he and Gail had had a fight and Gail ran out to cool off in the park.

"I wonder why she went out without her shoes on?" Bob wondered.

Marianne thought Bob's comment seemed odd, especially since he had told others that Gail had been wearing sandals when he last saw her. With a chill, she remembered Gail telling her about Bob choking her and how Bob had threatened her and that—unlike Claus von Bülow—he would not leave any evidence if he killed her. Marianne decided to press Bob for more details because his demeanor seemed weird.

"Did she have her rings on?"

"No, I found them in the jewelry box."

Bob had already told police Gail had been wearing her rings when she went out the door. He gave them descriptions of the rings and estimates of their value. When Marianne did not reply to his comment about Gail not wearing shoes, he told her in a confidential tone that Gail had been working on a school paper on depression and suicide. He said he was convinced that the work had actually made her suicidal.

"You know Gail tried to commit suicide when she was younger?"

"Yes," Marianne said, expressing doubt that Gail had killed herself.

"She became depressed working on the paper," Bob insisted, in a louder voice.

Again, Marianne disagreed, more strongly this time. She told Bob she knew Gail was happy. She knew because Gail had told her about her boyfriend Ken, but Marianne did not mention that—because she thought Bob did not know about him.

"I don't think so," said Marianne.

"How do you know that she didn't climb the gate of that reservoir?" Bob screamed at her, pointing at the gate, behind which the water was visible. "How do you know that she isn't lying at the bottom of that reservoir?" he demanded, still pointing west.

Bob's angry outburst startled Marianne—until she thought about it. Did Bob explode because of the strain of Gail's disappearance, or simply because he couldn't convince her that Gail had committed suicide? She decided it was the latter and was convinced that Bob had done something to Gail.

When the group returned to the apartment later that afternoon, Yvette spoke to one of the doormen. She asked him if he had seen Gail leave that day. He had not. He told her Bob had not questioned him about Gail's disappearance and he did not know which of his colleagues was working that day. Yvette confronted Bob in the lobby, demanding to know why he had not questioned the doormen and why he had not put posters up in his own building. Yvette, who also remembered Gail's stories of Bob's scary behavior, was outraged and began shouting at Bob.

"Why aren't there posters up in the hall? A concerned husband would make it his business to find out which door-man was on!" Yvette yelled.

Bob did not answer her.

Yvette had arrived at the same conclusion that Marianne had come to. She went down to the basement and looked in the incinerator room. She wasn't looking for Gail—she was looking for her body. She found nothing.

Upstairs in the apartment, as the group entered, a call was coming in and Gail's voice came from the answering machine—as if she were greeting them all.

"Hi," Gail said in her sweet, soft voice. "You've reached . . ."

Nettie Bierenbaum shrieked at the sound of her daughter-in-law's voice and began sobbing. Bob quickly shut the machine off, silencing Gail's ghostly voice in mid-sentence. The atmosphere in the apartment was charged with tension. Some people milled about nervously, others sat down.

"Where's the area rug you used to have here in the living room?" one of Gail's friends asked Bob, gesturing to the bare wooden floor.

"The cat got sick. I had to take the rug out to be cleaned," Bob replied.

"How could you find time to have the rug cleaned during the week your wife is missing?" Yvette demanded, obvi-ously implying that the rug was missing for a more sinister reason.

"The cat messed up and I had it cleaned," Bob shrugged.

Yvette asked what Gail took with her when she left.

"She took something to lie down on, which she does

when she's going to the park," Bob answered.

It was Yvette's turn to ask Bob what he thought happened to Gail.

"I think it's a possibility that she might have committed suicide or just run off," he said.

Yvette made a decision. She resolved to call the media the next day, because she believed Bob would not. She also intended to call the police. Someone had to tell them that this was more than just a Missing Persons investigation.

Someone had to tell them to investigate Bob.

CHAPTER 16

LAWYERED-UP

MARVIN was distraught when Bob told him about his police grilling and the fact that he had been asked to come back for further questioning the next day. Bob told his father that the police seemed to have stopped looking for Gail and seemed to be looking only for some way to pin her disappearance on him. Father and son suspected that Gail's family had decided Bob had killed her and hidden her somewhere—and the police apparently agreed.

Marvin went with his son to Police Headquarters the next day. Detective Virgillio Dalsass greeted the two doctors at 4 o'clock and asked them to be seated. Gail's parents Manny and Sylvia were already there, waiting. Virgillio began questioning Bob about his whereabouts the previous weekend in more detail. Manny just sat and listened—with accusatory eyes behind his black horn-rimmed glasses. Sylvia glared daggers at Bob and Marvin. Bob and his father no longer had any doubts as to where the police were getting their information. Bob asked what the police were doing to find Gail and he was assured that everything was being done to find her. Virgillio, who had been on "the Job" for nineteen years, then began at the same point as Tom had—Bob's story that Carlos the doorman had told him that he had seen Gail leaving the building on Sunday morning. Bob again claimed he had made a mistake and that Carlos had actually seen her at about 3 o'clock on the day before she vanished.

"Did you ask him what she was wearing?"

"No," said Bob.

Bob did not mention that Carlos had also informed him that Gail had had a man up to the apartment while he was at work. Virgillio, who casually pointed out that Bob was the last person to see Gail, told Bob that he needed all the help he could get—such as names and numbers of all of Gail's friends and associates, "anyone she might confide in, anyone she might stay with."

"I don't have her book with me," Bob claimed. "I'll get back to you later."

Bob did not want to give the cops a photocopy of Gail's address book because of a listing on the very first page: After "Alayne," the second entry read "Airport (Sky King)" and listed a New Jersey phone number, which Gail sometimes called to reach her husband. If a detective called the number, he would uncover the fact that Bob had flown that day—and then lied about it.

Virgillio, who knew that Bob had already been asked for a copy of the address book, went back further than Tom had. He asked Bob what he and Gail had done on that Friday. Bob detailed his trip to work, the car he'd borrowed from a friend, the car he'd borrowed from his dad, and his trip to the movies with Gail that night. Bob mistakenly identified *The Shooting Party* as *The Hunting Party* and Virgillio wrote it down that way. Virgillio then walked Bob through the weekend with Gail. Although this was still officially a Missing Persons case and had not been turned over to Homicide, it greatly resembled the "lock-in" phase of questioning of a murder suspect. The idea was to pin the suspect down to as many details of time and place as possible—and then hope his lies would later trip him up.

Marvin was helpful because he was able to speak up and tell the detective that Bob had arrived at the Social Security Administration offices on Saturday morning about 11:45, to pick up his Cadillac. Bob described lunch with Gail, running errands and arguing with her on the street. Dalsass asked about Gail's appointments that Saturday at the gynecologist and the hairdresser. Bob had brought some notes he had made from Gail's address book and gave the investigator the names and addresses of Gail's doctor and the hairdresser he'd found in the book—a local haircutting establishment a few blocks from her home that Gail had actually not gone to that day. Her actual hair stylist, Ouidad, was listed under "O" in the book, but without an address or identification as a hairdresser. Dalsass wrote down the information for later investigation. Bob then described dinner that night and a phone call from Francesca Beale the next morning, which he said had triggered the spat that caused Gail to storm out of the apartment.

"Was it the usual stuff that married people have—arguments over finances, things like that?" Virgillio asked in a friendly tone.

"I'd rather not discuss it," Bob said.

Bob added that Gail also had a fight with her mom the day before, on Saturday, the night he and his wife had "a romantic candlelight dinner" at home. Virgillio asked about their last dinner together and whether it meant they were making up.

"I don't want to discuss it."

Bob recounted a call from Debra after 11 on Sunday, after Gail had already left—which narrowed the time frame in which Gail had vanished. Virgillio asked if Gail took anything with her to the park.

"She probably took a towel," said Bob.

Marvin told the detective that Bob had arrived at the birthday party about 6:30 on Sunday night. Virgillio asked how long a drive it was from Manhattan to New Jersey and Bob said it was about an hour.

"So, you left your apartment on Sunday night around 5:30?" Virgillio asked.

"Yeah," Bob said.

Not only did Bob not mention that he had gone flying that day, but he shifted his alibi time ahead by exactly two hours—the amount of time he was in the air. Virgillio did not challenge Bob for the same reason that Tom had not confronted him the previous day—he had no idea that Bob had been up in an airplane on the day his wife disappeared.

Bob continued his account up until the time he reported his wife missing. Asked to describe her demeanor during their final fight, Bob replied: "Gail was more pissed than usual."

He said they had had arguments before but she had always returned within a half an hour. Marvin chimed in that Gail had been annoyed and displayed her temper at an anniversary party earlier that week. When asked what he thought had happened, Marvin replied, "Maybe she committed suicide," or ran off with another man.

Virgillio got phone numbers for Marvin at work and at home because he was now a witness as to his son's whereabouts. The detective did not ask about Gail's boyfriends or whether Bob had strangled Gail or her cat. Since Bob had not brought Gail's address book, Virgillio told Bob he would call him at home to get some numbers from him.

"Okay, but we're going out to dinner right now," Bob said, as he left.

"That's all right, I'll call you a bit later."

"Okay."

Virgillio tried Bob's number several times that night, until 12:30 the next morning—but got only the answering machine. Maybe, Virgillio thought, Bob was at his parents' place in New Jersey, so he called there. Again, all he got was an answering machine. That week, Virgillio left seven or eight messages for Bob but he never called back. During that same week, Gail's parents and sisters called him several times each. For a guy who wants to help us find his missing wife, the detective thought, Bob sure is hard to get hold of.

Marvin agreed with his son that the police did not seem to be exerting any effort to find Gail. Without any evidence, they seemed to have already decided what had happened and who had done it. He saw no reason to allow Bob's career and life to be ruined by vicious, unfounded gossip. He called a lawyer friend, who gave him the name of a Manhattan criminal attorney named Scott Greenfield.

Marvin gave the number to Bob, who made the call and set up an appointment for the next day. Scott was not a high-profile murder defender. Marvin did not believe he needed a murder lawyer because he did not believe that Bob had murdered anyone.

On Monday, Bob met his new lawyer. Three years younger than his client, Scott was getting a reputation around the Manhattan courts for successfully defending accused drug dealers. A handsome, aggressive, sharply-dressed young attorney with black hair and a mustache, Scott rose from his desk and shook Bob's hand.

Scott's first impression of the soft-spoken Bob was that he was obviously a smart guy but seemed a bit awkward, socially. The lawyer was struck by Bob's intense eyes. He looked weird. Scott wondered if Bob's odd gaze and social detachment had contributed to others' suspicions of him. It was a defense lawyer's maxim that, to be found not guilty, defendants should be good-looking and friendly—"Thou Shalt Not Be Ugly"—or, in this case, "Thou Shalt Not Have Weird Eyes." Unlike some of the defendants who had sat in the chair before Bob, Scott didn't think the guy would hurt a fly. It made a nice change to have a client who was innocent.

Scott, a heavy smoker, fired up a filtered Newport cigarette, took a deep drag, and exhaled.

Bob scowled at the smoke.

"Would you consider not smoking?" Bob asked.

"No," Scott replied, making it clear that that was the last time he expected to hear the question.

"They don't have any interest in finding her," Bob complained. "It's clear to me that they think I did something to her. They're wasting time with me."

Bob said he wanted the police to do their job and find Gail. If they did that, he felt all the suspicion and ugliness would disappear. Scott thought that that was a naïve point of view and that the Katz family's hatred might not ever go away. Scott believed it was possible that, even if they learned that Gail had committed suicide the next day, the Katz family would probably blame Bob. The cops had apparently done almost nothing in a search for Gail, believing her to be a mentally ill runaway—until her family convinced them Bob was a killer. Now they were concentrating on him, trying to fit him into the frame. To Scott, it sounded like laziness. Or maybe somebody in the Missing Persons Squad wanted to get promoted by breaking a big case. In any event, it was ridiculous—they had no body and no evidence.

"Okay, let's go through every inch of what happened during the day," Scott ordered, his cigarette in one hand, a pen in the other.

Bob recounted the previous weekend's events, as he had to the detectives, but without leaving anything out. He told his lawyer that, during his two-hour flight, he did not go anywhere of consequence but simply practiced landings and takeoffs at the Greenwood Lake Airport. He couldn't prove where he had been, because the tiny field had no tower, no controllers, and no tapes that could be checked. Bob told Scott about his decision not to tell police about his flight: he was already a suspect and the flight would look suspicious.

At that juncture, they could have made a clean breast of it to the police and told them what Bob had done that afternoon. The FAA tapes at the Caldwell Tower still existed and could have proved to cops that Bob did go flying that day and at what time. In a week, they would be erased and lost forever. If he had nothing to hide, the news would have extended Bob's alibi by several hours and shortened the time he could have done something bad to Gail, which might have been good for him.

But it would have alerted detectives that Bob had been flying and had already lied to them. It also would have focused attention on New Jersey and perhaps a very circumscribed area of the state dictated by his flight path—which might not have been so good for Bob.

Instead, Bob said nothing and did nothing for as long as possible—letting people's memories fade and keeping investigators away from the Garden State.

Bob told his lawyer that when he was talking to Carlos, after Gail had disappeared, the doorman informed him that

Gail had had men up to the apartment while he was working long shifts at the hospital. He now knew that Gail had been cheating on him but he maintained that he had not known before then, as Gail's family and the police implied. Bob said he knew that Gail had had male friends and colleagues but claimed he was the last to know she was unfaithful.

Bob turned several items he had removed from the apartment over to Scott for safekeeping, including the copy of Michael Stone's letter. He gave the lawyer two lists he had found in Gail's date book that detailed her surprise party plans and her moving out list. He also gave Scott Gail's book—with the listing for the Caldwell Airport—and her diary and a notebook. Bob held on to his flight log.

He told Scott that Gail was busy making all kinds of future plans. On the other hand, Gail had been cheating on Bob and had had a drug problem in the past—at least Bob thought it was in the past. Bob told Scott that, among Gail's things, he had found a pouch that contained a white powder that appeared to be cocaine.

"There's a lot of it," Bob said. "Maybe she was killed by drug dealers." It seemed Gail's dope stash only contained a few grams of the drug, which might have seemed like a lot to a straight arrow like Bob, but sounded to Scott like only a small amount for personal use. If Gail had brought druggies back to the apartment while Bob was in New Jersey, why would they kill her, clean up any evidence of a struggle, and take her body with them—but leave the drugs? It made no sense. Scott wondered why a woman planning to leave her husband—as her family now said—would be planning an elaborate surprise birthday party for him? That also made no sense. And it defied logic that Gail had suddenly gone off and killed herself. Her lists showed she was planning more than a surprise party—she was outlining a full life.

Perhaps somewhere on the list of names and errands, or in her address book, was the name of the person responsible for Gail vanishing. There was also another notebook that contained some of Gail's personal thoughts. In it were entries in which Gail had written uncomplimentary things about Bob—and about her family.

Scott read the letter from the psychiatrist, which made Bob sound like a dangerous guy. It seemed to him like a cover-your-butt letter designed to protect the shrink from a lawsuit. Fortunately, Scott knew the law protected confidential conversations between a doctor and a patient, so there was no way in hell the police would ever get a copy of the letter or of the psychiatrist's records. Bob described his encounter with Michael and said he walked out on the shrink after just twenty minutes—because he decided "it was a set-up" to make him the bad guy, which Gail could use to full advantage to force a divorce settlement.

Bob detailed what he said were exaggerated stories that Gail's family was telling the police—that Bob had strangled Gail and her cat. Bob said he had never strangled Gail's cat but actually had killed a cat belonging to a former fiancée—by accident. He said he had told Gail the story of the mishap with Marcy's cat in the car and she apparently had then told people that he had attacked her cat. Now all of Gail's lies were coming back to haunt him because she had disappeared.

After his initial meeting with Bob, Scott called Tom O'Malley to try and work things out. He wanted to convince Tom to focus his energy on finding Gail—and stop beating up on Bob.

"I know he's guilty," the veteran detective told the young lawyer. "Why'd he go out and get you—because he's innocent?"

Scott tried to explain that he was treating a nice Jewish doctor like a street punk by bracing him in a crude way.

"What did you think he's gonna do?" Scott asked. "He's gonna get a lawyer."

"I know your guy did it," said Tom, reiterating his gut feeling.

"You don't get it," Scott said.

Tom said he wanted to talk to Bob again and Scott made

an appointment for his client to speak to police in his office on September 12th. Scott told Tom he had no evidence of a crime and suggested he interview Carlos the doorman, and others, to nail down exactly what they did or did not see.

"Do your job," Scott ordered.

"Thank you, I'll take care of all that," Tom barked back. "I'll do my job."

CHAPTER 17

SIGHTINGS

TOM O'Malley, responding to reports from the public, was looking for Gail all over town. The afternoon after his conversation with Scott, a man called the Missing Persons Squad number and told the detective he had spotted Gail sitting in front of a brownstone on Washington Square Park at 12:30 P.M. She was sitting in a yoga position. Tom drove to the park and searched the area but did not find Gail.

A doorman at an apartment building on 52nd Street who saw Gail's picture on the MISSING poster, thought he had seen her. But when Tom showed him other pictures of Gail, he decided he hadn't seen her after all.

On Sundays, the divided families looked in the park for anyone who might have seen Gail. The Bierenbaums were hoping to find someone who saw Gail alive after she left the apartment. The Katzes hoped they would meet someone who saw Gail alive, but were also looking for someone who saw Bob do something suspicious or could disprove Bob's story.

On Sunday, July 21st, Tom placed MISSING posters in their neighborhood, outside movie theaters on East 86th Street, and interviewed another doorman, who said he did not recall seeing Gail. Calls had begun coming in from people who had read about Gail in the papers or seen her face on television or on MISSING posters around town.

According to the callers, Gail was spotted uptown on the subway, strolling downtown through Soho, and wandering around Tudor City. Numerous calls placed her in her own neighborhood and also on the streets of "Alphabet City" on the Lower East Side. One caller even claimed Gail was working as a prostitute in the Bronx. None of the sightings could be confirmed—or dismissed—by detectives.

The next day, Monday, July 22—Bob's birthday—

passed without the party that Gail had been planning, without any feast or punchbowl filled with piña colada. On his thirtieth birthday, Bob Bierenbaum, a man who had seemed to have it all, contemplated more than the ruin of his marriage. His wife was missing and police suspected him. His wife's family and virtually all of his wife's friends thought he was a killer. His life and his career seemed balanced precipitously, as if he were skiing in an avalanche zone.

That same day, at the Caldwell Airport, an FAA tower employee routinely erased the radio tapes from Sunday, July 7, destroying the only electronic record of Bob's conversations with the controllers.

That night, Bob got a second birthday present. Joel Davis saw Gail's face on a MISSING poster in an Upper East Side store, window and decided she was the sexy girl he had seen that Sunday afternoon.

"That's the one I saw at the bagel store," Joel told his girlfriend Sue.

The next day, before the sun was up, Joel called the Missing Persons Squad to report that he was certain he had seen Gail on the afternoon of her disappearance—two to three hours after Bob said she stormed out of the apartment. A detective took the information but Tom would not interview Joel in person for two months.

Bob, who had been incredibly stressed, began to relax as the weeks went by and nothing happened. Yvette Feis called virtually every day to check for news. Bob told her about his final argument with Gail.

"My psychiatrist told me to defuse argument situations, but this time I didn't defuse it," Bob told her. "It became explosive."

Yvette's stomach fell with fear.

"Bob, are you sure you want to be telling me this?"

Sylvia Katz knew about Michael Stone's 1983 warning letter but the police could not do anything about it because of doctor–patient confidentiality. Tom O'Malley told the family that, although he could not obtain a copy of the letter, they might. On Friday, July 26, Sylvia called Michael and began to explain about Gail's disappearance—but he already knew.

"You sent a letter to her at one time—we can't find it," Sylvia told Michael, her words pouring forth in a nervous torrent. "It's a piece of evidence. It's supposed to be in the strongbox but it's disappeared. This is the letter that Gail is said to have waved in front of Bob during their last argument, saying, 'I can destroy your career,' or words to that effect," said Sylvia.

"Could you please mail it to the police department?" Sylvia asked. Michael asked a few questions as she spoke.

"We're afraid he's killed her," Sylvia said. "It seems unbelievable. We knew him for three years. I never saw him over-excited, or anything. Gail said in early July she was going to leave him."

Sylvia gave Michael Detective Virgillio Dulauss' name and phone number and asked him to call.

"Gail did tell me he tried to strangle her two years ago," Sylvia said. "They had arguments all that last weekend. Sunday morning she supposedly went to the park—only no one saw her leave the building," Sylvia said.

"There's no hard evidence of what happened because no one saw anything. No one can even speak to Bob, because he's surrounded by lawyers," she told Michael. "The people at Missing Persons shook him up a lot because they emphasized he was the last person to see her alive, therefore, they were going to question him a lot. They didn't go so far as to tell him straight out he was a suspect."

Sylvia also gave Michael Tom O'Malley's name and phone number.

"Please do what you can for us," she pleaded.

Michael did not mail a copy of the letter to the police, as Sylvia requested, but he did send a copy to Sylvia, knowing she would show it to the police. When Michael spoke with the detectives after they saw the letter, they wanted to see his notes of his consultation sessions with Bob. Obviously, the detectives believed that Bob might have told the doctor some incriminating things in order for him to write a letter warning the guy's wife. The letter and those records might be enough to charge Bob with murder.

But Michael, obliged to protect his patient, retained a lawyer, who informed the investigators that he could not cooperate unless a judge issued a court order directing that Michael turn over his records. The police then subpoenaed the records and the issue went before a judge in Manhattan. Bob and his lawyer were not involved in the court case and were not informed about it.

The judge reviewed the matter and within days ruled against the authorities, saying that Gail was simply missing and that no evidence of her death had been presented. The jurist refused to violate the principle of doctor–patient confidentiality in a case where the missing person—gone less than a month—might return at any time.

It was very frustrating for the Katz family and the police. Michael sympathized with Gail's family and agreed with them that Bob was the prime suspect but he could not turn over his records without a court order. He wanted to help bring a killer to justice but his hands were tied. If he turned over the records, Bob could sue him and take everything he owned.

Bob, unaware that he had dodged a legal bullet, returned to work and resumed his routine. Many aspects of his life had returned to normal, out of necessity. He bought takeout food and groceries and rented movies.

He and his in-laws were not speaking to each other. It was impossible to continue a cordial relationship with someone who had called you a murderer or someone you believed to be a murderer. Scott hired a private investigator on Bob's behalf, who also began searching for Gail. If the private eye could find her, it would hopefully end the horrific situation, the Bierenbaums agreed.

On one Sunday in the park, the warring Katz and Bierenbaum camps caught sight of each other, while canvassing for witnesses. Sylvia, Manny and Alayne, along with Tom

O'Malley, spotted Bob and his parents. They all glared at each other and went about their separate business.

"We're putting posters up and they're taking them down," joked Tom.

CHAPTER 18

HAMPTONS FLIGHT

BOB called Dolores Erickson, the blond, beautiful owner of the house in the Hamptons in which he and Gail had a half-share. He told her about Gail and asked if it would be all right if he came out the next weekend alone. Shocked by the news, she expressed her concern and told him it would be fine. He also asked to spend the entire month of August at the house, for which he would pay extra.

When Bob arrived that hot summer weekend, Dolores and her husband—who ran a Manhattan ad agency—along with Susan D'Andrea and her husband, were relaxing on the porch. Bob again explained the situation to his housemates and answered their questions.

Bob said he had gone to look for Gail in the park after she went missing two weeks earlier—with only six dollars in the pocket of her shorts. A bit embarrassed, he said he'd discovered that Gail had a drug problem when he went through her drawers and found a bag containing cocaine. It appeared, he said, that she went off to meet some dope dealer and hadn't been seen since. They awkwardly expressed their sympathy and offered their help. That night, in an effort to cheer Bob up, they took him along to a comedy club, where Bob laughed uproariously at the comics. No one mentioned Gail that night. In contrast to the cheap weekends he had spent there with Gail in casual clothes, bicycling and eating in, Bob began dressing up and going out to dinner like a single guy.

On another weekend, Bob bought a case of wine and brought it back to the house. He went out on a date with Dolores' sister to a disco, where she and Bob had a great time dancing. They stayed up chatting and laughing in the living room past three in the morning.

Bob returned to the city during the week. At the hospital,

he spoke to Karen Caruana, the blond, blue-eyed nurse with a cute pixie hairdo, and took her up on her kind offer of help. He told Karen that the police had "searched my apartment" after Gail vanished, which was not true. "I'm clean, as far as any criminal investigation is concerned," Bob told her. "They came up with nothing."

When Bob found out from a mutual friend that Karen was going to be in the Hamptons that weekend, he invited her out to dinner, after assuring her that he was not dangerous. Karen, who had only known Bob for a few months, accepted and they met that Saturday. Karen drove to Bob's place and they chatted before going out to eat at a nice restaurant. After a pleasant dinner, Karen went back with Bob to his summer house. They went up to his room and began to kiss. Very quickly, they were in bed and naked. They made love—the first sex Bob had had in more than a year—and fell asleep in each other's arms. The next morning, they had breakfast and Karen went back to her friends' house.

Over the next month, Bob made advance plans for an important upcoming date. On Wednesday, August 7—exactly one month after he had gone flying from Caldwell—Bob drove to the nearby Easthampton Airport and rented a Cessna 172 for just one hour. It was the first time Bob had ever rented an aircraft from that airport. When he returned the plane, Bob took out his black pilot logbook and flipped the pages. The pages for 1982 and 1983 were dense with flight log entries, without spaces between them. But on the 1985 page there was only one complete entry and, several blank spaces down, a date. On the first line, Bob had logged a solo January 6 flight from Caldwell. Below that notation were two blank lines. On the fourth line was the date Bob had written in the box on the far left in blue ink on the morning Gail vanished, "7/7"

In the "Point of Departure" box on the same line, Bob had printed, in his bad handwriting, "CDW" for Caldwell Airport—which looked like "CDN" or "CPN." In black ink, Bob wrote over the 7/7 date, changing the first 7 to an

8 in the different color ink. But, because Bob always crossed his sevens to avoid confusion with nines, it was obvious the date had been changed. Bob then wrote "East Hampton" over CDW, obscuring it. He then filled out the rest of the boxes, noting that he rented a C-172 aircraft, registration number 68082 for one hour from the East Hampton Airport. In the "Remarks" column, Bob wrote "flight check." He recorded three takeoffs and three landings, which indicated he was practicing touch-and-gos—in which he took off, circled back, landed and then took off again.

Bob's personal log book now reflected that he flew on 8/7 instead of 7/7. A routine flight in a book of routine flights.

As the summer was ending, Dolores was walking by Bob's room when she noticed him through the open door. He was taking Gail's clothes out of the drawers—where they had lain neatly all summer—and packing them into a bag to take back into the city.

Bob was crying and Dolores noticed the tears in his red eyes.

"It must be hard for you," she said, quietly, suddenly sorry for the doctor who had lost his wife.

"Yes, it is," Bob agreed. "It was a hard summer."

CHAPTER 19

SMOOTH OPERATOR

Bob, dressed in blue "surgical scrubs," latex gloves and a blue mask over his mouth, stepped up to the green-sheeted table to begin the surgery. In the operating room, the surgeon was God. The doctor literally had the patient's life in his hands. He was the unquestioned boss; he oversaw all things. A large light illuminated the area to be opened on the patient's body. Rows of sterilized surgical instruments were arranged on adjacent tables by operating room nurses, who stood at the ready. Other OR workers attended to other equipment or tasks at the same time. An electronic monitor slowly beeped and displayed the patient's cardiogram blips, his blood pressure and a pulse-oximeter readout—the heartbeats per minute and the percentage of oxygen saturation in his blood. Everything looked routine and normal. A pop music song played softly in the background. The patient on the table had been sedated by another doctor, an anesthesiology resident named Roberta Karnofsky, at Bob's side. A very pretty young doctor with a halo of curly auburn hair, Roberta constantly monitored the patient's level of sedation and vital signs. Bob, who was one of Roberta's bosses, arranged for her to attend the same operations, and be on the same side of the table as him, quite often. Bob, who had a reputation as a surgeon with "good hands," started an incision and began the operation. The nurses and other staff noticed nothing out of the ordinary. Once the chest was opened, retractor clamps were used to hold it open, the vital organs glistening in the light, the heart pulsating in the center of the chest.

But, under the table, Bob was slowly, sensuously, rubbing his leg against Roberta's. Neither doctor let on to their colleagues that they were playing footsie under the table like a couple of teenagers, their loose, thin pants creating a pleasant friction on the naked skin of their thighs beneath the scrubs. To non-doctors, it might have seemed weird that a surgeon would try to woo a woman with his leg while his bloody hands were inside someone's body but, for Bob, it was just another day at the office.

That night, Bob returned to his empty apartment and noticed that the message light on his answering machine was blinking. He sighed, pushed the PLAY button and heard the familiar voice of Sylvia Katz shrieking a single word into the phone: "MURDERER!"

It was not the first time Sylvia had left such a message for him. Bob usually kept the answering machine on all the time, to avoid the calls. Sometimes, she just screamed a single word. In other calls, she tried to frighten Bob by claiming that the cops had discovered evidence of a murder and he was about to be arrested: "We know that you burned Gail in the furnace in the building," Sylvia said in one message. "The police know all about you."

It wasn't true. The police searched the building, including the furnace, but had not found any evidence of Gail or of a crime. Sylvia hoped her calls would keep up the pressure on Bob. She hoped it would drive him over the edge, that it would make him crack and confess. Bob neither cracked nor confessed to anything and seemed more confident and secure every day. But, with each call, Sylvia herself seemed to get closer to the edge.

"You're a doctor—how could you do this?" Sylvia moaned in one message. "You're supposed to save people."

Her voice was tormented and, like Gail, Sylvia was also lost. She thought of almost nothing else and would stop herself in a rare happy moment, as if she could never be happy as long as she did not know where her daughter was. The mother blamed herself and engaged in constant, guilty second-guessing of the past.

"I could have done more," Sylvia told her family. "I could have given her money to have her leave him and come live with us, or get an apartment."

Sylvia and Alayne were obsessed with locating evidence

against Bob. Alayne had postponed her life to seek closure for her family and justice for her sister. She put off taking her bar exams to help the police make a case against Bob. Her boyfriend also took a year off from the Harvard Business School to help her. Often, she went out with Tom O'Malley, following leads. In a sense, she had picked up where Gail had left off and she vowed to destroy Bob, even if it took forever.

Frustrated that the police were unable to act, the Katz family decided to follow the Bierenbaum family's lead and hire their own investigator. But he was unable to locate Gail or determine what had happened to her after she spoke to Francesca that Sunday morning.

Next, the desperate family contacted a psychic, who came up with even less.

Gail had taken a powder. She had completely vanished— as if a magician had made her disappear in a puff of smoke.

Bob told Roberta about his wife's strange disappearance and suggested that her mental condition was probably trance-like. "It's possible that she was in some kind of fugue state," wandering around, unaware of her own identity, said Bob.

On September 2, Tom called Joel Davis, who said he thought he had seen Gail in H & H Bagels. Joel correctly described Gail's clothing and said he recognized her from a MISSING poster in the neighborhood. Tom asked him if he could look at some other pictures of Gail but he said he would not be available for a while. Joel said Gail was wearing pink shorts and a white T-shirt with the word "APAR-ADOS" printed on the back. He also described her dark tan and her brown sandals.

On Thursday, September 12, Tom, along with Virgillio and another detective from the 19th Precinct, arrived in Scott Greenfield's third-floor office at 401 Broadway to talk to Bob. The doctor had been Tom's complaintant but now he was a suspect who wouldn't talk to him without his lawyer. By that measure, he had overplayed his hand by forcing Bob to protect himself. The investigators first asked about what Gail was wearing when she vanished and her distinguishing marks. Bob detailed Gail's scars on her arms from her past suicide attempt. They asked her blood type and he thought it might be type O-positive. They asked for any other medical details that might help identify her. Bob said Gail had had two abortions before their marriage.

Tom mentioned Anthony and Ken and said they were Gail's boyfriends. The detectives asked if Bob would agree to a polygraph exam. Scott, who thought polygraph tests were garbage, said no—twice.

So-called lie detector tests were not admissible in court and could be very unreliable and misleading. They did not measure lies—they measured nervousness. A nervous subject could come off looking guilty as hell and a cool psychopath—disconnected from his emotions—might beat it. A great deal also depended on the crafting of questions and the expertise of the operator.

Tom asked if Gail had ever been fingerprinted. He needed fingerprints for comparison if a body was found. Bob said he believed that had never been done.

"Her fingerprints are going to be all over the apartment," said Scott. "Can you do that?"

"Yeah," said Tom.

"Let's go," said Scott.

"We've got to make arrangements," said Tom, who agreed to get back to Scott when he was ready to search for Gail's prints.

Scott was a bit surprised. He assumed the detective would have been eager to get inside Bob's apartment. Scott did not know that Gail's brother had already conducted an unofficial search. Tom had no warrant and the search was to be conducted under the watchful eye of Bob's lawyer—but at least it was a search. They would be testing surfaces for traces of blood or looking for evidence of dismemberment in the plumbing. A week later, Scott agreed to let Bob stop by the Missing Persons Squad alone to provide a copy of Gail's address book and explain the names in it—to help the detectives search for Gail. Bob also gave Tom a detailed description of Gail's rings, her credit cards, and savings and checking accounts—which would be checked to see if they had been used after she disappeared. Bob said he thought Gail had a safety deposit box but did not know where. Some of the names in the address book Bob said he did not know.

"Ever know of a guy named Anthony?" Tom asked, pointing to an entry for Gail's boyfriend.

"Yes," said Bob.

"Was Anthony ever over to your apartment?"

"I don't think so," Bob said.

Virgillio and Tom began calling numbers in the book. Most of the interviews backed up what Gail's family was telling them, but no one had any direct knowledge of what had happened on July 7. Gail's psychiatrist, Dr. Elsa Fairchild, refused to tell them anything without a court order.

Bob and his lawyer braced for the reaction of the police when they found and called the second "Airport" number in the book and found out about his flight—but there was no reaction. Apparently no one bothered to dial the number, so the detectives did not learn about Bob's plane rental.

Within weeks of Gail's disappearance, Bob's operating room footsie with Roberta was followed by dating. The dating featured excursions in the air: taking women flying seemed to be a kind of expensive foreplay for Bob. He soon asked Roberta, whom he called Robbie, to live with him and she moved in that September, two months after Gail was last seen.

At the same time, unbeknownst to Roberta, Bob continued his part-time relationship with Karen Caruana for about six months, and had sex with the cute nurse several times, before they broke up after an argument at a Greenwich Village restaurant. Karen said something that challenged Bob—who verbally attacked her. Hurt by Bob's comments, she left the restaurant in tears.

From the start it was a strange situation for Roberta. She liked Bob but all of his missing wife's belongings still filled the apartment, as if she might return at any moment. It was a bit eerie, almost like a gothic novel where the husband was obsessed with the seductive, yet evil, dead wife—but Bob never seemed to do anything about trying to find her. Gail's coats, skirts, dresses, pants, blouses and underwear filled the closets and dresser drawers. Her toiletries, lipsticks, perfume and makeup were still in evidence in the bathroom and bedroom. Her books and schoolwork, photos and other possessions filled other closet areas, along with her skis and her bicycle. Her cooking equipment was everywhere in the kitchen and her smiling face beamed from photos on the walls, and especially from a large picture on a living room shelf of Gail in her wedding dress with Bob. Aside from the practical matter that there was nowhere to put her things, it was strange for Roberta to begin a new relationship with a man with so much baggage—literally. Obviously he had not put Gail behind him. There was no closure and he was still carrying a torch for his missing wife. Roberta gently suggested that perhaps it was time to move on, but Bob did nothing and she lived out of her suitcase for a while. Soon, she complained that she couldn't move in unless Gail moved out. Bob cleared out just two dresser drawers in the bedroom but that was it—as if Roberta were just there for the weekend. He never moved another thing out of the apartment until Gail's family demanded it.

Gail's friend Marianne DeCesare called Bob and asked him if there was any news. Bob said he had hired a private detective, who had turned up traces of Gail in California. "I think Gail is waitressing by a seaside community," Bob claimed.

Tom O'Malley finally interviewed Joel Davis on September 24th. Joel repeated the same information he had given Tom over the phone, but added that the woman he saw that day—who reminded him of his former wife—had been carrying a beach chair and a bag. The pretty girl was standing on line in the bagel shop and was next to another woman—who may have been her companion, Joel said.

Just as he had with other potential witnesses, Tom showed Joel several other photos of Gail. Joel looked at the snapshots and picked one out as being the woman he'd seen.

In October, Alayne left a message on Bob's answering machine that she wanted to come to what was now Bob's apartment to pick up Gail's things. Bob told Roberta that Gail's sister was coming and asked her to stay away until Alayne was gone.

Alayne's fury at Bob erupted into raw rage when she stepped inside the apartment and saw what Bob had done with Gail's belongings—he had dumped them into black plastic garbage bags, which were lined up, ready for her. Alayne looked in one open bag and saw broken perfume bottles and Gail's underwear mixed together, as if everything had been thrown there like garbage.

"I'm taking out the trash for him," Alayne thought.

A quick check of the bags showed that a lot of Gail's property was not there. Alayne demanded to know why Gail's 10-speed bicycle, her skis and her food processor blender were not included. Bob explained that he was keeping the expensive items. It drove Alayne over the edge to think that Bob's new girlfriend was riding Gail's bike, using her skis or making dinner with her food processor, but Bob would not give them to her. Alayne insisted that she wanted to take Gail's crystal platter, given to Gail by her Aunt Bea on the occasion of her engagement, but Bob said no. To anyone watching the tense scene, it might have seemed like a woman who simply wanted her missing sister's goods for herself or a husband who wanted to keep what he had paid for—but the clash went far beyond the objects.

"You killed my sister!" Alayne screamed. "You cannot keep her things!"

"I didn't kill her," Bob replied, coolly. "She was a tramp and is probably off living with another guy. You can't have it."

After her encounter with Bob, Alayne began writing letters to newspapers and television stations, demanding to know why they had dropped the story. She called Bob a killer but she got no response from the media, who were unlikely to call a doctor a killer without proof.

On Tuesday, October 29, Scott Greenfield met the detectives at Bob's apartment, and again Bob asked Roberta to make herself scarce. The cops were accompanied by Crime Scene detectives, who began searching for surfaces where Gail might have left her fingerprints.

Scott informed Virgillio that this would not be a forensic search after all—they could only search for Gail's prints. Period. Virgillio and the others were angry but not surprised. The investigators wanted to tear the place apart but all they could do was gather prints and look around—under the watchful eye of their prime suspect, his lawyer and his private eye.

In the kitchen, they found several glossy cookbooks that the detectives dusted with black fingerprint powder. They found several prints believed to be Gail's and "lifted" the latent prints with tape and transferred them to fingerprint cards. They found another good print on a makeup jar on Gail's dresser in the bedroom.

It was good to have prints to identify a body—if one was ever found—but the purpose of the visit had been to do a Luminol search for the presence of blood on various surfaces. Luminol is a chemical that made old, sometimes invisible, bloodstains glow under ultraviolet light. The investigators also intended to rip open the plumbing traps and search there for evidence of dismemberment. Without a warrant for a forensic search to determine if a murder or a struggle had taken place, the case was going nowhere, they knew.

The lawyer told the detectives they could not even look in the bathroom—the most likely place that someone would cut up a body. Virgillio did not want to leave without at least eyeballing it. At one point, he claimed he had to use the bathroom and went in and closed the door. Inside, he began to scan the surfaces and crannies, looking for old, caked blood with the naked eye—not a very reliable tool.

But his search was quickly interrupted by the private detective, who came into the bathroom. Virgillio didn't see anything suspicious but, of course, he would have noticed only the most obvious of traces—which were unlikely to survive for more than two months.

Meanwhile, the Crime Scene detectives used their brushes and black powder to dust for prints in several places, including the nightstand on Gail's side of the bed. When they found what looked like a good latent, they lifted it with tape and transferred it to a print card. The print powder made black soot-like spots wherever they brushed and Bob was clearly unhappy with the mess.

"Does this stuff clean off?" Bob asked.

"Yeah, yeah, we'll clean it up," one of the disgusted detectives replied.

One Saturday night that month, Bob, clad in his usual casual uniform of plaid cotton shirt, blue jeans and sneakers, took a break to visit his friends Amanda and Nick in New Jersey. When Bob walked into her kitchen, Amanda thought he looked like absolute hell. The pockets of his rumpled shirt and pants were bulging with personal papers, documents and receipts, as well as an old bulging wallet. There were dark circles under his eyes and he had lost at least twenty pounds. He looked like a broken man—but not a guilty one—to Amanda. Bob complained to the couple, and a few other friends, how unfair it was that Gail's family and others believed he was involved in Gail's disappearance. Bob said Gail had gone jogging to Central Park—where a stranger or possibly someone she knew did something to her. Bob did not talk about Gail's boyfriends. Amanda knew he was embarrassed by Gail's infidelity and deeply mortified that everyone knew about it. Bob expressed what seemed like genuine disbelief that anyone would consider him a suspect. He had learned that in his situation—just like in a divorce—everyone took sides. Nick made supportive noises but Amanda had discussed it with her husband and she knew he wasn't being totally honest. It was very awkward—as if there were an elephant in the room and everyone was supposed to pretend it wasn't there.

Not Amanda.

"Bob," said Amanda gently, "you have to acknowledge the fact that everybody is going to ask themselves the question, 'Did he kill Gail?' That's going to go through everybody's brain. You have to allow them to be human and think those thoughts. You're a suspect."

"But I didn't do it!" Bob protested.

"Everybody's going to wonder because there's no body. You would do the same thing," said Amanda.

Bob sighed. "You don't think I killed Gail?" he asked, in a pleading, hurt voice. "You don't think I could do that?"

No one else in the room said a word. Amanda took a deep breath and looked Bob directly in the face.

"Bob, I want to believe you but I have to ask that question. . . ." she said. "I liked you before all this happened. . . . I can't unequivocally say I'm certain you didn't do it. Did you kill Gail?"

Bob shook his head sadly. He was blown away that his friend could even consider that he was a killer. His family totally believed in his innocence—just as strongly as the Katz family believed in his guilt.

"How could you think that of me?" Bob asked. "How could people who know me think that of me?"

"If you did this, then you have to live with that," Amanda replied. "Looking into your eyes . . . I don't think you did. . . . If you did—I won't judge you."

CHAPTER 20

GAIL?

ROBERTA, under Bob's expert and patient instruction, held the controls of the airplane after their takeoff from Caldwell Airport. It was a beautiful Saturday morning, March 15, 1986—the Ides of March. Bob was giving Roberta her first flying lesson. The white Cessna 172 with a red stripe and the trademark Skyhawk on the tail was familiar to Bob. It was the same aircraft he had rented on the day Gail vanished.

Now, Roberta was sitting in the passenger seat, feeling the heft of the aircraft, having fun in the sky with Bob. They spent nine hours flying that day and Roberta got an introduction to what a pilot does, including keeping a flight log.

Exactly one week earlier, March 8th, on what would have been Gail's thirtieth birthday, Sylvia had called Bob and left a message on his answering machine. The anguished mother called Bob a killer and several other things, before she hung up and shared the pain of the day with her family. Nothing seemed to be happening with the DA's investigation so Alayne decided to renew her campaign against Bob. She would soon be ready to launch it.

Roberta happened to get home before Bob. She played back the messages and was shocked when she heard the mother shrieking that Bob had murdered her daughter. When Bob got home, Roberta told him about the call and he asked her not to play back the answering machine anymore. He explained again about Gail and her suicidal tendencies and her drug problem and how her family unfairly blamed him. Bob told her that the police had even looked in the building's basement incinerator. "They wanted to see if I threw her body down the incinerator but they didn't find any-thing," Bob said.

He also lied and said that detectives had grilled him about whether he had had his rug cleaned after Gail van-ished and he told them he had not. But Roberta, who had occasionally seen Bob's nasty temper flare, wondered if Bob was telling her the whole story.

Meanwhile, Alayne launched phase two of her campaign to nail Bob for Gail's murder. On April Fool's Day, 1986, she began sending hundreds of form letters, with individ-ualized greetings, and copies of Gail's picture, to every doctor who worked with Bob and everyone who lived in his building. Some of the more than 500 were sent by mail and others were delivered by hand. Alayne also went door-to-door, trying to find someone with that one piece of in-formation that might break the case.

"Bob initially gave only sketchy details about events of that weekend and has since cut off all ties with us. I fear that without his help, we will never find my sister or learn what happened to her on that tragic day," Alayne wrote. "As you can imagine, this is very hard on my family. I fear that the 'not knowing' will drive us crazy.

"I am writing to you because you may have heard or seen something unusual during that week or since . . . per-haps you have been reticent in contacting the police. No matter how small or seemingly insignificant the detail, my family would want to know it," she said. "I have lost my sister . . . and simply don't know where to turn."

Alayne included her address and phone number, as well as Tom O'Malley's number at the Missing Persons Squad.

Bob's neighbors and colleagues began to talk about him behind his back. Several told him about Alayne's letter campaign and showed Bob copies. The letter didn't actually call him a killer but it was obvious what Alayne's opinion was. Outraged, Bob called his lawyer and told him he wanted to sue Alayne for defamation of character. It was, he said, not good for a doctor's reputation. Worse than a charge of incompetence, was a charge—however veiled—that a physician was a killer.

"What do I do with this?" Bob demanded. "What do I do with this?"

Scott knew the letters would damage Bob and his career but he counseled prudence and patience. Yes, he told his client, he could sue. But it would probably go nowhere and Alayne would have a victory—publicity. Anything he did might also make Manny and Sylvia's pain worse. Ignore it, Scott recommended. There was no *Miss Manners* advice on how to act if your wife disappears and her family blames you.

"Bear in mind what they're going through," Scott said. "Try to move forward with your own life and hope she turns up."

Bob was also agitated that investigators were pestering his parents and going to his sister's office, announcing that they were investigating Gail's disappearance. Bob thought it was harassment. One of the investigators even contacted Roberta and warned her that she might be in danger because, her office believed, Bob had killed his wife.

Bob was not able to simply resume his life for many reasons. After Gail's disappearance, he began having trouble dealing with the occasional deaths of his patients. He had never liked it before, but it began to trouble him more and more, until he decided not to continue open heart surgery. He decided to take a residency in plastic surgery, where the mortality rate was much lower. Bob also liked the idea of doing some free work for disadvantaged patients. He felt an urge to help people, to do good and to improve their lives. He applied to Harlem Hospital.

Alayne got a flood of calls and letters. People offered sympathy and help but not a single one had seen or heard anything useful. It was an incredibly frustrating experience. In a sense, even though she had put her law career on hold, Gail's disappearance was Alayne's first—and most important—case. She would not give up. She would continue pressing authorities and the media to work on the case for two years, despite the fact that authorities told her they had no case and the media said they had no facts. Unfortunately, even the television shows that dealt in unsolved mysteries did not call her back.

No one cared.

Bob's neighbors looked at him oddly. Alayne's letters and calls made them all aware of Gail's mysterious disappearance and the Katz family's opinion of Bob. Some neighbors thought Bob had a lot of nerve to continue living there as if nothing had happened, and Bob was ostracized in the building. But at least one neighbor realized that that was exactly what Bob would do if he were innocent. To her, it showed strength of character.

Among Gail's things, in one of the garbage bags she got from Bob, Alayne found an inexpensive automatic camera that had belonged to Gail. She noticed that there was an unfinished roll of film still in the camera. Alayne finished the roll and took it to a photo store. When the film was developed, she received prints of Gail and Bob on a Caribbean vacation the previous winter. There were several shots of Bob and Gail in skimpy swimsuits, along with another couple, amid lush flowers. There was one odd picture, apparently taken by Bob. It was of Gail—who was not smiling at her husband. Gail was entering an endless turquoise sea, her head looking over her shoulder at the camera. The Katz family cried over the photographs—the last pictures taken of Gail.

At 2 A.M. on the morning of Wednesday, July 2, 1986, five days before the first anniversary of Gail's disappearance, Bob's phone rang in the dark. Bob and Roberta, who both worked long hard hours, were sound asleep, but he picked it up and answered in a sleepy voice. Roberta could only hear one side of the conversation, but it was obviously not the hospital.

The caller was an NYPD Missing Persons Squad detective, who asked if he was speaking to Dr. Robert Bierenbaum.

"Yes."

Detective Gerald Williams introduced himself and told Bob he had just gotten a call from the Port Authority Police at the World Trade Center.

"They are holding a woman believed to be your wife, Gail Katz Bierenbaum," and they needed Bob to go and identify or eliminate the woman as his wife, said Williams. The Port Authority cops said the woman looked like the picture on the MISSING poster.

"Do I need to come down right now?" Bob asked, turning on the light.

Williams thought Bob sounded annoyed at being awakened and strangely reluctant to come out in the middle of the night to see if his missing wife had been found. Perhaps he was not yet awake.

"Yes," said Williams, who said Bob should go down immediately.

Bob asked for Williams' phone number and jotted it on a bedside pad. He said he would call back in a few minutes. It sounded to the investigator like Bob didn't think the news was very important and could wait until morning.

When he hung up the phone, Bob was sleepy and seemed unmoved by the startling news. But Roberta was suddenly quite awake and very upset when Bob told her that police thought they had found his missing wife.

"If you're going down and that may be Gail, you might be coming home with Gail," Roberta reasoned, sitting up in bed. "What should I do? Do you want me to pack up and get out?"

"Don't worry about it," Bob reassured her. "I doubt it's Gail."

He told her to go back to sleep but Roberta was too nervous. Bob got dressed and called back the detective, and told him he would go down and identify the woman. Bob then left an uneasy Roberta inside the apartment. She wondered why Bob seemed so unconcerned. How could he be so sure it wasn't Gail?

Bob returned home at 3:40 and dialed Williams' number.

"It's not her," Bob told Williams. "Thank you."

Bob went right back to sleep but Roberta was still troubled.

When one of Roberta's girlfriends, also a doctor, later stayed at the apartment, Roberta told her about Gail and the calls from Sylvia one day while Bob was working at the hospital. She also mentioned the warning from the DA's office and that Bob did not seem to believe that Gail had been found on the night the police called. They began to speculate, almost as a joke, how Bob might have killed Gail. They hit on the idea that he might have dumped her out of an airplane. Roberta did not know that she had already been up in the same plane that Bob had flown that day.

"Does he keep a flight log?" the friend asked.

"Yes, he does," Roberta replied.

"Where does he keep it?"

"In the office."

"Well, let's go look at it," she suggested.

The two women entered Bob's office and went to his desk. On the floor next to the desk was a large stack of unused MISSING posters that featured Gail's face and the date she disappeared, July 7, 1985.

Roberta opened Bob's desk and took out the black book with "PILOT LOGBOOK and Flight Proficiency Record" written in gold letters. She opened it to the 1985 page and immediately saw a flight dated 8/7. But the women, both doctors and trained observers, noticed that the date had been written in two different color inks—it looked like the 8 had originally been a 7. If that was the case, then apparently Bob had changed a flight taken on 7/7/85 to 8/7/85. It looked like Bob was trying to hide the fact that he had flown that day. They noticed that Bob always crossed his sevens, so they could not be confused with nines. Even though it had been written over and changed into an 8, you could still see the cross on the original 7 if you looked closely. There were other strikeouts elsewhere in the book. Perhaps it was just a mistake. Also, if Bob was such a

genius, why did he use two different-colored inks? Any
idiot could see the date had been altered. Or was that Bob
being smart? If anyone ever noticed the change he could
say that if he'd had anything to hide, he would have done
a better job and used the same color ink. The women carefully put the log away in Bob's desk and discussed what it
might mean. Then they traded theories of how Bob could
have killed his wife. It was frightening to think that Bob
might have done away with Gail in the apartment but it
was also fun because it wasn't real. Roberta did not fear
him and never mentioned her discovery. But, one night after they'd had a fight, her murder hypothesis slipped out.
It was over dinner in a restaurant. After a few drinks, Roberta became angry with Bob and wanted to hurt him,
wanted to get a rise out of him. She wanted to see his
reaction to her idea. Roberta brought up the subject, out of
the blue, of Gail.

"Well, I have a theory, as to, if you had done something
to her, how you may have done it," Roberta told Bob in a
defiant tone.

Bob shot an embarrassed look around at the other diners,
to see if they were listening.

"Well, I think that if you did this, as some people seem
to think you did, and if it really happened, perhaps something happened in the apartment and Gail was hurt," Roberta said, deliberately using the word "hurt," rather than
"murdered."

Bob just stared blankly at Roberta, who plunged on, staring him right in the eye.

"You could have put Gail in one of those big flight bags,
as she was so small, and put her in the back of your car
and driven her out to the airport and put her on the plane
and then thrown her out of the plane," Roberta concluded.

She waited for his reaction but he gave her none. Bob
dropped his eyes to his plate and stared at his unfinished
entrée for a time. He said nothing.

Roberta was disappointed. Maybe Bob did not react to
the provocation because he wanted to deny her the satis-

faction. She had hoped her little theory would really yank Bob's chain. She thought perhaps he would become hurt that she thought he might be a killer. Or maybe he would freak out and become violent because she had figured out how he had done it. But all he did was stare at his plate. Of course, he didn't deny it, she realized with a chill. Why didn't Bob deny it?

CHAPTER 21

OPEN & SHUT

TOM O'MALLEY was convinced that Bob was the magician who had made Gail disappear. With nothing but weak circumstantial evidence—he didn't even have proof that she was dead, much less murdered—his gut instinct told him that Dr. Robert Bierenbaum was somehow responsible. Judges did not sign search warrants based on instinct and the District Attorney's office did not prosecute crimes without evidence. The case remained officially open.

The investigation had "homicide" written all over it, but detective supervisors refused to turn it over to the Homicide Squad—because there was no body. It wasn't classified as a possible murder because it looked like it might never be solved. Police brass did not want to saddle the department with another unsolved murder case, one of too many unsolved killings. If it stayed where it was, it was only an unsolved Missing Persons case and the department's murder-solving statistics would not suffer—not to mention the mayor's chances for reelection. Tom thought the political decision stank but he was just a detective who had to follow orders. He wanted to see it go before a grand jury. In confidence, he told the Katz family why NYPD would do nothing further until a body was found. Sylvia took the news particularly hard. The idea that the police believed he was guilty but that their hands were tied by law was a bitter pill to swallow. At that point the family decided to take action of their own.

Gail's cousin Hillard Wiese contacted his friend Robert Pitler of the Manhattan DA's office and made an appeal for a more thorough investigation. Hillard told Pitler that his family believed that Bob had killed Gail and that an investigation by his office was the only route to justice. Because of the double jeopardy rule, the DA was always reluctant to go to court without a case. If a jury found a defendant not guilty, he could never again be tried for that crime— even if authorities later discovered irrefutable evidence. Any DA that brought a murder to trial without enough proof was taking the risk that a jury would award a killer with what amounted to a pardon. One judge had already refused to order a psychiatrist to turn his records over to police because Gail might still be alive. Manhattan DA Robert Morgenthau had no intention of handing a get-out-of-jail-free card to a killer. He would not mount a weak prosecution against Bob Bierenbaum. But "Morgy" had another option. Although NYPD already had a Cold Case Squad, Morgy had what amounted to his own run by Chief Investigator Lieutenant Andy Rosenzweig, a former NYPD detective.

Andy Rosenzweig, born in 1944, grew up in the Bronx and worked on the mean streets there as a cop in the infamous 41st Precinct—better known as "Fort Apache"—in the 1960s. In his career, Andy threw a lot of crooks up against walls—the most prominent of whom was Godfather John Gotti, who was made to kiss the bricks of a building in Manhattan's Little Italy. In 1970, Andy and his partner became hero cops—as one of the first plainclothes "anticrime" teams. He later worked his way up to sergeant, and then lieutenant in 1980. A lover of mystery novels, he took nothing for granted, but he had the ability to read a case file and find what was not there, the gaps in the investigation. He had an eye for uncovering where previous detectives might have messed up or what they had left undone. At least one observer who heard his calm, measured voice was reminded of Humphrey Bogart, and, after he retired from the NYPD in 1981, Andy actually became a private eye. But eventually, he decided he wanted to return to a job where he could try to crack more important cases.

A few months after Gail vanished, he was hired as Morgy's chief investigator. His boss, Robert Pitler, who had spoken to Gail's cousin, called Andy into his office in

August 1986, told him about the Bierenbaum case, and asked Andy to take a look at it.

Andy's first step was to read the file carefully. The case looked like a murder but it remained a Missing Persons case. Why? Although it was scientifically possible that the victim had jumped in the river and was never found, it seemed too much of a coincidence that she had been cheating on her husband—who had choked her in the past and who was the last to see her alive. Also, there was a psychiatrist who had written a letter saying that the guy was dangerous and might kill her. Too many coincidences for Andy, or any other investigator. For him, the Bierenbaum case wasn't a who-dunit but a how-dunit. How did he get his wife, or her body, out of that building? Where the hell was the body? He noted that Bob was a brilliant guy who had a medical license, which gave him access to drugs, and meant he had the tools and the expertise to drug, kill and dissect a person.

According to Bob, he was alone in his apartment all day after Gail left at 11 A.M. That was either the truth or it wasn't. No one saw Gail leave that day but no one saw Bob leave, either. For that matter, they only had Bob's word that he was there all that time. If Bob was lying when he said he left home at 5:30 that night, that left almost seven hours unaccounted for. It was a hole big enough to drive a truck through. You could drive 150 miles and back again in that time—to lots of different places. Bob said he only went to a family party and a friend's house in New Jersey. But what if his nephew's birthday party was not his first destination—just his final one, where a whole house full of people could later swear where he was? What if Bob's alibi was a carefully-constructed, open-ended falsehood? Magicians performed disappearing tricks that seemed impossible until you realized they had a trapdoor and a secret accomplice, often one posing as a member of the audience. A lot of things became easier when you had help. It was a long shot but this was a cold case and Andy was in the long-shot business.

In September, Andy assigned rookie investigator Hope Wittman to the case. Hope also read the file and began to work, talking to everyone all over again.

Bob learned of the renewed probe after Hope re-interviewed his parents and sister that fall. Not happy to hear he was again being targeted, he met with Scott Green-field to discuss a DA request to do forensic testing on his car and his father's Cadillac. When Hope called to arrange a re-interview with Bob, Scott refused.

Hope interviewed Gail's family, and learned that Bob was a pilot. She passed the information along to Andy. He ordered Hope to go to small airports in New Jersey, find all the flying services that rented airplanes, and ask to look at their log books for July 7th of the previous year. It was a good, old-fashioned, wear-out-shoe-leather, wild goose chase.

On October 6th, Hope went to Teterboro Airport. She searched through the records but found no evidence that Bob had been th˜re that day.

On October 16th, she went to the Caldwell Airport and entered the office of the Sky King Flight Service. Hope asked to see the rental logs for that day.

Bingo.

She copied the plane rental log and the card for the Cessna Model 172N, with tail number N1223F, that Bob had rented for 1.9 hours and brought them triumphantly back to Andy in Manhattan. They then subpoenaed the rec-ords to obtain the originals.

Andy congratulated Hope and smiled at the first piece of hard evidence in the Bierenbaum case. It wasn't a smok-ing gun but it was a building block of a case. Bob had gone up in a plane from 4:30 to 6:25 on the night his wife went missing, something he forgot to mention when asked to detail all his activities on that day. Andy had caught Bob in what seemed like his first lie. Bob had said he left his home at 5:30 but he would have had to have left around 3:30 to get to the airport in Caldwell in time to rent the plane. When Detective Dalsass asked Bob what time he left for New Jersey, it looked like Bob had simply shifted his actual departure time by the exact time he was in the air. That looked like lie number two. Andy's long shot had paid off. They had found a hole in the investigation—one big enough to fly an airplane through.

But it was just the beginning. They would have to look for witnesses at the airport. Did anybody see Bob carry any suitcases or packages onto the plane—or would it be like at his apartment house, where nobody saw anything? The plane would have to be located and then an out-of-state search warrant obtained.

Manny, Sylvia, Alayne and Steve were buoyed by the news. Finally, more than a year after Gail was last seen, it seemed as if things were moving forward.

On February 4th, 1987, NYPD Crime Scene detectives went to Caldwell Airport and searched the Cessna N1223F, looking for evidence of blood, hair or other forensic evidence. Unfortunately, the aircraft had been cleaned and vacuumed many times before they got there. If there had ever been any trace evidence that Gail had been in that plane that day, it was gone.

The Crime Scene detectives, with Bob's permission, photographed Bob's Datsun and tested the interior for blood and other evidence two days later. The tests were negative, which was expected because that car had been in the shop when Gail vanished.

But, by the time the forensic team got to Marvin's Cadillac, it had been stolen, stripped, left on the street, recovered by police and taken to a Brooklyn auto body shop. It was covered with dust and grime and the front fenders, grill, hood and bumper were missing. They took their pictures and found three fingerprints on the interior side of glass windows but they found no traces of blood or tissue inside the car or trunk. Of course, considering the car had been stolen and had sat open on the street for a long time, only evidence of the most unequivocal kind would be of any help in building a case against Bob.

Many of Gail's friends and family were interviewed

again by investigators looking for something that was missed the first time around. They didn't find it.

More than ever, the investigators were certain Bob was involved in Gail's disappearance. Why else would he conceal his flight that afternoon? But that fact by itself was not enough to bring the case before a jury. By spring, Andy knew he did not have enough to go forward. One thing was certain. No one was rushing to confront the suspect with what they had uncovered—or failed to uncover.

Bob and his lawyer were not told that authorities knew about his flight that day. The investigators decided it was better to bide their time and let their bird believe he had flown free. Some investigators retired with unfinished business, frustrated by that one big case that could never be solved. Andy didn't want the Bierenbaum case to be "the one that got away."

Reluctantly, in April 1987, the DA's office closed the Bierenbaum investigation after nine months. The hardest part was telling the Katz family, whose hopes for justice and resolution were dashed by the decision.

"We know he's guilty, but we don't have enough evidence to indict him," Andy told Alayne. "We don't think we've got the evidence for a guilty verdict."

Andy took the failure very personally. The system had failed the Katz family and, for them, he was the system. He promised himself he would never forget the investigation. It would always be his case.

Sylvia took the closing of the second investigation even harder than the first. As flowers bloomed in her Long Island yard and the Passover holiday approached, she could not let go. While Manny kept his anguish private and ran the store, Sylvia wore her heart on her sleeve and clung desperately to any shred of hope. She kept hoping not just for the discovery of Gail's body, but for the possibility that her daughter was alive.

Every night, her son Steve lay in his bed, listening through the wall to the sound of his mother sobbing herself to sleep on his father's shoulder. Steve did not know what to do and the family did not talk about it. He wanted to help but he didn't know how. He felt so helpless, as though he had somehow let his parents down. At first, he had cried in his bed. But after weeks and months of hearing his mother's tears behind her closed door every night, he just felt an empty sadness. No matter what good things had happened at high school or in his life, his family's unresolved pain drained the color out of life after the sun had set.

Before Gail vanished, Sylvia had been a bit flighty, a bit of a "kvetch," like her daughter Gail, but proud of her appearance. Now, Sylvia sank into an obsessive depression. She talked to anyone who would listen about Bob, how he had killed Gail but the police couldn't arrest him because they didn't have enough evidence. She told her neighbor about how Bob must have used his plane to dispose of her body.

"He must have dropped the bag from the plane," she said.

Some neighbors and acquaintances believed her and sympathized with Sylvia. Others thought she was incoherent and acted like she was in a trance. They thought she was crazy. Everyone thought it was a shame and painful to see a mother unbalanced by grief. It was not usually possible to have a conversation with her—because all she would talk about was Gail and Bob.

"I know my daughter is dead," Sylvia told one sympathetic listener. "I know he killed her. She was so unhappy and he was so abusive to Gail. He even tried to kill her cat."

"Oh, my God."

"The police know all about him but they can't arrest him—because they have no evidence. I know he did it. I know he killed her!"

"Maybe she went to a girlfriend's house—maybe she'll turn up?"

"No. Bob killed her. I know he killed her."

The person listened and made sympathetic noises but

didn't believe a word of it. Neither did several others in the neighborhood. Why would Bob kill Gail and ruin his life—why not just divorce her? If Bob had done something to her, the cops would have arrested him, wouldn't they?

"He had to have killed her—she wouldn't just walk out the door with only the clothes on her back," said Sylvia.

Sylvia wandered her neighborhood, a lost soul, peering at faces in passing cars. She haunted shopping malls, walking around and scanning the faces of the women shoppers, the backs of their heads—looking for her baby.

One beautiful sunny spring day, Sylvia, her hair disheveled and a distant look in her eyes, stood around the corner from her home, scanning the faces of people in cars as they passed. Her neighbor Tess saw her and said hello.

"What are you doing?" Tess asked.

"Looking for Gail," Sylvia explained. "Wherever I go, I look for my daughter in a crowd," she told Tess. "Do you know what it's like to see people who look like Gail, and you run up to them—and it's not her?"

CHAPTER 22

ONE BODY

ROBERTA did not leave Bob after she heard Sylvia call him a murderer on his answering machine, nor did she leave him after she found the altered flight log. She did not walk out after his strange reaction to her speculation that he may have been a stone killer who dumped his wife's body out of a plane. She didn't even leave him when Hope Wittman warned her that she might be in danger. She was not afraid of Bob, whatever her suspicions might have been.

Roberta left Bob because she found out he was cheating on her.

She had answered the phone in Bob's apartment—a violation of Bob's standing orders. But that time it wasn't Sylvia—it was a young woman who asked for "Bobby." The call set off Roberta's suspicions that Bob was two-timing her in the apartment while she was on call at the hospital—just like Gail had done to Bob. While Bob was out of the apartment, Roberta had been snooping on him, going through his private papers and speculating about how he might have murdered his wife. Could it be that, while Roberta was out of the apartment, Bob had been having sex there with another woman—in their bed? Or, rather, in Bob and Gail's bed. Roberta confronted him with her suspicion that night and Bob did not just look at his food. He immediately confessed and told Roberta that her new theory was correct. Roberta, after quite a few choice words for Bob, packed up and moved to Connecticut.

After Roberta left, Bob dated several women, including a slim, sexy lawyer named Sandy Schiff, whom he met on a blind date in June, 1987, while he was still living with Roberta. Like Gail, Bob now looked for his next romance before ending the old one.

On their first date, Bob picked Sandy up at her apartment

and met her yapping brown-and-white cocker spaniel, An-
nie Fanny. At first blush, they seemed to be very different
people. Sandy was outspoken, Bob was shy and courteous.
Sandy liked to listen to Barbra Streisand and Frank Sinatra.
Bob loved loud rock 'n' roll and played soft folky and
classical pieces on his twelve-string guitar. Sandy loved
opera and Bob liked Hollywood movies. Sandy liked Bob's
gangly good looks and boyish manner. He liked her pretty
oval face, blue eyes and sarcastic sense of humor, something they shared. To Sandy, the handsome, brilliant surgeon who flew a plane, cooked, spoke several languages
and was a skier and a talented musician seemed too good
to be true.

"I wonder what other baggage he has?" she wondered.

On their second date, after Roberta and Bob broke up,
Sandy found out. Bob parked his Datsun in front of her
building and went upstairs to pick her up for dinner. When
they went back downstairs, Bob's car had been broken into.
A window had been smashed and glass pebbles were all
over the inside of the vehicle. The steering wheel had been
damaged in a failed attempt to hot-wire the car. Dinner was
postponed and the date was put on hold but Sandy was a
New Yorker and understood. Bob called a locksmith, who
came and fixed the broken ignition lock and Bob then drove
his date up to the Bronx to have his glass replaced. In the
car on the way back to Manhattan, Bob joked about what
a terrible date it was. Then he mentioned that he had been
married before but said it did not end well. He told Sandy
how Gail went missing, how it was, at first, a routine police
matter—until he became the target of the cops a few days
later. Sandy, who had represented criminal defendants, listened carefully. Bob described how the suspicion ate at him
and his family.

"Oh, this is bizarre," Sandy thought. "This is one I
haven't heard before."

She asked if he thought Gail was dead.

"I don't know," Bob replied.

He was sad as he described events. Clearly, the unresolved situation with his wife troubled him and he felt victimized by his wife's family and by the cops. Sandy believed Bob. They continued dating, spending time at each other's apartments.

Sandy never saw Bob being anything but affectionate to his two cats—Gail's Abyssinian, Katie, and a pale orange tabby named Emily. To her, he seemed like a real animal lover. Romantically, she felt he was kind and tender. In July, Bob began his residency in plastic surgery at Harlem Hospital, often arriving home after 11 at night. They would walk the dog and order a pizza or other takeout food.

They went flying almost every weekend that the weather was good. They would take cross-country flights down south or up to Martha's Vineyard for a weekend at the beach. Sandy brought her dog, who would doze off on the back seat. When not flying, Bob still liked to play with the Flight Simulator program on his laptop computer, where he also kept records of his patients.

Many times, Sandy and Bob would be eating dinner or settling into bed when Bob's beeper would go off and he had to rush back to the hospital. She saw him treat the victims of child abuse and was very impressed with his compassion toward his patients. Bob spoke Spanish to his Hispanic patients, who were surprised that an Anglo doctor spoke their language. Bob also spoke some French and Hebrew, although he didn't get much chance to use either. Many of the nurses were from the Philippines and Bob, in his spare time, learned the Tagalog language to communicate better with them.

Sandy, like Roberta, resented all of Gail's belongings around Bob's apartment. Once, while rummaging through it in 1988, Sandy found Gail's small jewelry box and a drawer full of photographs. She looked through the pictures, at the snapshots of Bob and Gail on their honeymoon, on vacation, their wedding. Sandy also found Gail's 1985 diary, which consisted of a date book calendar and an address book. Gail had jotted thoughts in a notebook and Sandy read through it. From her writing, Sandy thought

Gail seemed childish, immature. There were routine notes about school and errands. There were also notes about Bob and about Gail's family. Not all of them were nice or positive things. That evening, Sandy asked about Gail, and, as usual, Bob became sad when he spoke of his missing wife. Sandy was beginning to have strong feelings for Bob and she saw Gail as her rival for Bob's affection. It was tough to fight a ghost—especially a ghost that might still be alive. That night, like every night, Sandy noticed that Bob slept like a baby.

In 1989, Dr. Michael Stone testified at a civil trial, in which convicted killer Dr. Jeffrey MacDonald sued author Joe McGinniss on the grounds that the writer had betrayed and defrauded him by pretending to believe in his innocence. Michael testified that he believed MacDonald was a psychopath who stabbed to death his pregnant wife and their two young children—and then tried to blame it on "hippies." The psychiatrist took the stand and gave a diagnosis of the imprisoned doctor. He based his diagnosis not on any interview with MacDonald, but on transcripts of tape recordings made by the killer and sent to the author.

The practice of rendering a psychiatric opinion without interviewing the subject was a controversial one, one that garnered criticism from other psychiatrists and the press. In a scathing magazine article that criticized him, Michael defended the practice and said that psychopaths were incurable. He said there was a popular view that, "if we can send a man to the moon, surely we can make a psychopath go straight. But a person who has a propensity to murder is beyond the pale of psychotherapy. It is folly to think that a person like that could be corrected through the process of one-to-one therapy. He is a lost soul."

In the years since Gail's disappearance, Michael had become, to use his own term, a "murderologist." Frustrated that his warning to Gail had gone unheeded and her apparent murderer remained free, he had dedicated much of his spare time to analyzing and understanding killers. He had amassed a library of hundreds of true crime books about infamous murder cases and murderers and begun a large database of all the factors and parameters of murder and mayhem. It was his hobby but it overlapped his professional work and would soon find its way into a forthcoming psychiatry book by Michael, as a table of the "Gradations of Evil." Michael classified MacDonald, as well as Bob Bierenbaum, in the number 11 slot on the chart—as "Psychopathic Killers of People 'In the Way.' "

Bob had briefly been Michael's patient in consultation, but his sympathies were with Bob's suspected victim, Gail. Like the Katz family, Michael was outraged by the idea that Bob seemed to be getting away with murder. Occasionally, in the privacy of his home he resorted to dark humor to voice his frustration. One evening, lifting up a fork and large knife to carve a chicken for dinner, Michael gave his wife a twisted smile.

"I'm sure Doctor Bob could do a much better job."

On May 21st, 1989, just before 10 A.M., police on Staten Island found a pale object that turned out to be a human torso in the water between Pier 1 and Pier 3 on Front Street. The finding of a "floater" was not very unusual in New York. It was a rite of spring, when the waters warmed up and bodies of people who had jumped or fallen, or were dumped into the harbor or rivers floated to the surface. The Medical Examiner's office took charge of the decomposing hunk of flesh that had once been a young woman and an autopsy was performed the next day. The torso, which measured 27 inches long and weighed 32 pounds, was x-rayed and examined. It was partially decomposed, with portions of the ribcage and abdomen exposed. Two ribs on the left side and one on the right had been fractured but it could not be determined if the breaks had occurred before or after death. The pathologist identified the uterus, which did not contain an IUD, Samples were taken for testing for drugs and poisons. The most obvious thing about the remains was that the corpse had been "dis-articulated." The neck, arms and legs had been cut off, leaving sharp edges on the bones.

Suicides do not saw off their own arms, legs and heads. The autopsy did not immediately reveal a cause or time of death. The pathologist, who recommended that the torso be removed to the Kings County Medical Examiner's Office for further examination, made a note at the end of the report: "Cause of death: UNDETERMINED. Manner: HOMICIDE."

In Brooklyn, tests failed to find any drugs in the body tissues. New DNA testing was deemed not possible due to the advanced state of decomposition. The Missing Persons Squad was contacted and the family of Gail Katz Bierenbaum was notified, in an effort to determine if the body was Gail's.

A detective from the Staten Island precinct called the missing persons squad. The squad decided the torso was probably Gail Bierenbaum and the Katz family soon got the news. Through their tears, they heard a detective say that the "Jane Doe" body was the right age and size and the dismemberment was consistent with the way a surgeon would take a body apart. The pictures in Manny's and Sylvia's minds—of their baby cut up—sickened them. Their pain was great but it seemed that, at last, after four years, the case would again be re-opened and the law would catch up to Bob.

But, rather than clearing up any mystery, the unknowns multiplied. Sylvia had been searching for a living Gail. The reality of a call from police, the reality of a body removed the last vestige of hope.

The remains were tentatively identified as Gail, pending a positive ID. Alayne, at the request of the Medical Examiner's office, began a search for Gail's past doctors—who might have x-rays to compare with the body.

An anthropologist examined the records and the remains, which were stored in a stainless-steel pan and covered with a white plastic sheet. She estimated that the body was of a white female of 30 to 35 years of age. Using the state of decomposition, she estimated the woman had been dead for at least one month and as long as six months. That meant that the victim had been killed no earlier than November 1988. The time frame seemed to let Bob off the hook—unless he was somehow able to store Gail in a deep freeze or keep her alive at a secret location for 3½ years before killing her, cutting her up and dumping her in the bay.

Alayne located a doctor who still had x-ray films of Gail. The Long Island doctor compared the two x-rays and concluded that they were both Gail—because of the similarity of slight irregularities on a right rib, as well as a swelling of a shoulder bone.

But the torso had a well-healed fracture of the sternum—a bone that Gail had never broken before July 7, 1985—and there was no evidence of a fracture of the sternum in Gail's prior x-rays. However, the next day, the city certified the opinion. A death certificate was issued. It was official—the dead woman was Gail Katz Bierenbaum, despite the misgivings of the family and the anthropologist. The Katzes were horrified to learn from the Staten Island District Attorney's Office that radiological identification was good enough for a death certificate—but not good enough to prosecute a killer.

The Katz family now had closure—but they did not have satisfaction. They had Gail but the police could not get Bob. Circumstances even seemed to give credence to Bob's claim that Gail had run off with druggies—who'd killed her. Or had they? Sylvia and Manny and their family were immersed in grief and anguish. They thought they had Gail's body to bury—but who had killed her? Would Bob or anyone ever be arrested? Justice had already been delayed for years—would it now be forever denied?

CHAPTER 23

THREE FUNERALS

Bob was surprised to get a call from a detective, the first from the police in more than three years. He was shocked to hear they had found a floating torso that had been tentatively identified as Gail. The investigator said they wanted to question him and asked for pictures of Gail that might show any marks that would help identify the body. To Sandy, Bob seemed grief-stricken at the sudden news. Bob told her the little information he had received—that a torso had been found. Sandy listened and decided it was probably just the police trying to rattle Bob again.

"This sounds like horseshit," she told him.

Bob asked her if he should go down and try to identify the remains.

"There's nothing to look at," Sandy pointed out. "Would you want this to be your last memory of someone you loved?"

Bob said he should claim the body but Sandy disagreed.

"I don't think that's something you want to do," said Sandy, who suggested it would be better to let Gail's family take charge.

Bob called Scott. The lawyer saw the discovery as a good thing—but he did not trust the police and would not let Bob be questioned extensively until he had some facts.

Scott got on the phone with the police and the Medical Examiner's office but he didn't get very far. The detectives told Scott only that a torso had been found and the cause of death was unknown. He asked them for a copy of the autopsy report but they declined to give it to him. Scott was also unable to obtain a copy of the death certificate. The investigators did not mention that the body had only been in the water for a maximum of six months but Scott knew that a body could not have lasted that long. He told

Bob he wasn't getting any information but thought he had nothing to worry about.

"Bodies don't last in the water for three or four years," Scott said. "I don't think it's possible for this to be from 1985."

But despite the fact that it seemed Bob could have had nothing to do with the death, it appeared to the lawyer that police were still treating Bob as a suspect. Scott's fears were confirmed when the detectives repeatedly called Bob and showed up at his door—apparently trying to spook him.

The fourth anniversary of Gail's disappearance came and went while authorities slowly went about the scientific and bureaucratic business of confirming her identity. The body was not released until the next month. The casket was sealed.

Scott eventually learned that the Katz family had claimed the body and intended to bury it at the end of August.

"Should I go to the funeral?" Bob asked Scott.

"No. How can you go to the funeral? What can you do? These people hate you," Scott replied.

"But it's my wife."

"My advice is you don't go. Don't ruin it for the Katzes. Nothing good can come of you going to the funeral. Have your own funeral."

"How did she die?"

"I don't know. They will not give me a copy of the autopsy report."

"But I'm entitled to know," Bob protested.

"This is not the time to make a ruckus," Scott said.

Bob thanked Scott for all his help and said goodbye. As far as Scott knew, it was the last time he would ever have to speak to Bob Bierenbaum.

On Thursday morning, August 31st, 1989, Gail's family and friends finally gathered at a funeral home on Flatbush Avenue in her old Brooklyn neighborhood to say goodbye. Speaking in hushed tones, the mourners filed in and signed a guest book. The men donned yarmulkes they took from a table at the door of the chapel. The room filled to overflowing with relatives, friends and colleagues. If Bob had arrived, there would have been a riot. Even so, Alayne wondered why Bob did not just say to hell with everyone and attend his own wife's funeral. Isn't that what an innocent man would do?

Speaking to other friends before the ceremony, Gail's former boss Jane Dunne discovered that the role she had played as Gail's surrogate mother and confidante was also played by many other women—each of whom thought she alone was Gail's closest friend.

A rabbi performed the memorial service and gave a brief eulogy as her family sobbed in the front row. The recitation of each of Gail's unrealized hopes and dreams was painful. After the service, the red-eyed mourners spilled out of the air-conditioned funeral parlor and onto the sidewalk. It was a warm, sunny summer day, like the day she vanished. Gail's casket was carried through the 80-degree heat and into a waiting black hearse, for the trip to the Mount Zion Jewish Cemetery in Maspeth, Queens.

Unlike other old New York graveyards, Mount Zion was not the final resting place for the rich and famous. The best known residents were also victims—many of the 148 exploited women garment workers who were burned alive or leaped to their deaths, rather than be consumed by the flames of the infamous Triangle Shirtwaist fire in Greenwich Village in 1911. Mount Zion featured green grass, and rolling, park-like grounds graced with huge old stately oak and elm trees.

But just outside the northern fence, towering several hundred feet above the peaceful burial ground, were two huge yellow smokestacks of the New York City Department of Sanitation District 6 incinerator. Constructed of yellow brick, the giant twin tubes were blackened near the tips, like vertical cannons looming over the beautiful landscaping and quaint Victorian-style marble mausoleums. At the base of the smokestacks was a building constructed of the same masonry and an ugly nest of black boxes and tubes. The striking sight from the nearby elevated Long Island Expressway of the rows of graves leading to the incinerator often inspired remarks that it seemed to be some kind of factory of death.

The mourners arrived at the open gravesite. Next to the fresh wound in the earth was the pile of dirt that would cover Gail. A small ceremonial hand shovel was stuck in the brown mound. The coffin was placed on a metal frame over the waiting grave. Manny and Sylvia, who had never expected to bury their own child, leaned on each other as the rabbi recited the ancient Aramaic prayer of Kaddish.

"Yis-ga-dal, v'yis-ka-dosh sh' may rabo," the rabbi intoned.

At the conclusion of the graveside service, the casket was lowered into the hole and there were more tears and pained cries at the last goodbye. Several mourners grabbed the hand shovel, scooped fresh dirt and poured it on top of Gail's casket before walking away, drying their eyes with handkerchiefs. There was more embracing before the people returned to their cars. They met at the Katz house later, where the family would "sit shiva" for a week, receiving mourners in the old Jewish tradition that gave support to a grieving family.

The Katzes were dealing with more than Gail's death and finding her killer. Manny, 60, had been diagnosed with a brain tumor the previous year. He had received treatment but he was living with cancer. Sylvia had lost Gail and feared losing Manny, too.

The following week, another rabbi, this one from New Jersey, recited Kaddish again over the raw soil of Gail's new grave. There was no crowd for the second funeral service—just Bob and his father Marvin. After the simple service, Bob sat shiva at his parents' home for a week, as Jewish law required.

Gail's family ordered a large gray granite headstone and a small matching footstone for the grave. The large one was the family marker. It featured a chiseled lamp with an eternal flame and the name "KATZ." The smaller stone was for Gail's final resting place. It featured Gail's name in Hebrew and English.

GAIL BETH
BELOVED DAUGHTER
GRANDDAUGHTER AND SISTER
MARCH 8, 1956–JULY 7, 1985
FOREVER IN OUR HEARTS

The family had made July 7th as Gail's date of death— even though the body that rested underneath the stone had died several years later. That was the date they last saw Gail, the date they believed Bob killed her. Scientific evidence could not convince them that Bob did not kill her. It also reflected the Katzes' nagging concern that the body might not be Gail.

After the mourning period, Sylvia made it her business to bug the authorities and press them to do everything they could to eliminate any doubt about Gail's identity and prosecute Bob. At times, the fight seemed to be her only purpose in life, the only thing holding her fragile psyche together. She complained that a prosecutor in Staten Island had said that DNA testing was unlikely to be successful and was too expensive, and would not authorize funding for the lab work.

Three months later, just before Thanksgiving, 1989, Sylvia, 56, became ill and was diagnosed with cancer of the uterus. The disease spread quickly. Sylvia lost weight and became weak.

In February 1990, the Medical Examiner's office called Sylvia and said they agreed with her and wanted her authorization to exhume Gail's body to obtain samples for DNA analysis. The mother was glad the city would finally spend the money to find out whom they had buried but she did not like the idea of disturbing her child again. She told the pathologist she was "extremely unhappy" with how the police and his office had handled the case. But she said she would speak to Manny and they would agree—if it would aid identification and prosecution.

A week later, the Medical Examiner's office called back and said they had enough bone samples from the torso for DNA testing, and exhumation of the body would not be necessary. The news was a relief to Sylvia and Manny, who were told that after the DNA testing had been done, they would need blood samples from them to compare with the DNA of the body—to determine if it was Gail.

The next month, the bone samples were sent to the Life-codes Corporation in upstate Valhalla, New York, for DNA extraction.

The stress was high, but Sylvia's spirits were lifted by the possibility that, after so long, they were on the verge of certainty—whatever that might be. She seemed to rally at the news, despite the toll the disease was taking.

Her optimism only lasted until April, when the lab reported that the degraded samples actually did not contain enough human DNA to determine anything.

The bad news meant that Sylvia would never be sure if she had buried her daughter or a stranger. It also meant Bob would never be prosecuted and Gail would never be avenged. Justice had been delayed for too long. The blow was too much for Sylvia. She gave up. The cancer sucked the life out of her and she was dead in two months, on June 13th.

Sylvia was laid to rest beside Gail and for the third time in a year, a rabbi said the prayer for the dead at the Katz family plot in Mount Zion Cemetery. Alayne looked at the casket bearing the body of her mother, and at Gail's grassed-over grave. Then she looked at her ailing father, whose brain was slowly being eaten by cancer. She was filled with a consuming, burning hatred for Bob Bierenbaum whom she blamed for it all. Bob was killing her family, one member at a time.

The city Medical Examiner's office kept trying to do the right thing. They sent soft tissue samples from the torso to be tested but those were also degraded and useless. They gave up the following year.

Manny also gave up. He did not want to run the card store without Sylvia and closed up shop. He seemed lost without his wife and sat at home, as the tumor grew inside his head.

Alayne knew she had to get on with her life, no matter what was happening—for her own survival. She had begun to practice family law and sometimes acted as a Law Guardian—someone who protected the rights of abused or neglected children. She married and intended to have children of her own. She did not intend to let Bob destroy her life as well. It seemed as if it would be impossible to hold Bob accountable for Gail's murder but nothing that anyone said would ever convince her that Bob had not killed Gail.

She knew it in her heart.

CHAPTER 24

SIN CITY

BOB hurtled through the sharp, frigid air, trailing a cloud of pure white snow. For an instant, he was silently flying without an airplane between the clear, cobalt sky and the clean, colorless snowpack blanketing the mountain beneath him. When he came down, his skis dug into the powder with a whooshing sound. He stabbed the snow with his poles for balance and adroitly shifted his weight back and forth, expertly zigzagging at high speed down the snowy slope. The bright sun and the whipping thin air reddened his face as he flew downhill toward the Alpine village of Davos, Switzerland, far below.

Bob always joked about his fondness for "getting high" in an airplane or at a ski resort and it was true. He was high on the real thing. He loved the exhilarating feeling of complete freedom, soaring alone above the world.

Davos had been the site of resorts, spas and sanitoriums for asthma patients for generations. It had also become a center for medical research—and the perfect professional convention destination for doctors. Although he was a certified ski instructor and could ski rings around his colleagues, Bob stayed with his friends when they were on the slopes. He signed onto the 1989 Swiss ski getaway with his doctor friend Scott Baranoff and other doctors from Las Vegas for two reasons.

The first reason was that he did not want to pass up the chance to ski the Alps—or to escape his stressful situation back in New York. Gail had been laid to rest but Bob still seemed to be under a cloud as a result of the efforts of Alayne Katz, who, essentially, was trying to make good on her sister's threat to try and ruin him.

The second reason was that Bob was considering relocating to Las Vegas. Scott Baranoff, a urologist, had been trying to convince Bob for years that he should move to Vegas. He extolled the virtues of desert living: good medical opportunities, no snow—except at the nearby mountain ski resorts—and great flying weather year-round. On the ski holiday, Bob met Charles Vinnik, an established Las Vegas plastic surgeon. They hit it off and Charlie offered Bob an opportunity to join in his practice. He also told Bob how wonderful his town was. In the thin Alpine air and strangely warm sunshine—considering the temperature was well below zero—Bob listened to Charlie and Scott rave about Las Vegas.

Bob agreed to try the arrangement on a part-time basis and soon began commuting back and forth from New York to Vegas, beginning in October 1989. He would fly out to Nevada on a Sunday and assist in Charlie's office until he flew back to New York on Wednesday. He would then work on his cases there until Saturday and start all over again on Sunday. Bob applied for a Nevada medical license, which would allow him to operate in the state.

After five million years of desolate splendor, Las Vegas, the eternal hot desert valley ringed by a jagged bowl of rusty, mocha and velvety chocolate mountains, acquired the nickname "Sin City." It later acquired another name—"Second Chance City"—because so many people, including professionals like doctors, came there after having problems in other cities. In a sense, it was a place of retreat for those who had sinned elsewhere.

After flying over the starkly magnificent mountains on a commercial jetliner, the vast, ancient Las Vegas Valley is revealed, baking in the hot sun. As the plane descends, a grid of roads becomes visible and a strange sparkling skyline pops up in a row from the center of the desert floor. It seems to be a city but the buildings are somewhat garish for office towers and several are oddly shaped. It is "The Strip" of casinos, the glittering, plush factories for separating willing suckers from their money. Las Vegas is a company town and the industry is gambling and entertainment.

One thing a New Yorker used to damp seaside weather

notices right away is Las Vegas' hot, dry, crisp climate and crystal blue sky. The desert has a flinty iron scent and even the palm trees have a new, husky odor. Instead of pigeons, Bob was amused to see road runners and lizards zipping around. Another remarkable thing was how clean the city was—most of it seemed as spotless as Disneyland. Where was all the litter? Was Las Vegas better at cleaning up trash or were Las Vegans just neater—and prouder of their city— than New Yorkers?

Bob decided to relocate to Sin City and made arrangements to leave New York. It was hard to disengage himself because Bob was dating Sandy—and another woman named *Sonya.

Alayne Katz and her family had told authorities that Bob was a control freak who'd had to oversee everything Gail did. But Bob was still picking highly-educated, intelligent, independent, aggressive professionals as girlfriends. If Bob wanted to be a controlling brute, he was dating the wrong kind of women. It would have been a prescription for frustration.

But his love life had never been better. He had several girlfriends at once and was making up for lost time, despite his long hours at the hospital. He was certainly playing the field, something he was careful to conceal from his lovers— who did not know about each other. Since he was leaving town, Bob did not have to end either relationship or choose between the two women, who did not really want to leave Manhattan but wanted to visit Bob in Vegas. He had discovered, to his delight, that he was very eligible. There was no shortage of beautiful women who wanted to go to bed with a doctor.

For the six months that he went back and forth, Bob stayed at Scott Baranoff's house. When he moved to Vegas, he rented his own mission-style townhouse condo in a nice, walled development not far from the hospital.

Bob began his new life in a new town, which included renting a plane and flying to Lake Tahoe on the weekends for the best skiing. He loved hiking the rugged nearby canyons and went bicycling—up to ten miles a day. After he had engine trouble on a flight, Bob decided to save up for a twin-engine aircraft of his own. He began attending parties thrown by the doctors in his new circle of friends.

Bob worked at the University Medical Center on West Charleston Boulevard downtown and began paying his dues in the medical profession. He was on call at all hours' for emergency room pages. His beeper would go off and Bob would rush into the ER to find bloody, mutilated faces and bodies from car accident scenes to patch up and make whole and pleasing again. It was often a challenge but Bob was glad to lose far fewer patients than he had with cardiac surgery.

When Bob first arrived in the Emergency Room in his flannel shirt and jeans, and carrying his laptop computer, the nurses did not know he was a doctor. Nurse Patti McGill wondered who the fast-talking guy with the arresting eyes was, until he introduced himself. When Bob gave nurse Buffy Gustafson an order, she checked to make sure he really was a doctor before carrying it out. She thought he was another wiseguy New Yorker—until she saw the way he treated his patients. He talked with them—not at them, like all the other doctors.

*Dr. Fred Goodman, another surgeon, liked Bob instantly, although he thought the younger doctor seemed a bit naïve and idealistic. Bob didn't care if a patient had insurance or not, but then he would wonder why he was not being compensated as much as other physicians who did. "I'm every bit as good a plastic surgeon as they are," Bob complained to Fred. In Las Vegas, Bob discovered, there was a glut of plastic surgeons—most of whom made a living catering to the city's entertainers by performing breast enlargement and cosmetic surgery on showgirls and others. Bob and Charlie Vinnik performed their share of such operations but competition was stiff. Bob began to specialize in the more difficult breast reconstruction techniques needed to restore the figures of women who had undergone radical breast removal because of breast cancer. Charlie was impressed with Bob's credentials and thought he was some kind of genius. Bob had been chief of coronary care at Mount Sinai Hospital in his twenties—something that ordinary mortals did not achieve. Also Bob was better than most of the guitar players he had seen on stage.

"Were you ever married before?" Charlie asked idly one day.

"Yeah," said Bob. "It really didn't work out. She disappeared."

"So you're still, technically, married?"

"She's been gone for a long time," Bob shrugged.

"If she's been gone for so long, you're not married anymore?"

Bob said he didn't feel restricted and that he could remarry.

He was overjoyed to discover that his morning commute to work took just ten minutes, which, to a New Yorker, was like beaming up. As he rode to work, with music on the stereo, he saw giant, brightly-colored balloons rising from the northern part of the valley—balloonists silently riding the calm, morning air.

Now that Doctor Bob was in private practice, he began to have much more contact with his patients. His new patients responded to Bob's expertise and his informality. He was not rich but he did have a very good income. He bought sharp, expensive Armani suits and ties but his transformation from goofy, blue-jeaned resident to successful young surgeon was still incomplete. Although he wore the suits, the suits did not wear him. Bob's curly hair was still a bit too long and not quite tamed. His shirttails had a way of working themselves out of his pants, which were tugged down by the bulging wallet he kept in the back pocket. But to women, it was endearing. Bob seemed like a big kid, who wanted a woman's touch. Females wanted to straighten his tie, brush his hair and do things for him, especially when they saw him absently twirling one of his curls around his finger as he thought about something.

Bob got a cat and named her "Katy-Cat." He established himself as a pillar of the community with good works. He soon became known as a very skillful surgeon with a big heart and a brilliant guy who went the extra mile for patient and family—especially for anyone he knew. He was an activist for patients' rights and soon found his way into the *Distinguished Men of Nevada* book. He also became active in conservative Republican politics.

Bob's sense of humor sometimes displayed his sense of superiority. He once joked to Charlie that some people suffered from the condition of "micro-deckia"—that is, they weren't playing with a full deck of cards, or at least not with as much brain power as Doctor Bob. Charlie was an exacting surgeon but, next to Bob, he felt casual. Charlie joked that Bob was the finicky Felix Unger and he was the slob Oscar Madison from Neil Simon's *The Odd Couple*.

Many patients thought Bob was a great doctor who cared deeply about them—enough to administer tough love. But other patients did not respond well to Bob's orders. His approach to medicine was more holistic than traditional and he encountered difficulties because of his attitude. He believed you could not separate a patient's life into different boxes and simply perform surgery as if it were an isolated action. If a patient had other conditions or a lifestyle that might make it more difficult to recover, Bob strongly believed in addressing the problems. When he operated on a person, he expected that person to do everything possible to help achieve recovery, healing and the best result possible. It irked Bob when a patient who had been instructed to give up smoking started up with cigarettes again. He actually "fired" several patients who did not toe the line. It was, after all, for their own good.

Fred Goodman never saw Bob lose his temper in the operating room, although some of their colleagues were "OR screamers" and sponge-throwers. Once, Fred did see Bob lose his temper—big time—although it was in a good cause. Fred was also a pilot and Bob gave him some advanced instrument training. When Fred did his pre-flight check of the aircraft before takeoff, Bob watched him like a hawk. As Fred moved to step inside the cockpit, Bob stopped him and pointed to a piece of metal on the ground under the aileron. Fred walked over, picked it up and gasped—it was the small pin that held the aileron on to the plane.

"Are you trying to kill me, Fred?" Bob screamed.

"What?"

"I'm single, but you have a wife and kids—do you have a death wish?"

They both knew that a plane that lost an aileron in flight could fall from the sky. Fred began to stammer his apology—until Bob cut it short. Bob pointed to the aileron— the pin was in place. Because Fred had failed to check the aileron pins, Bob—who had one in his pocket for just such a possibility—had dropped it on the ground to teach Fred a valuable lesson, one that might save his life one day.

"The next time you do that alone, you're dead," Bob said. "It's as safe as you allow it to be."

Fred protested that there was actually no dangerous condition, that the pin had come from Bob's pocket—not from the airplane.

"Well, it can happen and that's why you're supposed to check it," Bob concluded.

Fred did not appreciate being dressed down but he knew Bob was right. Fred never neglected anything on his preflight check again.

New Year's Eve 1989–1990 was, for Bob, a ringing out of the old and a ringing in of the new. Las Vegas was a party town and New Year's was celebrated full tilt at thousands of blowouts, private and public.

At one such bash, Bob was introduced to a beautiful blonde in a sexy dress. Tall and slim, she had the face and figure of a showgirl, with high cheekbones, shoulder-length hair and a charming smile. Stephanie Youngblood was 31 years old and a successful chiropractor. Bob turned on his charm and something clicked between them. They talked and laughed and flirted as they told each other about themselves and their practices.

"Have you ever been married?" Stephanie asked.

"No," Bob replied.

Before they parted, Bob got Stephanie's telephone number and promised to call her soon.

After New Year's Eve, Sandy Schiff flew out from New York to spend the holiday weekend with Bob at his new home and renew their intimate relationship. On January 5th, Sandy and Bob were sitting in his kitchen as Bob wrote out checks and paid his bills. Sandy had insisted that she pay half of Bob's phone bill because she and Bob spent so much time on the phone.

"Do you believe this MCI bill?" Bob asked, holding up the paperwork.

The folded bill flipped open and stretched like an accordion to the floor. Sandy laughed and asked to see the bill but Bob said no. He changed the subject. Perhaps he was just being gallant but something in his manner made Sandy suspicious.

Later, when Bob was out on an errand, Sandy went into Bob's office and opened his desk. She found the huge phone bill. Next to the bill was a stack of letters. She recognized them as her love letters to Bob. There was a second stack of love letters to Bob in a handwriting she did not recognize. She looked at them and saw a signature—that of a former girlfriend of Bob's, a lawyer named Sonya, whom Sandy had believed he was no longer seeing. The dates on the letters said otherwise. She was shocked to read that Sonya was actually going to fly out and visit Bob the following weekend—after Sandy left. Furious, she opened the telephone bill and realized immediately why Bob had not let her see the list of New York phone numbers he had called over and over. One repeated number was her own. But the other number, about a hundred calls, was not familiar to her. She assumed all those calls were not to Bob's parents and suspected it was Sonya's phone. To confirm her hypothesis, Sandy dialed the number and got an answering machine.

"Hi, this is Sonya, but I'm not home right now . . ."

Sandy was not shy and she was angry. Bob had lied to

The Surgeon's Wife: Gail Katz Bierenbaum and Bob on their wedding day in 1982.

The Cessna 172 Skyhawk aircraft on the tarmac at Caldwell Airport in New Jersey. Prosecutors said Bob used it to dispose of Gail's remains.

"Place of Repose?" Scenic Wanaque Reservoir in northern New Jersey, surrounded by mountains and forest. Photo taken in 1988.
(Sam DeBenedetto)

MISSING

GAIL KATZ-BIERENBAUM

HEIGHT: 5'3"
WEIGHT: 107 lbs.
BROWN HAIR
HAZEL EYES

Graduate student at Long Island University.
Last seen 11 AM, Sunday, July 7, 1985.
May have been in the vicinity of Metropolitan
Museum in Central Park.

If you have information please call Det. O'Malley
at 374-6917.

REWARD for any information concerning her
whereabouts and leading to her return.

MISSING poster
Bob had printed.

DATE 19 85	AIRCRAFT MAKE & MODEL	REGISTRATION NUMBER	POINTS OF DEPARTURE & ARRIVAL	
			FROM	TO
1/6	C-172	48616	CDN grand CDN	
→ 8/7	C-172	68082	East Hampton	East Ha-ple
8/14	C-172	5490	CDN	CDN
10/27	C-150	82942	CDN	EEN
10/27	C-150	82942	EEN bridge CDN	
12/22	PA-181	43114	Republic	Republic

Bob's personal flight log, with the altered date (arrow) and
departure point.

Dr. Janet Chollet, the second Mrs. Bierenbaum, and her husband Bob arrive at a Manhattan court for his arraignment on murder charges in December, 1999. (Bolivar Arellano, *New York Post*)

Bob Bierenbaum *(right)* arriving for a 2000 court hearing in Manhattan, along with his father, Dr. Marvin Bierenbaum *(center)* and lawyer Scott Greenfield. (Jim Alcorn, *New York Post*)

Janet and Bob with their daughter Annah on a family outing while Bob was awaiting trial.

Bob and Annah playing on slide, caught by mom Janet.

"The Ice Princess," Acting Supreme Court Justice Leslie Crocker-Snyder, arriving at the Manhattan courthouse. (Tamara Beckwith, *New York Post*)

Anxious but optimistic, Bob and Janet leave the courthouse on their way to lunch, before the verdict. (Joey Newfield, *New York Post*)

Tearful but thankful, Steve Katz and his sister Alayne embrace on the courthouse steps after the jury's verdict of guilty. (Bolivar Arellano, *New York Post*)

her and she intended to shake up his cozy little situation. Speaking to the tape, she introduced herself to her rival and explained how she had obtained the number and discovered Bob was cheating on both of them.

"Look, I'm out here now and I understand you're coming out here next week," Sandy said. "I think you should be aware of the fact that this is not exactly what you had in mind. What are we going to do about it?"

When Bob returned home and changed to take her out to dinner, Sandy did not tell him what she had uncovered—or that she had called Sonya. She wanted to wait and watch him squirm in public, not unlike Roberta had done about two years earlier. Bob took Sandy to one of the best restaurants in town. Once they had ordered, Sandy, almost gloating, told Bob her recent discovery and how she had dialed his other favorite New York number.

Bob blanched. Once he realized Sandy was not joking, he set off his own beeper and excused himself to go make a call. Sandy was amused—though still enraged—to see Bob scramble. Bob kept beeping himself during the meal and trying to call Sonya in New York—to head events off at the pass—but was unable to reach her.

Sonya called back the next morning. Bob answered but she asked to speak to Sandy. Bob got on an extension and he and his two girlfriends had a three-way conversation, in which Sandy made accusations and Sonya demanded, "Is this true?" over and over.

"Yeah," Bob admitted into the phone.

Sonya cancelled her trip to Las Vegas and hung up on Bob. Then Sandy vented her anger at Bob and told him what she thought of him. It didn't seem to faze him much.

"I didn't fly out here—thirty-five hundred miles—for this!" Sandy screamed, winding up her fist.

She swung in her best tennis forehand style and punched Bob right in the jaw as hard as she could. Bob recoiled from the impact but did not strike back.

"You're like an unguided missile," Bob joked, rubbing his sore jaw.

Sandy thought her aim was pretty good. Bob was upset but seemed oddly calm, as if he was not too troubled. Of course, she did not know that Bob had met Stephanie a few days earlier and could not wait to call her. Sandy announced she was breaking up with Bob and he did not try to talk her out of it. She threw her things together and went to the airport to get on the first plane back to New York. She was so eager to get away from Bob that she spent twice as much money to get home—and flying through a southern city added hours to the trip.

When she got back to New York, she and her rival went out to see a movie about a man with two wives and decided they would be allies against Bob and never see him again. Later, Sandy thought about the police suspicions of Bob and his supposedly homicidal temper when a woman told him she was leaving him. In a strange way, it confirmed her belief that Bob, although a creep, was not a killer.

"If he would have strangled anybody, it would have been me," Sandy thought about their one-round fight in Las Vegas. "If I didn't push his buttons then, I don't know how anybody else could."

Sandy had thought she had Bob's heart and never considered the possibility that the reason Bob did not snap when she left was that he did not love her, as he had loved Gail.

CHAPTER 25

CUTTING OUT THE DEVIL

STEPHANIE received the full Bob treatment. Having obtained his twin-engine pilot's license, he took his new love on flying dates and whipped up gourmet meals for her. One thing they had in common was that they were both dynamos who approached their patients holistically, as complete human beings.

They soon became lovers and then a couple. Several months later, while Stephanie's home was being gutted in a renovation, she moved into Bob's casita condo. While putting something away in a closet after she moved in, Stephanie found a suitcase with a luggage tag bearing the name "Gail Bierenbaum." Later, looking through some of Bob's papers, Stephanie ran across a bank statement of an account for "Dr. Robert Bierenbaum and Gail Bierenbaum."

She decided to openly confront Bob over what seemed like a lie.

"Who is Gail Bierenbaum?" Stephanie asked, an edge of anger in her voice.

Bob was flustered by the question. He sighed deeply.

"That's very difficult for me to answer," Bob said, at last.

Stephanie noticed that Bob was suddenly upset and tears had appeared in his eyes.

"I was married," Bob admitted. "She disappeared one day . . . and she never returned."

Stephanie was taken aback. Bob told her he had had a fight with Gail at their apartment five years earlier and she had stormed out, never to be seen again.

"I was taken in for questioning a couple of times" by the police, Bob said.

Both he and the police believed that Gail had been murdered, he told her.

"In the course of the investigation," Bob added, "I found out she had a drug problem and she was having extra-marital affairs."

Stephanie quickly went from anger to sympathy as she heard Bob's tale of a wild, wayward wife and police suspicion focused unfairly on him.

"I believe Gail probably went to Central Park to hang out with her drug friends and it was probably a drug-related death," Bob concluded sadly.

Stephanie understood why Bob did not advertise his tragic past to everyone and realized he had been trying to avoid malicious gossip that might harm him professionally and personally. She felt a bit guilty for being so accusatory. Stephanie was one of the few people in Las Vegas who even knew that Bob had been married before, and one of fewer who knew that Gail might have been murdered. She accepted Bob's story and the incident brought them closer together.

Bob was working harder than ever but it was finally paying off. He and Stephanie were a golden professional couple and Bob was already in love. He was ready to marry and have children but she was in no hurry. Unlike most of his colleagues, Bob introduced himself to his patients by his first name and encouraged the first-name-basis familiarity that was anathema to virtually all physicians in the United States, who insisted that everyone but their mothers address them as "Doctor so-and-so." Many patients were uncomfortable addressing Bob so informally, so they called him "Doctor Bob." Some other practitioners frowned at the departure from tradition but Bob was so good he could get away with it. In Las Vegas, Bob was a bigger fish in a smaller pond and he reveled in it. The recognition of his skills inspired him to excel. As Bob achieved the success and financial rewards that Gail could not wait for, he was able to fully live the sophisticated, discriminating lifestyle that he was drawn to. He could afford the aged Bordeaux wines and prime cuts of meat and other gourmet foods he loved, not to mention all the skiing and flying he had time for. For the first time in many years, he was enjoying life. He even bought a house and a plane: a white, twin-engine Piper Cherokee.

One day, a colleague who stopped by Bob's new house was amused to see the transplanted New Yorker embracing the western lifestyle and thriving in the desert. Bob was out in the hot sun behind his new house, mowing his first lawn with a new lawn mower. He was wearing a pair of shorts, a pair of cowboy boots and a white cowboy hat.

Doctor Bob had arrived. There was a new doc in town and he was one of the good guys.

In the midst of the rewards, Bob acted on his social conscience. He joined his local chapter of the Rotary Club, and a group of physicians affiliated with Liga International, called the "Flying Doctors of Mercy," and became part of a squadron of flying physicians who went down to El Fuerte, Mexico—700 miles away—at least four times a year. Using donated equipment and supplies, the doctors and nurses of Las Vegas flew at their own expense and treated indigent patients for free.

Planning for the Mexico trips took many weeks. In the spring of 1990, the planes and pilots were lined up. The number of planes on the mission determined how many passengers and how many pounds of supplies could be transported. As if it were a surgical picnic, the medical group brought almost everything with them, including surgical gowns, instruments, bandages, medicine—even sterile water to clean instruments in because the local water was unfit to drink. Bob and his colleagues then recruited other doctors, nurses and civilians to go on the trip. Everyone was determined to make the hard work on the mission of mercy enjoyable and the atmosphere was part adventure and part vacation. "We're here to help people," Bob told a nurse on one trip. "But let's have a good time doing it."

Located in the state of Sinaloa on the Gulf of California, El Fuerte, like Las Vegas, was a city on a flat plain surrounded by mountains. But, from the air, the difference between the two cities was obvious. El Fuerte was not a pale desert pan but a fertile valley of rich green and brown located on the Rio del Fuerte river. There was no airport tower—pilots simply checked to make sure there were no other planes lifting off as they came in for a landing. In the distance, next to the runway, goats were munching grass.

Local officials met "the Flying Doctors" and arranged for transportation to their hotel. The honored guests had time for a shower or a nap or to go sightseeing before an evening get-together dinner in the small hotel's cantina.

In town they saw several local Yaqui Indians dressed in strange ancient native costumes. The elaborate pageant was a celebration of Lent, the period proceeding the fasting and penance before Easter, commemorating Christ's forty-day period in the wilderness. The public drama was an amalgam of ancient Yaqui mysticism and old Spanish Catholicism that would feature a mock-battle between the forces of good and evil.

In front of the Capri Bar, one costumed dancer appeared to be a good guy because he was clothed in white—although his human face was hidden behind a menacing horned mask. But a swirl of his white cape exposed black-and-white goat fur on his chest and he was revealed as a half-devil Sacred Clown, spotted with mortal sin. Suspended vertically from a belt around his waist was a skirt of what looked like scores of strings of pearls, but were actually hundreds of small bones. The demon silently went into his ritual dance for the tourists. As the supernatural spirit twisted his hips, his kilt of death gyrated rhythmically back and forth, making an unsettling clacking sound. In his right hand, he waved a large knife.

In the morning, after a night's entertainment, everyone went to three whitewashed one-story cinderblock buildings housing the "Centro de Salud" clinic operated by the Mexican Red Cross. Bob, who wore a white doctor's jacket over his scrubs, had become the only plastic surgeon in the state of Sinaloa. On his chest, he stuck a blue-and-white hospitality name tag, on which he had written: "Dr. Bob."

There was a line of hundreds of people outside, many

of whom had come from remote mountain villages to see the American doctors. They ranged in age from newborn children to a 115-year-old woman who wanted a growth removed so she could get married again. When the clinic opened, the people patiently filed in, filling the waiting room and lining the white walls, until it was their turn to enter one of the small examination rooms formed by orange curtains.

Bob hung his baseball cap on the wall and went to work. Some of the people in line had not seen a doctor in fifteen years. Bob saw a young boy with a cleft palate, a birth defect that disfigured his otherwise angelic face. Because he spoke fluent Spanish, Bob could talk to the worried mother and the child, reassuring them that the child would be all right. Bob held the boy's x-rays up to the window to catch the early morning sun, because there was no light box. Cleft palates split the gums, lip and face and could cause abnormal teeth, difficulty breathing, eating and chewing, ear infections, and even hearing loss. After the series of corrective surgeries to fix cleft palates, children were able to eat, drink and breathe normally for the first time in their lives.

Bob was told by a local doctor that a large part of the population in El Fuerte were dirt-poor Yaqui Indians, whose superstitious beliefs held that such deformities meant the child was inhabited by a devil. Kids born with cleft palates were stigmatized as pariahs, and could not attend school or church.

Bob gently palpated the affected area he was about to operate on. He smiled at his young patient and told him that he was going to be fine. The boy managed a brave smile back. Bob examined the other patients scheduled for surgery and then began. Bob liked the idea that his operations would be seen as an exorcism—as cutting the devil out of his patients with a knife.

Many times, Bob's skill prevented the amputation of a child's limb. When he was done, tearful parents would thank him for saving their child. To them, Bob had not just corrected a deforming condition—he had transformed their children from cursed outcasts into human beings. He had not saved them from death—but from an unhappy and blighted life.

"Finito—es todo," Bob would say, with a smile, to a child when he had finished. Over and over, Bob heard the word "Gracias, gracias."

"You are like saviors to us," the mayor told the doctors.

Rather than suing them for malpractice, their patients blessed them and prayed for them. It also felt good when money did not come between doctor and patient. As they walked around El Fuerte, they were treated like gods. Parents with tears in their eyes would hug them for saving their children. Bob and his companions were invited into the people's homes and offered food and drink and comfort.

"God will reward you every day," one thankful woman told them.

The trip had a major effect on Bob and he resolved to be a part of the mission of mercy, and a part of the lives of the people of El Fuerte, for as long as he could. He became a tireless organizer of the group and went on virtually every trip.

"The patients are truly appreciative for what you do," Bob said later to a reporter he invited along on another trip. "It's totally different at home.

"It takes half an hour or forty-five minutes out of my life. If I can do that a few times a year and make a change in somebody else's life, it's the least I can do."

CHAPTER 26

WIFE HUNTING

BOB and Stephanie began having problems beyond his wanting to get married and have kids while she was not ready. In 1993, their arguments became frequent. Bob had become very possessive and would sometimes go into a sudden fit of rage. The incidents frightened Stephanie. Parting seemed one obvious solution but Bob told Stephanie that he was very much in love with her. She suggested that they undergo therapy to work things out but Bob was reluctant.

"I went to counseling with Gail," said Bob, shaking his head. "It didn't work. It didn't help me."

They did enter counseling together but Bob was right—it didn't work. They continued to quarrel. Stephanie was now concerned about how much Bob would be hurt when she told him she wanted to break it off. Finally, she made up her mind. Just before departing for a scheduled professional trip, she told Bob of her decision.

"Don't be here when I get back," she said.

Bob was upset by the end of his relationship with Stephanie—which had lasted three and a half years, only about a year less than his relationship with Gail. He began socializing and dating regularly, in addition to his flying and skiing and trips to Mexico. He was seen around town, squiring dates and driving his sports car that had a "NIPNTUCK" license plate. Bob also had a four-wheel-drive SUV, with an almost identical license plate: "NIPNTRUK." To some, it seemed that Bob was living the frenetic life of a playboy—but that wasn't the whole story. He was having fun and engaged in an active search for beautiful, intelligent women, but he was no longer trying to be a swinger. He was intent on finding a beautiful professional woman to marry and have children with.

Over the next two years, Bob would date many women—even a stunning Las Vegas showgirl. But Bob wasn't like one *bon vivant* doctor in town, who performed breast enlargements on showgirls, attended their shows and dated them. With the exception of the dancer, Bob's friends thought he fell in love with every woman he dated. He actually got engaged to at least three of them. He became a good customer at his local jewelry store, who re-set a diamond several times, so he could offer different rings to different women.

"Who's Bob marrying this week?" one of his friends joked.

Fred Goodman knew Bob had been married before and just assumed he was divorced. When Fred introduced Bob to other physicians, they sometimes talked to him later about his new friend.

"Isn't he strange?" one asked.

"He's an oddball, isn't he?" said another.

When Fred's wife *Fiona first met Bob, he seemed like a low-key kind of guy—but one with a quiet intensity, whose eyes gazed unblinkingly at whomever he was speaking to. Fiona was not put off by Bob's eyes. She thought they indicated deep interest and sincerity. But she wanted to tell him to tuck in his shirt and comb his hair. Once she knew about his accomplishments, she realized Bobby was probably a genius. At one point, she introduced him to her sister and they dated a few times.

When Fiona gave birth to her second daughter, Bob came to the hospital room every day. He held the baby and cooed gently to her. Bob would come over to the house with bags of food, including some exotic delicacies. He would grab a chef's knife and begin slicing, dicing and chopping to create a terrific meal—there was nothing Bob could not do with a knife. After dinner, he would play with the girls and have a great time. It was obvious he loved children and wanted a family.

Once, when one of the girls fell and suffered a small cut on her chin, Bob insisted on cleaning and dressing the wound himself. Fiona even let Bob take a knife to her when she needed surgery. He also operated on her father-in-law. His professional life was prospering. More and more physicians in the Las Vegas medical community were trusting Bob with their family members—the ultimate compliment from a professional associate.

*Susie Cielo was another cute and smart young woman—but not a professional—and Bob asked her to marry him. One night, she brought him home to meet her parents and Susie's dad had a man-to-man chat with the doctor who wanted to marry his little girl after a short courtship.

"So, a nice, Jewish doctor like you, how is it you were never married?" he said with a friendly smile.

"I was," said Bob, a bit uncomfortably.

Of course, the dad asked how the marriage ended.

"She went out and she never came back," Bob replied.

Susie's parents were taken aback by Bob's story. Something seemed to be missing. They got weird vibes from Bob and expressed their disapproval to their daughter. Susie decided that Bob was trying to make marriage happen too quickly and that he wasn't so much in love with her as in love with the idea of getting married. They soon agreed that each disliked certain things about the other, and parted company.

At the beginning of 1995, Carole Gordon, a pretty, brown-haired clinical psychologist, went to a hockey game with a girlfriend, also in health care, *Ariel Cohen. There were a lot of men at hockey games and Carole, a single mom, noticed a tall, dark, handsome man sitting next to her. They began to chat and Carole was interested—until she found out the guy was a mortician. She turned to her girlfriend and whispered in her ear. "Everyone I met is a mortician or like a mortician," she complained, in a tone that said she despaired of ever meeting a good man.

Ariel told her friend that she knew a doctor whom she had dated a few times—a brilliant plastic surgeon, who was

also tall, dark and handsome. His name was Bob Bierenbaum and he flew his own plane, played guitar, was a gourmet chef, scuba diver, skier and flew down to Mexico to
operate on poor children. Ariel's tone made it seem like
there should have been a "but" in the sentence.

"So?"

Ariel said Bob seemed to be great but there was something off about him, although she couldn't give it a name.
They were not clicking. Carole realized she had already met
Bob at a bar mitzvah. She remembered that he was very
friendly and said he wanted to get married before he was
forty—which was that year.

"Well, I want to meet him—give him my name," Carole
said.

"You know the girl doesn't like you when she sets you
up with her friend," Bob told Carole when he called her
later.

They chatted and Bob turned on the charm, uttering a
romantic phrase in another language. Carole asked Bob if
he was bilingual.

"Actually, I speak eleven languages," Bob said.

They made a date to meet and have dinner at an Indian
restaurant. The food was great and Bob was a lot of fun
but Carole kept wondering if Bob was too good to be true.
After dinner, they went back to Bob's place, a slickly-
decorated home in the Pecole Ranch section. The living
room displayed Bob's impressive stereo and video equipment and the kitchen featured an array of gleaming professional devices and cookware. But upstairs, on the way to
Bob's bedroom, Carole noticed that several rooms were
crowded with unopened boxes, as if he had not finished
unpacking since he had moved in. She asked, and Bob said
he had been in the home for two years.

After they made love, Carole told Bob about her baggage and hoped he would tell her about his. She spoke
about her 9-year-old son and her work as a clinical psychologist. Then she asked Bob if he had ever been married
before. She had no idea about his background. Bob hesi-

tated and then said he had been married before and let it go at that.

If Gail had not vanished a full decade earlier, she would have become a clinical psychologist like Carole. If Gail had had a child, the kid would have been the same age as Carole's boy. In fact, Carole was a slender brunette—just like Gail—but there the resemblance ended. Carole pressed Bob, asking him about his first marriage.

"I don't want to talk about it," Bob said.

His abrupt rebuff startled Carole. After a long silence, she decided to prod Bob with a joke. "What'd you do— kill her?" she chuckled.

Bob's eyes widened and he turned bright red. He was obviously stunned by the question.

"What do you know?" Bob demanded. "What do you know?"

Of course, Carole didn't know anything—she thought she had made a joke. Bob's response made Carole very uneasy. After several minutes of denying that anyone had told her anything, Bob settled down and told her the story. He begged her not to tell anyone about his secret. Carole realized that Bob had come to Las Vegas to put his past behind him and she had accidentally asked the one question that pushed his hot button. She agreed to keep her mouth shut. Of course, she told her mother. Later, she would tell others

Carole was not scared off by the odd incident and dated Bob for six months. They had a very passionate relationship and a lot of fun. At first, Bob was very romantic and sweet but she later had occasion to see a display of his uptight temper.

Cleaning up after one of Bob's yummy gourmet meals, Carole accidentally broke a glass while unloading the dishwasher. Bob was furious.

"This is one of a set and I cannot replace it!" Bob snapped.

Carole could not believe how bent out of shape he was

over a glass. She pulled eight dollars out of her purse and handed it to Bob.

"Here, Bob—happy now?"

Later, when Carole mentioned his temper, Bob smiled and said that was nothing.

"My temper used to be much worse," he told her.

Bob dumped Carole in July 1995. She was very hurt when he coldly announced that he had never dated a single mother before and he didn't want to be involved with one. It was obvious Bob wanted to have a family but didn't care enough for Carole to embrace her son as his own.

Bob then became engaged to *Ronnie Denver, a pretty, elegant 25-year-old with short, straight dark hair. The young couple broke up after a weekend trip with *Dr. Stan Holmes, another flying physician, and his wife *Stacy. Bob went to meet his fiancée's parents during the trip and the meeting did not go well.

"The trip turned out to be a good thing." Bob said, making it clear that he was breaking it off with his fiancée because of something he claimed he did not like about her family. He declined to elaborate and the flight back to Vegas was a very long awkward silence.

Stacy had felt that Bob was trying a little too hard to make it work because he very much wanted to marry, settle down and have children—almost as if it didn't matter with whom he did it. What was his hurry? she wondered.

After Bob broke up with her, Carole met Ariel Cohen for dinner at a trendy restaurant in Las Vegas called the Mayflower. Ariel wondered aloud why Bob, a right-winger who supported a conservative local senator, didn't run for office himself.

"Skeletons in his closet," Carole replied. "Did you know he'd been married?"

"No!"

Carole told the woman who had introduced her to Bob about the skeleton in his closet—and that her name was Gail.

"Oh, my God, oh, my God," Ariel repeated over and over, as she listened.

That night, Ariel told her boyfriend *Peter about Bob and the torso.

"You dated him!" exclaimed Peter, who also knew Bob. "You dated a killer!"

Peter had noticed that Bob would either avoid looking him in the eye, or would look right through him—he now decided—with the intensity and darkness of an obsessional killer. From then on, the couple became a bit obsessed with Bob and could not watch an Alfred Hitchcock movie without discussing him. They began searching for any possible clippings about Gail's disappearance at their local library and on the Internet, but found nothing. When Ariel went to a medical conference that Bob might attend, Peter beeped her, typing the numbers 86776 into the pager—which on a telephone dial spelled TORSO. They passed the juicy tidbit of gossip on to many other members of the Las Vegas medical community. The whispers had begun.

In January 1996, Carole went to Bob's office to pick up a few things she had left at his place. Carole told Bob's office manager about the torso. The office manager told the receptionist. The receptionist called the former office manager, whom Bob had fired, and told her the news. Suddenly, any fit of temper, any strange mood of Bob's was invested with sinister meaning. The fact that, except for magazines, Bob had ordered his staff never to touch the mail now seemed very suspicious. Bob also told them that anyone who accepted a subpoena would also be fired. Most curious of all, the employees agreed, was the fact that Bob refused to advertise for business on a billboard or in a brochure.

"I want nothing in print," Bob had told them.

It sounded to the women like a man on the run, a man hiding from his nefarious past, almost like that old television show *The Fugitive*, about a doctor wrongly convicted of killing his wife. Those women told other women, who told others, and Doctor Bob and the torso became the hottest item of gossip in town.

CHAPTER 27

COLD CASE

MICHAEL tipped the hotel bellhop and looked out the window at the palm trees, the swimming pool, the women in bikinis and the scenic mountains beyond the city skyline.

Psychiatrist Michael Stone wondered what better place there could be for a psychiatric convention than Las Vegas, a city that hosted compulsive and casual gamblers alike and catered to every sexual and physical urge. Walking into the lobby, Michael had spotted row after row of gaunt, leathery old women attached to their slot machines. But Vegas was now also a family resort destination and a real pig-out city, where cheap all-you-can-eat culinary orgies attracted overeaters and bargain hunters.

After unpacking, Michael opened the desk drawer, where he found a Holy Bible and a phone book. He looked in the Yellow Pages under "Psychiatrists" to see if he knew any of the local shrinks.

He didn't recognize any of the names from school or from New York or any other conferences but a name caught his eye on the facing page. There, listed under "Plastic Surgery," was a "Dr. Robert Bierenbaum, MD, FACS."

"So this is where he is," Michael said aloud.

He looked out his window at the resort city again and shook his head—Doctor Bob had committed the perfect crime and was now living the good life in Vegas.

When he returned to New York, Michael again took out the Yellow Pages. He called a private investigator and had a consultation—to see how much it would cost to get a report on Bob. After being told that it would cost at least $5000, Michael let it drop. But it was never totally out of his mind.

In 1993, he was asked to speak at a psychiatric conference in Seattle and he considered what he should discuss.

The most frustrating case of his career was Gail Katz Bierenbaum. Every year, on the anniversary of the day she was
last seen, Michael ran the case over again in his mind,
sometimes taking out the case file that he had saved. It had
become an annual mental ritual with him to note that another year had passed and Bob had still gotten away with
murder.

Whenever Michael thought about Gail, he thought of the
two other women he had tried to persuade to leave their
abusive spouses. Michael had induced them to leave—but
they later went back, to their deaths. Gail, he was convinced, was also dead. Although he was legally blameless,
he regretted that he had been unable to dissuade the women
from their fates. No one was blaming him, but Michael felt
a duty to those women and their families. The ethics of his
profession strongly discouraged disclosing what patients
said in sessions—even if it involved homicidal impulses.
The Bierenbaum case was the point at which Michael de-
parted from his colleagues' insistence that doctor–patient
confidentiality almost always outweighed law. It was unfortunate that doing the right thing as a human being meant
doing the wrong thing as a psychiatrist.

Michael's apartment was filled with books and he col-
lected works from three major areas—the history of Juda-
ism, the history of psychiatry and the history of crime. The
straightforward moral universe of religious faith and the
Ten Commandments, as well as that of crime and punishment, had come into conflict with the more narrow code of
the descendants of Freud. Michael was not much for prayer
but he again remembered a hopeful quote by Oliver Wen-
dell Holmes: "May Justice triumph over Law."

Although it seemed that he could not help the authorities
put Bob Bierenbaum away, Michael felt he might do some
good if he could discuss the case with his colleagues. If it
saved one patient from a similar fate, it would be worth it.

At the symposium in Seattle, Michael presented the
Bierenbaum story—without the real names—as an example
of the difficulty of dealing with such a situation. But, even

though the names were changed, one of his listeners recognized the case.

In the audience, Jane Dunne, an award-winning re-
searcher and author and Gail's former boss and confidante
at Beth Israel Hospital, gasped.

"Oh, my God! He must be talking about Gail Katz!" she
exclaimed.

After Michael's presentation, he was approached by
Jane, who told Michael the real names of his sample case
and told him how she knew. They shared their outrage and
he told her how he had accidentally discovered that Bob
was living in Las Vegas.

Michael listened, as Jane told him, in a confessional
tone, that she thought she had seen blood on the rug in Bob
and Gail's living room after Gail vanished—but had never
told the police because she was afraid. Gail had vanished,
the rug had vanished and she didn't want to be next, she
said. Gail, she explained, had warned her that Bob and his
father were involved in a multi-million-dollar Medicare
fraud scheme. With so much money involved, Jane said she
was terrified to come forward—because that may have been
the real reason Gail was killed. It was the first time Michael
had heard a conspiracy theory of Gail's disappearance.

In addition to all the other provocations, said Jane, Gail
had told Bob—who was staunchly pro-Israel—that she had
also had a secret relationship with another doctor, of Arab
descent. The amazing coincidence was fascinating to Michael—but it was now even more frustrating to think that
there had been real evidence and Bob had still outwitted
the police.

Detective Tom O'Malley was no longer investigating Gail's
disappearance. Very unhappy with the way the department
had handled the case, he had left the Missing Persons Squad
and had been assigned to the 10th Precinct Detective
Squad. In March 1990, Tom busted a man who had stolen
the late Marilyn Monroe's furs. Later in the year, Tom
locked up a man who had made a phony 911 call that re-

sulted in the death of a cop who was rushing to the scene. The successful investigations and arrests and the credit he received were gratifying but, occasionally, something would remind Tom of Gail. The investigation of the chopped-up torso was the responsibility of a Staten Island precinct and it went nowhere. It was technically active in a file somewhere but it was dead—a "cold case."

After Bob moved out of 185 East 85th Street in 1990, Andy Rosenzweig arranged for a full forensic search of the empty apartment before anyone else moved in, which did not require a search warrant. The Crime Scene guys used Luminol to search for traces of blood and dismemberment and found nothing at all. Bob's claim that the cops had searched and found nothing had finally come true.

Five years after the fruitless search, Alayne Katz was back at another open grave in the bleak, leafless garden of Mount Zion Cemetery in Queens, as crows cackled in the cold shadow of the smokestacks. For the third time, she heard a rabbi intone the Jewish prayer for the dead on that same spot—now for her father Manny, who was killed by his brain tumor on February 16th, 1995. When the prayers had stopped, Alayne scooped dirt upon the casket and Manny was laid to rest beside Sylvia and Gail. Alayne now had a husband and children of her own—who had never known their grandmother or their Aunt Gail.

When Alayne heard that Bob had moved away, she hoped that it was her campaign of letter-writing and publicity that had chased him out of town. It gave her pleasure to think that she had made him suffer, even a little, but standing in a frigid cemetery looking at her family in the ground it was of little comfort. Of necessity she had moved on with her own life.

Still, she knew that Bob had killed Gail. And she firmly believed that grief, anguish and despair had lowered her parents' resistance to disease and, finally, their will to live. The police and the prosecutors had tried to do something about it, but Bob was too smart for them. He had gotten away with murder.

In the presence of her parents, part of Alayne felt ashamed that she, the lawyer in the family, had failed to get for them the justice they had prayed for. As a bitter wind froze the tears on her cheeks, it was hard to have faith that their prayers would ever be answered.

CHAPTER 28

WHIRLWIND

JANET extended her hand and Bob took it and shook it firmly.

"Hi, I'm Bob Bierenbaum," he said, loudly enough to be heard over the din of the other partygoers.

Janet Chollet, 33, turned her tanned face up at Bob, smiled and said it was nice to meet him. She brushed away one of her long, brown curls and sipped her drink. The gynecologist was pretty, a bit shy, a California girl, born to French-Canadian parents in Arcadia, and, in the summer of 1995, new in town.

Bob tried to persuade her to go to Mexico with the Flying Doctors. As they discussed the program, Janet was pleased to be speaking to a colleague who devoted so much time and effort to helping people. Janet told Bob she was considering accepting a position with WHO—the World Health Organization. The doctors also shared a distaste for managed health care—a system they felt was bad for both patients and physicians. Janet and Bob exchanged cards and agreed to speak again.

"Hope to see you on our next trip," Bob grinned, as they parted.

Janet's last job before moving to Las Vegas had been a residency in Los Angeles—where she was a consultant to a script writer for the hit network television hospital drama "ER." She and other residents shared expertise and experience with the author, who wrote a show called "Love's Labor Lost," which won an Emmy for writing after it aired in March, 1995.

Janet was proud that she had participated in such a successful writing project and decided she wanted to give writing a try herself some day. The things she had heard and seen in the emergency room and elsewhere were bizarre, interesting and even tragic. She felt there was a lot of raw material for a book.

She had accepted an OBGYN, obstetrics–gynecology, position with a Las Vegas medical group because she believed the practice involved almost no managed health care. She quickly discovered that that was not the case and had a falling out with her new employer, who she felt had misrepresented the situation to her. In December 1995, Janet ended her relationship with her employer and began searching for another position. Ideally, she wanted to find a place where she could make a living as a doctor without the restrictions of managed care. Her brother, who was a doctor in North Dakota, told her of an OBGYN position that would become available the following year at his medical center in the city of Minot.

On her medical license application to the state of North Dakota, in March of 1996, Janet was required to have two licensed doctors sign and attest that she was "a person of good moral character." One of them was her new friend Robert Bierenbaum. Bob also wrote a letter of recommendation that noted that Janet "has a good grasp of her scope of expertise and also of her limitations."

Bob and Janet soon discovered that they had a fondness for sports in common and both loved the outdoors. Bob asked Janet out and on their first date they went rock climbing at the nearby Red Rock Canyon, a beautiful landscape right out of a cowboy movie. They began dating regularly and Bob cooked for Janet and took her flying. Very comfortable with each other, their romance developed quickly. He told her about his first wife, and her disappearance.

Bob was very happy to hear that Janet was also interested in starting a family. Amazingly, Janet's brother told her that his community was desperate to lure a plastic surgeon to the area—who would be assured of a good living and virtually no competition. There were worse things than being a beloved, indispensable small-town doctor. Perhaps it would be like what Bob experienced in Mexico. It was too good to pass up. Minot seemed tailor-made for the new couple. Doctor Bob would become Flying Doctor Bob, piloting his plane almost every day and making a good living.

Bob took the diamond he had offered to two other women and had it set in platinum for luck. After a romantic dinner, he popped the question and Janet said yes. They were both very happy and planned a honeymoon at an exclusive Caribbean resort island that only hosted a dozen pampered guests at a time. After their whirlwind courtship, the couple looked forward to scuba diving on coral reefs and the beginning of a new life together.

Bob's friends threw him a going-away party in Las Vegas. He had just been elected president of the Rotary Club but now he was unable to serve because of the move. Bob assured his friends he would still go to El Fuerte from his new home. Ralph Carl Rohay was one of those who couldn't imagine why someone like Bob would want to move to North Dakota.

"It's a money thing," Bob explained, detailing how managed care was strangling medicine. Also, Bob knew rumors had been circulating about him and Gail in the Las Vegas medical community.

"It's too fast, Bobby," Fiona Goodman scolded. "You can't meet a girl and become engaged in three months."

"Well, why not?" Bob asked.

"It's too soon," the older woman repeated slowly, with a smile, as if to a child.

It wasn't too soon when you were in love, Bob replied.

"How are you going to take a big city kid like you away to a small town?" asked Stacy Holmes. "What's your life going to be like?"

"Well, I'll give it a try. I'll be the only doctor and my practice will build."

Laughing, Fred Goodman tried another argument: "Bob, you're going to freeze your nuts off out there!"

"Yeah," Bob agreed, with a chuckle. "But I'm going to be happy."

Looking at a marriage license application, Bob realized he would need proof that he was no longer married—which

meant proof of Gail's death—to wed. He called Scott
Greenfield in New York, who congratulated him. Scott obtained a copy of the death certificate and mailed it to Bob.
Janet's parents were dead, so the couple agreed to marry
in New York so that Bob's parents and sister could attend
the wedding.

When Gail's death certificate arrived by mail one week
before the wedding, Janet opened it. She scanned the document and noticed that the "CAUSE OF DEATH" box had
been filled in with just two words: "UNKNOWN (Homicide)."

Homicide? Bob had never mentioned that his first wife
had been murdered. Janet freaked out. She was a physician
and knew authorities would not have made such a determination without some evidence of murder—which Bob
had never mentioned to her. Why? She screamed at Bob
and demanded to know what was going on. His initial response did nothing to calm her.

Bob, who had never before seen the document, tried to
explain about the torso but the description of a surgically-
disarticulated body just upset Janet more. She immediately
had second thoughts about the marriage. It wasn't just a
matter of how Gail had died—and who had killed her—it
was also a matter of trust. Janet wondered if she really
knew Bob as well as she thought she did. How could she
marry a man she could not trust? Finally, Janet left.

"I need to take some time" to think, she said, as she
walked out the door.

Bob called Scott in New York.

"What can I do?" asked Bob, who suggested Scott speak
to Janet.

"I can't explain what it says," said Scott. "I can't make
it go away."

He suggested Bob sit down and tell Janet everything and
hope for the best. Bob called his former girlfriend, Carole
Gordon, to ask for advice, even though he had just dumped
her in a very cold and hurtful way, an action that was either
very naïve or very strange.

"If you'd get comfortable in your own skin, you wouldn't even need to marry Janet. You hardly know her. She's not Jewish and—North Dakota? For a gourmet cook who speaks so many languages? Please," Carole said, sarcastically drawing out the last word.

Bob ignored Carole's advice. He pleaded with Janet, who listened to his story. When he was done, Janet believed Bob and even understood why his experience had made him so cautious about revealing his past. They embraced, made up and resumed planning the wedding.

They were married in Ithaca, New York, on June 23rd, 1996, a warm, sunny day. Janet wore a white wedding gown and a white pillbox hat, with a veil. Because it was an out-of-town event, there were fewer than a dozen guests at the ceremony, including Bob's family and Janet's brother.

The low-key arrangements had the added advantage that Gail's death certificate, which had to be filed with the marriage license, did not become part of the public record in Las Vegas, or in Bob and Janet's new home of Minot, where it might do damage. It would remain in New York State. Also, the ceremony was held upstate—rather than in Manhattan or New Jersey, where it might have attracted unwanted attention from someone like Alayne Katz.

Bob's plan to live happily ever after was back on track and, at least in New York, he was still keeping a low profile.

CHAPTER 29

MAGIC CITY

BOB reached out and gently pressed the mole on the stranger's face with his finger, without first introducing himself or asking permission.

The husky man in work clothes with the mole was startled. In Minot, North Dakota, men did not touch other men—especially strangers.

"Hey, buddy, don't touch me," he said, recoiling from Bob's probing.

The man in the dark Italian suit quickly introduced himself and explained that he was the new plastic surgeon in town and he was simply checking the mole to make sure it was not cancerous—and it was not. No charge. The exchange ended with the man thanking Bob—but thinking he had just met a strange man, one who did not fit in, and stood out in the remote, rural town of 35,000 souls like a tuxedo at a taffy-pull.

It was not the only such encounter and soon the little burg was buzzing with anecdotes about the quick-walking, quick-talking doctor with the bullet eyes and a city-dweller's disregard for the personal space of others.

"That guy is nothing but strange," one local said to another after meeting Doctor Bob.

Some residents felt better about Bob when they heard he was from New York, as if all New Yorkers were like that. They also liked his casual manner and the fact that, for the first time in their lives, they were on a first-name basis with a doctor. The more they heard about him and his charity work and the way he put himself out for his patients, the more they liked him.

Others continued to think he was weird. But in a harsh and un-peopled landscape like Minot—which rhymes with why-not—people accepted newcomers and helped each other.

Even though the population density of the state was just two people per square mile, the little city had its own Minot International Airport because of the US Air Force base 13 miles north of town. The base was home for decades to a Strategic Air Command wing of B-52 nuclear attack bombers. Concealed among the far-flung wheat fields outside town were the hidden underground silos that housed America's Intercontinental Ballistic Missiles—the unused weapons of Armageddon.

Another New Yorker by the name of David Berkowitz had spent some of his time in the Air Force at the Minot base many years earlier. The carcasses of horribly mutilated animals had mysteriously appeared around town at the time. The puzzled residents did not know they had a killer in their midst until years later—when Berkowitz was arrested in New York for the "Son of Sam" slayings and the press came to Minot to talk about his sadistic habits.

Bob was happy to escape managed care in Las Vegas and was not unhappy to leave behind the dark rumors that had started circulating there about him and his first wife. He was attracted to Minot because of the unique opportunity and because it had the lowest percentage of managed care patients in the nation. That promised a better living and less interference from outside care managers and insurance companies. In many ways, North Dakota was a perfect state and they were moving from Sin City to Sinless City. The newlyweds, freshly tanned from their honeymoon on an exclusive Caribbean island resort, also had high hopes that the medical center would eventually become another Mayo Clinic, attracting the best physicians and researchers.

Minot was called "Magic City" because of its quick growth from the plains, after it sprouted on the route of the Great Northern Railway in 1887. Minot was originally popular for its brothels and saloons, which faded away as clean-cut homesteaders and sodbusters of Scandanavian stock built churches and schools and plowed a living out of the earth with wheat and barley and other crops. In the 1920s, the middle-of-nowhere spot was convenient for bootleggers running booze in from Canada to cities in the Midwest. At the end of the Twentieth Century, a strong local rumor had it that Minot was so small and so removed that the federal government used it as a secret relocation spot to conceal folks in the Witness Protection Program.

In other words, Minot was one of the best places in America to hide. The "Magic City" was an ideal spot to disappear.

Bob, like those who were born there, loved several things about Minot that distinguished it from the rest of the United States. It was quiet. The air was clean. The folks were warm and friendly and there were few strangers because everybody knew almost everybody else. There was no rush hour and no traffic jams—ever—even in the five-block downtown area that had a jail, a courthouse, a post office and two hospitals. In 1996, North Dakota had the lowest rate of violent crime in the U.S., which meant that some people forgot to lock their doors—a luxury of security only remembered elsewhere in the country by senior citizens.

Of course, like everything else in life, the rewards had a price.

In the winter, the clean air was chilled way below zero, which froze solid the contents of your nose with one painful inhalation. Entertainment and diversion, not to mention human company and conversation, could sometimes be hard to come by. Living in a town where everybody knew you also meant everyone knew your business—good or bad. No one complained about the lack of traffic jams but car batteries had to be warmed by electric blanket or taken indoors to avoid freezing in the sub-zero temperatures.

As in Las Vegas, some doctors who sought out Minot were rumored to be fleeing lawsuits or other problems. But Bob's medical record was impressive and spotless. Bob thought Minot was great. He loved the wide open spaces, even the tumbleweeds that blew on the small "downtown" streets. Janet drove a new, black Saab and Bob drove his Datsun 280Z sportscar with the "NIPNTUK" license plate. On the weekends, he drove his old, cherry-red Jeep Cherokee with the "NIPNTRUK" plates. When Bob lived in the Pecole Ranch section of Las Vegas, his rush-hour trip to his office took just ten minutes—a vast improvement over New York traffic. In the "Micropolitan Area" of Minot, his drive to the hospital took all of 90 seconds. He could drive anywhere in town in seven minutes.

Bob and Janet bought a large, $225,000 luxury one-bedroom condominium, very expensive for Minot. The home featured dark natural wood flooring, French doors, and a large deck with a lovely view of the large green lawn and the city on the flat horizon beyond. The right wall of the living room held Bob's expensive stereo equipment, CDs and hundreds of movies on laser discs that they viewed on a huge 52-inch television, a wedding gift from his parents. Bob still loved cooking and whipped up fresh bagels and gourmet meals at home.

Bob joined the local Rotary Club and made plans for future trips to Mexico, recruiting colleagues to accompany him. Janet had been raised a Catholic but Bob attended synagogue on the high holy days and attended a Passover seder at the home of Harriet Epstein and her doctor husband, who were originally from Queens, New York. For a time, Harriet ran the only bagel shop in town. After she closed, Bob was the only source of fresh bagels in Minot.

Janet and Bob worked at Trinity Hospital, a 250-bed facility associated with the University of North Dakota School of Medicine. Janet's physician brother Hillary Chollet also practiced at the hospital. His partner was Dr. Lee Trotter, who became Bob's closest friend in Minot. Bob first met Lee at the Minot Airport. They were both pilots and liked to talk about flying. Lee was a handsome guy with neatly-trimmed, sandy brown hair and matching mustache. When he first met Bob, whose unruly, curly hair flowed over his collar, Lee had no idea he was a surgeon.

They met again at a welcome dinner the hospital threw for Bob and Janet. Like Bob, Lee, a Mormon, neither smoked cigarettes nor drank alcohol. Hailing from sunny California, Lee had relocated to Minot after serving a hitch as an Air Force physician at the Minot Air Base. He and his wife Stephanie had three boys and two girls. Lee soon learned that Bob was a good surgeon. Bob was demanding in the operating room, as every surgeon was, but he was not a yeller or a thrower of sponges. The worst temper Lee saw Bob display in an operating theater was to employ sarcasm and tell his team, "Let's pretend we've done this before." But Bob, who assisted the hospital in trouble-shooting its mainframe computer, could be overbearing outside the hospital. Lee did not usually take it personally but many did.

Bob even made the Martha Stewart–type homemakers in town feel insecure because he could make meals that were better than any restaurant in the state. Besides his bagels, he made bread, soups, pizza and sushi—and other more exotic stuff—from scratch, and did so on a daily basis. He ordered many ingredients by mail from out of town, because the local culinary resources were limited.

Bob, who carried his laptop computer everywhere, was some kind of genius, and, like many geniuses, he had his eccentricities. Bob's Italian suit had dog hair on it from his new yellow Labrador named Gracie but he didn't seem to notice it. He often needed to be told to straighten his tie or to brush the canine fur off his dress shirt. Bob loved Gracie, and took her with him everywhere he could. Despite her tendency to misbehave, he did not seem to notice.

Bob and Lee and their wives socialized often and sometimes flew to Minneapolis or Las Vegas for a weekend. When Lee's wife needed gynecological care, she went to Janet. Lee thought Janet often came off as stone cold in social situations, but like Bob, she had "good hands" in the operating room.

Bob seemed dedicated to taking care of his patients and did it tirelessly. Most of his patients loved him.

Doctors learn a phrase in medical school that reminds them to stay alert for unlikely maladies that have ordinary symptoms: "Sometimes, when you hear hoofbeats, it's zebras."

Once, for Bob and his colleagues at Trinity, it was a tiger. A boy attending the state fair was attacked and mauled by a Bengal tiger, who slashed the youth's face near his eyes. Bob performed the delicate plastic surgery to carefully close the facial lacerations so that minimal scarring would result.

But, more commonly during the long winters, it was snowblowers that mauled people. After four Minot citizens lost fingers and parts of hands to snowblower blades, Bob made an appeal for safety in the local paper and cautioned operators to turn the power off before attempting to clear a jammed machine.

Lee and Bob gave a talk at Minot High School about medical careers and Bob mentioned his work in Mexico and the fact that he spoke fluent Spanish.

"I speak eight or ten other languages," Bob announced.

During a question-and-answer period, a student who was born in Samoa in the South Pacific, rose and asked Bob a question in his native language—hoping to trip him up.

"You think you can speak a lot of languages but you don't know what I'm saying," he said in his language, with a triumphant grin.

"I differ with you," Bob replied in the same language, also smiling. "I do know what you're saying—but you could be more polite."

"What was that all about?" Lee asked.

He translated the exchange and Lee was once again impressed with his friend.

Bob gave free flying lessons to his friends and colleagues and worked with the Civil Air Patrol. He was the only multi-engine instructor in the state.

Bob was always sending flowers to Janet when he realized he had done something insensitive, such as going flying and forgetting to call her. Once, Bob even sent flow-

ers to Lee's wife in a similar situation—and signed Lee's
name to the bouquet.

One weekend, Lee borrowed some "enroute" aviation
maps and approach plates used for landing at a particular
airport from Bob, on the condition that he replace them in
Bob's plane when he was done. Tired from his flight, Lee
forgot to return the navigational materials and went home.
Lee went to sleep—but was awakened at five in the morning by the telephone.

"Where's my approach plates?" Bob's angry voice demanded.

Bob was at the airport, about to take off and had noticed
he did not have what he needed. A sleepy Lee apologized
and said he had simply forgot.

"Well, fine—I'll just get some new ones!" Bob huffed.

"No, Bob, I'll be there in five minutes or less," Lee
protested.

When Lee arrived, Bob was waiting impatiently. He was
steaming mad. When Lee handed him the maps, Bob did
not say thank you. He stuck his face so close to Lee their
noses were almost touching and he screamed: "What kind
of person would take these and not return them? I could
have been up in the air and looked for them!"

Bob's implication was obvious—if he hadn't looked for
the maps before takeoff he might have gone astray or been
killed and it would all have been Lee's fault. Lee took the
tongue-lashing, which lasted several minutes, but felt it was
way out of proportion. Until then, he had not been the object of another of Bob's talents—the ability to make another person, even a very educated, accomplished person,
feel like an ant.

For the first time, Lee realized that Bob was governed
only by himself. He wasn't concerned about what other
people felt about him and he did pretty much whatever he
wanted to do. Bob was good at talking other people into
doing all kinds of things, but Lee couldn't remember ever
talking Bob into anything he did not want to do. He was
also very opinionated, as was Janet, and they seemed to

have a problem realizing their effect on other people.

When a nurse at the hospital proudly brought in a batch of her homemade fudge, Bob tasted a piece, as if he were a judge in a fudge-tasting contest, and told her she needed to add certain ingredients that would "make your fudge a bit better."

"Well, my fudge is just fine, thank you," the nurse replied.

The fudge incident was minor but, for Lee, it illustrated Bob's interpersonal blind spot—he was just trying to help her but she was insulted and felt he was an overbearing showoff. Other people took some of Bob's inconsiderate comments even more personally. When Bob was introduced to a new colleague, a young, attractive woman doctor, he sized her up with a gimlet eye and, as if she were a patient, and told her: "I was just noticing that your eyes are not symmetrical," explaining that it could be easily corrected by plastic surgery.

The pretty physician did not react well to Bob's unsolicited opinion.

"Bob, you can't be saying that kind of stuff," Lee told him later. "You really hurt her feelings."

The plastic surgeon assumed a colleague would realize that his job was to correct human imperfection with a knife. He fixed broken bodies and improved upon nature. Bob was genuinely amazed that anyone could be offended by the simple information that her face was crooked.

CHAPTER 30

BREAST MAN

BOB, a gleaming scalpel in his hand, looked down on the table, at the torso of a thin young woman, her small breasts smeared with red liquid.

The patient's head and her raised arms were shielded by green surgical sheets. She was also covered with draping below the ribcage. Her chest area was exposed in the brilliant illumination of the large overhead lamp, and her breasts had been swabbed with red Betadine disinfectant. The patient's sternum rose and fell gently, as she breathed slowly in and out. Under each breast, just above the crease, was a short, curved black line drawn there with an indelible marker that indicated where the incisions would be made. Bob scanned the monitors to check his patient's vital signs. She was fully under the sedation and all her signs were normal. Bob was wearing two pairs of surgical gloves and was dressed in blue OR scrubs, including a cap and mask. Upbeat jazz music filled the room and Bob was ready to begin his first augmentation mammaplasty—breast enlargement—of the day.

Other surgeons worked to reduce patient mortality—but accepted it. Bob did not. After Gail disappeared, Bob could not handle death and dropped out of cardiology. In North Dakota, the women to whom Bob gave bigger boobs never died, or even became sick. The patients, and even their husbands and boyfriends, were very happy with the outcome. He also reconstructed breasts for women who had undergone radical breast surgery to remove cancer and performed liposuction and breast reduction for women with painfully heavy breasts—but most of his work was lucrative breast augmentation.

In the slang of his profession, Bob had become a "Breast Man."

He still did work at the hospital Emergency Room—
such as hand reconstruction and other emergency operations—but, in elective surgery, the potential for bad results
and malpractice actions was low. Of course, patients sometimes filed frivolous lawsuits. Bob had seen it happen to
other doctors and he did everything he could to avoid becoming a victim himself. He was finally making a good
living but he was not on the cutting edge of medicine, as
many of his family and friends assumed he would be. Lee
noticed that his friend Bob catered to a very select clientele
because he seemed somewhat paralyzed professionally by
the legal aspects of being sued—even though he had not
been a target of a malpractice claim. Bob did everything
he could to reduce the chances of a bad outcome, which
meant he sometimes refused cases where patients were frail,
had complications or smoked. Lee assumed it was all part
of Bob's fear of litigation. He did not know about Gail's
disappearance and Bob's subsequent aversion to losing patients.

Janet, who was having second thoughts about her profession, shared Bob's fear of lawsuits and also tried to reduce her chances of a bad outcome. As a gynecologist, she
gave internal exams and breast examinations and delivered
babies, as well as performed surgery, such as caesarian section and hysterectomies.

Bob was pleased when his smiling face appeared over a
quiche Lorraine in the local paper next to an article about
his hobby of gourmet cooking. He remained active in conservative politics and a photo of Bob and Congressman
Newt Gingrich graced Bob's office. He continued his trips
to El Fuerte, Mexico which were covered in the local paper
after Bob alerted them to the charity medical trips.

But by the time Janet and Bob became settled the next
year, everything changed.

For several years, Janet had become more and more dis-
illusioned with medicine because of managed care, malpractice risks, and other issues. She had a dispute with a

colleague in Las Vegas and left the city because a "geographical clause" in her contract forbade her from practicing there if she left the group. In Minot, she had another dispute with colleagues and it all came to a head. Janet became concerned about low staffing at the medical center and felt it endangered some of her patients. She had a falling out with the administration over the issue. Lee Trotter thought that several male gynecologists in the area felt threatened by Janet because she was a woman and they were losing patients to her.

The net result was that Janet felt embittered and frozen out by her colleagues. She experienced a career crisis and decided to quit medicine. She told Bob of her decision and he supported her. Janet had always wanted to try her hand at the law and writing so she enrolled in law school at the University of North Dakota at Grand Forks and thought she would use her spare time to begin work on a novel based on her medical experience. Like Bob, Janet couldn't help being an over-achiever.

Janet's decision caused big changes in their lives. Grand Forks, a slightly larger town, was more than two hundred miles away from Minot. She would have to live there while she attended classes at the university. They flew to Grand Forks to go house hunting and Bob also applied to work at a hospital there. The plan was for Bob to continue working in Minot and commute to Grand Forks until he could find full-time employment there. Janet would stay in Grand Forks, attend law school and work on her book.

Janet's wishes to go to law school and to write were about to come true. Bob also had a wish he wanted granted. The couple agreed that while Bob supported them, Janet would have three jobs—school, writing and getting pregnant with their first child.

CHAPTER 31

FLESH MANAGEMENT

DOUG was standing next to the natural gas pipeline ditch in a remote stretch of prairie, stamping his work boots on the frozen dirt to warm his feet. His breath, exhaled from under the raised visor of his welding mask, frosted in the sub-zero air. He was waiting for the operator of the D9 crane vehicle to hoist another nine-ton section of pipe into the hole, so he could weld the three-foot-diameter tube onto the end of the last one.

Doug Willenbring suddenly remembered the date and realized it was twelve years to the day that his two best friends had been killed in a car accident. He glanced at his watch and noticed it was even the same time of day that they'd died. As he stood between the ditch and the pipe mover, he could see their smiling faces in his mind. For some reason, he began moving closer to the crane.

That was when the operator lifted the section, which weighed more than two cars, into the air. As the huge pipe swung over Doug's head, it tipped over and fell to the ground with a bomb-like boom. It came at him like a steam-roller. Doug didn't see it coming but he sure felt it roll over his legs and pin him to the back of the crane. He could feel bones snap painfully through his legs, thigh and pelvis. It only took a few seconds.

He was still alive. That was the good news. The bad news was he was hurt bad and trapped in a cramped spot on the cold ground with what felt like the whole world on top of him. His co-workers quickly realized that if they moved the crane, the pipe would crush him because of the incline. They could not move the pipe uphill by sheer man-power, so they had to get an ambulance and another piece of heavy equipment to the scene before they could get Doug out.

"What did I do to deserve this?" Doug wondered, as pain shot through his body.

He was 33 years old and working part-time on getting his college degree. His co-workers explained the situation to him—help was on the way, but he had to wait.

"I feel like a cat with no back legs," Doug joked.

His friends laughed and he bantered with them, as if he weren't in great pain, but every minute that went by seemed to stretch out like an endless pipeline. Although they didn't tell him, they did not intend to move the weight off Doug until the paramedics were there. They did not know how badly injured he was. It was possible he was all crushed and ripped up and that the only thing that was preventing Doug from bleeding to death was the weight on him, acting like a tourniquet. It was possible that when he was freed he would quickly bleed out and die.

Doug asked the time and was alert enough to know that it had already been half an hour, which seemed like half a lifetime he had been in his little hole under the cold rolling pin.

"Where's the ambulance?" Doug asked.

"It's coming, Doug."

"What are they—on dinner break or what?"

The other workmen laughed again and kidded him. Doug's crew hid their feelings and their fears: they were probably talking to a very brave dead man.

As he waited and waited, Doug went deeper into shock and passed out. He lay under the pipe for a full forty-five minutes before it was lifted off him and he was taken away in the ambulance to Trinity Medical Center in Minot, where he lived. The pipe that mashed Doug was later joined, welded and buried. Doug's fight to stay above ground was just beginning.

He was listed in critical condition in the Intensive Care Unit, suffering from a crushed leg and multiple bone fractures, including his tailbone. His pelvis was shattered in six places. Doug was given slim chances for survival and zero chances that he would ever walk again. But he was young and very strong and he refused to give up. He surprised the doctors by surviving the trauma and waking up. He underwent a series of operations over several months that used metal pins to piece his legs back together. But his mangled left thigh swelled up big as a watermelon and developed gangrene. The doctors advised him that amputation would soon be necessary to save his life.

"Doug, I can smell your leg," his stepmother Gaila Willenbring told him. "It smells like a rotting cow."

He began to cry. As he lay in traction in his hospital bed, smelling the rank odor of the festering hematoma, the young man decided he would rather die than lose his limb.

"I'd rather die fast than die slow," he told the doctors, refusing to authorize the amputation.

One of his doctors, Lee Trotter, told him he wanted to bring in another doctor, a friend of his by the name of Doctor Bierenbaum, who was a brilliant physician. If anyone could save his leg it would be him, Lee said. Doug said he'd like to see this smart doc.

Doug liked Bob immediately because he introduced himself by his first name and asked him a lot of questions before examining him very carefully. Bob told him there was a special kind of pump that he could order from New York that could suck fluids out of injured tissue, which might help the gangrene and save the leg. It was just what Doug wanted to hear. Bob ordered the pump and set it up on the leg.

Bob was an expert in techniques of "tissue management" for soft flesh and bony, cartilaginous tissues—which was a technical way of saying Bob knew how to control, treat, manipulate and reconstruct injured human flesh. Bob's calm manner comforted Doug and gave him hope for the first time, like he had finally met a welder who could put him back together.

Bob checked regularly on Doug to monitor his progress. He apologized for not being around on Saturday—when he flew to his new home in Grand Forks to see his wife—but he would appear at Doug's bedside just before midnight on

Sunday night to closely examine the healing flesh, touching it gently with his gloved fingers. The patient loved the fact that Bob seemed to be the only doctor around the hospital at that time of night, and that he sat and answered his questions, no matter how long it took—as if he were his only patient.

The leg healed and Doug felt he had only two people to thank—Lee Trotter and Bob Bierenbaum. Bob had not only saved his leg, he had saved his life. He still had a long row to hoe ahead—skin grafts, physical rehabilitation and Lord knows what, but he would always be grateful to Bob.

Later, when asked if Bob had saved Doug's leg, his stepmother replied: "You betcha. If it wasn't for Doctor Bob, I don't know if Doug would even be alive."

Bob seemed to be in constant motion. After visiting with Doug, Bob checked on a few other sleeping patients before calling it a night. During the week, he would fly wherever he was needed. At the end of the week, he would fly back to Grand Forks to spend the weekend with Janet before starting all over again. Flying Doctor Bob, a man who hated commuting by car, now had a 210-mile commute by air, twice a week, not to mention hundreds of air miles to fly to his far-flung patients.

In Grand Forks, Janet and Bob had paid $124,900 for a large, white split-level four-bedroom home on a quiet street. Several of the rooms were stacked with boxes, some of which had not even been opened since the move from Las Vegas.

Next-door neighbor Dan Sobolik greeted his new neighbors and was surprised to find out they were both doctors. He was immediately struck by Bob's intense eyes, which made his flesh crawl. He tried to carry on a pleasant chat with Bob but all the time he was thinking: "He has weird eyes. This guy is really strange."

Bob soon began to work at the Altru Medical Center in Grand Forks, doing breast surgery. Eventually, as he phased out patients in Minot, Bob spent more and more time in

Grand Forks, where he would drive home at midday, cook a gourmet lunch and prepare the dough for the water bagels that he would cook that night for the next morning's breakfast. Day and night the kitchen smelled great.

Janet was busy with classes at law school but, like Bob, she was driven. In her spare time, she completed chapter after chapter of her book, which featured a woman gynecologist as the main character. First, she called it *Sex* but later she changed the title to *The Anti-Clitoral Conspiracy*.

As Janet would finish a chapter, Bob would edit it, print it out and show it to his colleagues and friends, asking them to read it and tell him what they thought of it. Clearly Bob thought his wife's work was great and he was very proud. Several people who saw the manuscript were shocked by the content—such as a scene involving an emergency room patient with a billiard ball inside her vagina. The unpublished work was a unique, outlandish, satirical novel that centered on a feminist view of the transcendent sexual bliss of female masturbation and orgasm with the aid of an electric vibrator. It also detailed a specific male plot to keep women ignorant of their own bodies and deny them their potential for masturbatory ecstasy.

Needless to say, the subject matter was not for everyone. Some readers were uncomfortable at tongue-in-cheek parts of the book that appeared to advocate surgery on newborn children to equip them with colostomy bags—so the heroine would not have to change diapers. Also disturbing was the suggestion that childbirth could be made more palatable for mothers if the women were able to experience orgasm at the moment of birth—with their child acting as a kind of dildo. The vibrating flesh was vividly described in dry, detailed and technical medical jargon, which seemed to heighten its sexual content.

In Las Vegas, Charlie Vinnik got a copy from Bob. Charlie later sarcastically described the book as "a gynecological disaster. It's supposedly meant to be funny."

In Minot, another reader was also having trouble reading

the fleshy novel—and with what to tell Bob, who was eager
for praise.

"Oh, man, Bob. This is too much," Lee Trotter—the
Mormon—said after completing part of the book. "This is
not what I'm about or what I read."

"Yeah," Bob replied. "But—what do you think?"

Lee did not even know where to begin—it was too
graphic, way over the top. Later, when Bob handed him
subsequent chapters, he declined to read them, despite
Bob's urgings.

"Bob, c'mon—I'm not even interested," Lee said, ending the discussion.

Janet's book, which Bob edited and helped her write,
culminated in a dramatic and bizarre court trial. In one section, the gynecologist heroine announced she had no pity
for any man who perpetrated acts of violence against female victims. Such criminals, she said, were worse than
animals—and should receive the greatest possible
punishment under the law.

CHAPTER 32

HOT CASE

ANDY dialed Alayne Katz's phone number on December 3rd, 1997.

"Hello?"

"Miss Katz? This is Chief Investigator Andy Rosenzweig from the Manhattan DA's office."

"Hello. What can I do for you?"

Alayne did not recognize Andy's name after eleven years. She was a lawyer and had assumed that one of her clients was in trouble with the law.

"We're looking into your sister Gail's case again," he said.

"What do you mean you're looking into it again? What does that mean?"

Alayne was shocked and confused. Andy heard anger in her voice, which was not unusual for a relative in a case of presumed murder without an arrest.

"We'd like to re-open the case—what do you think?" Andy replied.

"You know, I've never been satisfied with the lack of resolution to this," Alayne said.

"Well, we certainly haven't, either," Andy agreed. "It always bothered me—knowing he did it and not mounting a prosecution: I want to try again."

"Do you know they recovered my sister's torso?"

"They what?" Andy asked. It was his turn to be shocked.

"They recovered her torso and we've buried it. I've buried my sister's remains."

"I'm chagrined to tell you I didn't know that," Andy said.

"You didn't know that? How could that happen?" Alayne asked.

"It's a big city," Andy offered. "It's a big system. The

left hand doesn't always know what the right hand is doing."

Alayne told him that DNA testing was not done but that Gail had been identified by x-rays. The Katz family had been told that the finding of the body was of no use to a prosecution. Andy told her he did not think that was true. Then she mentioned that her parents were dead and how Gail's disappearance—and no arrest—had affected them. She ended the conversation by saying she was happy to hear he was back on the case.

"Anything I can do to help, I will," she said.

Alayne hung up the phone. Before she called her husband or her brother, she smiled. The news had come three days before her birthday—she already knew this was the best present she was going to get.

Andy had not told Alayne the real reason the case had been re-opened. It was not because of important new evidence—like a "direct" admission by Bob to someone else that he had killed Gail, or other scientific proof. The office of Manhattan DA Robert Morgenthau had re-opened the Bierenbaum investigation because Andy was retiring and he wanted to lock Bob up before he did. Since twelve years had gone by, it didn't look like any more evidence was going to walk in the door, so the excuse that it was better to wait no longer applied.

He was saddened that Gail's mom and dad were not around to see the re-opening of the case. It strengthened his feeling of personal responsibility.

The news about the torso changed the whole nature of the case. Andy was not happy that NYPD had not informed him about it in 1989. If they had, he would have tried to prosecute the case then. After the phone call, Andy obtained the autopsy results and the record of the subsequent investigation of the torso. He was troubled: The pairing of the torso with Gail's Missing Persons report seemed to be a good piece of detective work but it stopped there. There was no real investigation into who the torso was, just whether it was or was not Gail.

Andy knew that an x-ray ID would not be good enough for an indictment and they couldn't go to trial with so much paper around that doubted the body was Gail. Also, the fact that the torso had only been in the water for a few months—which would apparently clear Bob—seemed to make it impossible to successfully prosecute him for the killing. Andy asked Alayne for permission to exhume her sister's body to obtain tissue samples. Without a strong determination that the remains were Gail, the case was going nowhere. The science of DNA testing had improved greatly in the intervening years and the time had come to try it.

It was also time to back up to the beginning and do it right. Andy had pulled Gail's file from the archives in July 1997, on the twelfth anniversary of her disappearance. He had been working with prosecutors Dan Bibb and Stephen Saracco on another cold case—a double homicide committed twenty-six years earlier, in which the fugitive killer had supposedly died.

Dan Bibb was a big guy. He was 6-foot-6 and weighed 200 pounds. He had neatly-trimmed, sandy brown hair and a matching mustache that crinkled up at the edges when he laughed, smiled or smirked, which was often. He had a deep resonant voice and an air of dignity that served him well in the courtroom. Like Andy, Dan took it personally when a killer walked free.

Dan himself had been the target of a murder plot, in the most serious death threat against an assistant district attorney in more than a decade. In 1991, a murder defendant had hired two hitmen to kill Dan. The mastermind, accused of the execution of a competing drug dealer, decided to bump Dan off because he had shown him disrespect by smirking, raising his eyebrows and rolling his eyes in a sarcastic manner at him in court. The hitmen attended a court hearing so they could see what Dan looked like. He was so tall, he was a great target, easy to pick out in a crowd. Fortunately for Dan, the drug lord gabbed to a cellmate—who was an informer—about the scheme. The informer told the police and Dan put the mastermind away for a long time.

Stephen Saracco, more than a head shorter than Dan, was a good cross-examiner, known for prosecuting "Preppie Killer" Robert Chambers for the strangulation murder of Jennifer Levin in 1986.

Andy had pushed to re-open the search for gunman Frankie Koehler, a small-time hood, because, when he read the file, he noticed there was no proof of his death—just statements from his family and friends that he was dead. It looked like the original investigators just gave up and closed the case because they couldn't find the bad guy. But, with the passage of time, Andy figured that Frankie Koehler might have resumed his life somewhere and maybe resumed some of his old habits. After a lengthy investigation that took Andy and other investigators from coast to coast, they tracked the killer down—living under another name in California and pretending to be one of his own relatives. He was finally locked up, after more than two decades of eluding authorities. What gave him away was that Frankie still celebrated his birthday on the day he was actually born. The arrest received a lot of publicity and Andy, Dan and Stephen were regaled as super-sleuths, operating their own Cold Case Squad and breaking impossible cases.

"When you get finished with this one," Andy had told the ADAs when Koehler pleaded guilty, was sentenced and put behind bars, "I've got another one for you."

After his work on the Koehler case, the prosecutors were ready to listen. Andy dropped the box containing the Bierenbaum's case on Dan's desk.

"I read the file," Dan later told Andy. "I thought he did it."

That was when Andy called Alayne and got the news about the torso. In a way, Gail's case was the opposite of the Koehler case. In the Koehler case they had two dead bodies—but no corpse for the supposedly dead killer. In Gail's case they had no body and they knew their suspect was alive. What was missing was the proof.

The re-opening wasn't exactly a reward to Andy for his good job on the Koehler case, but some in the office saw it that way—as the payoff of a "contract." One person close to the case said the office "opened up the investigation as a going-away present for Andy."

"That was the deal," said another member of the office. "They would do the Bierenbaum case if Andy brought in the double homicide."

But the prosecutors were not ordering an investigation of a man they believed to be innocent as a favor to a colleague. They were bringing an impossible prosecution against a man they believed to be guilty. One wag saw it as a "lose one for the Gipper" situation. The Bierenbaum case, as far as other prosecutors were concerned, was an un-winnable case.

"What, are they crazy?" was a typical response in the office when news of the new investigation got around. No other prosecutors volunteered to try the impossible case with the public watching and even Dan and Stephen would have their doubts as it progressed.

The detectives began re-interviewing the people in New York first—but not Bob's family. The less Bob knew, the better, although it was inevitable he would eventually learn of the renewed investigation. Andy wanted to start the case from the ground up, assuming nothing, because the original investigation had been weak.

Once Alayne realized that it was not new evidence that caused Andy to re-open her sister's case she asked him a question. "What're you retiring soon—and you don't want to leave an open case?"

Andy didn't answer. But later, he announced his impending retirement and admitted to Alayne that that was the only reason the case was re-opened.

In April 1998, Andy and Tommy Pon flew to Las Vegas to investigate Bob's life there—looking to score, not at the craps table, but with good witnesses. They were hoping to find a "direct"—a direct statement that Bob had made to another person that he had killed Gail. They knew that was a long shot, but if Bob had abused other women or had said different things about his past, it could be useful at trial.

They spoke to Carole Gordon. No, Carole said, Bob had never attacked her but she was glad to tell them about Bob's odd reaction to her "What did you do—kill her?" joke.

Andy's ears perked up at the story, which implied Bob's guilt. When they got back to the hotel, he related the tale by phone to Dan and Stephen back in Manhattan—who thought it would play well in front of a jury.

Stephanie told them she had been afraid to break up with Bob but the bottom line was that she eventually did tell him to leave—and he did not choke her to death and dump her out of an airplane. He took his food processor and left. They noted the differing stories Bob told his girlfriends, but as evidence, it was pretty thin. Several people gave accounts of Bob's strangeness or fits of temper but most of Bob's friends and colleagues in Las Vegas couldn't say enough good things about him to the disappointed investigators.

But gossip and rumors about Bob swept through the Las Vegas medical community like a hot desert wind. One wild story had Bob decapitating Gail, who was identified only by a serial number on a silicone breast implant.

One woman called the DA's office in Manhattan and claimed that Dr. Scott Baranoff, Bob's boyhood friend who lived in Vegas, had told her that Bob had confessed the murder to him. But Baranoff completely denied the story and told the investigators that the woman bore a grudge against Bob—who had fired her from her job. Andy and Tommy flew back to New York. Other than Carole Gordon's little anecdote—and the beautiful weather—they had pretty much crapped out.

CHAPTER 33

BLESSED EVENT

BOB arrived in the maternity ward where Janet was undergoing labor and opened a bag filled with hot, fresh bagels that he had just baked at home. The wonderful smell of the steamy bread filled the air, competing with the sterile scent of alcohol and disinfectant. Bob was thoughtful enough to also bring butter and cream cheese to smear on the bagels. The nurses and staff gathered round the food and dug in. There were ooohs and aaahs as they sampled the baked goods and praised Bob's skill as a cook.

On November 6th, 1998, Janet had been in labor for a grueling three days. She was exhausted and Bob was jumping out of his skin because he could not do anything to help her or speed up the birth process. After years of searching for a wife and hoping for a family, it was finally about to happen. But the wait was excruciating. Bob had to do something, so, he went home to shower and bake comfort food for Janet and the staff. The food didn't make Janet's ordeal any easier, but it kept the nervous dad-to-be busy and the doctors and nurses loved it.

When Janet went into full labor at last, Bob scrubbed up, donned blue OR scrubs and a cap and mask—like the other doctors and nurses—and entered the delivery room to observe. The maternity team did their job well and a wailing child emerged and was placed on a receiving table. Bob took a pediatric stethoscope and placed it gently on the pink infant's chest. When he heard the tiny heart beating normally, Bob pronounced her fine. He smiled at Janet and began to cry. He was a father. He had a daughter. He and Janet had brought a little girl into the world, a new life. They had already agreed on her name—Annah.

Later, one of the nurses told Janet that "When the father

cries in the delivery room, we know that the child has been born into a good family."

After they left the hospital, Bob took care of Annah twenty-four hours a day while Janet studied for her upcoming law school finals. Janet actually had to plead with Bob to hire a nanny so he could go back to work, since he was the sole support of the family. Beaming, Bob told Janet that he could give it all up and become a stay-at-home dad, a Mister Mom.

"I've never been this happy before," Bob said.

They agreed that Bob would take care of Annah until Janet's exams were over, when he would resume his practice. Until then, Bob basked in the proud glow of fatherhood, and the joy of caring for the beautiful little girl who was so completely dependent on him. He fed her, changed her, bathed her, cuddled her, sang to her, told her stories and called her "Annah Banana." Finally, Bob seemed to be living happily ever after. An excellent photographer, Bob e-mailed pictures of Annah to friends and family in New York, Las Vegas, and elsewhere.

On the last day of Janet's testing, Bob was in Minot with Annah, when a blizzard moved in. Janet wanted to hold her daughter, but the storm made flying impossible. Bob packed the baby up in the car and drove 210 miles through the blizzard to Grand Forks. Bob plowed into the driveway and carried the little bundle inside to Janet. He handed the baby to his wife and smiled.

"Thank you. She is perfect," said Bob.

Not long after Annah's birth, Andy and Tommy journeyed to Minot, where they interviewed Bob's friends and colleagues. They found even less than they had in Las Vegas, but they did stir things up. The hospital in Minot, without explanation, changed their attitude toward Bob. When his contract came up for renewal, Bob did not ask for a raise—but the hospital asked him to take a salary cut. Instead, Bob sadly made arrangements to leave. First Janet, and then Bob had been forced to leave Minot.

*   *   *

Bob and Janet planned to hire two nannies—a day nanny to take care of Annah while Janet went to law school and Bob practiced medicine, and a sleep-in night nanny. The night nanny was so Bob and Janet could get their sleep and would not have to wake up every few hours to feed and change the baby. They insisted the nanny be a non-smoker. The new parents hired and fired a series of care-givers. Several of the employees felt the couple were rigid perfectionists who "hovered" over them. One of the young women was startled to open her eyes in the middle of the night and find Bob standing over her bed in the dark. When she sat up, Bob left the room. She assumed Bob was just checking on the baby but it gave her the creeps.

Bob was very serious about protecting his family from the dangers of second-hand smoke—or even third-hand smoke. When one babysitter arrived at the Bierenbaum home after spending the weekend with her parents, Bob interrogated her about smoking.

"I can smell smoke on you," he announced.

Another sitter was forced to wash the clothes she was wearing because she had also arrived with the forbidden odor of tobacco on her.

The fifth nanny was Barb Scholler, a perky non-smoker with a cute, blond pixie hairdo, sparkling blue eyes and a friendly smile. Barb fell in love with little Annah, and called her "Sweet Pea."

Barb felt Bob genuinely loved his daughter, who would play happily at his feet while he prepared a gourmet lunch or dinner of strange foreign food. Bob was a dynamo and couldn't sit still. Always eager for feedback on his culinary accomplishments, he would often bring a spoon of the dish-du-jour to Barb's reluctant mouth. Sometimes it would be terrific and sometimes Barb would make a face at the strange tastes. She drew the line at sushi and weird stuff like that, but Bob's famous fresh bagels were wonderful.

In the fall of 1998, the investigators got around to Lee Trotter, who was interviewed at his office by an investigator for the state of North Dakota for almost two hours. Lee was asked if Bob had a volatile personality or if he had ever felt threatened by Bob. Several questions alluded to a first wife, which was news to Lee.

"Was Bob previously married?" Lee asked.

"I'm not able to discuss any information. I can't confirm or deny that," the cop said, mysteriously.

Lee asked if he should be concerned about the physical safety of his family, not to mention all of Bob's patients.

"No, he is not a threat to you or your family and, no, this is not an investigation of his professional life," the detective said.

"I would appreciate it if you wouldn't say anything to Bob about this," the investigator asked.

"Why is that?"

"Well, it would hamper the investigation."

"Am I under any kind of legal obligation?" Lee asked.

"No, but we would appreciate it."

Lee wrestled with the problem for three weeks before he picked up the phone and called Bob. Janet was in Grand Forks with Annah, who was not even two months old, so Lee went over and told Bob in person about the interview.

"Bob, I just don't feel good keeping this from you," Lee began.

Bob listened solemnly. He had a strange expression on his face that seemed to say "Here we go again." Lee did not know that he was bringing Bob the news that the investigation that began in New York and went to Las Vegas had just caught up with him in North Dakota. Perhaps the mysterious move by the hospital administration was no longer so mysterious to Bob. After he had gotten the weight of the secret off his chest, Lee waited for Bob to respond.

"You know, Lee, I'm really sorry you got involved in this," Bob said.

"Involved in what?"

"Nothing," Bob said, after a brief pause.

Lee's best friend got up, walked to the front door,

opened it and invited him to leave. Bob remained silent as Lee walked out the door.

In the summer of 1998, after many second thoughts, Alayne Katz had given permission for Gail's body to be exhumed, in order that more sophisticated DNA tests could be done. A medical technician from the New York Medical Examiner's Office had taken a blood sample from Alayne, for comparison with the body's—to determine, once and for all, its identity for use in court.

Alayne knew that it would be very difficult to prosecute Bob with so weak a case. She was concerned that Gail would be disturbed and everything dredged up again—the re-opening of a painful wound—for nothing. Ruining Bob's name and career seemed like the most they could hope for.

Her uneasiness continued until that fall, when she went to the office of the Chief Medical Examiner on First Avenue in Manhattan to meet with the "M-E," Dr. Charles Hirsch, and the prosecutors. They asked her if either she or Gail had been adopted. No, a confused Alayne replied.

The city's Chief Medical Examiner then gave Alayne the bad news—the mitochondrial DNA obtained from the tissue of the body her family had buried as her sister in 1989 did not match her DNA. The scientific test eliminated the torso as being the child of Alayne's mother.

The torso that had rested for 9 years under Gail's headstone in Queens, next to her mother and father, was not Gail. It was some unknown young woman, the victim of another killer who had murdered her, cut her up and thrown her into the ocean. He had also, apparently, gotten away with murder. Only in New York.

"I don't have an explanation for this, and I know that's not satisfying," Hirsch told a stunned Alayne.

He said the physician who had made the identification based on the x-rays, "was an excellent pathologist. I've never seen him make a mistake like this before—but the DNA doesn't lie."

Alayne couldn't believe it. The first investigation into

her sister's death had gone nowhere. The second probe, by the DA's office, also failed to result in an arrest and the case was closed. Now that they had re-opened the case, it looked like it had all fallen apart for a third time. It was even worse than that—Gail was no longer Gail.

"The one comforting thing I had was that I knew my sister was safe," an infuriated Alayne told Andy. "Now you've taken that and you won't convict him."

Alayne wished she'd never agreed to the re-opened investigation because it had shattered the only peace of mind she and her family had achieved. All of the horrible feelings came rushing back.

"It was so wonderful for me to bury my sister," she sobbed. "Now, my family's single shred of closure has been taken away!"

Dan told Alayne that he and Stephen were committed to the case and certain of Bob's guilt and that every effort would now be made and every resource of the district attorney's office was going to be brought to bear on the case.

"We can do it," Dan assured her.

"You'd better indict this man," Alayne said. "And you'd better convict him!"

The exhumed torso was not returned to Gail's grave, which was re-filled with dirt but remained empty. The now-unknown remains were re-tagged as "Torso—Jane Doe" and consigned for interment in Potter's Field on Hart Island by city jail inmates.

Throwing the torso out of the case was good and bad. Andy thought it was mostly bad. There was no longer a body that Bob could not have killed—but there was also no body at all. Murder cases are harder to prosecute without a victim's corpse that could tell a pathologist when and where and how she died. Andy felt that, without a body, it was going to be a challenge but Stephen and Dan felt they had enough to proceed. They hoped that the publicity that such a story would garner might help, that bringing charges against Bob might bring them the case—witnesses might come forward and strengthen it.

Alayne was grateful such sincere and dedicated professionals were on the job, but it was as if Gail had disappeared again—and it was almost as painful as the first time. She was glad that the new investigation would probably destroy Bob's comfortable life but she knew that getting a conviction with just circumstantial evidence and no body was going to be virtually impossible.

The prosecution interviewed Michael Stone, who was also happy to hear that authorities were investigating Bob again. Michael made a decision. He resolved to do anything he could to help justice triumph over law. He told the prosecutors about the conference at which he had presented his paper on the Bierenbaum case—and about Jane Dunne, who knew Gail.

"She said she saw blood on the rug in the apartment but never told police," Michael told them.

The startling news energized the prosecution. At last they had something new—a witness who had seen important evidence. It sounded like just the break they needed to win their un-winnable case. Stephen Saracco got on an airplane and flew to Seattle, where Jane Dunne lived, and knocked on her door.

But Jane told them that Michael was mistaken. She said she had only heard a rumor about blood on the rug but had seen nothing with her own eyes.

It looked like his long trip had turned out to be a wild goose chase. He continued his interview, hoping to find something.

Jane told him about Gail's glass casserole story and how Bob was supposed to be involved in some kind of big fraud, which only seemed to make things worse to Stephen. Either Gail's mother was some kind of monster or Gail exaggerated things. The fraud story sounded like baloney.

Just when Stephen was certain he had wasted a trip, Jane mentioned the red marks she had seen on Gail's neck from when Bob had choked her in 1983.

"At first, I thought they were hickeys," Jane smiled.

Then she recalled how Gail had wanted to move away

from Bob's abuse, and that she had written Gail a $500 check for a deposit on an apartment that was never cashed.

Stephen decided his trip was not completely wasted, after all.

Andy's investigators finally located and interviewed Dr. Roberta Karnofsky in South Carolina, where she had moved. Detectives had spoken to several of Bob's former girlfriends in New York and Las Vegas and, although many of them disliked Bob and were eager to help, they had little of value for a murder prosecution. As far as the detectives knew, Roberta would be no different.

The questioning began routinely, about her background and when and where she met Bob. When she mentioned Bob playing footsie with her under the operating table, the investigators' eyebrows went up. They began writing. She mentioned the screaming phone calls from Gail's mother, calling Bob a murderer, and asked them if they knew that Bob had altered his flight log to cover up a plane flight the day his wife vanished. The investigators looked at each other. They knew Bob had hidden a flight that day but they had no idea there was a record of it in his own handwriting—and of an attempt to cover it up. They wrote faster. As she talked, they peppered her with questions. She told them her theory about Bob's duffel bag, Gail's body and a flight over the ocean—and Bob's strange non-reaction to it. By the time Roberta related Bob's unusual reaction to the phone call from police that they had found his wife, the investigators knew they had a live one. She was an out-of-town witness but Roberta assured them she would be happy to go to New York to testify against Bob. Any time.

The investigators called Andy in New York, who found Roberta's story about confronting Bob with her theory of Gail's murder chilling. It meant he finally had a break in the case—a strong witness, leads to follow and the tantalizing possibility of finding vital documentary evidence in a thirteen-year-old case. Bob's disbelief that Gail had been found alive was the strongest evidence so far that he knew she was dead.

To Andy, it was a blessed event.

CHAPTER 34

HAM SANDWICH

ANDY and Tommy flew out to North Dakota on another long shot. On November 30th, 1998, they met up with state investigators and drove to Bob's medical office in Minot. They waited outside the main entrance until they saw Bob drive up and get out of his car. They intercepted him on the front steps. Andy wanted to see Bob's reaction, face-to-face, to the fact that the torso that he could not have killed was not his wife—which meant that Bob was fair game again.

Andy strode up to Bob, flashed his badge, and introduced himself as the chief investigator for the Manhattan DA's office. They had never met before. Bob, obviously surprised, stopped to listen. Bob looked intently at Andy, the man who was behind the investigation.

Several people, walking in and out of the clinic, noticed the odd scene of men with badges accosting Doctor Bob. Andy looked into Bob's flinty eyes and took his shot. He introduced Tommy and the state investigator and then got down to business.

"We'd like to talk to you," Andy said. "There have been some developments in your wife's disappearance."

Bob nodded at Andy, waiting.

"The torso was not Gail," Andy told Bob, watching for any reaction.

There was none.

"Talk to my attorney," Bob said, turning away.

"We'll see you again," Andy promised the man he had been hunting for thirteen years.

Andy and Tommy returned to New York right away. Andy did not really expect Bob to crack but he had hoped he would talk to them more. It was a long way to go for no result but at least Andy had finally looked Bob in the eye and let him know it was almost over. Andy's career was also almost over. He planned to retire the following spring and open a mystery book store called "Book 'Em" in Providence, Rhode Island, with his wife Mary.

On the way back to New York, Andy and Tommy's jet passed near Mount Rushmore, South Dakota, the national monument featured in the classic 1959 Alfred Hitchcock thriller *North by Northwest.* In the movie, Cary Grant played an innocent New Yorker who becomes a fugitive from a false murder charge, flees across the Midwest and ends up hanging off the chiseled presidential faces of the monument. Earlier in the film, the charming, brilliant villain James Mason proposes that the heroine be killed by throwing her out of a small, private plane into the ocean.

"This matter is best disposed of from a great height—over water," the urbane but evil Mason tells his smiling cohort.

After his encounter with Andy, Bob called Scott Greenfield in New York.

"The guy, the New York investigator, said that the body's not Gail's. Is this true?"

"No, he's full of shit," said Scott. "He's just bluffing. C'mon—they can't be that stupid. Frankly, I wouldn't believe it until I know a whole lot more."

Scott said he could not believe the burial of the torso as Gail could have been some kind of elaborate trick. He was furious about what he considered an ambush—an improper attempt to question a suspect who has a lawyer.

"It sounds like they're jerking your chain," he told Bob.

On December 1st, 1998, prosecutor Dan Bibb telephoned Scott and said they wanted to talk to Bob.

First, Scott made his opinion on the approach of his client abundantly clear: "What the fuck are you doing, having this guy ambush my client when he's represented by counsel?" Scott demanded.

"We're allowed to do that," Dan countered. "Why don't you see if your client will talk to us? If he's innocent, he has nothing to hide."

Dan suggested an informal conference call between himself, Scott and Bob. Scott had not the slightest intention of exposing Bob to the DA, but he asked what the whole thing was about—fishing for information.

"We know he went flying that day," Dan said.

"I'll have to talk to my client about this," said Scott, who then called Bob and told him the prosecutors had uncovered his secret flight.

"Yeah?" Bob responded.

Bob was extremely upset that the past was coming back to haunt him. He had endured years of gossip and whispering but it was all becoming frighteningly real. Scott believed that the DA would not dredge up an old case unless they had something solid—some witness or physical evidence. He wondered who or what it was. Gail's datebook and papers and Bob's flight log—which Bob had turned over before he left Manhattan— were still sitting in Scott's safe. Did they know about those? For years, Scott believed he had forgotten more about the case than the authorities ever knew—was that still true?

"What should I do?" Bob asked.

"Do nothing. There's nothing to do," Scott advised. "Is there anything, other than the torso, that anybody is telling them that's going to be a problem for you?"

"Not that I know of," said Bob. "Is it possible people would say something I never said?"

"Yeah, it's possible."

Scott dashed off a curt letter to DA Robert Morgenthau, informing him that Bob Bierenbaum was still represented by counsel and could not be questioned outside the presence of his lawyer.

Manhattan DA Robert Morgenthau, 80, known affectionately as "Morgy," had begun to "push the envelope" of murder prosecutions without a body. In 1998, the low-key DA indicted Sante and Ken Kimes—the mother–son "grifters" accused of murdering a wealthy East Side matron after scheming to gain ownership of her $5 million townhouse. There was no body, no witnesses to the crime, no confession and no forensic evidence. But there was a diary kept by Sante Kimes that tied together a whole web of circumstantial evidence that pointed to them as professional con men and killers who dumped the body in New Jersey. They had also perpetrated similar schemes elsewhere around the country and left other bodies in their wake. The pair were on trial in Manhattan as investigators assembled the circumstantial case against Bob Bierenbaum.

If Morgy could convict the Kimeses of murder, he could move the goal posts and widen the field of indictable behavior so that the ones that got away no longer got away with it. He could make history in the field of criminal justice.

But the case against Bob would be even harder. He was not a professional con man who had left bodies lying around the country. Bob was a plastic surgeon, husband, father, and benefactor of the poor, and had never been arrested. There was no diary that would serve as a roadmap for a jury. At least, not one the prosecutors knew about. In fact, besides the record of his flight on the day of the alleged crime, there was nothing they could hold in their hands.

Meanwhile, Andy retired from his third law enforcement career in May 1999. He kept in touch with the progress of the investigation almost daily by phone and offered suggestions.

In North Dakota, Bob called a doctor in Fargo whom he had never met, *William Wolfe. Bob introduced himself and said he felt like visiting Fargo that weekend and wondered if it was possible for Will to show him around town. A bit surprised, Will agreed and made a date to meet Bob at the Fargo airport and also invited Bob over to his home.

"Does anyone in your family smoke?" Bob asked, before agreeing to enter Will's home.

"Hell, no," said Will.

Bob seemed pleased by the answer. Will had never met Bob but he had heard a lot about the fanatically anti-smoking surgeon. Several patients had come to Will, complaining that Bob would not remove their moles because they were smokers.

Will and Bob introduced themselves in person at the airport, after Bob arrived in his piper Cherokee. He thought Bob was a strange dude. He was outgoing, perhaps to a fault, but also seemed like a cold cucumber, with piercing eyes. After lunch and a two-hour tour of Fargo, Will drove Bob back to his plane.

When Bob called another time, in the spring of 1999, and said he was flying into town again—with his dog Gracie—Will brought his 10-year-old son *George along.

"Do you want to go for a plane ride?" Bob asked George.

"Yeah. Let's do it," said George.

Bob took George up in his plane, while Will waited below. Bob made several passes at the field and then came back in for a landing. When they taxied back, Will noticed that his son's door was ajar and pointed it out to Bob, while George played with Gracie nearby.

"Oh, it popped open in flight," Bob said, nonchalantly.

"Popped open in flight?" Will asked, incredulously.

Will was alarmed that his son's door had opened up in the air and he was getting weird vibes from Bob. He shook hands and said goodbye.

"Don't be surprised if they start talking crazy," Bob said, out of the blue. "My girlfriend in Las Vegas is going around telling people I killed my wife . . . something about me throwing my wife out of an airplane."

That was it for Will. He hurried his son into the car and drove away as quickly as he could. He didn't know what the hell Bob was talking about—and he didn't want to know.

Bob's trip to El Fuerte in the fall of 1999 was also filled with drama and danger of arrest. En route, Bob and the other flying doctors were informed by radio that some Mexican doctors had threatened to have them arrested for stealing their patients when they landed. It took several phone calls to the mayor of El Fuerte and others to calm the local doctors down.

On the return trip, the group was held up at the U.S. border, where Mexican officials demanded bribes to let them out of the country. Bob agreed to pay the bribes to get his team home.

In New York, the DA convened a grand jury and began to present evidence against Bob. A September 22nd, 1999, letter from Dan to Scott made it official. Called a "target letter," it advised the suspect's lawyer that his client was the object of a criminal probe.

"The Grand Jury of the County of New York has been investigating the disappearance of Gail Katz Bierenbaum," the letter began. It made the usual invitation for the suspect to come in and testify before the grand jury, where he could not take a lawyer. Dan also requested that Bob's father Marvin appear voluntarily.

Scott called Bob and gave him the bad news; he would likely be indicted and arrested. That was how grand juries worked—a prosecutor could get a grand jury to indict a ham sandwich.

Scott wrote back that Marvin would not appear of his own free will before a body investigating his son. He also wrote that they would consider allowing Bob to testify, if he were granted immunity from prosecution—which was not much more than a legal joke, since Bob was the target of the investigation. Scott asked for more information, since he had no idea what kind of cards the prosecutors were holding, and also for a week's notice if an indictment was handed down. He warned that if they arrested Bob without notice, harm might come to his patients, unless they gave him time to arrange for other doctors to take over their care.

On Monday, December 6th, 1999—Alayne Katz's birthday—Bob was attending a luncheon meeting of the Rotary Club with Lee Trotter and other Rotarian leaders of the community in Minot. During a discussion of charitable projects and other business, Bob got a pager message to call

Scott Greenfield in New York. He excused himself and left the room to make the call.

"Bob, you've been indicted," Scott told him. "You have two days."

"Okay," said Bob, calmly. "What do I have to do?"

Scott told him he had to make plans to fly to New York. He would have to take his passport and his pilot's license with him, because the court was going to make him surrender both. Once again, he told Bob it was very important that he not talk about it to anyone.

"Let me call up and see if I can get reservations," said Bob.

When he returned to the table, Bob was pale and shaken.

"Lee, something really bad has happened."

Lee's heart sank. He immediately thought somebody was dead and hoped it was no one in his family or Bob's family.

"Bob, what happened?"

"Well . . ." said Bob, "they're arresting me for murdering my first wife."

"You're kidding me?"

"No."

"Bob, this isn't a joke—this isn't funny," said Lee, shaking his head and remembering some of Bob's bad jokes.

"No, I'm serious," Bob said, shaking his head. "I don't know why they are dragging this up fourteen years later."

Now it all made sense to Lee—the police investigation, Bob's strange reaction when Lee had told him about it.

"Bob, I don't know what to say. What can I do for you? What can we do?"

Bob said he didn't know. He had thirty patients to see that afternoon. Arrangements would have to be made for someone to cover his cases. A torrent of questions flooded into Lee's head and he began asking them.

"Lee, my attorney has asked me to not say anything," said Bob. "Please don't make it difficult for me by asking questions."

"Bob, just let me ask you one question."

"All right."

"Bob, did you do it?"

"Lee, I did not do this thing," Bob said, looking his friend right in the eye.

Later, Lee thought about it. He decided his friend could keep a secret and take it to the grave with him but it just didn't add up that Bob was a killer. Yet . . . maybe that's what it all was—the Flying Doctor Bob medical work, the charity missions to Mexico, the marriage, his daughter—atonement for a life taken long ago. Lee hoped it would all turn out right—but what way would that be? He hoped his friend would be acquitted—but what if Bob was guilty? Bob certainly had a volatile personality and a short fuse. But none of it meant that Bob was a killer. Lee knew lots of people, including physicians, with worse tempers and egos. Lee thought of Bob with Annah, or the time Bob ministered to his daughter when she had an injury. Bob loved his daughter and cared for his patients, which seemed to be inconsistent with some kind of monster who would kill his wife.

There was a part of Lee that almost hoped he did do it. Guilty or innocent, Bob's career, probably his life, was ruined. If he were guilty, at least he would deserve what was about to happen.

Bob informed Janet, who was in the middle of final exams in law school and would have to drop out until things were settled. Bob and Janet, who had been working together on a book that climaxed with a trial, were about to experience the real thing—with freedom, not orgasms, at stake.

The following day, Bob stopped in at the Minot airfield to pay his bill and Curt Hussey, whom Bob had instructed in instrument flying for free, noticed that Bob looked bad.

"Bob, you look sick," Curt told him.

"I just have a lot on my mind," Bob said.

He also had company. Bob was under surveillance by the FBI and investigators from the North Dakota Attorney General's office, to guard against the possibility that Bob would bolt to Mexico or nearby Canada, rather than fly to New York to surrender.

That morning in Grand Forks, Barb was getting Annah ready for the morning flight when Janet told her that Bob was going back east for a court appearance and there was a slight chance he would not be coming back for about a year. Barb held Annah and felt like crying because she knew what not having her daddy for a year would do to her. Janet said they would be moving out of Grand Forks in February and they wanted Barb to come east with them to help in the transition and to help select a new nanny. When she knew more, she would call from New York. Barb said she would do whatever she could to help.

Barb took them to the airport, while Annah talked happily in her car seat. Janet stared silently out of the window, lost in thought. She could not bring herself to tell Barb that Bob was going to be arrested for murder. Before she said goodbye, Janet made an almost identical declaration of wifely devotion that Gail had made fifteen years earlier: "I learned when I got married that you stand beside your spouse, no matter what, and work things out together."

CHAPTER 35

GROUNDED

BOB and Janet arrived at Newark Airport early on the morning of December 8th, 1999. They went to Scott's Manhattan office, where he prepared Bob for the day's events.

"Do not say anything to anyone at any time," Scott warned.

He explained that the cops would probably try to goad him and provoke him, hoping that he would reveal something or say something that would look bad in court. The lawyer then took Bob to surrender and went to the courthouse at 100 Centre Street to represent Bob at his arraignment. The agreement with the prosecution was that—because he was a polite citizen who had never been arrested before—Bob would be spared the indignity, not to mention the discomfort, of handcuffs. But, even without manacles, the sound of a cell door clanking shut like a cage door behind you was usually enough to unnerve even the toughest prisoner. A police photographer directed Bob against a wall and took his mug shot. After Bob was fingerprinted and processed, an officer plopped a bulging case file down on a table in front of him that said "Case Closed" on the outside, as if authorities had a mountain of evidence against Bob.

"We got you!" the officer said.

Bob said nothing.

"I bet you never thought that you'd be spending the night on Rikers Island?"

Bob remained silent and eventually, they gave up.

Scott did not know what bail would be set, so he used Marvin Bierenbaum's large stock portfolio as collateral to arrange for three separate bonds—one for $250,000, one for $500,000 and one for a million dollars.

In court, the New York press corps was out in full. A

brilliant and respectable doctor who broke his oath to heal and became a killer was a story, not just of passion and murder—but of the violation of a sacred trust in society.

The crowd hushed as Bob was brought into the courtroom to be arraigned. Janet, looking pale and very worried, took a seat, as did a haggard-looking Marvin and Nettie. On the opposite side of the court, Alayne Katz sat in the second row, weeping softly at the sight of Bob before the bar of justice after fourteen years. Her brother Steve was next to her. The clerk noted that Bob was charged with second-degree murder and asked how he pleaded to the charge.

"Not guilty," said Bob.

Prosecutor Stephen Saracco stood up and outlined the case for Supreme Court Justice Leslie Crocker-Snyder, saying Bob had murdered Gail on July 7th, 1985.

"He murdered her in the apartment, packaged her body and drove to Caldwell Airport where he took it up in a plane for disposal," Stephen told the attractive blond jurist. "He had access to areas of the Atlantic Ocean that extended from Montauk to Cape May. I believe her body still lies somewhere at the bottom of the ocean between those points," he said, asking that Bob be held without bail.

Dan Bibb told the judge that the prosecution had a "powerful and compelling" case against Bob. He asked that Bob surrender his passport and pilot's license, saying the defendant "frequently flies to foreign countries."

"What's he talking about?" Scott whispered to Bob.

"I'll tell you later," said Bob.

Scott told the judge that Bob, a "hard-working, law-abiding citizen," was innocent of the charges.

"Clearly, the charge is a very serious one," said Crocker-Snyder.

The judge with the golden hair and pretty face clipped Bob's wings. She imposed a bail of half a million dollars and told him he had to stay at his parents' home in West Orange, New Jersey, until the trial was over. She also confiscated his passport and pilot's license and ordered that he could neither pilot an airplane nor be a passenger in one.

She warned him to stay off "any kind of vehicle that flies."

Scott told the judge that the bail was reasonable "for a defendant who's not going to flee."

"I somehow believe he would, given the alternatives," the judge snapped back, not saying what she based her suspicions on.

For the first time in his life, Bob was denied his great love—flying. He was grounded. Bob was taken back to the holding cell area but it was only temporary—he soon walked out on bail. He ignored the shouted questions of a throng of reporters, cameramen and photographers on his way out the front of the building, passing under words chiseled into the polished stone above the door. "ONLY THE JUST MAN ENJOYS PEACE OF MIND."

Scott told reporters it was a case without a body and "a case with no evidence suggesting a criminal agency had any impact on Gail Bierenbaum. And, if there was a criminal agency, there is no evidence Mister Bierenbaum was involved."

In other words, they can't prove Gail is dead, they can't prove she was murdered and, even if they could prove those things—they can't prove Bob did it.

A tearful Alayne, now 41, told reporters that she was happy to see Bob charged with killing Gail.

"I'm extremely gratified that, after fourteen years, the person who murdered my sister is finally being charged," said Alayne. "From the very day that my sister disappeared, my family has believed that Robert Bierenbaum murdered her. I'm sorry that my parents are not here to see this. I hold him responsible for their early deaths."

Later, back at Scott's law office, the attorney told Bob he was furious at him for not telling him about his charity missions to poor kids in Mexico. His client had not mentioned that he was a part-time saint and the lawyer was unable to use it in court to argue for lower bail. Scott believed the only trial that mattered was in court and he did not believe in trying cases in the press. But Bob's medical mercy work in Mexico sure looked like an exception that might help Bob's new public image—which was otherwise bad.

"Why didn't you tell me?" Scott asked.

"Why would I?" Bob asked, in a confused tone.

Bob was instantly famous, or, rather, infamous. On the afternoon of his arraignment, the case was on the radio and it led the television news shows. The next morning, the case was in all the papers. Bob's arrest and his picture were splashed across the front page of the *New York Post*:

NABBED!
Doctor Charged with Murder
—14 Years Later

In Minot, in the doctors' lounge at the hospital, a poster appeared on the wall—a WANTED poster, complete with a mock mug shot of Bob, with numbers across his chest.

CHAPTER 36

HAND-TO-HAND COMBAT

SCOTT was not happy. His client had been vilified in the press around the country as a cat-strangling, wife-choking murderer. The men and women who would eventually sit on the jury to judge Bob were probably reading the stories that portrayed mild-mannered Bob as a two-faced monster—doctor by day, cat killer by night. Much worse was the fact that he had no idea what the prosecution had against Bob that had suddenly caused them to re-open the case after fourteen years. It had to be something—a witness or a piece of evidence—but they had revealed almost nothing in court.

The elimination of the torso as Gail meant that there was not even a death certificate for her. Technically, Bob was a bigamist, although it was not his fault because he had remarried after authorities told him Gail was dead.

Scott assumed they were going to try to prove that Bob did it when he went flying that Sunday, but they were being very stingy with their evidence. That was the game—to conceal your cards and only reveal what was required but as late as possible.

It was all part of the pre-trial battle phase, in which each side tried to learn what the other knew—while trying to hide as much as possible. The judge acted as referee and made rulings on what could or could not be used at trial. Some trials were won or lost before they began, due to rulings that helped one side or the other. Jurors rarely got to hear each and every fact and witness available in the case—just the ones the prosecutors and the defense lawyer wanted and the judge allowed.

When Scott received the prosecution's response to his demand for a Bill of Particulars, just after Christmas, there were few particulars. The letter from Dan Bibb refused to answer many questions but noted that Gail had two "adulterous" relationships with other men during her marriage, which gave Bob a motive to kill her.

Scott filed a thick motion with the court, asking, among other things, that the judge dismiss the indictment because the prosecution could not prove Gail had been murdered—much less that she had been killed in the jurisdiction of Manhattan. The judge denied the motion. Scott had once been on amiable terms with Acting Justice Leslie Crocker-Snyder but they had clashed in court and were far from being friends. Scott felt that she was a "results-oriented" judge whose rulings favored the prosecution and hurt the defense. He had a feeling there might be some friction between himself and the bench as the case progressed.

At the next court hearing in January, 2000, some shoes dropped. The prosecutors offered a copy of the 1983 report Gail had filed with police and said they wanted to show it to the jury at trial. Bob was surprised to see that there actually was a police report because he assumed it was one of Gail's exaggerations.

Next, they revealed a copy of Dr. Michael Stone's 1983 letter to Gail, which warned her of "the unpredictable nature" of Bob's "physical assaults" and that she might suffer "personal injury or death" at her husband's hands. They also introduced the records from Caldwell Airport that recorded Bob's flight and the amount of time he spent in the air.

In his office, Scott asked Bob if it was possible for one man to dump a body out of a Cessna in flight.

"Anything's possible," Bob shrugged. But, he told his lawyer it would be—if not impossible—a very difficult and dangerous stunt. Scott made a note for his private detective to check it out, then asked about the Michael Stone letter, and the psychiatrist's claim that Sylvia Katz told him that Gail was going to show the letter to Bob on the day she vanished.

Bob told his lawyer that he only saw Stone once, for just twenty minutes, and had no idea why the doctor had decided he was dangerous. The therapist, said Bob, "was off the wall." Bob said he'd gotten up and stormed out. That was it.

Bob said the police report was probably filed as part of a plan to prepare for a divorce action. Scott asked Bob about the choking incident and Bob said it wasn't really choking, that he didn't strangle her.

"So, this is all bullshit?" Scott asked.

"No, something happened. We had a fight. I was wrong. I was angry."

Bob described how he had used a judo move to render her unconscious and was then overcome with regret and shame. Scott could not picture it, so he asked Bob to demonstrate the move without knocking him out.

"Show me," said Scott, putting out his cigarette and rising from his desk.

Bob, who was taller than Scott, stood facing his lawyer. Bob put his hands flat out in front of his chest with the palms down, and the thumbs apart from the other fingers. He lunged toward Scott, straightening his arms. The palms of his hands slapped against Scott's shoulder blades and the sides of Bob's flat hands compressed the sides of Scott's neck and he was slammed up against the wall. Bob had obviously held back on the move—because Scott was still conscious and on his feet.

Scott was not a 5-foot-3-inch–tall Gail but it still scared the hell out of him. The lawyer agreed that it was different from choking someone by the neck, although the effect was the same—just quicker.

A few weeks later, while Scott and Dan Bibb were chatting on the phone, Dan informally offered a plea-bargain deal, which was a routine part of pre-trial interaction.

"Please take a plea," Dan asked. "I'll give you five-to-fifteen."

Bob faced twenty-five years to life behind bars for murder, which made just five or six years in prison a very good deal—for a guilty man assured of conviction. But Scott was confident of victory and felt his case was un-loseable. He saw the offer as a sign that Dan feared the prosecution case was un-winnable.

"Tell you what," Scott answered, sarcasm dripping from his voice. "Dismiss the charges, make a full apology and I won't make you look like a moron in court."

"Very funny," Dan said.

In March, Sante and Kenneth Kimes were convicted of murder—without a body. To prosecutors, the victory meant that fewer people would get away with murder. To Scott, it meant that Bob might be convicted of Gail's murder—despite the lack of evidence.

Bob, through Scott, made a request of the judge and asked that it be kept secret. Janet, the sole source of support for the family, had gotten a new job as a gynecologist in a hospital in another large city on the Eastern Seaboard and had moved there with Annah. Bob asked that he be allowed to leave his parents' home in New Jersey and live with his wife and daughter until the trial. The judge granted the motion and ordered that her ruling be kept secret—so that Janet would not lose her job.

After a court hearing in May, Alayne and a television reporter for a network "magazine" show confronted Bob in the hallway, while a TV crew filmed.

"Bob, why don't you tell the cameras—tell the public how innocent you are!" Alayne shouted, as Bob and Scott walked toward an elevator. Waiting for the elevator to arrive, Bob turned his back on Alayne. The television reporter looked at Alayne and she renewed her questioning.

"Bob, why don't you tell the public that you're innocent? Why don't you tell me that you didn't kill my sister? Fifteen years, I'm waiting to hear you say that you didn't kill my sister."

"He has no comment," Scott answered. "He's in the middle of a prosecution. We'll say what we have to say in court. After the trial, then you'll see that my client will be found not guilty."

On June 6, Scott found out about Mae Eisenhower, the woman who lived in the apartment underneath Gail and Bob. When he got a copy of the prosecution interview with the woman, it was obvious Scott would want to call her as a defense witness—to say the argument that morning had ended with a door slamming, an apparent corroboration of Bob's claim that Gail had stormed out. Combined with Joel Davis—the man who said he'd seen Gail hours after the prosecution said Bob had killed her—Scott was beginning to develop a case beyond just reasonable doubt. Things seemed to be looking up.

As the pre-trial hearings heated up, tempers flared on all sides. The judge angrily slammed Scott in open court after Scott filed legal papers that questioned the objectivity of the court. After she criticized him in public, Scott felt he had to do something to protect his client. He discussed it with Bob and they agreed that it would be better for someone else to be the lead attorney at trial, so that his differences with the judge would not impact on the defense. Scott suggested Bob retain David Lewis, a well-known murder defender who had more experience with murder trials than Scott did anyway.

Scott wrote a letter to the judge, naming David Lewis as co-counsel and charging that a footnote in her recent decision "exceeded the bounds of judicial propriety. It reflected an inappropriate personal attack, which calls into question this court's ability to fairly and impartially serve in this matter."

In court, on July 12th, Judge Crocker-Snyder issued a written opinion that would allow the prosecution wide latitude at trial. She ruled that hearsay evidence would be allowed because it was a domestic violence situation, despite defense contentions that Gail, with her multiple affairs, did not fit the profile. The DA would also be allowed to present evidence about Bob choking Gail in 1983, and about her intention to leave Bob. The judge said she would hold a hearing, at which Michael Stone would testify, in order to make a determination if she would allow the psychiatrist to appear before a jury. It was a series of defeats for the defense. But the judge also said she probably would not let

Bob's alleged cat attack be admitted at trial—the only glimmer of hope for the defense table.

However, if the defense put "character witnesses" on the stand, the prosecution would be allowed to introduce the cat attacks and perhaps other stories to prove Bob was a bad guy.

One week later, prosecutors issued a subpoena to Bob, demanding that he produce any and all personal documents "including, but not limited to, flight logs, flight records, and log books."

Obviously, Scott thought, looking at the subpoena, they knew about the flight log. Scott fought the demand in court, arguing that subpoenaing a defendant was unconstitutional. Again, the judge ruled against the defense. Scott filed an appeal but lost.

In July, Scott learned about the extraordinary conditions Michael Stone had required to treat Bob in 1983, from a journalist seeking a reaction. He immediately called Bob and asked him about the two tapes and the Lloyd's of London insurance policy to benefit Stone's children if Bob killed the doctor. Bob erupted into laughter.

"Scott, thanks. This was getting kind of heavy. I needed that," he said, still chuckling.

"No, I'm serious," said Scott. "This is what he said."

Bob claimed he never discussed the conditions—because Stone never mentioned them. He also denied that he had choked the fiancée he had before Gail, as Stone claimed. But he admitted to Scott that he had strangled a cat to death—by accident, explaining how he'd choked Marcy's cat in self-defense as it ran wildly about his car while he was driving.

When Michael heard the accidental cat strangulation story from a journalist later, he scoffed at it as "the rough-cat defense."

One magazine reported Bob had bragged that Janet was a virgin when he married her. Scott asked Bob if it was true.

"That's none of your business," an indignant Bob replied.

"Yeah, but . . ."

"No, it's not true."

Another magazine claimed that, at his bar mitzvah, Bob had kicked his father in the groin, a charge Bob also vehemently denied.

Scott also learned from a journalist that Michael Stone had claimed that Jane Dunne saw blood on Bob's rug. Like the prosecution, the defense quickly sent an investigator to check out the tale—which Jane again denied. Jane told private investigator Kathy Koch that she'd had a "false memory" about blood on the rug, but had seen nothing. Jane was somehow convinced that Gail had been killed to keep her silent about the non-existent multi-million-dollar fraud scheme Bob and his father had cooked up.

"You're going to tell them that I don't know anything?" Jane fearfully asked the private eye when they were done. "They're not going to come after me?"

The investigator asked her who she was talking about and Jane explained she meant Marvin and Bob Bierenbaum.

"Yeah, I'll tell the lawyer," she assured the psychologist. "Nobody's coming after you."

CHAPTER 37

STIFF UPPER LIP

JANET did not let her pain or anger show in public. Hardly more than three years earlier she and Bob had married, honeymooned in paradise and left Las Vegas for a perfect situation in North Dakota. That's what it had seemed like at the time. By the time they had settled in Minot, Janet was, professionally speaking, run out of town on a rail. She felt unfairly victimized by an Old Boy network. Embittered, Janet had left medicine and Minot, entered law school and worked on a book.

Again, by the time she and Bob had adjusted to the new conditions in Grand Forks, Bob was indicted and their lives became a chaos of professional ruin, humiliation, vilification, legal threat and impending debt from an approaching tidal wave of lawyers' fees. Some women in her situation would have left their husbands, filed for divorce and fled the horrific situation. Janet stood by Bob's side, took care of Annah and began a job search to fill in the spot of family breadwinner until after the trial, if there was one.

After the new millennium had dawned, Janet returned to Grand Forks with Annah. Barb returned to work as Annah's nanny. At the end of January, Janet and Annah flew back to New York for Bob's first court hearing. She told Barb she was confident the charges against Bob would be dismissed for lack of evidence, and he would be home soon. When they returned, Janet said, they would only be back for about a month to tie up loose ends and then they would be moving away—and they wanted Barb to come with them temporarily.

"Do you feel comfortable with that?" Janet asked.

"I don't have a problem with that," Barb told Janet.

Barb did have a problem with that but she did not want to say it. She felt sorry for Janet and Annah and wanted to help. Also, she was a lot less certain than Janet that a judge would just drop the charges against Bob. Barb had a feeling that Bob wasn't coming home any time soon—no matter what Janet said. As Barb drove mother and daughter to the airport again to catch a New York flight, Janet was silent. Suddenly, as if they had been having a conversation, Janet spoke: "Yeah, you know that reporter who is writing a book . . . Yeah, turns out he thinks it is a big joke and that this is a conspiracy within the NYPD."

When Janet returned to Grand Forks with Annah, she put Gracie on a plane to New York because she felt it would be good for Bob.

"Bob is really sad right now," Janet told Barb. "In fact, his mother is really depressed and was having trouble getting out of bed."

Barb's heart went out to Janet, who seemed to be blaming herself for the whole mess.

Janet's hopes that she would become an author were still just hopes. She had a pile of rejection letters from publishers. When she discussed her book with Barb, she recognized that the subject was not to everyone's taste. "Some might consider it pornographic," she said.

When Bob's next hearing was postponed until March, Janet saw it as a sign of a weak case against her husband.

"Yeah, they are doing this because they know they have nothing on this case," said Janet. "They have had two years to get ready for this date and they know they are grasping at straws."

Barb hoped Janet was right and that she was not the one grasping at straws.

In April, Janet again predicted that the charges against Bob would be dismissed. By then, Barb knew the charges were not going to be dismissed but she could not tell whether Janet was saying it to make her feel better or if Janet really believed it. Janet made plans to sell the Grand Forks house, Bob's plane and the $90,000 hangar in Minot—to pay legal bills and to make the move to the East Coast in April.

"It'll just be the three of us—me, Annah and you," Janet told Barb. "I hope you're comfortable with that?"

"That's fine by me," Barb agreed.

When Janet discussed their problem, she referred to it as "the Bob situation" and never mentioned Gail's name. Barb's husband and her family were strongly opposed to the trip.

"I won't even be in the same state as Bob," Barb assured them.

When Janet went to New Jersey to visit Bob, Barb was to stay at the new home, in a city hundreds of miles away. There was nothing to worry about, she told them.

Barb, Janet and Annah arrived in the new city just before Easter and had to stay in a motel for two nights, until the moving truck arrived and the new home was livable. As they drove to the new home, Janet turned to Barb.

"Bob's coming late tonight and he's bringing Gracie," Janet said, casually. "He'll be spending the weekend to help unpack boxes."

Barb smiled and nodded her head at the news but she was freaked out. Janet had sprung this on her when it was too late to back out, but she said nothing. Her mind was racing. Barb thought about what the prior nanny had said about waking up in the dark and finding Bob staring at her with those eyes of his.

That night, after Barb went to bed, she heard Bob and Gracie arrive and enter the house. Her door was locked. At breakfast, he was his usual, happy, friendly self—as if nothing at all had happened. It was strange but Bob put her at ease.

When Bob was up in New York, Janet and Barb interviewed prospective babysitters. After one interview, Janet mentioned how nice the lady was but stressed the importance of being careful and checking references.

"Yeah, because Gail really knew how to take advantage of people," said Janet.

"What?" Barb asked, confused at the sudden, out-of-the-blue reference to the first Mrs. Bierenbaum—the first time Barb had ever heard Janet use her name.

"Gail," Janet repeated. "She really took advantage of Bob and was manipulative."

Barb could not think of anything to say.

"I learned from my dad that you trust no one," Janet said. "They have to earn your trust."

Bob had not been convicted of anything, but his punishment had already begun. He was free on bail but he couldn't fly, couldn't ski and couldn't practice medicine—perhaps forever. For a can't-sit-still over-achiever like Bob, it really was punishment—although hardly enough to satisfy the Katz family.

Bob was convinced he would be found not guilty. He hoped to start his medical career again in a different state, perhaps even taking a residency specializing in hand surgery, but he didn't think it would be possible to practice in the United States again. The first thing he wanted to do was go to El Fuerte and finish the uncompleted surgeries on several kids who had been left in the lurch by his arrest. The couple felt the best way to begin healing would be to help others. They discussed their future and thought perhaps they would both go to Mexico and then perhaps another country—where Bob's scandal was unknown. They agreed that as soon as he was acquitted, they would have a second child and get on with their lives.

One day when Barb and Bob were in the car the news on the radio discussed a young man who planned to plead insanity to a recent racially-motivated mass murder. They discussed the case and Barb, without thinking, said she had just read about another man who was married to a woman for ten years and one day she vanished.

"Turns out, he had cut her up and fried her pieces in his restaurant and put the remains in a cardboard box out on the back porch," said Barb. "That is where the police found her . . ."

"Yeah," said Bob. "That's not good. No, not good at all."

There was an awkward silence and the subject was changed. Barb wondered what had made that come out of her mouth.

CHAPTER 38

PRIVILEGE

MICHAEL Stone was called to testify at an August 2nd
hearing on the subject of the privilege of doctor–patient
confidentiality. All doctors were good at keeping secrets but
psychiatrists and therapists were supposed to protect their
patients by never revealing their personal and sexual indis-
cretions, as well as their innermost desires, fears, insecurities and problems.

The prosecution contended that Bob, by allowing Michael to talk to his parents and to Gail about what they had
discussed, had waived his right under state law that his
doctor keep his medical secrets. They also made the unusual argument that, since Michael had simply seen Bob in
"consultation" and he had not entered treatment, Bob was
never his patient—so the confidentiality issue did not apply.

Bob's lawyers argued that Bob had not waived confidentiality and that it would be a violation of ethics and law
for Michael to even discuss any of it on the stand—as he
was about to do. The defense believed that the claim that
Bob was not entitled to protection because he had never
embarked on a full course of treatment was absurd—something they had never heard before.

Michael, the defense claimed, had already grossly violated the ethics of his profession by discussing Bob and
Gail with the press. Two psychiatric associations, who filed
a "friend of the court" brief with the judge, agreed with the
defense and called on the state to investigate Michael for
ethics violations. The judge overruled the objections.

On direct questioning by Adam Kaufmann, Michael testified that Bob allowed him to tell Marvin and Nettie Bierenbaum about their son's "dangerousness" and the
"significant risk" he posed to others, especially Gail. Mi-

chael also testified that he wrote Gail a letter warning her about Bob.

On cross-examination, Bob's lawyer David Lewis asked who had paid him. Michael answered that Marvin had paid him $1100 by check for ten sessions with Bob and Gail and one forty-five minute session with Bob's parents. The defense had one cancelled check—for about half that amount—from Marvin to Michael but they were saving it to confront him with at trial.

David next asked Michael if Marvin told him he had just returned from Taiwan and Michael agreed he had. The defense hoped to prove that Michael never spoke to Bob's parents and had reconstructed his notes at a later date. Marvin claimed he did not return from his conference in Taiwan until well after Michael claimed to have met with him in New York. Nettie had filed an affidavit, under penalty of perjury, that she had never met Michael in her life and was flat on her back with flu when he claims to have spoken with her. Under continuing questioning, Michael admitted he had no note detailing what he had told Bob's parents about his unusual conditions for treatment.

David asked if Michael could "sometimes make diagnosis of a person after meeting with them once." Michael said that he could.

David tried to grill Michael about the multi-million dollar life insurance policy he had demanded in order to treat Bob. But he dropped the line of inquiry after the judge warned that asking the question might result in the release of Michael's confidential notes.

David ended his re-cross and Michael stepped down after a few more questions from the judge. After Michael's testimony Crocker-Snyder told the lawyers she would not rule whether Michael would testify or his letter would be admitted at trial—until she had heard from the other therapists at a second hearing.

The lawyers argued several matters at length—including the prosecution subpoena of the defendant for his flight log.

"It's certainly the first time I have seen something like this," said Crocker-Snyder.

"It's funny to us," agreed David, laughing. "At least, on the surface. What we would like is time . . ."

"Mister Lewis can chuckle all he wants," snapped an annoyed Dan Bibb, "the subpoena was served in all seriousness."

Criminal defendants in America have a right against self-incrimination. When prosecutors are looking for something, they usually get a search warrant and look for it—rather than ask the defendant to surrender evidence against himself.

After the hearing, Michael spoke to *The New York Times* about how it only took one session with Bob for him to discern that he was dangerous.

"People who kill large animals . . ." he stopped himself in mid-sentence.

Bob's "accidental" strangling of Marcy's cat had not been made public. But Michael, according to the article, did say that Bob "spoke of homicidal impulses toward his wife and acknowledged past violence."

When another journalist asked him how he could diagnose Bob as a psychopath in less than an hour, the professorial shrink quipped: "It was a piece of cake."

After the first hearing, Michael's lawyer called Scott Greenfield and asked Bob to agree not to sue Michael if the psychiatrist stopped talking about him. Scott rejected the offer—which he felt was too little, too late—and vowed to sue.

The following month, on September 7th, the parties met again for the second hearing. The defense said all of the therapists were bound by the doctor–patient privilege and could not discuss their consultations with Bob. The shrinks, who were represented by lawyers, had—unlike Michael—refused to testify voluntarily.

The prosecution's position was that three other therapists had consulted with Bob but not entered into a course of treatment—which put them in the same position as Michael. They argued that they all could testify because their professional relationship with Bob had been ended.

"Your Honor," said David, "we're prepared to prove at a later point in the hearing that Doctor Stone has perjured himself and that part of the notes that he has referred to on the stand are fabricated."

The judge said she wanted to hear from the witnesses first. Adam argued that Michael's letter must, somehow, be admitted at trial because Gail's use of it provided "a very explosive motive for the defendant to kill her."

The judge asked Michael's lawyer, Jonathan Svetkey, to step forward. She asked Svetkey about a "weird letter" she had received from his office, stating that Michael was no longer cooperating voluntarily with the prosecution—despite the fact that he had already handed over forty pages of his notes from Bob and Gail's sessions to the court. Previously, Michael had told a journalist that he'd received free legal advice from Alayne Katz, who told him he had nothing to worry about.

"I think we are trying to put the genie back into the bottle, so to speak," said Svetkey.

"I think you would agree that the genie is really out of the bottle," said the judge. "Doctor Stone has already testified on these issues and this letter appears to me to be too little, too late."

"That may be true," Svetkey agreed.

The judge then ordered Manhattan psychiatrist Dr. Stanley Bone to testify.

"Good morning, Doctor Stone," the judge said to the witness.

"Doctor *Bone*," said the witness.

"Doctor Bone, pardon me."

On direct, the reluctant Bone told Adam that he had seen Bob twice in consultation in November, 1983, and had also spoken to Gail and Marvin Bierenbaum. He agreed that he had warned Gail that she was in danger.

The judge asked him to recall the specifics of Bob's

authorization, and the psychiatrist balked, saying he was "very troubled, for all kinds of reasons, about testifying."

The next witness was Brooklyn psychologist Shelley Juran, who also did not testify of her own free will. She refused to answer questions about her warning to Gail.

Crocker-Snyder told her she had to answer the question.

"This is over our objection," David put on the record.

"So, I'm directed by the court to reveal this information—even though it's privileged information?" the witness asked.

The judge told her that she should answer.

The witness took a deep breath.

"I wanted to hear her voice because I was concerned for her safety," said Juran.

"Did you feel at that time that you had an ethical duty to warn her that she might be in danger from the defendant?" Dan asked.

The defense objected but the court allowed an answer.

"I didn't feel that was the purpose of my phone call," Juran said.

"Well, you just said—I don't understand that answer," said the judge. "You said, a moment ago, you were concerned for her safety."

"I didn't know if I would hear her voice," Juran said quietly.

Everyone paused, as the implications of what the therapist had said settled in. She wanted to hear Gail's voice because she feared she might already have been murdered. Bob's face betrayed no emotion.

"Well, I don't want to go too far with this, but let's ask another question," the judge said, ending the silence.

Everyone in the courtroom—except those at the defense table—wanted to hear more.

"I think I have to go to the next logical place, Your Honor," Dan said. "Did you think, at that point, that there was a potential that she had already been harmed?"

"Objection!" said David. "Goes straight, right into the area—past what we're doing."

"I'm going to sustain the objection," said Crocker-Snyder, finally closing the barn door.

After court, Scott Greenfield told a journalist that if Michael Stone testified at the trial, he would be destroyed on cross-examination. "He will leave that courtroom a broken man and bring disgrace upon the prosecution and himself." Scott predicted, anger in his voice.

The following week, David produced a plane ticket that he said proved Marvin Bierenbaum got on a plane to Taiwan on November 25th, 1983, to attend a medical conference and did not return until December 2nd. That meant, David said, that it would have been impossible for Marvin to have met with Michael Stone at the end of November, as Michael had testified under oath. The defense claimed that the only strange, devious doctor in the equation was Michael—who, they claimed, made up most of what he said about Bob for ego gratification.

The prosecution admitted that Michael might have been mistaken about minor details. The judge ruled that it was simply an honest mistake after the long passage of time. The judge finally ruled that the prosecution could not admit Michael's warning letter to Gail or the police report Gail filed after the choking incident. The defense heaved a big sigh of relief but the judge's further rulings banished any feelings of triumph. Crocker-Snyder made the prosecution happy by ruling that, although they could not show Michael's letter to the jury, they could call witnesses to give hearsay testimony about what Gail told them about the letter and what she was going to do with it. Even though they could not put the police report in the jurors' hands, the prosecutors could call a witness to say that Gail had filed a police report after the strangling episode.

In other words, the prosecution got to have its cake and eat it, too. They would be able to introduce damaging testimony about Bob but the defense would be limited in their cross-examination. The defense wanted to savage Michael Stone on cross-examination—not Alayne or Gail's friends.

In some ways, the judge's rulings were the worst possible result for Bob's defense. Scott held the opinion that the judge was biased in favor of the prosecution. He pointed out to the press that she once made an argument the prosecutors had apparently forgotten to make—and then ruled in their favor.

"Leslie *is* the prosecution," he declared.

Crocker-Snyder decided against trying to re-write New York State law and ruled on September 12th that the psychotherapists who had warned Gail could not testify against Bob at the trial—because it would be a violation of the privilege of doctor–patient confidentiality.

She lamented that she had to exclude the testimony of the three therapists and limit the "truth-finding function" of the court. In an impassioned tone, she regretted that the chilling testimony that she had heard would not be presented at trial. The implications of her words hung in the air—because of doctor–patient confidentiality, the jury would never have the privilege of hearing compelling evidence that Bob was dangerous.

They would not hear the truth and Bob might go free.

CHAPTER 39

KILL THE ICE PRINCESS

LESLIE Crocker-Snyder's car pulled over to the curb at the courthouse at 100 Centre Street in Lower Manhattan. Her burly police bodyguard—made more husky by the bullet-proof vest under his shirt—got out of the vehicle quickly, opening his jacket so he could reach the nine-millimeter pistol in the holster at his waist. He scanned the pavement with trained eyes in every direction, looking for anyone or anything suspicious. When he saw nothing out of the or-dinary, he opened the door. A very attractive woman with shoulder-length blond hair in a simple flip and wearing a bare-shouldered white dress stepped out into the sunshine and strode over the sidewalk. Crocker-Snyder pulled the arms of a white cashmere sweater over her shoulders, wear-ing it fashionably like a shawl. A photographer from a daily newspaper took her picture, as she gave a friendly grin. Crocker-Snyder was 58 years old but most observers thought she looked twenty years younger. Several passers-by wondered who the pretty celebrity was. When one cu-rious man stopped to gawk at the good-looking blonde having her picture taken, the bodyguard pivoted toward the stranger, placing himself between the man and the judge, as she walked up the steps of the courthouse.

In 1999, just before Bob was to go on trial for second-degree murder, Crocker-Snyder's career had never looked better. She had been mentioned in different press articles as a possible candidate for police commissioner and for the spot that would be vacated by her old boss, Manhattan DA Robert Morgenthau, when he retired.

Crocker-Snyder had begun her career in the criminal jus-tice system as an assistant district attorney in the Manhattan DA's office back in the 1970s. She felt a special affinity for the most helpless victims of crime—children and women—and eventually was named director of the Sex Crimes Bureau.

When she became a judge in 1989, she saw the worst of human nature and the nastiest criminals New York had to offer. She quickly became known as a tough judge—but one who retained her femininity and even wore stylish chokers above her black robes. She was the cool judge who got all the hot cases—including the most savage, murderous drug gangs in a city where that profession was a growth industry. She was very tough on killers and dope dealers and was often controversial. Some of the controversy was probably the result of sexism—a woman being criticized for doing what male judges did without opposition. But she also seemed to garner a bit more than her share of publicity. When a newspaper ran a big story about acting justices and how the use of such appointed—rather than elected—jurists was bad for the city, only three judges were pictured, including Crocker-Snyder.

But most of her press concerned the horrific criminals who appeared before her—and their fury at the severe sentences she meted out in her husky voice. Most handcuffed felons who were ushered into Crocker-Snyder's courtroom thought they might put it over on the cute lady judge. They quickly discovered that that was hardly the case and the room—1313, appropriately—proved doubly unlucky for them. They often vented their hatred at her and vowed revenge.

The one bizarre exception was the case of vicious killer John Royster, who had bludgeoned one woman to death and savagely assaulted another. The tougher Crocker-Snyder was, the better Royster liked it. He began sending her demented, steamy love notes, which found their way into the press.

One letter addressed, "Dear Leslie," told the judge that she had a "delicious body." He claimed the jurist was making "advances" at him and he invited her to "come to me of your own free will to get what you want."

In another macabre mash note, the twisted killer told

"Leslie" to "search your inner feelings, search your heart.
I can get that sizzling hot sensation through my body when
I think about it, too." He ended the letter with another
creepy sexual invitation: "Whenever you want me, just call
me back and I'll come running—like a shiny, black, brand-
new 44-magnum gun—locked, cocked and ready to fire."

Somehow, Crocker-Snyder managed to resist Royster's
charms and sentenced her admirer to life in prison without
the possibility of parole. Royster reacted by yawning and
stretching his arms—and smiling at his favorite judge.

But he was the only defendant to get "maxed-out" and
take it in stride. Time and time again, a sly crook would
be tried before her and receive the maximum sentence. Leslie Crocker-Snyder had become the nemesis of evil, the
nightmare of drug dealers and killers. She gave one convicted killer 75 years behind bars. "I hope you will suffer
every day of your life," she told the murderer, in a frosty
voice.

She gave a paralyzed drug dealer 175 years up the river
for shooting a cop in the arm. In a strange tribute, a Bronx
drug gang put a picture of the lovely jurist on their product,
over the brand name "25-Years-To-Life."

Nicknames for the tough-cookie judge who threw away
the key began to circulate on the streets of Harlem and
Washington Heights and in jails. They called her "The Ice
Princess" and sometimes "Judge 232"—for the number of
years in prison she gave to the head of a Jamaican drug
gang called "the Jheri Curls."

In 1995, she presided at the trial of nine members of the
"Wild Cowboys" crack gang—one of whom was represented by Scott Greenfield. She sent one of the murderous
thugs away for 158-years-to-life, telling him he was "unfit
to live." They felt the same way about the judge and took
a contract out on her life, prompting authorities to give her
permanent round-the-clock police protection at home and
at work—the only judge in the state who had it. The security at her courtroom was also beefed up beyond the three
armed officers who checked ID, searched bags and ran

hand-held metal detectors up and down the bodies of everyone entering the court—with special attention to defendants and their family and friends.

In August 1999, the month before Bob was to go on trial, another angry defendant, who used a pen instead of a gun, also marked the Ice Princess for death.

Stewart Winkler, an accused 100 million-dollar stock swindler who wore expensive suits and button-down shirts, was re-arrested in his cell and charged with hatching a jailhouse plot to have his judge bumped off—before she could give him the max. He also wanted another judge because he hoped to get his 1.5 million-dollar bail reduced and get out of the lockup. Both the *New York Post* and the *Daily News* featured the murder plot on the front page with identical banner headlines: "KILL THE JUDGE."

The white-collar Winkler had been as dumb as the drug gangs who'd tried to have Crocker-Snyder killed—he hired another criminal, who wore a "wire" and ratted him out to police.

"Do it. It's a done deal," Winkler told the rat. "Don't worry about it—just don't get fucking caught!"

Instead, Winkler was charged with conspiracy to commit murder and was ordered held without bail by another judge. It looked like the accused con man was going to be in jail for quite some time and the closest he would get to white-collar, button-down shirts would be in the prison laundry.

Once again, the Ice Princess had escaped death and triumphed over evil.

CHAPTER 40

OPENINGS

LESLIE Crocker-Snyder's courtroom, 1313 at 100 Centre Street had additional security outside the wooden double doors but jurors who crowded inside were not searched again. More than 120 citizens of Manhattan, of all shapes, sizes, colors and origins filed into the room. They sat on the dark walnut pews, adjusted their newspapers, paperback novels and pocketbooks and chatted amongst themselves. For a few in the jury pool, whose eyes roamed around the large room, it was the first time they had ever been inside a higher court of law.

Carved wainscot panels of walnut woodwork lined the walls. There was also a wooden rail between the audience and the well of the court, and a wooden jury box, a witness box and the judge's bench. Over the judge's head, halfway to the ceiling twenty-five feet above, was a tall wooden panel, flanked by American and New York State flags, with the raised gold letters: "In God We Trust." On the right side of the room, high over the jury box and partially extending into the public area, were four tall windows.

A court clerk called the proceedings of September 18th, 2000, to order and Judge Crocker-Snyder, clad in the traditional black robe, entered from a door at the front left of the courtroom and mounted the bench. She sat in a large black chair and, with a charming smile, greeted the prospective jurors, wished them a good morning and began to explain the jury screening process. She said that the prosecutors had obtained an indictment against Robert Bierenbaum, who was charged with killing his wife Gail fifteen years earlier, a charge he had denied.

"The case is entirely circumstantial," and "involves domestic violence," the judge continued. "There is no death penalty involved in this case," because the crime occurred a decade before New York State re-instituted capital punishment. The jurors listened silently. When the judge told the pool, "I anticipate it will be four to six weeks" to complete the trial, the room erupted in groans. One by one, some seventy jurors asked and were excused because they couldn't understand English, had a mental defect, would suffer undue financial hardship if kept away from their jobs that long, and several other excuses. Slowly, the pool was whittled down to a much smaller group. Jurors-to-be were quizzed on their opinions about the merits of a wholly circumstantial case and were not chosen unless they said they could vote to convict a man of murder without the proof of a victim's body, without forensic evidence, witnesses to the crime or a confession.

Potential jurors were excused for various reasons but a yes answer to one particularly strange question automatically excluded anyone from the jury: "Do you own a cat or are you a cat lover?"

Judge Crocker-Snyder had earlier ruled that no testimony would be allowed about Bob's alleged choking of Gail's cat or the killing of his previous girlfriend's pet. But it was always possible a witness might blurt it out while on the stand or that circumstances would change and the court would allow it to enter the record. Implicit in the decision seemed to be the supposition that people might be objective about a man charged with murdering his wife—but not about a man who might have roughed up a pussycat.

It took less than two weeks to pick those who would decide Bob's fate—a twelve-member jury panel, along with six alternate jurors. In the front row of the jury box, seated on the right, close to the public seating, was a young, attractive woman juror who resembled Gail Katz Bierenbaum enough to be her sister.

The judge set Monday, October 2nd, 10 A.M., for opening statements.

*   *   *

At the opening, the courtroom was filled. Janet, dressed in a tan dress suit, sat in the front row behind her husband. In addition to the new suit, Janet had gotten her hair cut, lightened and curled for the trial. Bob, dressed in a gray suit and tie, sat at the defense table on the left of the courtroom with David Lewis, Scott Greenfield and a third lawyer, Kathryn Kase. Bob's mother stayed home and his dad was not in court because he was going to be called as a prosecution witness.

David, a husky gentleman with a full beard and a bald spot on top of his head, was referred to—behind his back—by one member of the press corps as "Friar Tuck" because David would cross-examine a witness cordially, even reverently—and then out would come the sword. David had become well-known by defending unpopular people like "Fatal Attraction" killer Carolyn Warmus, ousted Panamanian dictator Manuel Noriega and the "Pizza Connection" drug dealers. One star prosecution witness who had been skewered on the stand by David referred to the shaggy lawyer as "a wild animal in a three-piece suit." David, with a wry smile, responded that the witness who made the comment "knows I've never owned a three-piece suit."

The prominent lawyer, who once referred to cross-examination as "a blood sport," had never tried a case before Justice Crocker-Snyder. But he and the judge had dueled over legal matters on the "Charlie Rose" television show, during which David got in the last word by saying, "I'm not in your courtroom, so listen to me." Now, he was in her courtroom.

Prosecutors Dan Bibb, Stephen Saracco and Adam Kaufmann were seated at the prosecution table on the right, next to the jury box. Adam's parents, proud to come and see their son on opening day of his first big trial, sat in the front row behind the prosecutors. Gail's brother Steve Katz sat behind the Kaufmanns in the second row. His sister Alayne was not present because she would appear as a major prosecution witness and was not allowed to listen to testimony until after she had left the stand.

Reporters from newspapers, radio and television stations and courtroom artists, busily sketching the participants in colored pastels on large drawing boards on their laps, filled the other front-row seats. In the back of the courtroom, his back to the wall, sat the judge's armed bodyguard, his eyes scanning the crowd.

Judge Crocker-Snyder took to the bench without ceremony or a call to stand in her presence. Above the collar of her black judicial robe, her long, pale neck was circled by her fetching black choker. She began the proceedings, which were promptly delayed by legal wrangling—something that would become common during the trial.

David objected when the prosecution dumped more than 100 pages of documents on the defense table. The stack was "discovery" material, which the prosecution was required to furnish to the defense. David demanded time to review the pile of paper before making his opening statement—in case the last-minute submission contained a "Shanghai Surprise" that might throw a monkey wrench into the defense case. The judge granted them just twenty minutes to check out the new information, which they did in the adjacent witness room.

The jurors filed into the court from the rear, left door, walked single-file across the well of the court and filled the jury box. Many of the jurors looked around the crowded courtroom and several glanced at Bob. They would soon be asked to listen to the evidence and then judge him for an alleged crime committed fifteen years earlier. Although witnesses would testify about events, deeds and conversations that took place in 1985, no one in the court of law—including the witnesses—was the same person he or she had been fifteen years earlier. In 1985, Bob Bierenbaum was a brilliant, intense, hot-tempered, socially awkward 29-year-old surgical resident with shaggy hair, long sideburns and a turbulent marriage that featured alternating periods of fun and fighting, sex and estrangement, reconciliation and conflict. That young man was the defendant the jury would actually have to judge—not the balding, bespectacled, accomplished 45-year-old surgeon and father sitting before them in a conservative gray suit, white shirt and red tie.

The judge explained to the jurors that they would now hear opening statements but that the statements were not evidence—that would come from witnesses. Crocker-Snyder then told Assistant District Attorney Stephen Saracco that he could begin the prosecution's opening statement. Stephen rose and stepped behind the prosecution table to the wooden lectern next to the jury box and greeted all the participants and the jurors.

"The evidence in this case is going to explore the short, unhappy marriage of this defendant and Gail Katz Bierenbaum," Stephen told the jury, referring to notes he had placed on the podium. "It will reveal a relationship that was deeply troubled, almost from the beginning. The testimony will demonstrate the root of this trouble was the defendant's controlling nature and that he felt a compelling need to control each and every aspect of their relationship, including minor things, of her behavior. The evidence will also show that, when this control was resisted by her, that the defendant would react in an abusive and sometimes violent manner," said Stephen.

He told the court that Bob "is a zealous anti-smoker. Nothing wrong with that." But Stephen said Gail was a smoker who had been forbidden to light up by her husband—who, in 1983, "when he caught her smoking, that he choked her because of her smoking and because of her resistance to his controlling nature that she shouldn't smoke. He choked her to the point of unconsciousness."

Stephen told the members of the jury that on Sunday morning, July 7th, 1985, "the conditions of the marriage had reached a flashpoint, the various things were converging. You will hear that a situation developed that morning—in the defendant's own words to a woman to whom he described that morning, some months later—that the situation became 'explosive.' "

Gail, Stephen said, his volume rising, his words coming quicker, "had enough and she was going to tell him the relationship was over and that she was going to walk out and she was leaving. It is the People's contention at this point that the defendant saw his control of her evaporate.

"On that Sunday morning in the apartment, around 11 A.M., the marriage was terminated—not by divorce—but at the hands of this defendant . . ." Stephen said, pointing an accusing finger at Bob, ". . . when he killed his wife in the apartment, removed the body from the apartment, took it in his father's Cadillac to an airport in New Jersey and had it packaged, possibly in a duffel bag, where he rented a Cessna 172 for approximately two hours in the areas where he had access—the depths of the ocean extending from Montauk Point to Cape May in New Jersey, and he dumped the body into the depths of the ocean, where it remains to this day."

The courtroom was completely silent until Stephen resumed his statement, reminding the jury that there was no body or forensics in the case, ". . . no murder weapon, no bloody clothes, no fingerprints, no brain matter, no body part ever found . . . Well, the purpose of this opening is not to tell you what we don't have. . . . Basically, the People have to prove two things in this case. The two things are that she is dead and that she is dead because the defendant killed her."

Some witnesses would be called to establish Gail's death, some would be called to establish that Bob killed her and some would do both, he explained.

"It was her intention to leave her husband on July seventh, 1985—it was not her intention to drop off the face of the earth," Stephen said in a voice filled with rising indignation. "You will hear that she was not—as the defense may claim, as the defendant claims—suicidal; that she was looking forward to a life without him, that her career was what was paramount in her mind."

From the outset, he said, Bob "engaged in a pattern of deceit to cover his tracks" and waited for thirty hours to alert police to his wife's disappearance—only at the insistence of one of Gail's friends. Stephen began listing items he said were part of the pattern of deceit: Bob claiming incorrectly that a doorman had seen Gail leave that Sunday morning; Bob concealing his plane flight that day from everyone, including police; Bob shifting the time he said he left his apartment to two hours later—the same amount of time he spent in the air.

"He never tells anyone—his family, her family, his friends, his acquaintances, people he works with—never tells anyone through the years," Stephen confided to the jurors, striding up and down in front of the jury box.

Not only would the prosecution prove that Bob made a secret flight that day, he said, but they would also show that Bob had altered his personal flight log to cover up the fact that he flew on the day of the murder.

Stephen told the jury about the letter from psychiatrist Michael Stone "which indicated she was in danger, in physical danger, in the relationship and that she should leave the relationship to avoid coming to harm at the hands of her husband. She indicated she was going to use this letter as leverage when she left. She was going to confront him with the letter and tell him that she was going to get what she wanted.

"I submit to you that if you use your reason, your logic and your common sense and you look at the evidence in its totality, that the only reasonable conclusion that you can come to is that the People have proven this defendant's guilt beyond a reasonable doubt and we will ask you, on behalf of the People of the State of New York, to find him guilty of the murder of his wife. Thank you," said Stephen taking his seat.

It was a strong opening. The prosecution intended to pile on the circumstantial evidence so that it was overlapping, comprehensive, compelling.

David then took to the podium to deliver the defense opening.

"Good morning," David said pleasantly to the jury.

"What you have heard is a theory—a theory that the People say that they can prove to you. But you will discover in the course of the trial that, as to what happened to Gail Katz Bierenbaum, their theory is as good as almost any other theory, in that it could just as well be true as false. Your job is to determine whether the theory ever rises to the level of proof beyond a reasonable doubt—that determines your verdict."

David told jurors that the defense did not dispute that Gail died sometime that Sunday and would not try to argue that Gail was alive somewhere.

"What is disputed by us—so it's clear—is that Gail Katz Bierenbaum, on July seventh, 1985, sometime after eleven in the morning, was alive." David paused for emphasis and said it again.

"She was alive. She was seen by a man named Joel Davis, who you will hear testify. Joel Davis says . . . 'I saw Gail Katz Bierenbaum. I saw her at H & H Bagels on the East Side of Manhattan' and he tells Missing Persons that."

David said his witness would testify about being shown photos of the missing woman and identifying a picture of Gail Katz Bierenbaum as the attractive woman he saw that day on line in the bagel shop.

"There is more evidence, a different kind, evidence which will show Gail Katz Bierenbaum's dark side—in which she engaged in what is still called risky behavior, as recently as the day before the seventh of July.

"We also want you to know that the evidence will show that this was a lousy marriage, that these two people did not get along, that they didn't like each other, that she was not a loyal, wonderful woman and that he had a temper," said David.

"You will learn that, from the evidence, and—as to whether or not who is controlling who—you will learn that . . . before the seventh of July, Bob Bierenbaum wanted to visit his friends and Gail would not let him do it. So who was controlling who is going to be one of the issues," he said.

David said that the 1983 choking incident "was so severe that it frightened him and sent them both to counseling. You will also hear that it was a constant theme for Gail Katz Bierenbaum that she was leaving Dr. Bierenbaum, that it wasn't just on the weekend of July seventh—that she talked about it regularly, to as many people as possible."

He noted that Gail was planning a surprise party for Bob at the same time she told people she was thinking about leaving.

"Now, did he ever tell anyone about flying a plane on July seventh, 1985? The evidence will show you, and we concede, he never did. He didn't tell anybody."

In Bob's first police interview, David said, Detective Tom O'Malley asked about Gail's movements—not Bob's. In the second interview, "the story changes, and, at that point, the questions asked tell Dr. Bob Bierenbaum this is no longer a Missing Persons inquiry. He's the target and when he's the target, he decides he is not going to tell them anything else—because why should he? They are no longer looking for Gail Katz Bierenbaum."

"Objection! This is argument," Stephen shouted.

"Yes, be careful. I will give you some latitude but don't argue," said Crocker-Snyder, sustaining the objection.

David resumed his statement, saying in a calm, confident voice that Bob did not try to conceal the fact that he went flying. Also Bob himself gave police the number for the airport's flight service—which was on the first page of Gail's address book that Bob copied and gave to detectives after they asked for it. He said the defense would introduce one of Bob's cancelled checks in payment for an August 8th, 1985, plane rental from the East Hampton Airport on Long Island—proving that Bob did, in fact, fly on that date also. The check implied that Bob simply made a mistake on the log—not a clumsy attempt to cover up his secret flight.

The lawyer told the jury that there was a body in the case—the wrong body. He told them about the armless, legless, headless torso found washed up on Staten Island, about how the corpse was buried as Gail—which led Bob "to the conclusion that his wife had met foul play" that he later told to girlfriends in Las Vegas.

"Objection! That is argument," Stephen protested again.

"Overruled," the judge replied.

"You will also learn that she had a drug issue and you will learn from one of what they gently call romantic relationships . . . at least one of the lovers Gail Katz Bierenbaum took behind Dr. Bierenbaum's back was also someone she shared drugs with—and you will learn it from his own testimony," David promised.

He told the panel that the police conducted forensic examinations of Bob's apartment, his car, his father's car, his friend's car, and the airplane Bob flew on July 7th—"and found no evidence of blood or any other biological determinations that would ordinarily support the idea—the theory, if you will—that the People have put forward, because the point is this case also turns on lack of evidence. While the People call it a theory, the question for the jury is, 'you have to prove this to us—not just tell us the story.'

"You will also see that the case turns on Bob Bierenbaum's behavior, as judged by his ex-girlfriends, and I am not allowed to argue what that would mean to at least some of us," David said, with a slight smile at the edges of his mouth.

"Not only that, it turns, in part, on the judgment of some of the girlfriends of Gail Katz Bierenbaum. And so, the witnesses—like in a wedding—divide into those on Gail's side and those on Bob's side. Was she leaving him that weekend? As I said, the evidence will tell you about the party being planned, about her talking about leaving and whether she was going to go or not. So what happened? Ironically enough, there isn't anybody who can tell you. We can give you a theory, just like they did. We know that Joel Davis saw her and if you believe Joel Davis . . ."

"Objection!" Stephen said, leaping to his feet.

"I will withdraw 'We know.' I apologize. That's wrong," David said.

It was becoming clear that David was using a two-pronged defense—reasonable doubt and Joel Davis.

"You will learn and then maybe you will know that Joel Davis saw her on that date and once Joel Davis sees Gail Katz Bierenbaum alive on the afternoon of July seventh, then the theory washes away," David said, looking each juror in the eye, one after the other.

"And once the theory washes away, the question for you becomes, 'If Gail Katz Bierenbaum is alive on the afternoon of July seventh—then who killed her? Because Bob Bierenbaum didn't," David said, pointing at Bob.

"In the end, the fact is that we may know nothing more than Gail Katz Bierenbaum is dead and that no one knows who did it," said David.

"If that's what the conclusion of the jury is at that point, then the verdict which you speak, which we will return to ask you for, will be a verdict of not guilty and will be a verdict consistent with the evidence, the law and justice. Thank you."

CHAPTER 41

THE PEOPLE'S CASE

BOB and Janet paused with the lawyers just inside the rear exit of the courthouse to get ready. The lawyers and Kathy Koch, a private detective who had been sitting with Janet in court, formed a phalanx in front of the defendant and his wife—in preparation for running the gantlet of media photographers waiting outside for shots of the accused killer. Bob took Janet's hand and they stepped outside. Once on the sidewalk, a television reporter reached over the private detective's shoulder, shoved a microphone in Bob's face and began peppering him with questions, including "Did you kill your wife?" Bob's face remained impassive and he said nothing. All of the media covering the trial knew he had never said a word, on the advice of his lawyer, but the reporter wanted confrontational film of Bob ignoring him for his piece for the evening news, so he kept asking. Scott Greenfield brushed the mike away from his face and the reporter reacted loudly with righteous indignation.

"Don't touch me!" he shouted.

The lawyers and Bob and Janet kept walking with other photographers snapping away, walking backwards in the street.

"Who's that?" one man on the street asked a reporter.

"The doctor on trial for killing his wife," was the answer.

"Oh yeah—he dumped her out of a plane, right?"

The photographers swarmed in front of the defense group for two blocks—until they entered "Part F"—Forlini's Restaurant, a popular hangout for lawyers, judges and prosecutors from the nearby courts.

After lunch, the prosecution began the People's case. The first witness they called to the stand was Gail's cousin

Hillard Wiese, now 53, and a law clerk for a judge in the Bronx. His black beard had gone gray in the intervening years between the time Gail told him about Bob's violence and the time he finally had an opportunity to tell a jury about it. Like all witnesses, he stood in the witness box between the judge and the jury box while a court officer held up a Bible. Hillard placed his left hand on the Bible and raised his right hand to take his oath—spoken aloud by Court Clerk Rocco DeSantis.

"Do you swear the testimony you are about to give in the case against Robert Bierenbaum, the defendant, is the truth, the whole truth and nothing but the truth?"

"I do," Hillard swore, taking his seat and adjusting the microphone in front of him. The direct examination by the prosecution began and Dan Bibb asked Hillard about the 1983 call he had received from Gail.

Hillard answered that Gail told him that Bob "had choked her into unconsciousness, that this was not the first time he had choked her but it was the first time she was rendered unconscious and that she was extremely upset." He told the court about advising Gail to leave the house immediately and go to her grandfather's house in Brooklyn.

On cross-examination by David, the lawyer asked Hillard if, in that first distraught phone call, Gail had asked "you about her concern that she would lose rights to her marital property?"

"She did," Hillard answered.

"And you advised her, for her own safety, to leave, right?"

"Correct."

"And not worry about marital property?"

"Correct."

Dan next called Detective Virgillio Dalsass to the stand. In 1986, Virgillio had left NYPD after 21 years on the job and become the chief operating officer of a security firm. On direct testimony, Virgillio described his interview with Bob on July 8th and the fact that Bob told him his wife had been hospitalized for a condition "that might be pertinent to this investigation."

He said that Bob claimed it was a minor spat that resulted in Gail walking out that day and that he said he stayed home all day until he left for New Jersey. Later in his testimony, Dalsass mentioned that Bob told him that Gail had been hospitalized in the past "possibly for an attempt at suicide."

Several jurors looked up in surprise, suddenly very attentive at the news that their alleged murder victim once tried to kill herself.

Dan asked if Bob ever mentioned "whether he had flown a plane that day, or in fact, whether he was a pilot?"

"No," Virgillio replied. "He never mentioned it."

Virgillio told the court Bob's version of events and also told the jury about how Bob several times refused to discuss what he and Gail had been arguing about that weekend. He said he was frustrated because Bob repeatedly said, "I don't know, I'll tell you later," when asked for information. After the ninety-minute interview, Virgillio said he told Bob he would call him at home later that night—to get the information Bob had promised. Bob, he said, told him he was going out to dinner with his father but would be glad to give him what he wanted by phone. But when he called, Bob's answering machine was all he got.

"Was that all the information you got from the defendant about his wife?" Dan asked.

"That was it," said Virgillio.

Dan asked if the fact that Bob had gone flying that day would have been important information to him.

"Objection!" said David.

"Overruled," said the judge.

"Absolutely," said Virgillio. "It would have been helpful. . . ."

As part of the investigation, Virgillio said he spoke to Gail's friends, who had not heard from her.

By that point, the judge's bodyguard had dozed off in the back of the courtroom, one of several people, including jurors, who seemed a bit sleepy. Crocker-Snyder, in a loud voice, interrupted the proceedings with a smiling admonition to the jury to "please stay awake." Her bodyguard also got the message.

Virgillio told the jury that when he met with Bob and his lawyer Scott in September 1985, he believed that they had a deal that allowed police to conduct a full forensic search of Bob's apartment. But, when he arrived at the apartment on September 30th, Scott informed him that they could not use Luminol to search for the presence of blood—or conduct any other forensics tests. They would only be allowed to collect Gail's fingerprints to be used in identifying her body—if it was ever found. Virgillio said the detectives were not allowed to examine the bathroom and a defense private detective followed him all over the apartment.

He said he pretended to need to use the bathroom, hoping that he might find obvious signs of blood—but the private eye followed him in.

On cross-examination, David asked the detective if the normal procedure was for police to gather enough evidence and then go to a judge and "get a search warrant?"

"Yes," Virgillio answered.

"That did not happen here?"

"That's correct."

"Despite the fact the lawyer stopped you, you tried to do it anyway—didn't you?" David asked, an edge in his voice.

"As much as I could," Virgillio told David, with a defiant glare in his eyes.

David then asked the veteran investigator if Bob had told him Gail was unusually upset the day she vanished.

"Did he say, 'Gail seemed more pissed than usual?' " David asked.

"No, he did not," Virgillio said, decisively.

In fact, Virgillio had written those very words—coming out of Bob's mouth—in his notes of his session with Bob.

David then asked Virgillio about his interview of Gail's boyfriend Anthony Segalas.

"Did he tell you anything about using cocaine with Gail Katz Bierenbaum?"

The eyebrows of several jurors went up.

"Objection!"

The judge called a sidebar conference, in which all six lawyers, the judge and the court reporter with his small typing machine, convened in the far left corner of the courtroom—where neither the jury nor the spectators could hear them. After the sidebar, Crocker-Snyder stepped back up to the bench and said, "The jury is to disregard the question, at this point."

David did not resume his cross-examination. He did not spring the traps he had set to show the jury that Virgillio made mistakes and that Bob had cooperated with him.

After Virgillio stepped down, the judge excused the jury for the day. The jurors filed out and the judge told the lawyers that she would not let the jury hear about a statement Bob made to police that Gail used drugs, saying it "was self-serving and will not be allowed."

After several rounds of wrangling between the lawyers, Crocker-Snyder pretended to be enraged by the bickering and she pulled a gigantic gag gavel—as long as a sledge hammer—from underneath her bench and threatened to use it to quell the argument. Laughter filled the courtroom at her stunt.

The prosecution then responded to a subpoena served by the defense on Alayne Katz—which demanded items of Gail's that Alayne told the Grand Jury she had found among her sister's belongings. The subpoena named several things, including Gail's pocketbook and her address book. The main reason for the subpoena was for the defense to determine if the prosecution knew that the defense actually had the address book and the daily diary, as well as the notebook in which Gail wrote her thoughts. If the prosecution had a copy, or knew what was in the diary, they would be required to say so now. But Dan said that, while

Alayne did have the address book at one time, it had apparently been thrown out, "although, she told me she would look for it."

Scott suppressed a chuckle—because the book had been in his safe for fifteen years. Of course, the address book was not as interesting as the notebook in which Gail jotted thoughts about the people in her life. To the prosecution, the judge and the spectators, it seemed like a pointless request by the defense but it wasn't pointless at all. Dan told the court that the other items were "no longer in existence ... except for one minor article ... a brass toothpick in some type of case, that, evidently, Gail Katz carried around in her pocketbook."

"Do you want the toothpick?" the judge asked David, with a chuckle.

"No, Your Honor, we don't need Miss Katz's toothpick," David grinned.

That night on television and the next morning, in the papers, the press led their stories with the prosecution's charges. *New York Post* reporter Laura Italiano wrote that Bob "wasted no time dirtying up the wife he's accused of killing ..." by calling her "a pushy, promiscuous cocaine addict," in a story headlined: "DOC'S VANISHED WIFE SMEARED BY LAWYERS IN SLAY-TRIAL OPENING."

Juror Robert Johnson was taking a cab home when news of the trial came on the cabbie's radio. He asked the driver to turn down the volume or change the channel but, being a New York City cab driver, he refused. The juror stuck his fingers in his ears for the rest of the ride—and gave a bad tip.

CHAPTER 42

COMIC RELIEF

BERNICE peered through reading glasses at a crossword puzzle clue, ignoring the bustle around her in the courtroom on the second day of the trial, as people filed in, took seats and chatted before court began. Gail's "Aunt Bea," Bernice Backan from Connecticut, sat in the front row on the right side to represent the family and note the testimony because Steve Katz could not attend that day. A thin, pleasant woman with silver hair and a warm smile, Aunt Bea was Manny Katz's sister and Steve and Alayne's only living blood relative. When Alayne argued with Bob over Gail's possessions, she fought to get a crystal dish given by Aunt Bea to Gail and Bob for their wedding. The elderly woman looked up from her puzzle book to peer at Bob and Janet, who had arrived and took seats across the aisle on the opposite "defense" side of the courtroom. As the lawyers gathered in front of the room, Bob, a tight expression on his face, stood up. Janet also stood, her nervousness evident on her face. She kissed Bob for luck and he walked forward to take his seat at the defense table. Aunt Bea watched Bob pass with a cold eye.

"Their family is suffering now, and I know I shouldn't say it, but it makes me very happy," she said, returning to her crossword.

The first witness of the day was Jane Dunne, who was nervous until she walked to the stand with every eye in the hushed courtroom on her—then she was scared. After she was sworn in, she spotted Bob at the defense table. An unreasoning wave of fear rushed over her when she saw him. But she realized this was not the gawky young doctor she had met fifteen years earlier. He was an attractive man, a good-looking professional in a suit. The fact that the judge was a woman was a bit comforting to Jane and her fear faded as Stephen Saracco, a familiar face, began to take her through the paces of her direct testimony. She described being Gail's boss and how the younger woman had confided some of her problems—such as the time Bob choked Gail. Unlike her earlier descriptions of Gail's neck bruises as looking like "hickeys" on either side of Gail's neck, Jane testified that the bruises "didn't have the amorphous shape of hickeys—they seemed like fingers." Jane told of being alarmed that Gail intended to threaten Bob with ruin by using the psychiatrist's letter—and also threatening to expose his father for supposed fraud.

"She said there were millions of dollars involved and that she was going to threaten to reveal this to Bob . . . because she was angry. It made no sense to me that she would do that."

She described writing a $500 check to Gail just before she disappeared, for Gail to use as a security deposit on an apartment.

"She never cashed the check," Jane said.

On cross-examination, David asked her about Sylvia's glass casserole, casting doubt on Gail's tale in an attempt to demonstrate that it was one of Gail's exaggerations. He asked if Jane had information, other than Gail's bizarre claim, that "her mother actually put glass in a casserole . . . ?"

"I don't know if it was there," Jane replied. "I had no reason to doubt it."

On re-direct by the prosecution, she said Gail did not appear to be fibbing but was sobbing when she asked, "There were big pieces of glass in it—what does that mean?"

Jane, who suddenly seemed to be testifying as the clinical psychologist she was, then answered Gail's question for the jury. "It means her mother had been careless with her . . . it makes the adult child careless" such as when Gail planned to provoke and threaten Bob.

As she spoke, several jurors shook their head in agreement with her. The testimony certainly painted Gail as a troubled, reckless young woman but it also suddenly gave the jury an insight into why Gail was the way she was—a reason to forgive her behavior: the drugs, the men, the exaggerations.

When she left the stand and looked at Bob one last time, Jane no longer saw a man she feared. She had doubts about whether he had really killed Gail. From what she knew about the case, it didn't seem as if the prosecutors had a case beyond a reasonable doubt.

"What if I'm wrong?" she asked herself, as she walked past Bob. As she left the court, Jane felt bad, not just for Gail, but for Bob.

There had been no mention of blood on the rug or of "false memories." David did not try to discredit her by asking why she had told people she had seen blood on the rug. After a brief recess, the former police aide who had filled out Gail's complaint that Bob had choked her into unconsciousness in November 1983, took the stand to testify about the document—which the judge had ruled could not be entered into evidence. For the jury, it was a distinction without a difference.

Next on the stand was a reluctant prosecution witness— Bob's father, Dr. Marvin Bierenbaum. The thin, gray-haired doctor with a florid face walked slowly to the witness box. He did not look well.

"My, did he get old," Aunt Bea whispered as he passed.

Marvin swore to tell the truth in a weak, shaky, raspy voice and sat down.

After preliminary questioning, Marvin was asked by Dan Bibb about the family birthday party that Bob attended on the day Gail vanished and if he had "any knowledge whether there was any problem in their relationship?"

"I had no knowledge," Marvin testified in his wobbly voice—his eyes glaring strongly at Dan. His answers were short, dripping with anger—not surprising for a man forced to testify against his son in a murder trial. He was asked if he had tried to talk his son out of marrying Gail Katz.

"I thought they should take a little bit more time before

they got married . . . it was our observation that Gail was a very tense lady. He didn't answer me and they were married shortly thereafter."

In tense, terse exchanges, Dan asked Marvin about the 1983 choking incident, which the father described by allowing: "They were having some difficulty adjusting to each other."

Dan asked if Bob had told him that the fight had resulted in "physical contact."

"Yes, he told me that," Marvin said.

Dan asked whether Marvin had asked Bob who physically contacted whom in the altercation.

"I did not."

Incredulous before the jury, Dan asked if his son had ever told him whether Bob had "put his hands on her or her hands on him?"

"No, I do not recall that," Marvin said.

Marvin said that on July 7th, 1985, Bob showed up at the party alone, about 6:30 that night.

"He came by himself," said Marvin.

"Did you ask him where his wife was?"

Marvin did not, but "the subject came up, though . . . he said that she had gone out earlier in the day and had not returned. . . ."

"Did he ever tell you that he had an argument with his wife that morning?"

"He didn't tell me that," Marvin said, his eyes trying to bore holes in Dan Bibb. When he left with his wife about 8:30 that night, Bob "was lying on the couch, sound asleep."

Dan asked whether, in subsequent years Bob had told him "what he says happened that day with regard to Gail's disappearance?"

"No."

He also asked if Bob had told him why she left or what the argument was about. He answered both questions with a no. Marvin said that Bob gave no details of what happened that day and Marvin did not ask him for any information.

"Did he ever tell you he flew a plane that day?"

"He did not," said Marvin. "I don't see why he would, it was so routine." Marvin's eyes seemed to glint slightly.

"Objection, Your Honor," Dan protested. "I move to strike that as non-responsive."

The judge did just that, ordering the court stenographer to strike Marvin's words from the record and the jury to disregard them. The tension—in the courtroom and between the witness and the prosecutor—rose with each question.

Dan and his witness then sparred over whether Marvin remembered what he told investigators for the DA's office in 1986 about what time Bob showed up at the party. Marvin said he did not remember.

"Were you as truthful and accurate as you could be . . . ?" It was a question lawyers asked before they presented you with something you'd said years earlier—that was different from what you had just told the court.

"The answer to your question is yes," Marvin said, coldly.

Dan showed him his earlier statement and asked him if it refreshed his memory as to what time Bob arrived at the party.

"Not any more . . . I must have said that to them. I have no recollection of that."

Dan then repeated his question about whether Marvin had been as truthful and accurate as he could be, a polite way of asking him if he would admit to being a liar.

"I always try to be as truthful as I can . . ." said Marvin, his wobbly voice suddenly steeled by rage.

"I have no further questions, Your Honor," Dan said, sitting down.

The defense took the opportunity to cross-examine their client's father, not to grill him but to score backhanded defense points. First, David asked Marvin if he or Bob had had anything to do with Medicaid at their jobs at the Social

Security Administration—a question aimed at Gail's unfounded claim to Jane that Bob and his dad were major
Medicaid frauds.

"No, sir."

David then showed Marvin two 8-by-10 color photos,
which he identified as being taken that night at the party.
One showed Bob at his sister Michelle's dining room table,
a big grin on his face for the camera, his nephew on the
other side of his uncut birthday cake. It was still light outside the window. Bob's watch on his left wrist seemed to
read 7:10. The second photo was taken later at the same
table, the cake cut, fading light outside, almost dark. Bob's
watch seemed to read 7:30.

The defense wanted the pictures in evidence because
they feared the prosecution intended to say Bob may have
finished flying later that night—to get around the expected
testimony of Joel Davis. If Davis convinced the jury that
he had seen Gail as late as 3 o'clock in the afternoon—
how could she get home in time for Bob to kill her, package
her and drive for an hour with her body to the New Jersey
airport? Joel Davis was crucial for the defense and the pictures might prevent the prosecution from making an end
run around his testimony.

David also showed Marvin a cancelled check with an
illegible, scribbled signature. It was a check for an August
7th, 1985, flight from an East Hampton airport—a plane
rental by Bob exactly one month, to the day, after Gail went
missing and Bob flew from Caldwell Airport. In their opening statement, the prosecution said that Bob altered his personal flight log, crudely writing over a 7 and changing it
to an 8 with another color ink—as part of his brilliant plan
to cover up the fact that he had flown on July 7th. The
defense hoped the check would show the jury that there
was a real flight and the prosecution was trying to turn an
everyday mistake into a sinister cover-up.

"Do you recognize the signature?" David asked.

"It's unmistakable," Marvin said, smiling at the illegible
scrawl. "It's my son's."

"Thank you. No further questions, Your Honor."

After lunch, the prosecution had a surprise for the defense. Prosecutor Adam Kaufmann said the next witness, a friend of Gail's, had suddenly remembered—after 15 years—something important the night before her testimony. She recalled that Gail had told her about a psychiatrist's letter that warned her that Bob had the potential to be "homicidal."

David objected, noting that the judge had excluded the letter and Michael Stone from the trial and that the prosecution had not notified them of the upcoming testimony, as the law required.

"I don't think this is fair to spring this—three seconds before the witness is to appear," Crocker-Snyder scolded the Assistant DA. She ordered a mini-hearing without the jury, to hear what the witness had to say.

Denise Kastenbaum, a thin psychologist with frosted hair and glasses, took the stand and told the judge that Gail had told her about the letter's warning that she was in danger if she stayed with Bob.

David cross-examined her and had her confirm on the record that she had never told the police or any other investigators in 1985 or at any other time, right up to her appearance at the trial. Denise left the stand and returned to the witness room, while Stephen defended what seemed to the defense like a fast one.

"I have no doubt that your motives are pure but . . ." the judge said to Stephen, with a smile—and then allowed the testimony, over defense objections, saying, "I find the witness to be credible."

After the jury had filed in, Stephen, in a loud voice said, "The People call Denise Kastenbaum."

Denise walked across the room, past Aunt Bea, who confided, disapprovingly, that she thought that "anyone who goes into psychology has something wrong with them." The listener was too polite to point out that her niece Gail had been one of those people.

Denise told the court that she had met Gail in junior

high school on Long Island and they had become close friends. Gail, she said, had told her she was unhappy and had related the choking incident to her. Once, at a party at Denise's apartment in July 1985, Bob displayed controlling behavior. "Bob wanted Gail to stay sitting on his lap. Every time she would get up, he would draw her back."

She claimed she was the last friend to see Gail alive on Saturday, July 6th, when she met her at the hairdresser's that afternoon and later did some window shopping. Gail, she said, was looking in a newspaper for apartments because she was leaving Bob.

"She said she was going to tell him that weekend," Denise said.

She said Gail told her of an affair she was having with someone at Beth Israel Hospital.

On cross-exam, David asked Denise if Gail had said she was planning to move out that weekend.

"No, that she was going to tell Bob of her intention to move out."

David asked if Gail had ever told her before that she intended to move out.

"Not exactly."

He asked if Gail had told her that she was moving to Connecticut, to stay with a friend.

"I don't recall."

He then asked her if she had read about the case in magazines and newspapers, which she had—implying that her testimony was influenced by the articles, that she was inserting herself into the case.

"Did the prosecution come to you or did you come to them?"

"I don't remember."

Gail's gynecologist, Dr. Mary Wilson, testified next. The doctor, clad in a dark skirt, white silk blouse, and gold-crested navy blazer with gold buttons, testified in her German accent how Gail came to her for implantation of an IUD birth control device on June 21st, 1985. Two weeks later, when Gail returned to check placement of the device, the patient was in good health with no apparent disease and made an appointment to return in six months for a routine checkup.

Usually Gail was "withdrawn and introverted" but on the morning before she disappeared "she was quite happy, she was quite jovial—I don't know why," the physician told Adam Kaufmann on direct questioning. The prosecution had shown that Gail was not suffering from any disease and was planning on a sex life and further doctor visits after July 7, and, hopefully, that she had no intention of killing herself.

Adam next called Ian Wilson, the doctor's husband—who managed her practice—to the stand. When he entered the somber courtroom, Ian had a humorous air about him. He was short and chubby, with a red, round face and tousled brown salt-and-pepper hair. One wing of his collar was askew and his fat, out-of-style tie only reached halfway to his belt. Ian seemed completely unfamiliar with the American courtroom and the oath process, stirring a few titters in the court. In a charming English accent, Ian described how he ran the gynecology office and knew Gail. Adam then asked a question with perhaps not quite the right word that was about to prove that, as George Bernard Shaw observed, Americans and the British are two great peoples separated by a common language: "What was the nature of your relationship with Gail Katz Bierenbaum?" Ian's eyes popped open.

"Relationship? Certainly not! I didn't have a relationship with Gail Katz—outside of the office!" Ian protested indignantly.

The courtroom filled with gales of laughter from the jury, the judge, the lawyers, the press—even Bob and his wife Janet. It was a welcome respite from the deadly serious business of the trial, a relief of the built-up tension.

Ian settled down and described Gail as a moody patient—until the day of her last appointment.

"What I saw on that day was a cheerful girl," Ian said.

On cross-examination by David, Ian, who seemed not to

understand that he himself wasn't allowed to ask questions, revisited the funny misunderstanding.

"I was asked if I had a relationship with Gail Katz—I wouldn't be here if I did," he volunteered, provoking another wave of laughter in court.

David, attempting to return to business, asked Ian to read a statement he had made to police.

"Does that refresh your memory?" David asked.

Ian accepted the piece of paper, squinted at it carefully and then looked up and announced: "I haven't got my glasses. I'm sorry, I would very much like to confirm this, but I don't have my glasses with me."

Again, there was laughter.

The judge, also laughing, took the document and read it to the witness so he could answer. David asked more questions but Ian interrupted the lawyer: "You haven't let me answer the questions before you ask them."

David laughed, shook his head, and tried to press on with his cross-examination.

"Are you a masochist?" the judge asked David, with a big smile.

Again, the court echoed with laughter. David threw in the towel and sat down.

"Thank you, it's been a pleasure," said the judge, with a chuckle. "You may step down."

Grateful for his release, Ian got up, accidentally knocking over the boom microphone, which hit the floor with a loud, amplified BOOM!

Every person in the courtroom was laughing harder—except the judge, who no longer seemed amused at the comic relief. After Ian left, she scolded Adam for the breech of decorum and warned the prosecutor that if his witnesses did not conduct themselves properly in court, they would not take the stand.

Outside court, Ian, apparently still concerned that someone might think he had slept with Gail Katz, told a columnist that he felt the "relationship" question was "very inappropriate. It's not like "Law & Order" at all, is it?"

Francesca Beale was next up and told the jury that Gail wanted to leave Bob and had asked if she could stay with her, because she was afraid of Bob.

"She expressed fear that something would happen to her because of her husband," Francesca said. "She was afraid of him and that he had a terrible temper."

Francesca was the last person other than Bob to speak to Gail, who she said was "cheerful" on the phone.

But on cross-examination, she admitted to David that, in 1985, she had described Gail as being "flat and depressed" that day.

After the jury was excused for the night, the judge reprimanded Dan Bibb and ordered him to caution Steve Katz and other family members in the audience, because they had been making faces in response to defense questions during testimony. The jurors could see the rolling eyes and sarcastic expressions and the judge said she would not permit it. It was the second time Steve had been warned. The families on both sides were ordered not to sit in the front row for the duration of the trial.

CHAPTER 43

FRIENDS & BOYFRIENDS

LESLIE Crocker-Snyder cleared her courtroom of the press and the public before the trial began, to explain the murder trial and the criminal justice system to a rapt audience—a class of grammar school kids from Manhattan Public School 116.

When the lesson was over, the trial resumed with another surprise for the defense from the prosecution. Adam Kaufmann announced that the first witness of the day, Marianne DeCesare, had also just remembered something sensational the night before she was to take the stand. Gail, she said, had told her that Bob threatened to kill her if she ever left him and that Bob had said that Claus von Bülow, another husband accused of trying to kill his wife, had been convicted because he failed to "get rid of the body, so it could never be found and traced back to him."

David Lewis objected to the convenient last-minute memory, saying the inflammatory alleged statements were far more prejudicial to his client's defense than they were probative—that is, providing proof or evidence.

"I think it's far more probative than prejudicial, Mister Lewis," the judge replied, with a grin.

Lewis also protested that the von Bülow statement was double-hearsay—what Gail had told someone Bob had said—and should not be admitted. The judge overruled the strenuous defense objections and ruled that the witness could give the double-hearsay evidence in a murder trial.

Marianne wore a black dress suit that contrasted with her blond hair. She described her background and friendship with Gail, how she socialized with her and Bob, and how Gail had sought her advice when the marriage soured.

"When it was good, it was good," Marianne remembered. "When it was bad, there was fighting. Bob had a bad temper."

She said Gail told her that Bob had threatened to strangle her to death if she ever left him. She also told her about the 1983 choking incident, after which Gail claimed that Bob "had a problem trying to revive her and he had to call 911."

Closer to the time she vanished, Gail asked her friend what she would do if her husband threatened to strangle her if she left him and Marianne told Gail not to be afraid to leave.

"She was afraid and, I guess, she was asking me should she be afraid? He said he would kill her . . . he told her she couldn't leave."

After seeing a movie on the von Bülow case, Marianne said Gail had told her, "Bob said that the problem with the von Bülow case was that he had left evidence and that [Bob] would not leave evidence."

Her words hung in the air, in complete silence until Adam asked his next question. On the Tuesday before she disappeared, Marianne said she had spoken to Gail, who "was very happy. She told me she was going to ask Bob for a divorce." Gail also mentioned that she was working on a paper on depression and had met a psychologist and had a "pretty serious" relationship with him. Gail asked Marianne if she thought it was all right to have guys up to her apartment when Bob was not there.

"I told her I didn't think that was a good idea." She also described Gail's paranoia that Bob was having her followed. When asked why Gail was happy when she'd last spoken to her, Marianne replied: "She was happy because of the person that she had met, Ken. I think it was the first time that she really, sincerely was in . . ."

"Objection!" shouted David, protesting that the witness was volunteering something that only Gail could testify to.

"Sustained," the judge said.

Adam rephrased the question, asking her belief on why Gail was happy.

"Because she was in love with Ken Feiner."

She also testified that Gail confided she was "prepared financially" to leave Bob—because "she had ten thousand dollars in a safe deposit box that Bob did not know about . . . to pay for the first year of graduate school, once she had left him."

Marianne told the jurors that she'd asked Bob where he thought Gail was and that he replied that she was probably "on a shopping spree at Bloomingdale's—you know what a JAP she is."

Strangely, she said, Bob asked her, "I wonder why she went out without her shoes on?" Bob also told her about Gail's 1979 suicide attempt and claimed that Gail had become depressed while working on a paper about suicide. When Marianne disagreed, Bob got angry and asked, "How do I know that she didn't climb the gate of the reservoir, how do I know that she wasn't lying at the bottom of that reservoir?"

On cross-examination, Marianne said she struggled with her conscience but went to police because she felt it was her duty as a citizen and to Gail. David asked her if she had encouraged Gail's affair with Ken.

"Encourage? How did I encourage? No, I did not."

David asked if she'd told police that Bob told her that maybe Gail had become depressed while working on the suicide paper—not the definite statement she had just given.

"Bob was pretty adamant about it."

David showed her the police document, in which she said Bob used the qualifying word "maybe"—more a guess than a statement—but Marianne did not want to take anything back.

"I don't remember him saying 'maybe.' "

David asked, incredulously, why she had never remembered the von Bülow exchange when speaking to police over the years—but Marianne stuck to her story.

Because Marianne's testimony about a TV movie that inspired such damning words from Bob came at the last minute, the defense was unable to quickly determine a crucial fact: The only movie made about Claus Von Bulow, *Reversal of Fortune*, was not released until 1990—five years *after* Gail vanished.

At a sidebar conference, the defense lawyer and the prosecutor almost came to blows. Stephen took issue with a statement by David—about the sudden appearance of the dramatic von Bülow testimony—that the prosecutor felt impugned his ethics. He lunged toward David, who snapped: "You've got to be kidding! You do that again and I'll drop down on the floor in front of this jury—and you explain it."

There was no more jostling at the sidebars.

Nurse Karen Caruana testified that three weeks after Gail disappeared, a mutual friend set her up on a date with Bob in the Hamptons and that they went to bed on the first date. Now married and a mother, Karen seemed ill at ease discussing her sex life fifteen years earlier. She was the first of several witnesses who were now married with children who would be asked embarrassing questions in public.

"We went out to dinner, then we came back . . . and we had sex right after that," said Karen.

Several jurors shot glances at Bob, who was making notes on a yellow pad, not looking at the witness or jury. That August, Karen said, Bob told her that he had hired a private investigator, who found evidence of Gail in California. Bob, she said, told her he thought Gail was in hiding and receiving money from her family. He told her he had been a suspect but that police had searched his apartment for blood and clues and cleared him.

When it became time for cross-examination, David told the court he had "no questions." Karen looked relieved.

The next witness, Susan D'Andrea, looked like a beautiful, blonde actress playing the part of a witness in a murder trial. She strode to the witness box on long, shapely legs, looking a lot younger than her 47 years. She told the court about Bob coming out to the Hamptons and surprising everyone with news that Gail was missing. Bob told the story that he had gone to Central Park looking for Gail but found only her suntan lotion and her towel. She described asking Bob if he thought Gail had been kidnapped and Bob shrugging his shoulders and saying he didn't know.

"There was no remorse," Susan blurted out, her voice dripping with anger.

"Objection!"

"Sustained," the judge agreed. The witness was volunteering to tell the jury what was going on in Bob's mind—only the guilty should feel remorse.

"He wasn't upset, very low-key," Susan explained.

Next, she described Bob going out and having a good time without his wife. Her hatred of the man was palpable.

When cross-examined, she admitted to David that her original description of Bob's mood that weekend was very different. She was shown a statement in which she had described Bob as "dull and somber."

"Those could have been the words I used," she said, looking up from the document. "Yeah, and not upset, nor sad."

"You thought he was socially inept . . . ?" David began.

"Objection!"

"Overruled."

"Yes," said Susan, reluctantly admitting her distaste for Bob.

On re-direct, Dan Bibb tried to underscore several points but Susan couldn't resist condemning Bob, despite the reaction of the defense and the court the first time.

Bob, she volunteered again, "was not the least bit remorseful or sad."

"Objection!"

"Sustained."

Moments later, she did it again, saying that such a short time after his wife vanished, "I would have thought I would see some remorse or sadness."

"Objection!"

"Sustained."

* * *

Another slim, attractive blonde, Dolores Erickson—owner of the summer house—took the stand to add to testimony about Bob in the Hamptons. After only a short association with her, Gail had complained to Dolores about her doctor husband. "She couldn't stand the thought that they didn't have any money." Dolores related that Gail couldn't wait for Bob to start making big money. "Oh, that's going to take too long," Gail told her. "That'll take more than three years—I can't wait that long."

Several jurors shook their heads from side to side. Dolores said Bob told her that Gail left with only $6 in her shorts. She said he told her he realized Gail had a drug problem when he went through her drawers after she left and found cocaine.

"He thought she went off with drug dealers and disappeared," she said.

She recounted Bob going out with the group, with her sister as Bob's date. The couple stayed up late, chatting and laughing in the living room, she said. Departing from his habit of wearing casual clothes and eating in, Bob—after Gail disappeared—dressed up to go out to dinner and even splurged on a case of wine. At a comedy club, Bob laughed his head off and had a good time, she testified.

On cross, David asked if it wasn't true that Bob bought the case of wine as a gift for the house.

"No," said Dolores.

David asked if, at the comedy club, Bob laughed at jokes that Dolores did not think were funny.

"Yes."

Then she described walking by Bob's room and surprising a teary-eyed Bob, who was packing up Gail's clothing. She testified that she said to Bob that it must be hard for him and he said it was. On re-cross, David tried to bring out Dolores' dislike of Bob, by asking if the first time she met him, "you thought he was creepy—didn't you?"

"Objection!"

"Sustained."

When David asked her why she asked Bob the question, she replied: "I thought it would be difficult to pack someone's clothes after they had disappeared. He seemed to be upset while he was packing the clothes. He seemed like he was teary-eyed."

After her testimony, the jury filed out to eat lunch. Once the door was closed behind the jurors, David made a motion to the court:

"Based on the von Bülow testimony, I move for a mistrial."

"Denied," Crocker-Snyder said immediately.

The first witness after lunch was Ken Feiner, PhD, Gail's former boyfriend. Like the nurse who had testified that morning, Ken—an established, middle-aged professional—was visibly nervous and uncomfortable talking about his love life before he was married. He told the jury how he'd met Gail on the subway. Despite his prior statements to police and to the grand jury, under oath, that he and Gail had been lovers, Ken testified that he and Gail had never had sex. His claim caused a brief stir and a whispered conversation at the defense table. Ken claimed that Gail had come to his apartment several times—but not for sex, for intellectual chats. He said that the last time he saw Gail they began to kiss but "I stopped it."

When asked directly by the prosecutor if he had had sex with Gail, who was obviously not around to dispute what they did or did not do when alone, Ken replied: "No, we did not."

Ken said he knew that Gail, who told him about all her problems, was married but wanted to divorce Bob. He said he and Gail had also made plans to meet secretly in the Hamptons on July 13th. He admitted that he visited Gail at least two or three times in her apartment while her husband was at work but insisted the visits did not include sex.

"Did you have a sexual relationship?" David asked on cross.

"We did not consummate the relationship," Ken replied. "I don't know what you mean by sexual relationship," the judge told David and asked for a sidebar conference between the lawyers. After the sidebar, David confronted Ken with his grand jury testimony, in which he was asked if his relationship developed into a sexual relationship.

"I said yes," Ken replied, frowning and squirming in the witness chair.

"Is it true?" David asked.

"I have to give it a fuller answer because this is not comfortable for me to talk about . . . it's embarrassing testifying about it . . ."

The judge interrupted and asked him why he had told the grand jury that he had sex with Gail but now said under oath that they did not have sex. Ken's brow wrinkled.

"I gave that answer because I didn't want to talk about it in detail," he said. "It seemed easier to say yes."

Several jurors had quizzical looks on their faces. One member of the press in the first row whispered, "He sounds like President Clinton."

"So, what was the nature of the sexual relationship?" David asked.

All Ken would admit to was that they kissed, that "it went a bit further" than kissing and "we held each other."

David had the classic opportunity for a cross-examiner— to hit the jury between the eyes with the conflicting testimony. Was he lying before the grand jury or was he lying now? Why should the jury believe an admitted liar—who wanted to convict Bob? But David believed in the intelligence of the jury and did not want cross-examination to result in a jury backlash. He moved on to the time Ken and Gail had picked each other up on the subway. On his direct testimony, Ken had made it seem that all he was interested in was the article on self-mutilation that Gail was reading— not in the sexy girl reading it.

"She was an attractive woman, wasn't she?" David asked in a friendly way.

"An attractive woman reading an article on self-mutilation!" laughed the judge, causing a wave of laughter in the court. David, who also smiled, asked Ken again if

Gail was pretty—and that was also a reason he spoke to her.

"Yes," Ken admitted, grudgingly.

David asked if Gail had told Ken that she hated Bob.

"At some point, yes."

"Did you tell Gail that as long as Gail was living with Bob you couldn't have anything to do with her?"

"If I told it to her, this is fifteen years ago . . ." said Ken, pleading a poor memory.

Another one of Gail's boyfriends—Anthony Segalas—was next on the stand. Dressed in a trim Italian suit, with his gleaming black hair swept back from his handsome face, Anthony also looked like an actor playing the role of the hunk boyfriend. Now married with three daughters, he also could not have been comfortable discussing his past romantic life, but he presented a figure of a strong witness as he discussed his background. He described picking Gail up at a luncheonette and listening to her troubles. Anthony claimed that he'd never noticed a wedding ring and didn't know Gail was married until later in their relationship. He openly admitted it was a sexual relationship, but protested that they didn't have sex every time they met.

"I think we went out to dinner once," he said, causing a few chuckles in the courtroom.

"She really felt trapped," but stayed in the marriage so her husband would pay for her graduate school, Anthony said.

He talked about drifting apart from Gail and then how they "re-connected" in the spring of 1985 at the coffee shop where they had first met, which renewed their affair. He also admitted that "On about two occasions we did cocaine." He related a nighttime call in late June from Gail, who'd invited him over to snort the drug and have sex while Bob was working overnight at the hospital.

"It wasn't much of a marriage but Bob was treating her better," said Anthony.

He said they'd agreed to talk later. When he found a "hang-up" on his telephone answering machine the day before Gail disappeared, Anthony said he thought it might be Gail and called her back.

"I asked Gail to see if she had called me," said Anthony. "She said she had not. It sounded like somebody else was there—maybe Bob was there."

He then described how Bob had called him after Gail vanished and left a message asking him to help look for her. When Anthony called back, Bob "knew who I was . . ." and never asked if Gail was with him.

This was potentially incriminating: If Bob didn't even bother to ask Gail's lover if he knew her whereabouts, was it because he already knew she was dead?

"He asked if I was over at his apartment with her recently."

"What did you say?" Dan Bibb asked.

"Yes."

David cross-examined Anthony and put on the record that he'd shared drugs and had sex with Gail in the apartment while her husband was not home. Anthony agreed that he had told police that Gail was "needy" and "high-maintenance," and "needed a white knight" to rescue her.

"She wanted you to be the white knight?"

"Possibly."

"And you didn't want to be that?"

"Correct."

"At some point, Gail told you to ask for Doctor Bierenbaum and not her—to conceal that you were coming there for her and not him?"

"I don't recall that. . . ." Anthony replied. When shown a police document, Anthony agreed that he had said that.

The last witness of the day was Yvette Feis, who took the oath, adjusted her brown hair and sat down for her direct questioning. She testified about Gail as her student at Hunter College and how they had come to be friends.

In the year of the vanishing, Gail "told me that she was not interested in having sexual relations" with Bob. "She wore clothes to bed to reduce the likelihood of having sex," said Yvette. She told the jury that Gail had told her about

Michael Stone's written warning and that "she intended to use the letter as leverage in a divorce proceeding . . . she would use the letter to get more of what she wanted" or else "She would use it to ruin his career. She said she would show it to the department chairman where he was working or anywhere he was working in the future."

When Bob called Yvette after Gail went missing, she said she'd "strongly urged him to call the police and report her missing. He didn't seem very interested."

"Objection!" David protested.

"Overruled," Crocker-Snyder said.

"He put off taking actions. He had excuses," Yvette continued.

She said she—not Bob—had called the press to get publicity and she even searched the incinerator room looking for clues. She also called police to "alert them to what I felt was more than a Missing Persons investigation."

One week after Gail disappeared, after a search of Central Park, Bob said he had taken a rug at the apartment out to the cleaners.

"I was surprised," said Yvette.

"Objection!"

"Sustained."

"I asked how he could find time to have the rug cleaned during the week his wife was missing."

"He said the cat had messed up and he had it cleaned." She said Bob's tone seemed phony.

Two or three weeks after July 7, Yvette said she spoke to Bob on the phone about his final argument with Gail and that his "tone seemed more genuine to me."

She said Bob told her that his psychiatrist had told him "that he should try to defuse" argument situations "but that, this time, he did not defuse it. He said the argument had become explosive."

She said she'd responded to Bob's confidence by saying, "Are you sure you want to be telling me this?" to Bob. "I was scared," Yvette said, looking at the jury.

"Objection!"

"Overruled," said the judge.

On cross, Yvette said she knew about Gail's boyfriends Ken and Anthony. She also admitted that Bob had called the police, called all of Gail's friends and searched for Gail.

"I urged him to hire an investigator but I know he hired a lawyer first," Yvette sniffed.

"You know there's nothing wrong with hiring a lawyer, don't you?" David asked.

"I was surprised," Yvette shot back defiantly, answering the question in her own way.

As she walked away from the witness stand, Yvette glared at Bob. He looked away from the loathing in her eyes.

CHAPTER 44

ALAYNE

DAN Bibb announced in court that Alayne Katz would also make a surprise statement—that Gail told her that she had actually threatened Bob with the psychiatrist's warning letter and said she would ruin his career. David angrily objected to what seemed to him like another prosecution trick but, once again, the judge allowed the testimony.

Alayne, who had her short, spiky blonde hair dyed a more conservative brown for her appearance, entered the courtroom and was sworn in. She wore a black dress and a somber expression on her gaunt face. She crossed her legs, clasped her hands on her lap and turned toward the jury as she described her background and her family history. In a dramatic, breathy drawl, she described meeting Bob in 1981, after Gail had told her that he "was athletic, he was smart, he was charming, he was successful, he was good at everything." She added that Gail "was enamored of him."

When Alayne related the strangling incident, her voice quivered with emotion as she remembered her hysterical sister on the phone after the attack.

"She didn't know what she should do," said Alayne, pulling a tissue out of her purse and dabbing at her eyes. "She was unhappy and scared and ready to leave."

Some four to six weeks before Gail disappeared, Alayne said, they spoke on the phone.

Dan Bibb asked Alayne if Gail had told her then about threatening Bob with the shrink's letter.

"She told me she had done so. She told me that she had told Bob that if he didn't give her the things she wanted . . . that she would use the letter to expose him to his superiors as being psychotic."

For the first time, the jury heard that Gail had in fact threatened Bob with the psychiatrist's letter. But the prosecution had opened by saying that Bob had snapped and killed Gail because she threatened him with the letter for the first time on Sunday, July 7th. How could Bob be surprised and enraged by the news if he had already heard the threat more than a month earlier?

Alayne cried when she spoke about a lost opportunity to see her sister at her parents' house the week before she was last seen.

"Did you ever see her again?" Dan asked.

"No," said Alayne.

"Did your parents ever see her again?"

"No," she said, sobbing.

She testified about the search for Gail and, later, about picking up her sister's belongings from Bob at his apartment. "It was terrible," said Alayne, anger now in her voice. "There were trash bags all over the place with her things. I felt I was doing him a favor and taking out his trash."

"Objection!"

"Sustained."

She described yelling at Bob that he had killed her sister and couldn't have her things.

Dan asked if Bob had responded.

"He said she was a tramp and she was off living with someone else." Alayne broke into tears again. She had left out an important part of that encounter that she had told several journalists—that Bob had denied killing Gail. She then described taking off from law school and writing letters and searching for proof to have Bob arrested.

"I got back lots of letters and lots of phone calls . . ." but not one person had seen Gail.

When Dan finished the direct exam, he sat down and the court informed David that it was his witness. He asked the judge for a minute to confer with his client and the other defense lawyers. The defense team was very happy with Alayne's testimony. She had said that Gail had threatened to ruin Bob with the letter—and he had done nothing. It seemed like a complete gift for the defense. The victim's sister had just testified that the very thing they said had provoked Bob to murder was nothing new to him. A star prosecution witness had testified that the People's theory was wrong. Also, Alayne had said that Bob told her Gail was probably off living with someone else. It was an implicit denial by Bob—provided by Alayne. They had what they considered strong material to call Alayne's truthfulness or memory into question on certain issues—but why use it and take a chance it might backfire or that the jury would resent a grilling of the sobbing sister of the victim? After a hushed, animated discussion for several minutes, David addressed the court.

"Your Honor, the defense has no questions."

There were several gasps of surprise that the defense would not cross-examine the witness. Alayne seemed shocked. The reporters felt cheated out of a heated and dramatic courtroom clash. Alayne shot Bob a fierce look on her way out of the court. He looked away. After a ten-minute recess, Alayne, now able to attend the trial, returned to the courtroom and took a seat in the second row.

*Oscar Asner, owner of Sky King Aviation at the Caldwell Airport in New Jersey, testified that Bob Bierenbaum had reserved a 4:30 to 7:30 P.M. time slot for that day but only operated the aircraft for one hour and fifty-four minutes. He said Bob could have driven his car on the tarmac up to the rented plane, which was not visible from the rental office.

He talked about the "hands-off" flying of the Cessna 172 that Bob flew and estimated that he could have flown ninety miles away from the airport before turning back, indicating on a large aviation map a circle of flight that could have taken him southeast—out over the ocean.

On cross-examination, David—also using a pointer on the map—asked if the circle of flight might also have taken Bob north toward New York's Catskill Mountains, or west toward Pennsylvania, or even in circles in New Jersey.

"Yes." David did not mention the Greenwood Lake Airport or the Wanaque Reservoir and he did not point them out on the map.

CHAPTER 45

RINGING THE BELL

ELSA Fairchild, Gail's former psychologist, was a striking figure with jet black hair, shocked with Bride-of-Frankenstein ripples of white on either side. As she sat in the witness box, she observed Bob and thought the defendant looked ghoulish, his eyes seemed empty.

She testified that Gail's everyday conflict was "her fear of staying and her fear of going . . . she was extremely afraid of his anger."

Gail failed to make her Monday, July 8th, 1985 appointment, recalled the therapist—who strongly rejected the notion that Gail was suicidal. On her last visit, a few days before she was last seen, the psychologist noticed something that she felt ruled out suicidal intent: "She'd had a pedicure," said Elsa. "No suicide had a pedicure. I remember the color of her toes."

Ten minutes after 12:30—the time of Gail's appointment—Elsa said Bob had called and told her that Gail had gone off after an argument and asked if she was there. She said Bob never asked if Gail was suicidal and she never told him that. On cross-examination, she said that for three years she neither encouraged Gail to leave or to stay with her husband.

"I was trying to help her discover where she was going with her internal conflict . . . so she could come to her own decision. She landed more on the side of leaving him."

She admitted that Gail was a bit manipulative and said Gail had told her she had a rich friend who would guarantee a lease on an apartment.

Tall, lanky and balding, Ralph Sugarman—Bob's best man at the wedding—was sworn in as a prosecution witness against his medical school colleague and former best friend. To deflate the defense's cross-examination, Adam

Kaufmann asked Ralph about losing his medical license in 1997, which Ralph said occurred after he improperly wrote prescriptions. Also, Ralph admitted that he had been arrested for selling valuable antiques that belonged to a patient —and keeping the money.

Ralph said Bob had told him that Gail wanted a divorce after the choking incident but that he wanted to keep the marriage intact. He said Gail called to complain "that she was frightened . . . of potential violence" from Bob.

He told about meeting Bob on the street in 1985 and Bob telling him "that he hated her so much that he could kill her."

Ralph said that in Gail's absence, Bob told him "that he believed that she had been seeing someone" but that Bob was "very concerned about her disappearance."

David also declined to cross-examine Ralph.

Clinical psychologist Ellen Schwartz brushed aside a strand of her curly strawberry blond hair and took the oath before testifying that her friend Gail wanted to leave Bob but was afraid of him. She said she was going to tell Bob she was leaving the weekend she was last seen alive. She testified that she had told Gail she could move in with her until she got settled—even though it wasn't exactly convenient to live in Connecticut and go to school in Manhattan. She said Bob called her and asked if Gail was there. On cross, she said she remembered Bob telling her that he was concerned that Gail "would do something to hurt herself."

The jury took an afternoon break, while the judge and the lawyers briefly argued about keeping the alleged cat strangling away from the jury.

Crocker-Snyder assured David "that the cat issue . . . will not come in."

"I'd rather not litter the record, Your Honor," David replied, with a smirk—prompting laughter from the judge and several others.

After the recess, Detective Tom O'Malley, burly, silver-haired and florid-faced, stepped into the witness box. A friendly witness, Tom looked a bit like Santa Claus without a beard. He detailed his 28-year career in NYPD, his fluffy white eyebrows arching and straightening like snowy caterpillars as he remembered details. He described his initial interview with Bob and the questioning on July 13th—when Tom had confronted him about the doorman and Bob told him he had made a mistake and the doorman had not seen Gail leave that day. He recounted how Bob refused to discuss what he and Gail had fought about, saying, "I don't want to talk about it."

"I told him I wanted him to tell me everything he did that day," said Tom.

Stephen asked if Bob had told him that he'd rented a plane that day.

"Absolutely not."

Did Bob say he thought his wife might have committed suicide? Stephen asked.

"Yes, he did . . . He said that she was depressed and that she was suicidal."

Tom said Bob mentioned nothing about Gail's drug use, or drug dealers, which might have been of use in an investigation. Tom also talked about running down reports of sightings of Gail and not finding her.

On cross-examination, David elicited that in 1985, identifications were done from fingerprints—not DNA evidence. Tom also agreed that some bodies found around the city went unidentified and were buried in unmarked graves in Potter's Field on Hart Island in Long Island Sound. But when David tried to get Tom to admit that he spent much more time on Joel Davis' sighting report than the others, Stephen objected and the judge agreed.

"You did more than . . ." David began.

"Don't even ask it," the judge warned. Then she turned to O'Malley and took over the questioning. "Did any witnesses have any credibility whatsoever?"

"Objection!" David shouted. The judge was about to torpedo the defense case before it was even presented.

"No!" the judge replied, wagging her finger at the defense lawyer, warning him to shut up.

"Objection!"

"I think it needs to be asked," Crocker Snyder said, sternly.

"No!" David protested, incredulously.

After another round of strong objections, the judge silenced David and asked Tom her question in front of the jury. "You decided you did not believe Joel Davis, is that correct?"

"*Objection!*" David yelled, angry.

"Sustained," said the judge, apparently realizing she had gone too far. She ordered a sidebar conference. The lawyers went to the far left of the court well, followed by the court stenographer and the judge. The spectators and the jury could hear a whispered argument and see anger on the faces of the lawyers, though they could not hear what was being said—but it was obvious that David and the judge were engaged in battle.

David demanded a mistrial, saying the judge had used her position to destroy the credibility of a key defense witness—before he took the stand.

"I think the question was inappropriate. I think the rephrasing of my question in that fashion was inappropriate," David said. "I think it is the level of interference in the trial rises to the point where this defendant could not get a fair trial because you now matched this detective's credibility against the witness, not allowing me to inquire as to the basis of his determination."

David said that the prosecutor had "opened the door" to the question of alleged sightings of Gail by the public and Joel Davis "was approached three times by this detective. He initialed and identified the photo of Gail Katz Bierenbaum as the person he saw."

"Okay. Your motion for a mistrial is denied," the judge snapped, in a voice the jury never heard. "Say whatever you want, the record will bear out what the record bears out. You did not ask proper questions, in my view. I made my rulings."

She told David that during the People's case there was "no way in which you are going to bring out exactly what this detective did with this particular person."

The judge then severely limited David's cross-examination of O'Malley on the issue of Joel Davis. The sidebar ended and David tried to continue but felt that his hands had been tied. The prosecution had opened the door but the judge would not allow him to go through it.

"You may ask . . . what I've indicated," the judge said.

David asked Tom if he had interviewed Joel Davis.

"Yes."

"Did you interview anyone else three times?" David asked.

"Objection!" Stephen interrupted.

"Sustained," said the judge. "Don't argue—ask your next question."

David began asking general questions about how Tom investigated sightings, trying to figure out how to show the jury that Joel Davis was very different from all the others who reported sightings of Gail—without violating the judge's orders.

"Your Honor, I need a moment," he said.

"Take a moment, take more," said the judge, with a friendly smile.

"Thanks for your generosity, Your Honor," David said sarcastically, smiling back.

"Isn't that from "Ally McBeal"?" the judge joked, provoking a few chuckles from the jury.

"I don't know, Your Honor, I don't watch TV," David shot back.

The judge's law secretary Teresa Matushaj whispered something into the judge's ear.

David backtracked and went over points raised during the prosecution's questioning, thinking on his feet as he went. He stopped at the podium, thought for a moment and then shrugged. There was no way he could get what he wanted out of Tom O'Malley without violating the judge's instructions.

"Your Honor, I have nothing," he said, with a shrug.

"I need to have another sidebar on something we were talking about earlier," the judge announced.

At the new sidebar, the emotions were not as high but the issue was the same and just as important

Crocker Snyder, said she had decided that she was being unfair. She granted a prosecution request to strike her question and O'Malley's answer—to avoid a mistrial.

"I shouldn't have asked the question," she said. "It is my fault. I'm the judge. I shouldn't have asked the question just to remedy my annoyance of your question."

"To be very blunt about it," David replied, "I tried very carefully to not do what you believed I was doing. I know . . ."

"Let me think about this. . . ." the judge said.

"Here is the problem," David posited. "I don't know if you can un-ring the bell, folks."

Once the jury had heard Joel Davis discredited, they couldn't un-hear it, no matter what the judge said.

"That is not your problem," the judge said. "That is my problem. You asked for a mistrial, I denied that."

"Judge, we believe that you cannot un-ring the bell. Therefore, whatever curative action, whatever the court decides to do, we will just renew the mistrial motion," David said.

"I understand that," the judge responded, breaking up the sidebar. "That is your opinion. I will do what I think I have to do."

Back in open court, David decided to stop his questioning.

"That concludes our examination," he said, sitting down at the defense table.

Tom O'Malley was excused and stepped down. With the press watching and taking notes, the judge ate crow in front of the jury—the first time in her career she had been forced to do so on such an issue. Judges usually only apologize to juries and strike their questions when they realize that to fail to do so might result in a reversal of a conviction by a higher court. She told the jurors with a tight smile that, in reflecting on the heated exchanges, she had become a little cranky because it was past her usual lunchtime.

"I feel that I should not have asked that question. It was an inappropriate question on my part . . . it was not evidence," she said, before sending the jury home for the night.

Bob and Scott had a conversation about justice and politics after Bob complained that the judge seemed completely biased toward the prosecution and against him.

Crocker-Snyder, "is a perfect judge—according to your pal, Newt Gingrich," said Scott. "Suddenly, the other guy is you."

The lawyer told his client and friend that Bob's longtime support of conservative, right-wing law-and-order politicians had, ironically, helped to "create a system that will deny you any semblance of fairness."

CHAPTER 46

GIRLFRIENDS

ROBERTA Karnofsky, sporting a round, curly auburn hairdo and a blue dress suit and pearls, was next up. She told the jury that in 1985, Bob, who was one of her bosses, had arranged for her to be in his operating room—so he could flirt with her during surgery. Bob, she said, "would make sure I was on the same side of the table . . . sometimes he would rub his leg up against mine as we were doing the case."

One of the jurors in the front row smirked and there were several titters about a doctor playing footsie with another doctor over an unconscious patient on the operating table.

Roberta said Bob had asked her to move in with him less than a month after Gail disappeared and she actually moved into the apartment in September. Bob, she said, told her he thought Gail "was in some kind of fugue state," in which sufferers "don't know who they are or where they are. He said that he knew she had some affairs during their marriage, even though it was very short," she said.

She described how she and Bob were awakened in the middle of the night in 1986 by a phone call from the police.

"A woman had been found at the bus terminal the Port Authority thought may have been Gail," and the cops wanted Bob to go down "and identify whether this was Gail."

Bob, she said, had replied, "Do I need to come down right now?"

Roberta said the police wanted Bob there. The call, she testified, "was disturbing, to some degree, because I was living in his house. I said, 'If you're going down, and that may be Gail, you might be coming home with Gail. What should I do? Do you want me to pack up and get out?' "

She said that Bob replied, "Don't worry about it—I doubt it's Gail."

It was very quiet in court and every juror was looking right at her.

Roberta also testified that Bob told her that police had looked in the building's basement because "they wanted to see if he threw her body down the incinerator and they didn't find anything." She said Bob also claimed cops asked him if he had his rug cleaned and he told them he had not.

During a minor spat, Roberta said she was annoyed at Bob and decided to goad him about Gail. She said she'd told him her theory about how he might have killed Gail. She described "how he may have done it," by putting Gail "in one of those big flight bags, as she was so small, put her into the back of your car and driven her out to the airport and put her on the plane and then thrown her out of the plane."

Bob, she said, had no reaction—he looked down at the table and neither denied the theory nor responded. Discussing events with a friend, who also moved into the apartment, Roberta said she and her friend pulled out Bob's flight log and discovered what looked like an altered date, which was changed from 7/7/85 to 8/7/85.

"It was quite apparent to us that the date of the entry had been changed," said Roberta.

On cross-exam, Roberta admitted that her relationship with Bob did not end in an entirely amicable way but said she and Bob had stayed in touch.

"It ended because you discovered he had a relationship with someone else in that apartment . . . while you were on call?" David asked.

Yes, Roberta answered, "She called and asked for him when I answered the phone."

"That's how the relationship ended, right?"

"Objection!"

"Sustained."

"You went into his office, into his files to look into his flight log . . . into his drawers?" David asked.

"No, sir, it was on the desk."

He asked her if she ever told the grand jury or police the opposite—that Bob had changed the day in his flight log, not the month.

"I may have said that . . ." Roberta said, claiming a mistake.

David then attempted to characterize Bob's non-reaction, not as a stunned admission of guilt, but as Bob ignoring an absurd, provocative "theory." He hoped to demonstrate to the jury that it was a case of an angry girlfriend trying to annoy her boyfriend—not expose him as a killer.

"What you were trying to do was get a rise out of him, right?"

"I would say that's correct, that's part of why . . ." said Roberta, who also admitted she did not rush to move out and "did not have any personal fear" of Bob, despite her theory— which was now the prosecution's official version of events.

After a few more questions and a re-direct, in which she looked at and identified Bob's altered flight log, Roberta stepped down. Her testimony—that he'd flirted during operations right after his wife went missing, that he'd altered a flight log, and especially that he'd somehow seemed to know his wife could not be waiting for him in a police station—seemed very damaging to Bob.

Or would the jury believe the defense take—that a spurned girlfriend would lie under oath and put her cheating ex-lover behind bars for life, out of revenge?

In between witnesses, Dan announced that the prosecution would soon introduce a videotape showing a lone police pilot dumping a 110-pound duffel bag out of a Cessna 172 into the ocean.

"I suspect we'll object," said David.

"I suspect I'll allow it," the judge smiled.

"I suspected that, as well," David replied.

Carole Gordon Fisher told the jury about asking Bob on their first date if he had been married before. When he hesitated in an odd way, she made light of it: "I asked him . . . 'What'd you do—kill your wife?' He was stunned. He looked pretty shocked."

She said Bob became pale and asked what she knew.

"I didn't know anything. I thought I had made a joke," she said.

Several jurors shook their heads.

She said Bob then told her his tale of woe about Gail's vanishing, about her drug problem, and seeing other men. She said he confided in her that he had once had a bad temper.

The cross-examination was very brief and concerned the dates of their relationship and the fact that she did not fly with Bob on all his flights during that time.

Dave Ostrow told the court about his attempt to cajole Bob to come to New Jersey or to get together for a reunion with him and Scott Baranoff two nights before Gail was last seen.

"I started to break Bobby's balls," chuckled Ostrow, who said he could hear Gail "hen-pecking him. She was screeching that he couldn't go out, that they had a date. He was conflicted. I said that he was pussy-whipped."

"Ahhh," uttered one juror. Several others laughed, as did many observers in the audience.

The prosecutor asked if Ostrow had seen Bob during his visit home.

"No," said Ostrow, who began an account of what followed. The judge, apparently concerned that more x-rated slang might pop out, cut the witness short:

" 'No' will be good."

After a few more questions, he was excused and the jury was shown the flight log. Paper clips marked the spot where an 8 had been superimposed on a 7 in a different-colored ink and "Easthampton" had apparently been written over something else. Although the People did not call their handwriting expert to validate their theory, it was clear the number had been changed. The DA said that Bob had covered it up to hide his flight, which meant that he would have had to write the full date of 7/7/85 in one color ink and then conceal it with a crude alteration in another ink. The jurors silently scrutinized the log and the entry carefully, passing it to the next juror when they were done. When they were finished and filed out of court at the end of the day, none of them looked at Bob.

After court, out of sight of the jury, Bob hugged his old friend Dave Ostrow, the prosecution witness, and the two sat down for a friendly chat before parting. His testimony was damaging to Bob—if the jury decided that Gail keeping Bob from a reunion with friends on Friday night and a party on Saturday night were some of the last straws that had led Bob to kill her.

Outside court, several members of the media were discussing the line of women—including Gail—who'd sought relationships with the doctor, despite believing bad things about him. One reporter told a sardonic joke about a single Jewish woman, who saw a good-looking Jewish man surrounded by photographers on the courthouse steps.

"Why are they taking your picture?" the woman asked.

"I'm the doctor charged with killing my wife," the man answered.

"So . . ." the woman smiled flirtatiously. "You're single?"

CHAPTER 47

MURDER MOVIE

CHARLES Hirsch, the chief medical examiner of New York City, was the first witness on the seventh day of the trial. Adam Kaufmann asked Dr. Hirsch how long it would take for a trained surgeon to dismember a human body.

"Objection!"

"Overruled."

Hirsch detailed how the ligaments that bound the skeleton together at the joints could be easily sliced. Adam again asked how long that would take to accomplish.

"Objection!"

The judge interceded, saying the question was "overly broad—why don't you break it into several parts?"

There were a few muffled chuckles at the judge's choice of words.

Hirsch said a person would not even need a scalpel and could dismember a body using "only a knife." Adam asked Hirsch to say how long it would take a person "trained as a surgeon" to do it.

"Objection!"

"Sustained."

Adam switched his question around, asking Hirsch how long it would take him to dismember a dead person.

"Given a sharp knife, I believe I could dismantle a body in . . . ten minutes or so," said Hirsch.

He then testified that before rigor mortis sets in, the body "is extremely pliable." He said that a small, thin woman like Gail would be "easily foldable at the waist" and her body could be tied with a cord or belts—making a package less than 36 inches long and weighing 110 pounds. In fact, he said, he had seen such a thing done to several murder victims.

On cross-examination, Hirsch admitted that people other

than surgeons could also accomplish such a deed.

"Perhaps even lawyers?" who knew a lot about murder, David asked with a smile, causing a ripple of laughter to sweep the courtroom. Hirsch said that was possible but qualified his answer: "I'm not sure you can learn that in a courtroom," he said.

"A cook or a butcher certainly has that knowledge, yes?"

Hirsch said it was possible but again qualified his answer, saying that the bones of man and animal "are structurally different."

He also said "approximately ninety to ninety-five percent of recently dead persons will sink in water." Some five to seven percent will float, especially overweight persons with a lot of body fat.

David asked if it was a fact that many bodies, or even parts of bodies, later rose to the surface after gases produced by decomposition made the corpse buoyant. The judge interrupted, calling the questions "hypothetical" and wondered whether the witness had not been given enough facts for "an informed answer." To further settle everyone's breakfast, Hirsch then discussed the "activities of marine animals" that might devour a body. Finally, David asked if many variables were involved.

"I'd agree with that," Hirsch replied, concluding his testimony.

In from Las Vegas, Dr. Scott Baranoff told the jury that he had been Bob's friend since boyhood. Bob had told him that his marriage "was in turmoil." Gail and Bob, he said, argued frequently over "His time, his money. She had certain things she expected . . . that a young resident couldn't offer his wife." He said Gail wanted "money to spend" and there was "a lot of yelling and screaming." Scott said he'd told his friend to "get a divorce and be done with it." He described coming home on the night Gail disappeared and finding an unexpected guest there—Bob. Stephen asked if Bob had told him that he had gone flying that day.

"No, he didn't," Baranoff said.

David also declined to cross-examine Baranoff.

Also in from Las Vegas was the svelte, beautiful blond chiropractor and former fiancée of Bob's, Stephanie Youngblood, who described meeting Bob at a 1989–1990 New Year's Eve party in Vegas.

Dan Bibb asked her if she'd ever asked Bob if he was married.

"He said no" but she eventually found out he'd had a previous wife when she came across luggage with Gail's name on it.

"I asked, 'Who is Gail Bierenbaum?' He said it was very difficult for him to answer. He was upset. He was a little bit teary-eyed and he told me he had been married. He said . . . she had disappeared one day. He was taken in for questioning a couple of times. He felt that she had been murdered. . . . In the course of the investigation, he found out she had a drug problem and she was having extra-marital affairs, so I felt he was the victim," Stephanie remembered.

She said Bob told her that Gail had gone to Central Park "to hang out with her drug friends and it was probably a drug-related death."

Stephanie said Bob never told her he had flown that day. She testified that she had been flying many times with Bob, who always logged the flights in his log book.

David also did not cross-examine Stephanie.

The jury filed out for a recess, as the lawyers argued over the prosecution's intention to introduce their video re-enactment of a police pilot dumping a weighted duffel bag out of a Cessna 172 into the ocean.

The video, David argued, "is not evidence—it is a demonstration."

"It's evidence—of a demonstration," the judge smiled, overruling the defense objection. After lunch, Sergeant Matthew Rowley, the pilot featured in the video, took the stand to testify about the video. A cop for seventeen years and a police pilot for thirteen years, he said the lack of an autopilot would not prevent such a maneuver. Then he stepped down in front of the jury box and narrated the video for the jurors. The prosecution had wheeled in two large television screens on a cart and played their movie in the darkened courtroom. It showed Rowley at the Caldwell airport in New Jersey, loading two 50-pound bags of kiddie "play sand" and an "easy to carry" 10-pound bag of long grain rice into a black duffel bag and then hefting it, with difficulty, into the passenger seat of a rented Cessna to simulate Gail's folded 110-pound body. When Rowley was in the air, he slowed the plane and the "package" was easily pushed out and into the ocean below.

"Ahhh . . . !" exclaimed one juror as the black bag vanished toward the blue Atlantic.

Obviously, for the audience in the jury box, the prosecution's film was a hit.

A second plane and a police helicopter shadowed the Cessna, filming the reconstruction from both sides. Bob seemed as fascinated by the video as everyone else in the courtroom. Rowley narrated the show, describing how he slowed the aircraft, raised the nose, and how he was able to "push the bag out the door—it's gone." He did it a third time, pulling the bag across his lap with great difficulty. It got caught on the steering wheel and he was forced to move his seat back to get it past. He then shoved it out the pilot's-side door—just to cover all the bases. That time, the bag got stuck and Rowley had to free it before it went into free fall toward the water. Now the jury had seen that it was possible to dump such a load out of a plane. By doing it three times, Rowley made it look almost easy. Since the defense was not disputing that it was possible to do such a thing, the video should not have been a big blow to their case, but many observers, including the press, saw it that way.

The jurors now had a movie of the murder in their minds. For most of the time inside the plane, the pilot's face was not visible. The prosecution hoped the jury would decide that seeing is believing—and superimpose Bob's face on the man pushing the black bag into blue oblivion.

Back in the witness chair, Rowley said he was not able

to use the actual plane Bob had flown that day—because it had been "in a crash and it was totaled."

On cross, David noted that the re-enactment was done, not on the busy Fourth of July weekend, but just a few weeks earlier, in the fall, after the pleasure boating season had ended. The lawyer also noted that a tanker was visible in the water in the video when he dumped one of the bags. Rowley admitted that he and the other two aircraft had visually "cleared the area" before the bags were dumped.

"So you wouldn't hit anything?" David asked.

"Yes."

He then asked if anyone on a boat below would have seen the big splash of the weighted bag hitting the water in broad daylight.

"Objection!"

"Sustained."

After Rowley stepped down, the judge read two legal stipulations, in which the prosecution and defense agreed to certain facts to save them both the time and effort required to prove them. It also saved the jury the time they would have had to listen to witnesses on the subjects. Crocker-Snyder told jurors about the torso found in 1989, how it was mistakenly identified as Gail and buried and then eliminated as Gail by DNA years later. The second stipulation was that Bob's nephew's birthday party was held at Bob's sister's house in Upper Montclair on the day Gail disappeared. Before excusing the jury for the night, the judge admonished them not to discuss the case or read newspapers or watch or listen to accounts of the trial on radio or television.

"The media continues to amaze me but it should not be amazing to you," she said.

The testimony was over for the day but the arguing was not. David told the court that Mae Eisenhower, the neighbor on the eleventh floor who had heard a door slam at the end of Bob and Gail's argument the morning she disappeared, would not be testifying for the defense. "Mae Eisenhower has successfully evaded process" servers and was not to be found, David said, the disappointment obvious in his tone.

During a break, Alayne said, "It was disturbing," to see the video. "Seeing a visual depiction of the way my brother-in-law apparently disposed of my sister's body is just different than thinking about it. I suspect that's probably how my brother-in-law regarded my sister that day— as an object to dispose of."

Not surprisingly, Scott Greenfield had the opposite view: "They've proven that you can throw one hundred and ten pounds of rice out of a plane," he said. "Now they're only missing the evidence that this ever happened."

Back in court, the defense argued about being able to stipulate that Bob had helped police by providing them with a copy of Gail's address book.

The judge angrily denied their request "to show the defendant had been forthcoming" and shouted she would not allow them "to make some kind of dramatic show before the jury." Such an argument "in no way refutes the concept that he didn't tell anybody that he went flying," said Crocker-Snyder. "You may not make an argument . . . that the defendant has been forthcoming in any way," she said. The jurist then threatened that she would allow the prosecution to introduce evidence "That, when they made inquiry, they were, in fact, stone-walled." The defense, she yelled, was "trying to say the defendant was forthcoming— which is ludicrous . . . because he wasn't forthcoming."

She warned David that, if he used his contention in the closing argument, she would allow a very unusual event. After the defense summation, she said she was putting the defense "on notice" that the prosecution would be able to present evidence of Bob's alleged uncooperative behavior— and the defense would not be able to challenge it before the case went to the jury. If David even mentioned in his closing that Bob helped police by giving them a copy of Gail's address book—that had the phone number of Sky King Aviation on the front page—the judge would allow prosecutors to call witnesses to say Bob stymied their investigation.

To any defense lawyer, it was a death threat to his client's case.

CHAPTER 48

FOR THE DEFENSE

DAVID finished cross-examining the last person called by the prosecution on the eighth day of the trial. The longtime superintendent of 185 E. 85th Street testified about entrances and exits from the building. The jury learned that there were several ways in and out of the building and that there was no video camera at the entrance in 1985 that would have caught anything suspicious.

The judge then read four more stipulations to the jury before the prosecution rested. One concerned the fact that Bob had provided Gail's address book to Detective Tom O'Malley. Another agreed that the average driving time between Bob and Gail's apartment and the Caldwell Airport in New Jersey was between 50 minutes and one hour and 10 minutes.

"That is the People's case, Your Honor," Adam Kaufmann said, ending the prosecution portion of the trial.

"All right," said the judge. "Please come to the sidebar for a moment."

Away from the ears of the jury, the press and the spectators, the lawyers had a sidebar and the defense moved to end the trial by dismissing the charges, claiming the prosecution had not made its case. It was routine and certainly not a motion the defense expected to be granted.

"The motion is denied," said Crocker-Snyder.

Dan Bibb asked the judge to prevent Joel Davis from testifying that he had seen the word "APARADOS" on Gail's T-shirt—as had been reported in the newspapers at the time. He also demanded that the court order the defense to bring in its private investigator who interviewed Joel Davis so the prosecution could interview the private eye away from the jury. The defense protested but the judge granted the prosecution request and ordered the defense lawyers to call the investigator. Clearly, the prosecution was very worried that Joel Davis might destroy their case and ensure an acquittal. At one point in the sidebar, the judge referred to Joel as the "star witness" of the defense.

"I was hoping to have the defendant testify, myself," Crocker-Snyder smiled.

"I know," David smiled back.

"I gather that is not going to occur?"

"Who said you don't get what you want?" David laughed.

"Or wish what you want," the judge chuckled.

"The People have rested," the judge said to the jury, returning to open court.

During the People's case, the defense strategy had been to let prosecution witnesses make points for them and then underscore those same points and others on cross-examination. The one over-riding point was that no one had seen Bob do anything and there was not a shred of physical evidence. The other points were that Gail had engaged in risky sex and drug behavior, that she'd lied or exaggerated, that she'd hated Bob and intended to blackmail and ruin him. In short, she was a whining, complaining shrew who didn't love Bob and was only out for his money. The good news was that the District Attorney's witnesses provided a lot of proof on those points, but it was also the bad news. All of the claims about Gail's character and behavior were true—but they were also proof of motive. Those aspects of the defense case might sound more like an explanation or a confession, instead of an exculpation. Worse, it could anger a jury who believed a killer was putting his dead victim on trial. It was time to introduce a different type of evidence—one that juries often put great stock in, despite the fact that it was actually among the most unreliable— eyewitness testimony.

The pared-down defense case depended on the testimony of two witnesses and one basic principle of American law. Bob's best chances of acquittal were contingent on the testimony of Joel Davis, the man who said he'd seen Gail after the time that the prosecution claimed Bob had killed her, and Mae Eisenhower, the woman from the eleventh floor who'd heard an argument that morning that had ended with the sound of a slamming door. The legal safety net was reasonable doubt—the fact that there was no physical evidence against Bob, no witnesses, no body and no confession. But Eisenhower had avoided process servers for the defense—who believed the woman was hiding from them so she would not have to testify. Without Eisenhower, the defense had only two shields left—Joel Davis and reasonable doubt. Since the jury had already agreed in selection that they could convict Bob on circumstantial evidence alone, Joel Davis was Bob's last best hope.

"The defense calls Joel Davis," David said.

A husky man with short gray hair and dark eyebrows entered the courtroom from the witness room. He was wearing a dark suit and a rep tie was snugged-up to a white shirt collar whose right wing was askew. He smiled a nervous smile as he took the oath and sat down. Joel described his birth in Brooklyn, his work life and his retirement to Florida. He seemed like a likeable man and several jurors smiled back at him when he smiled at them. Both the defense and prosecution teams, of course, were watching the jury like hawks—to see if they liked the witness, whether they were buying it or rejecting it. After describing his time in the US Army, Joel described being attacked by a man on a St. Louis street, who came at him with a broken bottle. Several jurors wrinkled their brows, wondering what was going on. Joel said he'd defended himself and the other man fell injured. David asked if the other man was moving.

"I don't think he was alive after that," Joel said.

Whispers swept the courtroom. The star defense witness had just confessed to killing a man. Joel said a policeman was a witness to the brawl and told him to leave the scene. Obviously, the defense was bringing the incident out on direct questioning to deflate any use by the prosecution on cross-examination. David then walked Joel through his sighting of the woman who looked like Gail. He described

being seated at a table at the bagel store with his girlfriend
Sue, when Gail entered. Joel said he didn't remember Sue's
last name—despite the fact that she had been his girlfriend
for several years. He was very convincing when he described Gail and her clothing and the foreign phrase on her
T-shirt in great detail. He described seeing Gail's picture
on a MISSING poster and calling the police. He then recounted a visit from Detective Tom O'Malley, who showed
him several other pictures of Gail.

"I said, 'That's the woman!' " Joel remembered.

David asked him what time he saw Gail that day.

"Two or three o'clock in the afternoon, on Sunday . . .
the seventh of July," Joel replied.

The defense lawyers looked at the jurors as Joel testified
and were very reassured by what they saw. The prosecution
was just as worried. David sat down and the court took a
break so that the prosecution could prepare to cross-
examine Joel. For some reason, the People withdrew their
request to interview the defense investigator. Joel had been
a good witness and the jury seemed to like him. If they
believed him, one man would blow away a long line of
prosecution witnesses. If the jury thought Joel was reliable
and Gail was getting lunch between 2:30 and 3 that day—
Bob could not have killed her and packaged her in time to
start that plane engine in New Jersey at 4:25. In short, if
the jurors believed Joel, Bob would walk.

During the break, a courthouse employee rushed back
into his office and told his co-workers that they had to come
to the Bierenbaum trial because the lone defense witness
was very strong and that Bob would be acquitted.

"He's fuckin' not guilty," the worker said. "You've got
to see this." All of his co-workers followed him back into
the courtroom to see the drama.

Stephen Saracco opened the cross-examination with a
smile and polite questions about the time Stephen had interviewed Joel in Florida the previous week. He began asking Joel where he was before the bagel store and what time
he arrived. He also asked about his girlfriend.

"And how long had you been going with this woman before July seventh, 1985?" Stephen asked.

"Six months, eight months, maybe a year. I really don't remember."

"And how long did you continue to go with her after July seventh, 1985?"

"Probably another year or two. We were friends afterwards."

"And do you know where this woman is today?"

"No idea."

"Do you know what her last name is?"

"No."

"You went out with her about two years?" Stephen asked, in a skeptical tone, before moving on to the woman he identified as Gail.

Joel testified that the women were carrying beach chairs and bags and Gail kept "turning around and they were talking, very happy. You could see they were very close friends."

But Joel could remember nothing about the other woman. Stephen pressed Joel, asking if he remembered how tall the other woman was.

"I don't remember. I was looking at the other one."

"I just asked you if you can answer my questions, yes or no?" said Stephen sternly.

"Yes."

"You think you could do that?"

"Oh, sure," Joel said in a friendly voice.

"If you can't . . ."

"Right."

Stephen asked if the other woman had black hair, blonde hair, red hair, short hair, or long hair. To each question, Joel replied:

"No idea."

Stephen was apparently fishing, which is a risky enterprise in open court. It was a lawyer's maxim never to ask a question unless you already knew the answer—because the answer might backfire against your case or open a door you did not want opened. Prosecutors only went fishing if they were desperate. Another tactic of cross-examination, of course, was to bait and badger a witness, hoping he would get confused and appear unreliable. Joel said he wasn't looking at the woman's face for the whole ten minutes she was in the bagel shop.

"No, I was looking at her shirt. That's what really . . ."

"What was interesting you was the T-shirt?" Stephen said, a note of disbelief in his voice.

He was in the printing business, Joel said, and the shirt was "very distinctive, probably a European-printed pattern, which was done in a magnificent way. That's what turned me on and then I looked at her as a man. I found her attractive and her body was very attractive, so I noticed her."

"Your girlfriend didn't mind this at all?" the judge interjected, introducing another note of skepticism about Joel in front of the jurors.

"She, well, she was a little jealous, Your Honor, because I asked her to turn around and look at the woman's T-shirt and she said, 'I can't turn my head,' meaning why are you looking at her and why aren't you . . ."

"I understand that," the judge replied, conversationally.

"Well, I was foolish, but I'm a man, I mean, I can't help it," Joel shrugged.

"Excuse me," David interrupted.

"The T-shirt," Stephen said, getting back on the beam.

"It's the court's questions, I think," said David, masking his objection in front of the jury.

Stephen asked Joel about the design on the T-shirt.

"It was either a map or something like an island. It was very distinct. It just turned me on when I looked at it."

"The T-shirt turned you on, or . . ." Stephen asked with raised eyebrows, sparking muffled laughter.

"No, actually, it was the print on the T-shirt because that was my business for many years."

Stephen then grilled Joel on the size, shape, color and wording of the shirt. He also asked if Joel had seen the

back of the shirt but Joel said he saw flashes of the back
when the woman turned around to talk to her friend. Stephen then confronted Joel with his statement the previous
week that he never saw the back of the shirt.

"I think what I meant was that . . ."

"Do you recall telling us . . ." Stephen interrupted.

"I object," said David, protecting his witness, who was
not allowed to finish his answer.

"I didn't mean to interrupt," Stephen claimed.

"Overruled," the judge said.

Joel seemed confused by the exchange.

Stephen grilled him again, asking if he recalled telling
the prosecution that he never saw the back of the shirt, as
if it were a crucial issue.

"I saw the back of the shirt," Joel said. "Maybe it's the
way you asked the question that might have confused me
Friday . . ."

"So, your answer is you don't recall?"

"I don't recall anything on the back."

"No, my question is, do you recall telling us you never
saw—by us, I mean Mister Bibb and I . . ." Stephen said,
not finishing his sentence.

"I don't remember . . . I might have but maybe the question you asked I might have taken it in another way," said
Joel.

"If I had asked the question, 'Did you ever see the back
of the shirt?' would that have been confusing to you?"

"Objection!"

"Overruled," said the judge.

"Would you have understood that question?" asked Stephen.

"Sustained," said Crocker-Snyder, changing her ruling
on the hypothetical question. "Go to another question."

Stephen asked Joel to describe the "physical character-
istics" of the woman in the T-shirt. Joel said she was built
like his ex-wife—petite but with a "very good body."

"May I just have a moment, Your Honor?" Stephen
asked. "See where I'm going with this?"

After a whispered conference with the other prosecutors, Stephen trailed a baited hook in front of the witness, a cast in the dark.

"Mister Davis, would it be your testimony that the woman you saw in H & H Bagels with the T-shirt with the design and the lettering was ... had a well-developed chest?" Stephen asked, gesturing with both hands in front of his chest to indicate large breasts.

"I think so, yeah."

Joel had taken the bait but Stephen did not yet yank on the line—he wanted to set the hook. Instead, he played out line and asked if the woman or her friend were wearing bathing suits. Joel said they might have been wearing bikinis under their clothes.

Joel then recounted seeing the MISSING posters and calling his girlfriend and phoning the police.

"Do you recall that you made this phone call at five to five in the morning to Missing Persons?" Stephen asked, tugging on the line.

"I don't remember," said Joel. "That sounds very early but maybe I did. I don't remember."

Stephen hit him again and again with the same question, as if anyone up at that time of the morning must be up to no good. David did not object or ask the judge to stop it on the basis that the question had already been asked and answered. Of course, objections sometimes flagged an issue for a jury, who might think the lawyer was trying to hide something. Then Stephen noted that the original police report of his call said he had seen the woman who looked like Gail between 1 and 3 o'clock.

"It's possible you did see her as early as one?" Stephen asked.

The timing was crucial. At one, Gail still had time to get home and be murdered by Bob. At three, it was very unlikely.

"I think it was probably from two o'clock on, possibly," said Joel. "It's so many years ago, truthfully, I don't remember."

"I understand," said Stephen, who showed Joel the police card that had the 1 to 3 P.M. notation.

"Okay. Possibly, yeah. Possibly one to three, or could have been between two and four also."

Stephen was reeling in loose line. Joel had admitted that his 2:30 to 3 estimate on direct exam might not be right. The prosecutor then tried to land the witness, showing Joel a police document that quoted him as saying he had seen the woman between 1 and 3 P.M.

"I don't remember," Joel said.

"All right, let's move on," said the judge.

He then quizzed Joel on the clothes the woman was wearing and the photographs he was shown of Gail.

"Isn't it a fact, Mister Davis, that you told Detective O'Malley when you selected a photograph that 'It could have been her but I'm not sure'?"

"That I don't remember, don't remember that," said Joel.

"Are you denying . . ."

"Whatever I saw, that was the woman," Joel protested.

"Is it your testimony that you told Detective O'Malley 'That is positively her'?" Stephen demanded in a loud voice.

" 'That's her,' yes."

"Do you deny telling Detective O'Malley that, 'I think it could be her. It could be her but I'm not sure'?"

"I don't remember that. It was her. It was her," Joel insisted, his voice also becoming louder.

"That's not my question. My question is what you told Detective O'Malley."

"Objection!" David said.

"Overruled. Mister Davis, you have to answer that specific question," said the judge.

"Yes, say it again, sir," said Joel, confused by the questions.

Stephen started over and ran through the session where Joel was shown photographs. The defense did not protest that all of the questions had already been asked and answered at least once. But Joel, although shaken, held his ground.

"My next question is, do you recall commenting on the photograph that you pointed out to Detective O'Malley?"

"Yes, sir, 'It's her.' "

"It is your testimony today that you told Detective O'Malley that you were positive that this was the woman?"

"Yes, I was positive."

"And are you denying that you told Detective O'Malley that this could be her, but you're not sure?"

"No, I never said that. No."

Joel was unshakable on the point but the jury had heard over and over that he was absolutely positive about the identification and was never unsure. Next, Stephen asked Joel if he had told a defense investigator that he never saw any pictures. He began demanding answers from Joel, not about what he had seen fifteen years ago, but what he had said a few months earlier.

"His question was not clear to me. No. Yes, I remember that," Joel said, sounding rattled.

"So you told him you never saw pictures?"

"Possibly . . . At that time, I didn't realize it was the detective who was at my house. I thought he just meant on the telephone call. I had other calls from different people. I was confused."

The prosecutor jerked his fishing line hard.

"Nobody can show you photographs over the telephone," Stephen smirked.

"No, no but the thing was, I was confusing other investigators besides this man."

The answer made little sense and Stephen asked for a moment to confer with his colleagues. Stephen asked about a tape recording made by that private investigator and a transcript that Joel had reviewed before coming to court. Joel, who seemed a bit confused, said the transcript was 99 percent accurate.

"Mister Lewis . . . Mister *Davis*, I'm sorry," said Stephen, momentarily confused himself.

"I'm Lewis," David smiled from the defense table.

Finally, Joel admitted he had told the defense investigator that he had never seen pictures. "But I did see the picture, you know."

"Do you recall describing the woman to the jury, just now, that she was petite?"

"Her height was petite. She . . . she was a well-developed woman."

Stephen suppressed a smile. The hook was set and his fish continued to spin on the line. The prosecutor went back to the interview that year with the defense investigator.

"Do you recall saying to him, 'She was gorgeous, she was tall, statuesque'?"

"I was confused when I said that. If I can explain?"

But Stephen did not let him explain and neither the judge nor the defense came to the aid of the witness.

"Do you recall?"

"I said that, but it was a mistake."

"Do you recall describing the woman to him?"

"Yes, I did," Joel admitted.

"That she was gorgeous?"

"Right."

"That she was tall?"

"And I was mistaken, yes."

"Do you recall telling . . ."

"Yes, I did," said Joel, answering the question before it was asked.

"Do you recall describing her as statuesque?"

"Yes," said a weary Joel.

"Can I just have a moment?" Stephen asked the judge before another huddle with Dan and Adam.

Stephen sat down and the three prosecutors put their heads together. It was time to net the fish, a tricky moment in a boat or in a courtroom. In both pursuits, the goal was to snag your prey—without losing it when you reached for the net or the hook. Stephen stood up and returned to the podium. He asked Joel if he remembered describing to the defense investigator "what physical attributes you look for in a woman."

"Yes."

Joel Davis' preferences in women's bodies should have been irrelevant but the defense could not object—it all came from the tape and transcript of their investigator that they had provided to the prosecution. It was now obvious to the defense that the prosecutor was going to try to portray Joel as lecherous, hoping to discredit him before the jury—not on the facts of the case, but on his personality. Lying on an evidence cart next to Stephen at the podium, was a large white sign with black letters several inches tall, that spelled out Joel's words that Stephen read to the court:

"I'm a leg and ass man. This broad was perfect, yes. I couldn't see her ass because she had a thing over it, but she was gorgeous, she was tall, she was statuesque."

"Yes, I did [say that]," said Joel, his face red, obviously flummoxed and embarrassed.

"You are talking about the woman you identified in the shirt, is that correct?" Stephen asked, his voice dripping with scorn.

"Not correct."

"Who are you talking about?"

"After fifteen years, I confused her, I confused my ex-wife's body in which she was five-foot-one, with my friend's ex–sister-in-law, who is tall but had her face," Joel stammered.

Two male jurors in the front row laughed at his bizarre answer, as did many others in the court. Even the judge suppressed a smile. Several spectators asked their neighbors to explain what they had just heard. One of the defense lawyer's head dropped.

"So I was confusing two different women in regards to that," Joel continued to sputter. "She was petite. She had a nice body, nice-looking face. That is what I noticed."

He opened his mouth to speak again but no words came out, like a fish out of water.

"Sit down," Dan Bibb whispered under his breath to Stephen.

"I have nothing further," Stephen said, ending his cross-examination with the barely-suppressed triumph of a man who has landed the big one with fake bait.

"Are you kidding?" one of the courthouse workers whispered to his colleague who had insisted that Joel Davis would get Bob an acquittal. "This guy is the star witness?"

David stood up and tried to resuscitate his star witness.

"Do you remember the woman's face that you saw in H & H Bagel?" David asked Joel.

"Yes, I do," said Joel.

"Is it the face on the poster?"

"Yes."

"Would you agree, Mister Davis, beauty is in the eye of the beholder?"

"Objection! Leading."

"Sustained," said the judge.

Joel agreed with David that police documents refreshed his memory about being shown photographs. After a few more questions, David concluded and the prosecution declined to question Joel any further. The lawyers had a sidebar conference, after which the judge asked David, "Does the defense rest?"

"The defense rests," David answered, sitting down next to the other lawyers and his client—who seemed shell-shocked by the implosion of his only defense witness on the stand.

The judge announced that, after a brief recess, the prosecution would present rebuttal witnesses. During the break, a shaken Bob, his face flushed, sat with his wife Janet in the second row, while the court buzzed. Scott Greenfield saw Bob's hangdog expression and gave his client a chin-up signal and a smile.

Adam Kaufmann called the first rebuttal witness, Alayne Katz, who was shown People's Exhibit 33—a picture of her sister Gail in a bikini. Her body, in profile, showed without a doubt that she was flat-chested. Alayne looked at the photograph.

It was odd and somewhat undignified that the size of her dead sister's breasts had become an important issue in the trial and strange that the half-sad picture of Gail about to enter the sea had become the most important exhibit. The picture of Gail had been taken by Bob on a Caribbean vacation in 1985. In the picture, Gail was standing in a black-and-white polka-dotted bikini, with the hot Montserrat sun profiling her body—wading into the warm turquoise water. Gail was looking directly at the camera over her left shoulder, sad, pausing before entering the endless sea behind her. A gentle tradewind caressed her thin, lithe body and played with her long, curly brown hair. She was not smiling but wore a conflicted, half sad, half Mona Lisa smile. Perhaps the ambivalence reflected in her pretty face was the result of looking at her husband while they were alone. To some, her face seemed to bear the imprint of someone caught in dark reflection, about to return to the waiting sea. It had seemed odd that Gail was not smiling in the holiday snapshot but now, to some, it made a strange sense. It was as if Gail, from the grave, had given the film to Alayne and now the victim herself was the final crucial witness against Bob, providing evidence to destroy the defense of her killer.

Alayne testified that Gail was just under 5-foot-3-inches tall, hardly statuesque. Adam asked her if she knew Gail's bra size.

"An 'A' cup," Alayne declared. She had heard Joel Davis' testimony and knew exactly what she was refuting—his claim that Gail was "well-developed."

Adam ended his rebuttal and asked that the haunting picture of Gail be shown to the jury. Several jurors nodded their heads when they saw the photo.

"The defense has no questions," David said.

The prosecution then re-called Detective Tom O'Malley, who testified that Joel Davis only told him that the picture of Gail *might* have been the woman he saw. A vigorous cross-examination failed to shake his testimony that Joel

Davis was unsure, despite the fact that the defense pointed out that Tom's reports on the subject were conveniently missing. To most observers, it seemed that Joel Davis had not just been landed—he had been blown out of the water. And a jubilant Stephen Saracco had done it with the help of an interview by a defense investigator and a photo of Gail taken by Bob.

After the jury was sent home for the night, Steve and Alayne spoke in the hallway about their strong opinions and emotions at the end of the case. Steve ridiculed Joel Davis and said his testimony was not credible.

"He had a girlfriend for six months to a year and he doesn't even remember her name—but he remembers seeing my sister in a bagel shop for a few minutes fifteen years ago," Steve scoffed.

"It's been such an incredible trial," Steve said. "It seems so overwhelming a case against Bob that a not-guilty verdict will be very difficult to accept."

Alayne spoke of her emotional exhaustion and how she had a second sleepless night the previous night. Her first sleepless night, she said, was the evening before she first testified. Despite developments, she said she was very worried about the outcome.

"I wish it wasn't really over," Alayne said, the tension evident in her voice. "I wish there was twice as much evidence as there was to make it easier for the jury to convict him."

The prosecution team celebrated the end of the case— and Stephen Saracco's demolition of Joel Davis—with drinks at Forlini's. The defense team had nothing to celebrate and worked on its closing argument.

That night, an editor at the *New York Post* wrote a headline for the next day's story about the meltdown of lone defense witness Joel Davis on the stand and how his claim that Gail had a "well-developed" chest was refuted by the flat-chested photo of the victim: "SLAY-CASE DOCTOR'S SOLE DEFENSE WITNESS A BUST."

CHAPTER 49

LOGIC & EMOTION

BOB was very optimistic when he spoke to his friend Dr. Lee Trotter by phone on Saturday, October 21st, two days before closing arguments in the case. While he was concerned about the jury getting caught up in emotion instead of the facts, he was not expecting a guilty verdict. Whether Bob was convicted or acquitted—whether he killed Gail or did not—it wouldn't change the way Lee felt about Bob. He was still his friend.

In contrast to Bob's hopeful mood, Dr. Michael Stone was almost desperate about the impending verdict. The Ethics Committee of the American Psychiatric Association was investigating whether Michael had violated the ethics of his profession by speaking to the press, the police, the prosecution and the Katz family about the supposedly confidential sessions with Gail and Bob in 1983. He feared both losing his license and a civil lawsuit from Bob after an acquittal. Despite his impressive collection of rare Judaica, Michael was not a religious person—but he actually prayed for a guilty verdict. Michael knew that if Bob was acquitted, he would probably go after him in court. He could still sue if convicted, but it would then be a lawsuit by a convicted killer—which might not be looked upon favorably by a jury. The night before the last day of the trial, Michael spoke to a journalist about his fears that his stance for justice—rather than law—might ruin his life, and those of his children.

"Well, it would certainly be a cruel irony," the journalist replied, "if the only doctor to suffer in this case were you."

On Monday, October 23rd, 2000, David Lewis and Dan Bibb were ready to give their closing statements to the jury. All of the male lawyers—prosecutors Dan Bibb, Stephen Saracco, and Adam Kaufmann, as well as defense lawyers

David Lewis and Scott Greenfield—were sporting short, new haircuts. Getting a haircut before closing arguments was something of a local lawyer superstition but, of course, only one side could win. Unless, of course, there was a hung jury. The judge had not gotten a haircut but she was not wearing her gold-rimmed glasses—she was wearing contact lenses for the event.

That night, New Yorkers were looking forward to another World Series baseball game between the Yankees and the Mets. David Lewis was first up at bat and he used America's pastime as a metaphor for the circumstantial case against Bob.

"Maybe it's the season, but you're out at the ballpark and you decide you want to go out for a hot dog, get up and go out," said David in his quick, gentle, friendly voice to the jury. "The batter at the plate, when you leave, is standing there ready to hit. When you come back, he's on first base. We all know the only way he could have gotten to first base is that he hit a single—unless, of course, you think about it for a minute and then it could be it was a walk or he got hit by a pitch, not so unusual, if you've been watching."

David said the only way to know what happened was to look at the official scores and the replay.

"How Gail Katz Bierenbaum came to die is what this case is all about," said David. "The People's theory is that Robert Bierenbaum did it but, given the evidence in the case, we know that while we were at the ballpark there may be lots of reasons. In life, too, there are lots of reasons something happened," but the jury were "the official scorers" for the trial.

He spoke of how Bob was cloaked in a presumption of innocence and told them they had to believe the prosecution theory completely before tearing that cloak away. The judge interrupted David when he began to describe reasonable doubt, saying he had said things that were not accurate and warning the lawyer, "please do not go into my area."

"Fine."

David then began a rundown of the evidence from the defense perspective. He said that one witness said that Gail had told her Bob was going to be a plastic surgeon, although "at the time of that conversation, not even Bob knew he was going to be a plastic surgeon—because the evidence by stipulation . . ."

"Objection!" said Dan Bibb, protesting that David was alluding to facts not in evidence.

"Sustained," said the judge. "Don't do that."

David then attacked the DA's theory about the flashpoint of issues—that Gail was killed after she told Bob she was leaving him for another man and tried to blackmail him with the psychiatrist's letter. All of the prosecution's claims, David said, were refuted by their own witnesses. The lawyer noted that Alayne testified that Gail told her that she had confronted Bob with Michael Stone's letter and threatened to ruin him four to six weeks before she went missing.

"So, the idea that it was shown that morning and caused an explosion is belied by the evidence," said David.

Divorce, he said, had already been discussed and Bob wrote a check to a divorce lawyer for Gail, "so divorce wasn't something that came up that day" for the first time. Also, there had been testimony that Bob knew before July 7th that Gail was cheating on him.

"She was seeing other men," said David. "You heard— Ralph Sugarman told you that Bob believed that that was happening but we don't know when that was . . . it appears that that was a later conversation. The flash-point theory doesn't work because those things didn't come to a flashpoint."

The defense seemed to be trying to have it both ways— Bob knew she was cheating, so it wasn't a surprise but maybe that was later and he didn't know on July 7th. The detectives had testified that Bob had told them that he still didn't know his wife was cheating on him, almost a week after she vanished. The prosecution, of course, claimed Bob knew about the adultery and lied—and that it was a motive for murder.

"What about the controlling theory—that Bob had such control that losing the control would set him off?" David asked. "Well, we know that Gail apparently wasn't that controlled; that she was cool enough to entertain her lover in the marital house, in the marital bed; talked to Bob on the telephone with Anthony there, and according to Anthony's testimony took cocaine and had sex with him."

He also noted that Gail prevented Bob from going out to New Jersey for a reunion with his friends.

"So, the theory that Gail was somehow controlled by Bob is belied by the evidence," said David.

Next, David targeted a third theory, what he called "the Karnofsky theory" that Bob dumped Gail out of the plane.

"The problem with the theory is not that it's not appealing, because it is. It's a nice video. We got to look at it. They were able to show us how it could be done," David said.

"The problem with the theory is, there's no proof of it and proof is what we agreed we were looking for. There's no proof that there's a single duffel bag owned by Bob capable of holding one hundred and ten pounds . . . and there's no proof that Bob carried anything from the apartment of the elevator . . . no proof of Bob with a duffel bag at the door, on the street or the two blocks to where his car was parked," he said.

Roberta testified that Bob could carry such a weight but David said Sergeant Rowley "was in pretty good shape and he had to struggle to get it in the Cessna.

"There's no proof of Bob having a duffel bag at the airport at Caldwell . . . no proof of Bob driving a car onto the tarmac, no proof of anything being loaded onto the plane . . . no proof of the direction of Bob's flight . . . no proof of anything seen falling from a plane on one of the biggest boating weekends in the summer . . . no proof in the surfacing of a body off the Rockaways or washing up . . . no proof of any of this or even a hint of it—and there's no blood or human tissue found in the car, in the airplane or even seen by Detective Dalsass when he looked in Bob's apartment in September," he said.

"So, what's the videotape? What's the videotape mean? Well, it's a piece of circumstantial evidence," David said, with a hint of a smile.

"It's the same as if I got up here and told you that I killed a grizzly bear with a pen. When you ask me to prove it, I say, 'Here—here's the pen! What more could you want?' " David shrugged.

"Because it's not proof of what happened," David said, answering his own question. "It's a theory and it's a theory represented by a videotape, by a film. There are lots of films that you could talk about. You can talk about *The Panic in Needle Park* because of the drug use in this case. You can talk about *The Shawshank Redemption* about someday a real killer will confess. You can talk about *Looking for Mr. Goodbar* when someone's picked up, by risky behavior, as Gail was picked up outside the coffee shop by Anthony or on the subway by Ken. All those films could be shown."

David did not mention the middle-of-the-night phone call in 1986 from police who thought Gail had been found—and Bob's odd response. David had seen the jury's reaction when Roberta said that Bob told her to go back to bed because it probably wasn't Gail. David believed that was the most damaging testimony of the trial.

Instead, he then addressed what he called the version of events from the "friends-of-Gail," who came in to court to repeat Gail's claims that Bob was dangerous, even if Gail's descriptions were at odds with the Bob they saw. Gail, David told the jurors, exaggerated things. For example, Gail told her cousin Hillard that Bob had choked her several times but she told her boyfriend that it only happened once. Gail's claim to Jane Dunne that Bob and his dad were involved in a multi-million-dollar Medicaid fraud together was completely false. Gail told another friend that she got a $10,000 loan and stashed it away but there was no evidence that it ever existed.

"She told Anthony she had an unhappy childhood," said David. "That's not the same childhood described by Alayne Katz. And then there's the story about glass in the casserole . . . even when you get to the choking incident, Gail blows it out of even the terrible proportion it's in—that 911 was called, that EMS was called, that she was hospitalized, possibly. Those things never happened or we would have seen evidence of it.

"There are some other mysteries to this," said David. "For example, she talks about the lovers. We know about Anthony, we know about Ken. There appears to be a third one. She says there is a new man."

Denise Kastenbaum, he said, testified that Gail told her she had a boyfriend at Beth Israel—but Ken was at a different hospital and Anthony wasn't at any hospital.

Also, Gail's psychiatrist said that Gail—just days before she vanished—mentioned for the first time a mysterious rich man who would bankroll her new apartment.

"We don't know if there is a third person or not," said David. "From Gail talking, we could assume there may well have been."

The story that Gail told about Bob saying that he would be smarter than Claus von Bülow and not leave any evidence was just another one of Gail's tall tales, said David.

Bob was being castigated for telling different stories to different people but that is just what Gail did also, said David. Gail, he said, hid her drug use from Jane, hid her romance with Anthony from another girlfriend. She told friends that she and Ken talked about the future together but Ken said they never did.

"Of course, she hid Anthony from Ken," said David.

Also, Gail hid her relationship with Anthony from her psychiatrist, he said.

"When Gail disappears, Bob gets three pieces of devastating news. First, about her drug use. Second about Ken. Sex behind his back with Anthony in the apartment. When all that information comes in, how is Bob to behave?" asked David.

"The man is not a cardboard cutout. What does he have when she walks out of the apartment? He is lonely, abandoned and he is betrayed. He doesn't know how to behave. There is no way to behave. If you think that he had something to do with her demise, how do you account for the fact he left all of the clothes in the apartment where they were? Everything is there as if she would come back."

All jurors' eyes were on David.

"What is the feeling of a man abandoned by his wife—what are you supposed to feel? Should he be angry? Should he feel betrayed? . . . He is struggling with his explanation, to tell himself and others what happened each time a new external event comes to his attention. Does he get on with his life? Does he want her back? Does he react when he finds out Gail has cheated on him?

"Does he rebound to Karen Caruana—the sex in the summer of '85 that he has with her, which could be so horribly damning on one level? If you think about it, she left him, he has found out she wasn't faithful. With all the available evidence, he was faithful to her. When you learn of her secret life, what is required of you?"

Essentially testifying for Bob, David told the jury that Bob did not find out about Gail's infidelity until after she vanished. He tried to explain Bob's odd statements that his private investigator had found evidence of Gail in California, that her family was financing her and hiding her, that Gail could be a waitress in a seaside resort.

"Because, on some level, he is waiting. If you ever waited for a child to come home or a spouse to come home, it takes longer than it should, the things that go through your mind. Suppose you don't get it resolved that night, that evening—suppose it's never resolved? The explanation changes, not talking to other people, but to yourself. You are trying to understand why you are left behind, where they have gone.

"It is not evidence you have killed them—it is evidence that you don't know the answers. But there is an explanation that he does give, when Alayne Katz comes to the house to pick up her sister's things: She says to him, 'You killed my sister.' He says right to her face, 'No, I didn't. She is a tramp and she is probably with someone else.' A true expression of both people," David said.

"Confronted with an accusation, he tells the sister to her face, 'I didn't do it.' He tells her what he thinks of her sister.

"What happened to Gail Katz Bierenbaum? Bob Bierenbaum's answer—'I don't know.' How are you supposed to behave when you are innocent, when you didn't do it? How do you meet people? What are you supposed to say? 'I'm Bob Bierenbaum, my wife disappeared. I did not kill her. Here is our entire marital story.' Is that what is expected of Bob for his entire life? Is that what satisfies? Do you have to disclose intimate details of your failure at marriage to the first person you meet? Or do we not tell everybody everything because we want . . . a chance, not with our past but for our future? If you do that, if that is the requirement the prosecution sets at you not to be guilty of murder, then you have quite a problem on your first date— of what to disclose," David said, a sarcastic tone in his voice.

Gail, he said, might have been killed by drug dealers in Central Park in a city that was not as safe as today.

He ridiculed testimony that Bob enjoyed himself in the Hamptons just weeks after Gail went away.

"Wow! He went out to a comedy club, went to a discotheque. Wow! He was laughing . . . Bob decided his life had to go on. He wasn't dead himself."

The lawyer then read to the jury part of his cross-examination of Detective Virgillio Dalsass. The investigator, said David, did "a full turn-around," on the stand when he admitted that, despite his direct testimony, Bob had in fact told him that he and Gail had argued and Gail was "more pissed than usual."

David tried to convince the jury that the cops were not telling the truth—that they were grilling Bob, who realized when they asked him about choking his wife, that they were not looking for Gail but were looking to build a case against him.

"Our common experience tells us, even if you come to the conclusion Bob lied, didn't tell you he flew a plane out of Caldwell, common sense tells us even an innocent person, as he was,—after the O'Malley interview and looking to protect himself, not to look guilty in a situation, not to make it look worse than it was. Bob had good reason to answer only what he was asked, although he never said anything about flying a plane."

There it was—Bob was Dr. Richard Kimble, of *The Fugitive*, the doctor wrongfully accused of killing his wife, trapped in a web of circumstance. Bob did not forget that he flew a plane—he kept it a secret because he knew it would make the cops more suspicious of him. David was masterful, trying to draw the jurors in with reason and logic, to get them involved in solving the mystery with him, as if he were playing the part of fictional detective Nero Wolfe. He then explained away Bob's altered flight log by reminding the jury of the dated check that paid for the August 7th flight and noting that the log was full of omissions and alterations.

"The check and the log match the story, and their version doesn't," David contended.

Bob may have told people Gail was suicidal because Gail was capable of pretending to be suicidal to manipulate Bob, even if she wasn't.

"What do we know?" David asked, sounding a bit like a detective. "We know the marriage was terrible. They were too young to marry, they were both immature. She, in part, wanted to be some sort of princess. Anthony said she was looking for some white knight to play Sir Lancelot to her Guinevere. We know from Anthony—white knights and white powder. From Kastenbaum—a new man, perhaps. Gail Katz's life was a double life and a mystery."

David said the 1983 choking incident scared both Gail and Bob and sent them into therapy.

"We know Bob has a temper. We know he was a resident working all hours, a lifestyle that was inadequate for his wife. He was working two jobs. The idea he was up working all these hours doesn't make him a nicer man or make moods any better," said David.

In his rapid, conversational style, the lawyer then addressed the time Bob told Ralph Sugarman he was so angry at Gail he could kill her.

"If you think about it yourselves, there may be times in which you said those words yourself and the anger in saying them—you can't predict what the future holds."

Gail, he noted, was preparing a surprise party for Bob at the time she was supposedly planning to leave him.

"Bob loved her. Gail hopes the marriage would get better. In the spring and early summer, she says things were getting better, Bob was treating her better. She tells Yvette Feis there is no sex between them because she is not letting Bob have any—but things are still getting better," said David.

Returning to the witnesses, David called Roberta "bitter" and politely accused her of perjuring herself, saying she "colored her story about Bob" because she hated him. Other women hated Bob and shaded their testimony, he claimed.

"The question is, do you have to leave what the cats leave on your rug to satisfy Yvette that you are innocent?" David asked, sarcastically.

He called Roberta's confrontation of Bob a "crackpot theory" that Bob simply ignored—not "an admission of guilt by silence."

When Carole Gordon made the joke about Bob killing his wife, Bob reacted strongly, asking what she knew, because he had been burned by Alayne's campaign of vilification. "The one thing he is absolutely convinced he has put behind him, back in New York," and was suddenly fearful that it had started anew, David said.

When Stephanie Youngblood asked Bob who Gail was, after finding her name on luggage tags, Bob "got weepy about it" five years after Gail vanished. He had first denied being married before, said David, because "It's not what

you tell a woman unless you really have to, especially when
he thought he had put it behind him."

When nurse Karen Caruana saw Bob at the hospital after
Gail vanished and he was disheveled, unshaven and suffering from a lack of sleep, "is that real or has he made it
up for consumption someday in the courtroom?" David
asked.

He also asked whether Bob crying over Gail's clothes
in the Hamptons was just an act. When Bob leaves all of
Gail's things in the apartment—is it for show or is it a sign
of grief? Then David broached the subject of Joel Davis.
He said he called Joel because he saw Gail and the jury
deserved to hear him.

Joel, he said, was "tested by the principle of cross-
examination, tested by a very able examiner, Mister Saracco—who is able to take Joel Davis and, in some way,
make Joel Davis look like a fool but, you know, you've
got to be careful even with that description."

Joel testified that Gail had a well-developed chest and
"he still doesn't know what she looked like—but he knew
in '85 that's who he thought he saw and he's got no axe
to grind and no reason to come in here, except he believed—he believed that's what he saw.

"So, you can either accept Joel Davis or toss Joel Davis
aside. If you toss him aside, the People's burden doesn't
change. So, what happened to Gail Katz Bierenbaum?
Somewhere, she walks out of that apartment that morning,
the doorman says he never saw her . . . no one saw Bob
Bierenbaum leave the apartment either and we know he left.

"Did the way she led her life and the things she did,
meet in misadventure—a man who approached her like Anthony did out of the coffee shop or Ken did on the subway?
Did someone talk to Gail and did Gail go off with them
while Bob Bierenbaum was in his airplane or in New Jersey
. . . or even in the apartment?

"All of those things are reasonable inferences that flow
from a double life, from risky behavior that catches up to
you," said David.

The torso that turned up in 1989 was buried as Gail and later eliminated and sent back to an unknown grave. It was unclaimed to that day, he said.

"That body is a human being and no one knows who that is now," said David—which proved that it was just as reasonable that Gail's body had never been found or was itself in another unmarked grave somewhere.

"We know that Gail's dead. We tell you that it's a horrible and terrible tragedy. When there is a tragedy like that, there's an urge that runs through us that someone must pay. But if there's not enough evidence beyond a reasonable doubt to tell us who it is—by a verdict of not guilty you may end up re-opening this investigation.

"In this country of ours, people have struggled to get to these shores from all over the world," David said. "They fought in the streets, they fought in the legislatures for dreams. The dream is not of wealth, nor privilege and not of power—it's a dream of justice."

He noted that every time the jury entered or left the courtroom Bob and the defense team stood for them.

"We stand for you because you stand for justice and because you stand for the very living democracy we've come to expect. The job you have is very difficult and we wish you all the skill, all the knowledge and everything else. We will not flinch from what you decide, whatever. All we can tell you is that we wish you good luck in this endeavor and, really, Godspeed."

David had delivered an excellent summation—one that depended on logic and the complicating possibilities of various scenarios—but it seemed he was a detective who could not solve the mystery.

After a brief recess, it was the turn of Dan Bibb, a detective bearing a much more emotional message, who, of course, had a simple—even elementary—solution for the jurors.

Dan told the jury that, as he sat in his chair listening to David, he wondered, "was he listening to the evidence I was listening to? Was he sitting at the same trial that I sat in on or were the facts that I heard from the witness stand the things that he heard? And I think, to a large extent during his summation, he distorted the record. I believe that he has even . . . gone so far as to make some facts up, to put some things in some people's mouths, but that's for you to determine. . . .

"First, I want to talk about some of the things Mister Lewis raised in his summation and, unfortunately, I am not going to talk as quickly as Mister Lewis did, so I'm probably going to be up here just a little bit longer," Dan grinned down upon the jurors, in his easygoing manner, adopting a kind of no-nonsense Abe Lincoln demeanor.

He said the idea that they had to believe every part of the People's theory was just not true—all they had to believe was that the defendant killed his wife and that he intended to do it.

"Mister Lewis talked so fast that I found, at times, that I wasn't able to take notes but there's just a couple of things that I want to address."

First, he said, was the issue that Bob never had control of Gail.

"The fact was that he wanted it and it always eluded him when it came to his wife. He wasn't in control—he always sought it.

"Now, and to a large extent, what he did during the summation was to blame Gail Katz, to blame her for her death on July seventh," blaming risky behavior, drug use and adultery.

"Evidence shows that he knew in advance about Ken and Anthony," said Dan, seemingly abandoning the opening position that Bob did not know until July 7th—but embracing the defense gift that Bob knew in advance, which was his motive for killing Gail.

Bob never asked Ken or Anthony what their relationship with his wife was—because he already knew, Dan said. He made fun of the scenario in which Gail is rubbed out by drug dealers, saying she was a novice at drugs and that there was no such evidence. The defense lawyer, he said, spoke of how consistent with innocence Bob's behavior was, giving innocent explanations for everything.

"Everything the defendant does and says, taken out of context, has an innocent explanation," said Dan amiably. "But that's not the way you should look at the evidence. . . . When taken as a whole, the things that he does and the things that he says have no innocent interpretation. The only reasonable inference is that he's lying and covering up—because he killed his wife."

Dan ridiculed David's proposition. "What's a guy to do? What's Robert Bierenbaum to do when faced with a disappearing wife? He's betrayed, he's hurt. It doesn't matter what the status of their relationship was. Any normal, innocent human being does everything in their power to find the person they've spent at least the last four to five years of their life with.

"Robert Bierenbaum does nothing," Dan said loudly, gesturing toward Bob. "He posts a few posters in Central Park at someone else's urging. It even takes someone else's urging to get him to report her missing."

Bob's lawyer, Dan reminded the jury, asked them how many of them had said they wanted to kill someone, as Bob had said he wanted to kill Gail.

"But how many of you, how many of your relationships with either significant others or spouses, where you've said that—where your spouse or significant other ended up dead? So, taken out of context, yeah—but in this context, there's nothing innocent about it."

The defense lawyer was trying to parse out the evidence, he said, disconnect it, take it apart and tell them that every little piece meant nothing. But, taken as a whole, it all spelled out Bob's guilt.

"The fact remains that every piece of evidence in this case points to the defendant. He's the only person in the case with motive to kill her. He's the only person that has in the past displayed a capability to harm her, an intent to do her harm. He is the last person to see her alive. He has, I suggest to you, an even stronger motive when she is dead to get rid of her body," as well as the ability to dispose of Gail's body, Dan said, his voice charged with indignation.

He spoke of Bob's words and deeds and lies after Gail's death, his pattern of deception.

"Circumstantial evidence goes beyond the reasonable doubt that he is the only person on the face of the earth who could have killed his wife. There is no other inference to be drawn from the evidence and how could Mister Lewis, with a straight face, get up here and tell you that in the spring and early summer of 1985, things were getting better in the marriage when Gail Katz is in love with Ken and seeing Anthony?

He told the jury they simply had to ask themselves, was Gail dead, when did she die, how did she die—and who killed her?

"Well, she's not sunning herself at some seaside resort," snorted Dan. "She's not in California . . . She's not married to some reclusive billionaire. She hasn't been spending the last fifteen years in Central Park. She's certainly not waiting outside that door to end this trial here," said Dan, sweeping his hand toward the motionless double wooden doors at the back of the courtroom. The jurors' eyes followed the gesture.

"You don't need any scientific evidence, you don't need any forensic evidence to know to a certainty that Gail Katz is dead. The evidence is simply overwhelming."

On the day she was last seen and heard from, Gail's life "was like a book that was yet to be written," Dan said. "She was intent on closing the chapter on Robert Bierenbaum, but there were many more chapters yet to be written."

She was looking forward to her career, her new patients, to a "life without fear . . . to her life without the defendant. She's got no reason to simply drop off the face of the earth on July seventh, 1985," said Dan, who quoted Gail's psychiatrist: "suicides don't get pedicures."

"Suicides also don't get haircuts the day before they kill themselves. Suicides don't go looking for apartments. They don't get new birth control devices. They don't plan on being sexually active, they don't make plans with lovers and boyfriends. They don't look forward to the first patients of their career," he said.

Of course, the jury had heard virtually nothing about Gail's attempted suicide and how she had gone out of her way to make plans with those she knew just before she tried to take her own life.

"Suicides are incapable of disposing of their own bodies," said Dan. "She wasn't run over by a taxi, hit by a bus or bike messenger or subway," and did not die of natural causes.

Bob, he said, had one story for the cops and others for Gail's friends and his later girlfriends. Bob knew Gail was cheating on him. His motive was Gail's threat to ruin him with the psychiatrist's letter if he did not give her what she wanted in a divorce, despite the fact that Gail was the one committing adultery. Gail married Bob, he said, because she was "dazzled by the package . . . he's a doctor, he flies, he speaks languages, he plays guitar, an expert skier. He's perfect—what can go wrong?"

But when she's ready to leave, years later, she threatens Bob with the letter. Dan, speaking as Bob, talks about what he supposedly said about von Bülow leaving a body: "Von Bülow's mistake: He left evidence that can be traced to him. If I'm going to do it to you, Gail, I won't make that mistake."

Then Dan spoke for Gail: "She said, 'You know, I've had it. I'm leaving you. I'm having an affair. I'm in love. Not only that, there's been more than one affair . . . and I'm going to have a life . . . without you. . . . I have the letter. You know what it means. And if you don't let me go, *if* you don't give me what I want in the divorce, I will use it, I will use it to show to every head of every department and ruin your career.' And the defendant sees everything evaporate—everything he's worked for, everything he's strived for," said Dan.

"His career is going up in smoke and the person doing

the threatening is his wife and, ladies and gentlemen, this time she's not just smoking a cigarette. And what does he do? He places his hands around her neck and begins to choke her. But he chokes her much harder than he'd done when she was only having a cigarette, chokes her much harder than when he had only strangled her into unconsciousness. He chokes her to death."

Bob, he said, had solved one problem but created another, but not one he can't solve. Bob is a doctor and knows the strangulation left bruises and damage to Gail's neck that an autopsy will reveal. He can't claim it was an accident. But Bob has lots of time to get rid of the evidence—which is what Gail had become—and still have the life he wants for himself. Bob must dispose of the body and make up a story for the police, one in which his wife is missing all day and he does nothing but sit at home and then go to a party, where a photo was taken showing him laughing.

"Look at the photographs with a big smile on his face," said Dan. "It's all a show. He does nothing to find his wife. He does nothing to show any concern, whatsoever. A normal human being . . . maybe let her go and cool off for a while but, as time goes on during the day, an innocent person goes and looks," said Dan, his voice getting louder and louder with anger.

"I don't care how bad the wife is—simple human decency. You would expect that the defendant is going to be concerned at a minimum for the safety of his wife, but he sits and he waits and he flies and he parties," Dan accused, pointing a finger at Bob.

"That's just that day," said Dan. "He does nothing to try and find her. He does nothing to try and find her because he knows she's not coming back. He knows because he killed her."

Bob, he said, knew he had to get rid of the body.

"He's got to get it in the elevator down to the first floor, a simple task. He's got to get it out the first floor to his car," by putting his father's car in front of the building and just boldly carrying the bag out to it.

"He goes through the lobby . . . through the service entrance . . . a couple of feet out into the street and into the car and off to Caldwell Airport," said Dan.

He said Bob rented the plane, drove the car up to the plane, "puts it right in the passenger seat and he's off and flying in a matter of minutes."

Gail's body was never found because Bob dumped it into the ocean, he said.

"I'm not suggesting it wasn't difficult but it's certainly not impossible—especially if you are determined and the defendant was determined. And the thing is . . . this is all done without leaving a shred of forensic or scientific evidence behind. Strangulation, ladies and gentlemen, choking someone is not going to leave blood or brain matter."

Afterwards, "within days, he's out in the Hamptons, partying up a storm. In days, he's at a disco, a comedy club. Within weeks, he's having an affair with Karen Caruana. Taken individually, it may be subject to interpretation. Taken all together, his behavior indicates that he knows his wife isn't coming back. He knows his wife is dead."

Although Bob later showed evidence of emotion in the months and years that followed, "where was the sadness in July of 1985?" Dan asked.

When he arrived home on the night Gail disappeared, Bob went to sleep and then he went to work the next morning. He didn't call the cops until Yvette Feis told him he had to. And then he told the detectives he stayed home all afternoon—but he told some of Gail's friends that he looked for her in the park and found her towel and suntan lotion.

"She never went to Central Park," said Dan. "He never found her towel and he never found her suntan lotion. He never tells this to the police. You have to agree that that would go in the category of 'nice to know' if you're a detective investigating the disappearance of Gail Katz."

Dan said Bob came out with "unguarded moments of truth"—such as when he said Gail was a JAP on a shopping spree with his money at Bloomingdale's, and how she could be lying at the bottom of the reservoir in Central Park.

When Bob and Roberta are awakened in the middle of the night in 1986 by police, who say they think they found Gail, "The defendant doesn't jump up and say, 'Oh, my God, this is the first ray of hope in a hopeless situation—I'm going right away.' He doesn't question the officer, 'Is she okay physically, mentally? Are you sure it's her? Do you know it's her?' None of the questions that you would think an innocent man, someone whose wife had recently disappeared, would have asked."

Instead, Bob asked if he needed to come down right away "as if waiting until morning is the appropriate thing to do," said Dan. "His response isn't 'I'm on my way.' His response isn't 'I hope it's her,' His response isn't 'I don't think it's her.' His response is to turn to Roberta Karnofsky and say, "Don't worry, it's not her,' " said Dan, leaving the crucial word "doubt" out of the sentence that Roberta said Bob spoke that night.

"And the reason he says that, ladies and gentlemen, is because he knows for a fact, beyond any doubt, that it can't be her—because she was dead on July 7th, at his hands."

As David had predicted, Dan said that Bob's failure to deny Roberta's theory proved he was guilty.

"Under the circumstances," said Dan, "an innocent man would have simply looked us straight in the eye, and, probably with an epithet, told us, 'You're crazy. I didn't kill my wife.' An innocent man, especially this defendant, would have angrily denied it. An innocent man with this defendant's temper, may have violently denied it—but he didn't.

"Had you, ladies and gentlemen, been accused, said nothing? It is as if he is admitting the truth—another unguarded moment of truth."

Another moment of truth was the altered flight log, and the second flight in August—exactly one month after July 7th—which Bob arranged "to cover up for his impulsive, obsessive entries into his flight log," making the alteration "even more sinister and dark."

Joel Davis, he shrugged, "is simply mistaken. A nice man, a bit eccentric . . ." who described her with a well-developed chest—in direct contrast to photographic evidence. Davis, he said, was confused about Gail's height, among other things. He saw a woman he thought had a nice tan, a nice body and a nice T-shirt that day—but it wasn't Gail.

Dan told the jurors that Bob intended to kill Gail.

"He knew, in July of 1985, what it would take to kill her. He didn't stop when he knew he was hurting her, he didn't stop when he knew she was unconscious. He only stopped when she was dead. He stopped when it was too late to apologize, too late to ask for forgiveness," Dan said.

Bob, who had been watching Dan, turned away and gazed straight down at the table in front of him.

"Think about the closeness of strangulation . . . how close up you are with a person that you are choking. It's not a bullet from twenty feet—it's not that impersonal. It's not a knife thrust into the stomach, it's not the simple act of shoving somebody in front of the subway train. Strangulation is up close and personal—you watch as you literally squeeze the life out of another human being. Think about him looking at her while he squeezes the life out of her. Think about him standing over Gail Katz as she feels and watches the life ebbing from her body," said Dan.

As he paused, the courtroom was utterly silent. At the defense table, Bob's hands fidgeted slightly. His neck, face and bald spot flushed with blood.

"Now you know what his intent was. Now you know what he meant to do was squeeze the life, choke the life out of Gail Katz," Dan concluded.

"Mister Lewis is correct—no one can tell you. There was no witness in the apartment—there was no fly on the wall to tell you that this is exactly what happened," said Dan. "The only reasonable and rational inference from the evidence is that the defendant intentionally killed his wife on July seventh of 1985. And I ask you, in the name of the People of the State of New York, to find the defendant guilty of murder in the second degree. Thank you."

After Dan's dramatic closing, the judge sent the jury out to lunch, after which she would issue her mandated charge to the jury on the law—the marching orders for jurors. After lunch, the judge noted:

"I got so excited. . . . I forgot to say that Mister Lewis' motion for a mistrial is DENIED," emphasizing her final word and then giggling.

The jury then entered and the judge began her charge. A judge charging a jury is generally considered to be one of the more boring events in the known universe, far more potent than sleeping pills—especially in the afternoon after lunch. But, of course, justice and a man's liberty were at stake and the issues of law were deadly serious. She spoke to them about reason, logic and common sense. In an hour-long charge, she explained the standards to determine guilt beyond a reasonable doubt, and what intent and motive were. She discussed circumstantial evidence and told them they could reach a guilty verdict on that alone, if they so decided. A judge's charge can be custom-fitted by agreement among the lawyers and there was an unusual charge in this case—confession by silence. The jurors were told they could decide that Bob showed a consciousness of guilt when Roberta confronted him with her you-dumped-Gail-out-of-the-plane theory and that his silence was a confession. At least one juror wore a puzzled expression at the instruction that a man could confess to a murder by saying nothing. When she had completed her charge, the judge dismissed the six alternate jurors and sent the twelve men and women into a room to decide Bob's fate. As they left, Bob and the defense team stood out of respect for the jury, as they always did. Several jurors looked at Bob as they passed.

Now, for Bob, for Janet, for Alayne and her brother, for the lawyers and the press came the hardest part—waiting.

One of the alternate jurors told a *New York Times* reporter outside the court that the jury was divided and that he and other jurors felt the prosecution case was weak—because there was no body or direct evidence against Bob. He said he felt the defense lawyers might have made a mistake by admitting that Gail was probably dead. The 1983 choking incident, he said, was not damning, because "everybody has fights in their marriage. Where's the body?" the juror asked. "How do you even know she's dead?"

To the defense, the report was great news. It held out hope of a not-guilty verdict or a hung jury, which would result in a new trial—a lengthy, tiresome, expensive process—but one in which the defense would already know the prosecution's worst. To the prosecution, it seemed to be terrible news. One part of the jury did not buy the circumstantial case. All juries are divided until they reach a consensus—but which group would prevail?

CHAPTER 50

VERDICT

ALAYNE was exhausted and numb. Standing in the hallway outside the courtroom, she was seething with outrage that the defense tried to blame her sister for her own murder. It had always been difficult to stand in the same hall as Bob, his lawyers and Bob's second wife—but now the tension in the air was palpable. One reporter joked to another not to get in the line of fire whenever Alayne glared at Bob, just in case looks could kill.

Steve and Alayne were approached by two of the alternate jurors, including the woman who resembled Gail, who had just been excused. It was seen by the press as a possible indicator of how the jury was thinking—since the jurors did not approach Bob or his lawyers. But those jurors were now out of it and the jurors who were deliberating were beyond reach, beyond prediction.

Inside the jury room, the jurors elected juror number one as the forewoman and decided to take a vote. On the first ballot, eight jurors voted for guilty and four were undecided. No one spoke out to suggest that Bob was not involved—but several jurors did not want to convict without a body. A majority of the jurors felt that Bob's concealment of his flying on the day Gail disappeared was crucial evidence of his guilt. Roberta Karnofsky's testimony that Bob seemed certain that the police had not found Gail made it seem that Bob knew Gail was not coming back—and there was only one way he could have been certain about that. After a discussion that lasted a few hours, the jury sent out their first note to the judge.

Later that afternoon, the judge announced that the jury wanted to hear a read-back of the testimony of Bob's father, Marvin, and the DA investigator who later interviewed him about the day Gail vanished. The jury filed back in and the same jurors glanced at Bob as they passed, although most did not. The court stenographer then began reading back the testimony, playing all the parts. After the laborious read-back was complete, the jury returned to their deliberations. They next asked for People's Exhibit Number 6—the Hobbs Meter log that showed how long Bob had used the rental airplane that day. The jury appeared to be concentrating on Bob's flight and what it meant—but why? Were they trying to convince someone of something or trying to change their minds? Guessing didn't count but everyone did it. The jury worked until just after 7 that evening when the judge sent them to a hotel for the night.

The next morning, the jury requested copies of the lawyers' stipulations, the photos of Bob and Gail's building that showed entrances and exits, and the check that Bob wrote to Gail's divorce lawyer. It seemed, like most dutiful juries, they were methodically working their way through the case. But they also asked for read-backs of the testimony of Scott Baranoff and the cross-examination of Joel Davis.

The prosecution was buoyed and the defense was wary. Scott Baranoff was most likely a continuation of their interest in the day in question—but the meltdown of Joel Davis on the stand was something different. Was the jury leaning toward guilt? Why else would they listen to Joel Davis? Scott Greenfield thought it meant Joel Davis might still be alive as a viable witness. The problem, as always, was why a jury asked for something—to prove or disprove, to convince or dissuade? As court stenographer Joyce Hounsell read back Joel Davis' demolition in the courtroom, the jurors were literally on the edges of their seats. They looked like a jury on the edge of a verdict. One juror listened intently, eyes closed. Bob also leaned forward, leaned his cheek on his right hand, reading along on the transcript that was in front of Scott Greenfield. The judge applied lip gloss and read a newspaper, keeping it below her bench. Alayne and her brother Steve listened carefully in the second row. In the last row of the courtroom sat the

excused alternate juror who looked a bit like Gail. She had
returned on her own time to see the case through to the
end.

" 'Gail' is in the back today," whispered one reporter to
another.

When the read-backs were over, the jury retired to continue their deliberations.

In the hall, reporters, lawyers and others milled about,
chatted and waited. A courtroom artist slept on a wooden
bench with a coat over her head, her pastel drawings of the
morning's proceedings resting nearby. Some members of
the press went out to lunch, others to the Press Room on
the first floor, to wait it out.

Not quite a half an hour later, the jury sent out a new
note. They wanted to hear a third read-back—the direct
testimony of Joel Davis. The judge's announcement created
a stir in court. The defense lawyers' spirits seemed to lift
and the prosecutors looked worried. Scott Greenfield
thought the jury would either acquit Bob or become dead-
locked, with the latter more likely. If the jurors wanted to
hear Joel Davis' strong testimony that he saw Gail, did that
mean that they had found their reasonable doubt and were
on the edge of acquittal? Or was the flip side the real reason—to show holdouts that the reasonable doubt they
sought was not there? Alayne and Steve were in a panic—
going from the cross to the direct was not the order they
wanted to hear on Joel Davis. It seemed like the jury might
believe Davis, something Steve and Alayne found incom-
prehensible.

Two male jurors again looked at Bob when they filed in
to hear the read-back. As they filed out afterwards to resume their job, the same two jurors looked at him. Courthouse superstition held that jurors looked at defendants they
favored and did not look at those they intended to convict.

The atmosphere outside the court was charged. Bob and
Janet looked cautiously optimistic. Alayne and her brother
looked very apprehensive. They tried to console each other,

prepare each other—because they expected the worst. Steve
was a pessimist—he couldn't help it when it came to this
case.

"No matter what, we changed this guy's life, we have
maybe lost the war but won a battle," Steve told his older
sister. He reminded her that Bob might never practice medicine in the U.S. anymore. They were cooperating with the
medical boards of North Dakota and Arizona, in an effort
to have Bob's medical licenses pulled. He tried to sound
positive but the words tasted bitter in his mouth.

Steve didn't get very far with his pep talk. Three minutes
after they entered the jury room, the jurors took a final vote.
In just three minutes, the jury came back with a unanimous
verdict, after a total of 5 1/2 hours of deliberation. They
sent out a note, telling the judge they had a verdict. The
surprise news spread like electricity through the partially
empty court and hallway. People who had just walked out
of the courtroom turned around and went back through security and hurried into seats. The court officers very carefully searched everyone, giving special attention to running
the metal detector all over Steve Katz's body.

By prior arrangement, Janet left before the verdict. She
nervously kissed Bob in the hallway.

"Good luck," she said, before rushing off with the private detective, to avoid the onslaught of the press after the
verdict—whatever it would be.

Janet had been there every day for Bob—listening to a
line of people who said terrible things about the father of
her child. She wanted to stay but she knew it was for the
best. Bob sat at the defense table and took a small color
photo of his daughter Annah out of his wallet. He placed
it on a yellow legal pad in front of him and just stared at
the picture of the child who loved him.

But the judge noticed the little picture and ordered Bob
to put it away before she brought the jury in. Reluctantly,
Bob put the snapshot away.

Alayne sat next to Steve in the second row and grabbed
his hand with both of hers and held on for dear life. She

could feel fifteen years of rage, hatred, frustration and sadness welling up inside her. It now seemed easy to come to the trial every day and tell reporters that she was glad to finally be there and that it didn't really matter what the verdict was. But Alayne realized, once she heard there was a verdict, that it mattered a great deal. She was very scared. For fifteen years she had worked and fought and prayed for this moment. Now that it was here—she wanted to wait another week. She wasn't ready. She was a lawyer and she knew how difficult it was for a jury to come in with a beyond-a-reasonable-doubt guilty verdict without a body or eyewitness or forensic evidence. Alayne thought she was prepared for the worst, but she knew she wasn't.

One journalist in the front row whispered to a colleague from television: "The read-backs must have been to convince a few holdouts not to believe Joel Davis and the last read-back did it. A majority can convince a few holdouts in a few minutes but a few holdouts can't swing the rest of the jury so quickly. It's got to be guilty."

For the first time, the two jurors who had looked at Bob virtually every time they went in and out of the courtroom did not look at him as they passed. Like the other members of the panel, their eyes were straight ahead.

"They didn't look at him this time," the journalist said. "It's got to be guilty."

Alayne overheard the whispering journalist but did not want to get her hopes up. Tears welled in her eyes. She tried to suppress her emotions but muffled cries escaped in spasms.

"Will the foreperson please stand?" asked the court clerk. The woman stood up in the jury box, her hands at her sides.

"Please answer my question with a yes or a no answer. Ladies and gentlemen of the jury, has the jury reached a verdict?"

"Yes, we have," the forewoman replied.

"How say you as to the first count, charging the defendant, Robert Bierenbaum, with the crime of murder in the second degree—guilty or not guilty?"

"Guilty," she declared.

A gasp went up in the courtroom.

"Yes!" hissed Alayne, triumphantly.

Bob blinked and the color drained from his face. He looked frozen, like a man in a daze.

The defense team also seemed stunned—they had lost the un-losable case.

If anything, the prosecution seemed even more surprised—they had won the unwinnable case.

Alayne sobbed uncontrollably in the second row and huddled with her brother, while the court clerk polled the jury: "Juror number one, is that your verdict?"

"Yes," she agreed.

The clerk polled all the jurors, who agreed on the verdict.

"Ladies and gentlemen of the jury—hearken to your verdict as it now stands recorded," the clerk announced. "You and each of you say you find the defendant, Robert Bierenbaum, guilty of the crime of murder in the second degree, and so say you all?"

"Yes," all twelve jurors answered at once.

The judge thanked the jurors for their task: "It is always difficult for one human being to pass judgment on a fellow human being. We are very grateful to you for making our great system—imperfect though it may be, the best system we know of—work."

She excused the panel and they filed from the room for the last time. Adam Kaufmann requested that "the defendant be remanded, having been convicted of murder."

"The defendant is remanded," said Crocker-Snyder.

Judge Leslie Crocker-Snyder ordered Bob into custody. Several court officers approached Bob, who stood up. One officer took a pair of handcuffs off his belt and clicked them onto Bob's wrists. It was the first time in his life he had ever been handcuffed. When he surrendered ten months earlier, the cops did not bother to cuff him. In the second row, Steve Katz smiled at the sight. A door on the left side of the courtroom opened, revealing a room with barred cells. The officers led the manacled Bob through the door and shut it behind them with a thud. Spectators and press flooded out of the courtroom.

The smiling prosecution team declined to comment to the clamoring press. They hugged Alayne and Steve and returned to their offices.

"I'm just so relieved," Alayne said, through her tears, hugging the alternate juror who looked like her dead sister.

"I have a sister who I'm close to and I can't imagine what she's going through," the juror sobbed.

"He's a pretty cold, emotionless guy," Steve Katz said of Bob. "I guess I have to admit I'm surprised that anyone could face a guilty verdict and be just stone-faced. I know that I was supposed to be stone-faced and I couldn't be stone-faced.

"I heard the cuffs close around his hands—I have waited for that sound for a long time."

A television reporter asked Alayne what she would say to Bob.

"I've nothing to say to Robert Bierenbaum. He's irrelevant. I have people I want to thank. I don't care about Robert Bierenbaum."

The same reporter asked what she might now say to her sister, if she could.

"I'd also like to show her that she—who felt he was so good on paper, when she stayed with him for all the wrong reasons, that during the trial, he—looked blacker than coal, and she looked like an innocent victim."

Was Gail resting easier tonight? another television reporter asked.

"I hope so," said Alayne.

"Our client was extremely disappointed by the verdict," and would appeal it, Scott Greenfield said.

Janet "chose not to be present" for the verdict because "it was too emotional for her," said David Lewis.

David was disappointed by the verdict. He did not like to lose.

Cheers and applause erupted in Foroni's a few blocks away when the prosecution team entered. They were local heroes.

"I love the smell of Napalm in the morning. It smells like victory!" Adam Kaufmann said, quoting from the hit movie *Apocalypse Now*.

"Doctor Bob's smelling victory!" Adam exulted.

The libations flowed, toasts were toasted and the somber faces of Alayne, Steve and many of Gail's friends broke out in a joy they thought they had lost. For the lawyers, it was a career-topper. They were no longer the guys who brought the impossible case—they were the cutting-edge hotshots who had won it. They had pushed the envelope for homicide prosecutions in New York and elsewhere and were now the experts on how to put someone who had committed the perfect crime behind bars. The celebrants stayed four hours, ending up at a large round table, hashing over the testimony, the evidence, the verdict—all but pinching themselves to see if they were dreaming.

"I knew he was guilty the first time I came face-to-face with him," a jubilant Tom O'Malley told a reporter.

O'Malley remembered the patronizing, superior attitude he got from Bob the genius who thought Tom was just a dumb flatfoot who would go away.

"Yes, it took fifteen years," said Tom, beaming, "but who is dumb and who is brutal—who is in jail?"

Uptown, Dr. Michael Stone heaved a huge sigh of relief at news of the verdict. Justice, he thought with a smile, had triumphed over law.

CHAPTER 51

THE UNDERWORLD

BOB'S eyes were vacant and he wore the hopeless expression of one recently damned to the criminal pit of prison. Dazed, dressed in a tan "Tombs" jumpsuit and orange sneakers issued by the jail, he greeted Scott and asked his lawyer the same question over and over again:

"What happened? How did this happen?"

Bob could not comprehend how he could be sitting behind bars when the prosecution did not have any evidence.

"We failed you," Scott said, sullenly. "You believed in the system, you believed in your lawyers and we failed to protect you from the insanity. You trusted me and I failed."

"But, I'm in jail," Bob said, as if he were stating an impossibility, something that went against the laws of nature.

"I know," said Scott.

Three days after Bob's conviction, Scott sent a letter to Michael Stone's lawyer regarding *Bierenbaum vs. Stone*, threatening to sue the psychiatrist for breach of physician–patient confidentiality, calling his numerous press interviews and court testimony "unethical."

It was a threat letter—offering to settle out of court with Michael, or his malpractice insurer, before Bob went to court. Scott gave Michael thirty days to respond to the threat. Michael's lawyer had no intention of giving Bob any money and did not respond.

The only thing Bob liked about jail was that there was no smoking in the brightly painted, twelve-story "Tombs." The city's most comfortable and modern lockup was attached to the Centre Street courthouse and housed fewer than 500 inmates.

In the fall, Bob usually piloted his own airplane through a blue sky to a ski resort, where he flew down a snowy

slope. Instead, he was confined to a dark 8-by-10-foot cell
with a stainless-steel toilet and sink.

Bob, the gourmet chef, was being forced to eat stale
baloney-and-cheese sandwiches. But that was not the worst
that a correctional institution had to offer someone who was
not from the mean streets. Jail is not a nice place— it is a
cage filled with criminals.

On October 27th, one of those criminals, a violent felon
named *Lamar Lake recognized Bob from television as the
rich doctor who had killed his wife. Bob was out of his
element and made the mistake of not surrendering his gold
wedding band when he was incarcerated. Lamar noticed the
gold on Bob's left index finger. When Lamar tried to remove the ring, Bob resisted. Lamar tussled with Bob and
bit him in the chest. Some of Bob's judo moves came back
to him and he spun his attacker away. Lamar then came
back with fists and punched Bob in the nose, drawing
blood. When Lamar pulled out a knife, Bob broke free and
escaped. Bob thought his nose was broken but he examined
himself and concluded it was not. The bite gave him some
concern but his assailant did not appear to be an AIDS
sufferer, although visible symptoms meant little. He had
human teeth marks on his chest and a huge bruise developing on his face from the punch. It was nothing, compared
to the damage he might have suffered if Lamar had con-
nected with his prison "shank" knife.

Bob told Scott about his initiation into prison culture but
he did not report it to authorities, for fear of breaking the
criminal code and being labeled a snitch—with deadly results. Scott took Polaroid photos of Bob's injuries and convinced him he had to report it on some level—in order to
be moved into protective custody. Authorities said they
would treat Bob's information confidentially and not file
charges against his attacker. But an officer later went to
Bob and announced, in front of other inmates: "Bierenbaum! Get over here. We want to question you about violence by other inmates."

Bob, alarmed, called Scott and told him what had happened.

"Are they trying to kill me—or are they just morons?" Bob asked.

Bob was later transferred to the Queens House of Detention in a routine move, along with other inmates. Several inmates told Bob they had been approached by authorities— who wanted to know if Bob had told them anything. Scott was surprised at the news because jailhouse informant tactics were used by prosecutors before a trial—not after one. It appeared as if the prosecutors feared Bob might get a new trial on appeal and were already preparing for round two.

Later, a "Bloods" drug gang member approached Bob and said he would not make up a story about Bob confessing to him—if Bob gave him money.

Bob had already heard that several inmates had made statements to prosecutors—fabricating statements and attributing them to Bob.

After the conviction, Dan and Stephen were the experts on how to make impossible murder prosecutions possible. They were contacted by prosecutors from other DAs' offices for advice on how to heat up their cold cases without a body or forensic evidence. Most DAs' offices around the country had an unsolved missing wife case that had gone un-prosecuted due to lack of evidence.

Connecticut prosecutors called Morgy's office, seeking their expertise on how to go forward with their own affluent husband–missing wife case. Three years before Gail went missing, another pretty young bride vanished. Her wealthy husband was a suspect but no body was ever found. After consulting with the Manhattan ADAs, the Connecticut authorities changed their murder scenario from New York City to a Connecticut lake, in a new theory that mimicked the Bierenbaum case. They dragged the lake near the couple's cabin and then announced that they suspected the husband had dumped the body into the water—where it was destroyed by decomposition. Water plus fifteen years could make many troubling prosecutorial problems vanish.

Gail's family and many of her friends came to court for Bob's sentencing on November 29th, as well as investigators who worked on the case, such as Tommy Pon and the retired Andy Rosenzweig—who had promised Bob he would see him again.

Steve and his wife, and Alayne and her husband, sat with Gail's friends. On the opposite side of the aisle, sat a somber Marvin and Nettie Bierenbaum, along with their daughter-in-law Janet, who was holding hands—for support—with Bob's former girlfriend Sandy Schiff. Next to them was Bob's new appeals lawyer, Diarmuid White.

Three burly court officers brought an apathetic-looking Bob into court from the holding cell area. He was wearing a suit and his surgeon's hands were handcuffed behind his back. One officer unlocked the cuffs and Bob sat next to Scott Greenfield at the defense table.

David Lewis was not in court. Scott, who had begun the case for Bob fifteen years earlier, would end it by speaking for him.

One journalist who had read Scott's thick and impressive pre-sentencing memo—which contained glowing letters from a state supreme court justice and a United Nations ambassador, among many other prominent people—joked that it read more like a nomination for the Nobel Prize than a plea for mercy for a killer.

"I am broken by what has happened to my husband," Janet wrote to the judge. "However, I am grateful that our child is too young to understand where her daddy is. His family will never give up on him. Despite all the allegations, I will forever love my husband. I will not leave his side. I beg this court to take into consideration all the good Bob has done over the last 15 years and impose the minimum sentence possible."

Marvin and Nettie also composed a moving letter to the

judge, in which they expressed love for their son and pride for his dedication to helping others.

"We probably will not live long enough to be there when he completes his sentence, no matter what sentence you impose," they wrote. "The pain of this situation is unbearable to us, as it is to his wife, Janet, and the miracle of our lives—our granddaughter Annah, who will grow up without a father to love and guide her. The sentence is imposed upon all of us, for Robert is part of us and we cannot detach our lives from him."

The judge only had a decade of discretion when it came to the sentence of second-degree murder. The minimum sentence under the law was 15-to-life and the maximum was 25-to-life. The defense team and the press assumed Crocker-Snyder would give Bob the max and the prosecution and Gail's sister and brother hoped they were right.

When the proceedings began, Prosecutor Dan Bibb called Alayne Katz to the stand—to make a Victim's Impact Statement to the court before sentence was imposed. Alayne stepped to the podium and addressed the judge, reading from a prepared statement.

"On July seventh, 1985, Robert Bierenbaum pronounced sentence on his wife and my sister Gail—death and defamation. On me—life without my sister," Alayne said.

Gail's "crime," she said, was that she planned to live a happy life without Bob, who would have had to make a costly financial settlement with her. Her sister was killed because she was going to tell the truth that would have ruined her husband—that he was violent and mentally ill.

Alayne said that Bob might say he will miss major events of his daughter's life and noted that Gail had missed all of the events in the life of her family after she was slain. The difference, she said, was that Bob's family could visit him in jail—unlike the Katz family, who were left with an empty grave. She said Bob had neither confessed nor shown any remorse and deserved the maximum penalty of 25-years-to-life behind bars. Bob sent the judge letters from friends and family who claimed he was not dangerous,

Alayne said, "while he prohibits the psychiatrists to whom he admitted his violence from testifying in this courtroom.

"I submit that any showing of leniency by this court is tantamount to agreeing with the decision that Robert Bierenbaum made on July seventh, 1985—*that he was, and is, more important than Gail Katz, that his life is worth living but hers is not.*"

Alayne showed the judge snapshots of Gail and her family and described her life from childhood.

"She fell in love with Robert Bierenbaum and, despite the evidence of his deep character and psychological problems, she stood by him—believing that her love and understanding would change him, would cure him," said Alayne.

"Instead, Robert Bierenbaum changed Gail. His violent, controlling and judgmental behavior embittered Gail."

Alayne then read the love poem Gail had written to Bob early in their relationship, the one in which she told Bob that he was capable of "Soothing all my feelings of confusion and sadness, And promising me love and friendship and happiness."

Alayne pointed out that Bob's defense had been to blame his victim and defame Gail and her family in the press.

"Robert Bierenbaum killed my sister to prevent her from exposing him as a violent and twisted man," Alayne concluded.

She then asked to read Michael Stone's warning letter to Gail—hoping to make it a permanent part of the court record—but the judge would not allow it and Alayne sat down.

Dan Bibb rose to say that Bob's position during the trial and the sentencing had been "to blame the victim, to blame Gail Katz—almost to put the responsibility for her death on what they describe as risky behavior . . .

"But, I think it's safe to say that, for a matter of moments, the defendant held his wife's life—literally—in the palms of his hands," said Dan, his voice tinged with indignation. Bob, he said, "was close enough to his wife to see her life ebbing from her, as he strangled her."

Bob sat expressionless at the defense table, staring idly at his clasped hands and slowly twiddling his thumbs.

Bob viewed Gail's death, Dan said, "not as a tragedy, but as an opportunity—an opportunity to live without the baggage that Gail Katz represented to him, and without the threat that Gail Katz presented to the remainder of his life," said Dan.

"For that . . . it is the People's position that the minimum sentence in this case would be a travesty of justice, that substantially more than the minimum sentence is appropriate and we ask the court to impose such a sentence."

Scott, who had taken a back seat during the trial, at last rose to speak for Bob—who also got to his feet. He told the judge that Bob maintained his innocence and was already preparing an appeal—therefore he would not speak or express remorse for a crime he did not commit. He said Bob's silence "should not be construed as callousness or arrogance on his part—it's out of respect for these proceedings and out of respect for the Katz family.

"Alayne Katz has spoken for the Katz family and eloquently expressed their grief and their loss and their anger and the defendant takes no issue with the feelings she's expressed," said Scott.

The lawyer said he asked the court to consider "who the defendant is who stands before you—what has he done with his life, is he a threat to society?"

The probation report and Bob's testimonial letters attested to the fact that Bob was a caring, compassionate and charitable person, he said.

"Not charity in the sense of a yearly donation to the Red Cross," said Scott, "but charity in the sense of the missionary, where it's become a significant part of his life."

Several reporters in the front row circled the word 'missionary' in their notes—any time a convicted killer was called a missionary, it was worth printing. In her seat,

Alayne seethed. "Bob never performed such acts of charity until after he killed my sister," she thought.

"I've known this defendant for more than fifteen years," Scott continued. "Over that time, I've gotten to know him very well. He is one of the most extraordinary human beings I have ever had the privilege of knowing. Bob Bierenbaum has done more to help others than anyone else I have ever known. And the things he's done, the burdens he's endured to help other people—particularly the children of Mexico—are truly monumental."

Scott said he was "in awe" of Bob's deeds and denied that Bob did it so he could one day tell a judge about it.

"What he did, he did solely for the people of Mexico, the children, particularly—and he never asked for anything in return," Scott said.

"It's also been suggested that this work in Mexico is his way to atone for the death of his wife. If this is so, what's wrong with that? If a sentence is intended to pay a debt to society, then there's nothing wrong with someone voluntarily paying that debt to society," he said.

"There will be no winners here today. There will be no cause for celebration tonight, no matter what happens," the lawyer said. "Bob Bierenbaum is prepared to accept the sentence of this court today. His life is in shambles, his reputation is ruined, his medical career is at an end and his family is heartbroken. His proclamation of innocence is of no consequence today," said Scott.

"I beg this court to consider the person standing before you—not just the defendant, but the human being—and balance the good he's done. Please sentence Bob Bierenbaum to fifteen years to life. Thank you."

"Mister Bierenbaum," asked Rocco, the court clerk, "would you like to say anything to the court before sentence is imposed?"

"No," Bob answered.

He and Scott remained standing, as the judge spoke.

"I want to make the comment that the evidence of this

defendant's guilt—in my view—is overwhelming," said Crocker-Snyder.

She referred to excluded testimony of the barred psychotherapists who warned Gail, including the one who called her "immediately—to make sure that she was still alive," and warn her "of the extraordinary danger she was in." The judge told Scott, "you are aware what is in that privileged material, the defendant is aware of it, I am aware of it."

That and the evidence presented at trial "make overwhelmingly clear that this defendant killed his wife" as a result of the "dark side" of Bob's personality, she said. The judge then went beyond facts alleged by prosecutors or proven at trial and declared that the crime was premeditated, as well as "vicious" and "blood-curdling."

"There's every reason to believe that he dismembered Gail. He squeezed her into a bag, He rented a plane—because he had the privilege and the wealth to know how to fly a plane. . . . He dropped her body in a manner so that it would never be found, in the ocean," said Crocker-Snyder.

"Is this a kind and considerate human being? Maybe he was kind. I accept that he was kind to children in Mexico. That's a wonderful thing—but he wasn't kind to Gail or her family. He didn't exercise any charity toward Gail or her family or her friends. They had to wonder and search for her for years, with no closure.

"Who knows why a person commits good acts, who has a dark side, an evil side? Who knows? Did he commit these acts of charity in Mexico to expiate his guilt? I don't know. Did he commit these acts of charity because he's a good human being? Maybe part of him is, but we know that part of him, certainly, is evil. Did he commit these acts because his ego-gratification was so important that this was the way he received it? I'm not a psychiatrist. I don't know."

The judge noted that "Gail was destined to have no resting place and her family no knowledge of her final repose," and compared Sylvia Katz to Demeter, the mother of Persephone in ancient Greek mythology, who ate forbidden fruit and was consigned to the Underworld. Her mother was doomed to "wander in search of her daughter in the other world," the judge said.

"This defendant went about disposing of Gail like she was a piece of meat: cut it, saw it, package it, dump it—it's garbage—and cover your tracks. Tell no one about the plane trip. Lie about it, lie about it to numerous people. Tell different stories to numerous people. . . . that was the conduct of this defendant," Crocker-Snyder said.

"This is a very difficult sentence," the judge said. "What's the right, fair, just thing to do?"

She said Bob's superior education advantages meant he could seek help from a psychiatrist—and had done so. It also meant he could have hired a divorce lawyer. In fact, she said, he used his "superior, advantaged" background, not to obey the law—but to break and thwart it by committing the worst crime and becoming "a successful criminal and a successful murderer for a long time."

"The defendant has never shown any remorse, any regret," said Crocker-Snyder. "In fact, he has shown no emotion whatsoever from the first time I have seen him until now. He has been defiant—he has brazened out his position.

"The lack of emotion that I have seen here is exactly the lack of emotion that this defendant employed in killing Gail—brutally and coldly, over hours and hours—cutting up her body," the judge said, which was at odds with the prosecutors' theory that Gail was bloodlessly "folded" in ten minutes.

"Despite his fifteen years of freedom, despite his fifteen years of avoiding justice, this sentence is to punish a brutal, calculated evil and the total failure to accept responsibility," she said.

"This was a horrible case—horrible to everyone, a tragedy for both families. I believe that the appropriate sentence, and the one I now impose, is twenty years to life. That is the sentence of this court."

Many people were surprised by the sentence—either because the judge showed some unexpected mercy or because she failed to give a killer all that he deserved.

The court officers clicked the cuffs back on Bob's wrists and took him back to jail.

"I was extremely satisfied with the sentiments expressed by the judge as well as the sentence," Alayne told the press outside the courtroom.

Gail "would not be satisfied" with the sentence, Steve said.

"Gail would have wanted no mercy—she would only want the worst for him," agreed Gail's psychiatrist, Dr. Elsa Fairchild.

After the sentencing, Alayne and Steve hosted a victory party at the nearby Forlini's Restaurant, which was attended by Gail's family, friends, the prosecutors and even two women alternate jurors from the trial. They toasted to Gail and to victory, with Kir, one of Gail's favorite liqueurs. One celebrant complained that Bob had only received twenty years, instead of the death penalty. Someone from the prosecutor's office explained that the death penalty was not enacted until a decade after Gail vanished and that Bob never faced it.

"But don't worry, it might as well be a death sentence," the person laughed. "I have no doubt that he'll be killed in jail."

That night, Janet went back to her new home in another city and that night delivered several babies at the hospital to happy families.

The verdict and sentencing stripped Bob of his freedom and his medical licenses. The day after Christmas, Bob was designated as state inmate number 00A7114, and sent to a prison in upstate Fishkill for one day, before being transferred to the imposing Elmira Correctional Facility, an antique maximum-security fortress that opened in 1876.

At Elmira, his mental and physical condition would be evaluated and his final prison would be chosen by authorities. Because of the attack on him at the city jail, Bob was assigned to a Special Housing tier and removed from the general prison population.

Bob would not become eligible for parole until August, 2020, and his earliest release date would not be until two months after that.

Steve Katz believed his mother was happy at last and his family seemed to have emerged from the nether world, now that Bob had been removed from society and sent away. It was like Bob had taken their place in Hades.

The judge had spoken about his mother searching the Underworld for Gail and now it was Bob who was consigned to the Hell of prison.

On each and every day of those twenty years, Steve thought, Bob would know that he didn't get away with murder and, as smart as he was, there was no such thing as a perfect crime.

EPILOGUE

BOB Bierenbaum is currently serving his 20-years-to-life
sentence at an upstate prison, and is appealing his conviction. The odds are against success with any appeal. But,
considering some of the controversial rulings in the case,
he may have a better shot than most. Of course, if Bob
does win on appeal, he would not win his freedom—merely
the right to have a second trial before the same judge and
a different jury. He has also demanded a different judge.

If that happens, it would be interesting to see if his lawyers mount a full defense the second time around. The original jury never heard a word about cat stranglings—but it
also did not hear anything about Bob's trips to Mexico.
They heard nothing good about the man, although it may
not have made any difference. Even an army of character
witnesses would only have proved that Bob was a very
charitable and dedicated physician and good father—years
after Gail disappeared. The law is not self-service. It does
not allow citizens to get away with murder and sentence
themselves to perform charitable deeds which, in any case,
would be a very light penalty for robbing someone of his
or her life.

Perhaps a second trial, if there is one, will have a different result if Bob takes the stand. He could look the jury
in the eye and tell them he did not kill Gail. But, with his
famous strange eyes, would they believe him? He could tell
them about what a terrible person Gail was—the lying, the
cheating, the drugs, the goading, the attempted blackmail.
But that approach, blaming the victim, might backfire the
same way it did in the first trial. David Lewis did not mount
a full defense but slip-streamed behind the prosecution—
cleverly cross-examining their witnesses to score defense
points. It was a defense more suited to a Mafia chieftain

than a wrongfully-accused surgeon. But the more points the defense scored on what a scheming, unfaithful, dishonest wife Gail was, the more they proved the prosecution's motives for murder. In short, the "She was-asking-for-it" defense did not work the first time and it probably will not work a second time.

The verdict that sent Bob to prison meant that the jury believed Bob carried Gail's folded body out of their apartment house inside a duffel bag and down a Manhattan sidewalk in broad daylight. He then drove her to New Jersey and loaded her into a plane at a public airport. It was an incredibly brazen series of acts, which a person of lesser intelligence and gall would have thought impossible. Perhaps it only proves the adage that "He Who Dares, Wins."

The prosecution "theory" that Bob dumped her body into the ocean was made official by the jury but that does not mean that is what actually happened. The burial-at-sea solved many problems for the prosecution. They picked the ocean because the "VFR" flight area Bob used included the waters off New York. The Atlantic Ocean is presumed to have swallowed the victim, freeing the DA from producing her body. The mighty tides and currents could have carried the body to Europe or it could have been gobbled up by fish or crabs or bacteria. But that meant that Bob—the genius—dumped a body into open waters off a busy port, an area teeming with thousands of ships, charter boats and pleasure craft on a sunny holiday afternoon. One thing that non-boaters should understand about mariners is that most are, of necessity, an observant and alert lot. In the prosecution re-enactment video, filmed in late autumn, a large vessel had a clear view of the dumping of the "body." And that was after the aircraft—aided by two police helicopters—looked for the best spot available. Would a genius who had succeeded that far without detection, simply shove the body out the door and hope that a sailor was not reading his tail number with binoculars and repeating it by radio to the Coast Guard?

A body would have most likely surfaced, after bloating

with decomposition gases, within weeks. It might have washed ashore in New Jersey, New York, Long Island or New England—but it did not. Why? There are only two possibilities: Either it was swallowed up, possibly because it was weighted, and consumed by the blue hole of the sea—or it was never there.

In the almost two hours he ran the Cessna's engine, Bob could have flown anywhere within a 90-mile circle of the Caldwell Airport and back. That covers thousands of square miles of territory, most of it over land. He could have flown over the rolling, forested Catskill Mountains in New York or the city of Kingston, or east to Connecticut, almost to Montauk Point on Long Island, down south to Philadelphia or west to Scranton. But a killer looking to dump a body would have avoided populated areas and major airports that had air traffic controllers and tracking radars that were re-corded.

It is possible that Bob was even more daring and original than even the prosecution suspected.

Based on evidence I developed after the trial on alternate dumping sites—including Bob's claim that he had flown to the Greenwood Lake Airport that day to do touch-and-go's—it is possible that he disposed of Gail's body in a New Jersey reservoir.

Bob had been to the Greenwood Lake Airport before and knew the countryside, which featured opportunities for several of his favorite activities—skiing, hiking and bicy-cling. A straight, line-of-flight, north-by-northwest course from the Caldwell Airport to the Greenwood Lake Airport in rural Passaic County, would have brought Bob's rented Cessna directly over the Wanaque Reservoir within ten minutes after takeoff, just before he arrived at the second airport. The field is a small one, without a tower or air traffic controllers. Pilots flying under visual flight rules must make a radio call on a specific frequency to alert other pilots in the area that they are about to land or take off. There would be no taped record of the radio transmissions, which would have freed Bob, not to do touch-and-go's, but to search for the best location for his incriminating package. As James Mason said in *North by Northwest*, Bob had a problem that was "best solved from a great height—over water."

While it is always possible that Bob had a willing accomplice meet him at his destination to relieve him of the body, that would have meant trusting another person with a deadly secret, an unlikely event. My guess is he traveled solo that day. It is also possible he dropped Gail into a wilderness area but a body on land was much more likely to be discovered, no matter how far off the beaten path.

My alternate theory is based on information the police and the DA never received. I believe the reservoir theory is just as likely—possibly more likely—than the ocean disposal theory of the prosecution. In fact, considering how close Greenwood Lake Airport is to Caldwell Airport, it is certainly possible that Bob did do several touch-and-go's while scouting out the reservoir for the safest spot to lose his cargo. He would have had more than an hour to find the most deserted spot on the reservoir to deposit his burden. The more time he spent running his engine, the more likely investigators would assume he made a long trip that day—if they ever discovered he went flying. It would have been a very clever piece of misdirection, and that was what actually happened—the prosecutors told the jury that Bob flew out over the ocean.

The Wanaque Reservoir is very remote and surrounded by deep woods and fencing. The Boontown Reservoir, near the Caldwell Airport, is only two miles long but is also surrounded by a fence and woods and would also have made a good backup dumping site—but not as good as the deeper, more remote Wanaque Reservoir. Almost seven miles long, Wanaque is the longest reservoir in New Jersey. It has more than 2,300 acres of water, surrounded by thirty miles of shoreline and 4,000 acres of forest. Its clean, cool waters range from 37 to 90 feet deep. Because Wanaque supplies drinking water to one out of four people in New Jersey, there is no fishing or boating allowed. The ban on recreational fishing and boating would have made it a more attractive dumping spot than any of the many lakes in the area, where a fisherman might inconveniently hook a duffel bag containing a grisly surprise. Wanaque Reservoir is not subject to strong currents or daily tidal forces like the ocean. Properly weighted and ventilated, a body would sink to its depths—and stay there. Because authorities were never alerted to the Greenwood Lake Airport trip by Bob, police never questioned anyone at the airport or the nearby Wanaque Reservoir. They never dragged the Wanaque Reservoir, or the Boontown Reservoir near the Caldwell Airport. Either body of water—even on a sunny holiday weekend—could have been used as a repository for the body of an inconvenient wife and no one would have seen or heard the splash.

The remains of Gail Katz Bierenbaum may repose in the scenic Wanaque Reservoir, the "Place of Repose," but the chances of authorities locating a body after the passage of so many years is probably very slim. The odds are that Gail's final resting place will never be confirmed—unless the one person on earth who may know, Bob Bierenbaum, decides to tell us.

Perhaps he already has.

I find it fascinating that, in a careless moment of anger, Bob Bierenbaum made an unusual point. When frustrated by one of Gail's friends in his attempt to posthumously portray her as suicidal, Bob pointed west toward the Central Park Reservoir—and also in the same direction as the Wanaque Reservoir—and blurted: "How do you know she's not lying at the bottom of that reservoir right now?"

Indeed.

If Bob Bierenbaum is guilty, his guilt was betrayed to the jury, not by scientific evidence, but by circumstance—especially by his suspicious behavior. The most suspicious behavior of all was the fact that Bob Bierenbaum, to this day, has yet to act like an innocent man. He has never publicly protested his innocence or his outrage at being falsely accused.

He hid his plane flight that day from everyone he could. Why? Gail's friends and family, who turned against Bob, had all been flying with him and Gail but it did not occur to a single one of them that Bob had used an airplane to get rid of Gail's body. No detective deduced that Gail was thrown from a plane, hardly an everyday occurrence, even in New York City. It took authorities one year, two investigations and a bit of luck to discover that he had been up in the air. The only reason they considered it significant was that Bob had concealed it. In fact, the only person on the planet to initially think Bob's flight was suspicious was Bob himself. He wanted to keep the police looking in New York and away from New Jersey, and, possibly, from one particular reservoir. It appears he began to log information for his flight that day but did not complete the entry, for some reason. He later altered the date and location of his flight by arranging another plane rental on a day exactly one month later from a Long Island Airport. That was clever. Again, Bob wanted to divert attention away from New Jersey. If police learned where he had actually been, a dredging of the reservoir so soon after Gail disappeared might have been inconveniently successful.

The fact that Bob removed papers he did not want police to find from his apartment, and turned them over to his lawyer to be locked in a safe, was not introduced at trial but is hardly consistent with innocence. It was understandable that Bob wanted to avoid a scandal that might ruin his career. But concealing a letter from a psychiatrist that said he was dangerous, as well as lists that showed his wife was planning on moving out was also consistent with guilt.

The jury also gave great weight to Bob's reaction to the phone call from police, who thought they had located Gail in 1986. Although Bob had had such false alarms before, it had been almost a year since the last such sighting. He told his lawyer that he never went out that night and claimed that he called a Port Authority Police lieutenant, who told him first that the woman was probably not Gail, and, later, that it was definitely not his wife. Roberta remembers no such calls and swore Bob left the apartment to see if it was Gail. If Roberta told the truth on the stand, Bob could have had no special knowledge that the woman police were holding was not Gail—unless he had killed Gail and knew it was a false alarm, which is exactly what the jury believed.

Bob was the obvious suspect from the start, as most killers are. He was the last person to see Gail alive and the only person who had attacked her. He had a bad temper and he lied to police and concealed evidence. He hired a lawyer and refused to take a lie detector test. He gave different stories to different people. His wife, a charming user, had lied to him, cheated on him in their own bed and attempted to blackmail him so she could take him to the cleaners in a divorce—enough provocation to drive Captain Kangaroo to murder. From Gail, Bob got one copy of Michael Stone's letter, which he gave to Scott Greenfield. It is possible that, in a safe deposit box somewhere, is the other copy of the letter and a copy of the police report that Gail put aside to blackmail Bob.

While researching this book, I rented a Cessna 172 and a pilot and made a flight under virtually the same circumstances as Bob Bierenbaum did on July 7th, 1985. By trial and error, the pilot and I were able to discover how to dump a large package out of the passenger door—me. It was accomplished by slowing the aircraft to near stall speed, which makes it harder to control, tilting to starboard, and shoving the package against the unlocked door at the same time. I held on and stopped once I was leaning out the open door and looking down at suburban New Jersey two thousand feet below. Although the pilot was an experienced flight instructor, the aircraft rocked, wobbled, and rose and fell violently during several of our attempts. I do not recommend it as recreation.

Several sources said that Dr. Michael Stone diagnosed Bob as a psychopath and he said so in at least one published article. In an extensive interview, Dr. Stone read directly to me from his notes from Gail's sessions—because he had received written permission from her family to do so. He gave me his reactions to Bob but declined to read from his notes of Bob's sessions or directly quote him.

The psychiatrist was castigated by the defense and some in his own profession, for cooperating with authorities to bring a killer to justice. He took a stand for justice but no one praised him. He still faces a possible legal battle with a convicted killer. He hopes that his jury, if a civil lawsuit is filed, will not find for Bob Bierenbaum and, if they do, will only reward Bob with one dollar.

A forensic psychiatrist I consulted about the case, Dr. Michael Wellner, had some reservations about Stone's conclusion that Bob was a psychopath. Bob's charity work after he left New York was inconsistent with the self-serving behavior of a psychopath, but might have been more in line with someone suffering from a Narcissistic Personality Disorder, or "malignant narcissism." Of course, the mercy missions took place years after Bob saw Stone. No psychopath would have a conscience or remorse and sentence himself to community service, Wellner believed. Also, most true psychopaths cannot function professionally for long without messing up their own lives. But Bob's medical career was unblemished and he never again exhibited violent behavior over a period of fourteen years—a near-impossibility for a hardcore psychopath.

Or did the physician heal himself? Did Bob atone for his sins and change his behavior so he was functionally no longer a psychopath—like an alcoholic who never touches another drink? If so, it may have been his greatest accomplishment. Although psychopaths often mellow in middle age, the current accepted wisdom is that they can't change their spots. But, as Bob said, anything is possible.

Whatever the diagnosis, it was obvious that both Bob and Gail had deep, perhaps untreatable, emotional problems that each complemented the other in a malignant way. What started out as infatuation and then love, quickly degenerated into vicious cycles of fear and loathing, dependency and manipulation. Bob and Gail were both addicted to and poisoned by each other. But they reconciled again and again, rather than part—as if they loved hating each other more than they loved loving each other. In the end, it was Gail's decision to end the cycle that sealed her fate.

Michael Stone believes that Gail, suffering from the so-called "Carmen Syndrome," precipitated her own murder—which is not a defense under New York state law. Even if Gail had begged Bob to kill her—which she did not—Bob was still required to dial D for divorce, not M for murder.

There seems to be little evidence of premeditation in the case and most signs point to a crime of passion. If Bob had planned ahead, why would he enter the date of the flight in his log—and then clumsily write over it a month later and then be forced to set up a second flight to cover the altered date? Obviously, if the log book proves anything, it shows that Bob did not know he had to conceal that flight—until after he had begun writing. I am convinced that if Bob Bierenbaum set his mind to committing a premeditated perfect murder he would have accomplished it without mussing his hair. Why not simply arrange to give an unsuspecting Gail an overdose of drugs before going to work and then return home that night, "discover" her body, call 911 and be seen performing valiant attempts at resuscitation when the paramedics arrived? Gail had a history of mental problems and suicide attempts. I doubt the police would have looked twice at the case.

Curiously, Andy Rosenzweig is not so sure the unidentified torso from Staten Island is *not* Gail. After a conversation with the Medical Examiner, Andy thought that the torso might have survived for four years in the water—if it had been in a watertight container for most of that time. Alayne Katz also still subscribes to this against-the-evidence theory and hopes to someday fill Gail's empty grave.

A few days before she disappeared, Gail told her therapist that she had met a rich man who was going to guarantee her apartment rent. Was he a figment of Gail's imagination, *or* had Gail finally picked up the wrong guy—

a twisted monster who lured her to her death? I was unable to find anyone who has a clue to the identity of the mystery man, if he existed—the best candidate, according to Bob Bierenbaum's lawyers, for "the real killer."

Dr. Janet Chollet told her nanny that I thought the whole case against Bob was a big joke and that I thought the NYPD was corrupt. I have never had a conversation with Janet Chollet—therefore, her impressions, if they were sincere, could only have come to her secondhand.

I never thought the case was a joke, although I did believe the prosecution had no case, other than circumstantial evidence, against her husband. I started out giving Bob the full benefit of the doubt and I set out to find evidence that Bob was not guilty—or that someone else was.

I never found evidence of Bob's innocence but there was evidence of his guilt.

For personal reasons, I hoped Bob was innocent—because it would have made a nice change for me and it would have made a better book, if I could have proved he did not kill Gail. In a personal sense, both Scott Greenfield and I were looking for an innocent man—after careers filled with guilty defendants. It was Scott's openness, so unusual in a lawyer representing a client charged with homicide, and his confidence that Bob would be acquitted, that initially led me to suspect it was possible that an innocent man had been accused of nature's worst crime.

Until the trial, I believed Bob Bierenbaum would be acquitted—not necessarily because he was innocent, but because the prosecution had a weak case. At the trial, I predicted the verdict. After the trial, I came to the conclusion that, although I probably could not have voted to convict him, Bob was probably guilty. It is still possible that he is innocent, but I fear he will never be able to prove it, if he is. Bob twice refused to take a lie detector test in 1985. After his conviction, I asked Scott Greenfield if Bob would be willing to take a polygraph exam to prove his innocence. Not surprisingly, the lawyer said no—claiming the tests were unreliable and would prove nothing.

Anyone familiar with my career knows that I definitely do not think the NYPD is corrupt, although, obviously a few cops have occasionally been guilty of that. In fact, I believe that the vast majority of cops are hard-working, honest and doing a thankless job that most of us depend on but would never do ourselves.

Three months after the sentencing, in a "60 minutes" TV profile of Judge Leslie Crocker-Snyder, Scott Greenfield said that "There are no other judges like her in New York." He charged that the presumption of innocence in her courtroom was "kind of dubious and I think that's unfortunate." Crocker-Snyder replied that "anything that man would say, I don't have a need to respond to."

This case sparked a lot of bizarre rumors and ghoulish theories. One was that Bob had somehow arranged for Gail to be dissected by a class of medical students, a rumor for which there is no proof. One of Bob's friends is convinced he used a scalpel to de-flesh Gail's corpse in their apartment and then used her food processor to liquefy her tissue, which he simply flushed down his toilet—leaving only bones for disposal. Again, no proof whatsoever. There was also a rumor that Gail might have, at some point, become pregnant by a boyfriend, or even aborted Bob's baby—also no evidence.

Gail's family said Bob made medical mercy missions to Mexico just to polish his image, against the possible advent of future criminal charges in Gail's disappearance. If that were the case, it would be truly Machiavellian—but would not explain why, after working for ten years to make himself look good, Bob failed to introduce it at his trial—or even mention it to his lawyer. The jury never heard a good word about Bob and they acted accordingly. Bob may be a deranged psychopath but he may also be a complex, troubled and flawed human being—possibly suffering from "malignant narcissism"—who felt remorse for his evil deed and labored to do good in the world. As his lawyer said at the sentencing, what's wrong with that?

Gail took an entire course on psychopathy and got an

"A" just two months before she dropped off the face of the earth. Unfortunately, she flunked her final exam in real life and was apparently slain by the psychopath she married. Since most of the evidence against Bob at the trial was hearsay, he was convicted largely by Gail's own words. In a strange way, it was also Gail—in the bikini picture introduced at the trial—that finally destroyed Bob, as she threatened to do so many years ago. The photo in Gail's camera that Bob threw away and Alayne found, trashed the testimony of Joel Davis, who claimed he saw the big-breasted Gail alive after Bob had killed her. Just before entering the calm water, with her Mona Lisa smile, Gail proved to some observers that love and hate can be stronger than life and can survive death.

My heart goes out to the Mexican children whose faces are still frozen, waiting for Doctor Bob to return and cut out the devil, as well as to Janet and her daughter—who also have done nothing wrong. The "Flying Doctors of Mercy"—Liga International at 1464 N. Fitzgerald, Hangar #2 Rialto, CA, 92376, will use any tax-deductible donations to try to help those kids, and others.

The doctor–patient privilege has been bruised by the case because a precedent has been established that a New York court can call therapists into court and ask them if a particular person was their patient and if they warned that person's spouse about potential violence—and the psychiatrists must answer. It is a frightening prospect for most psychiatrists and many patients and will remain a hot topic for some time.

The jury found Bob Bierenbaum guilty of intentional murder solely on circumstantial evidence, something that should chill everyone who hears about it. The fact that he had a weak defense and is probably guilty of a terrible crime should not be enough to allay the fear that, someday, as a result of this case, an innocent man or woman might be consigned to hell for a crime he or she did not commit— a travesty that already takes place in this country, although rarely.

In the Bierenbaum case, the convicted man may be granted a new trial and may even win his freedom with a not-guilty verdict, but he will almost certainly never be able to prove his innocence—because there are no "hard" facts to disprove.

I hope to hell Bob Bierenbaum *is* guilty of the crime for which he is serving twenty years to life behind bars—it's the only way I can sleep tonight.